The Way Life Should Be?

The Globalists' Demographic War on America with Maine as a Microcosm

By John Q. Publius

Foreword by Kevin MacDonald

Ostara Publications

The Way Life Should Be?
The Globalists' Demographic War on America with Maine as a
Microcosm
By John Q. Publius
Foreword by Kevin MacDonald

ISBN 978-1-64713-566-9

Contents

Dedicated to Dirigo.

John Q. Publius is a New England native whose work has been featured in numerous publications both print and online. His work focuses on neo-liberalism's devastating impact on all the world's unique peoples and ecosystems. He envisions an independent homeland not just for his would-be countrymen in New Albion, but for all the peoples of the world so that they may pursue their respective destinies unmolested.

Foreword

by Dr. Kevin MacDonald

The power of the pro-immigration lobby is well known and often written about. The vast majority of this writing concerns events at the center of American political culture, at the federal level. There is good reason for this. Most immigration policy is produced at the federal level, and states such as Arizona and California that have attempted to enact legislation limiting immigration in one way or another have been slapped down by the judicial system.

In general, the pro-immigration forces have gotten their way. The main players are well known: the ethnic lobbies seeking more of their people as immigrants, leftist activist organizations seeking to alter the demographic and political balance of the U.S., together with big business interests intent on importing cheap labor.

The uniqueness of John Q. Publius's *The Way Life Should Be?* is that it delves into how the pro-immigration forces have penetrated down to the state and local level. It focuses on what may seem like an unlikely target—the state of Maine which, as of this writing, remains around 95 percent White. It is also the most rural state east of the Mississippi, with a population of around 1.4 million.

But Maine is nevertheless the target of an extensive network of NGOs and various other religious and secular groups masquerading as charities that have focused their efforts on importing as many Third World peoples into the United States as possible. In this effort the NGOs are joined by business, political, academic, and media elites.

Maine is thus a microcosm of what is happening in the rest of the country. The only group left out in all this are white middle-and working-class Americans who bear the burden of this onslaught in terms of increased taxes and a deteriorated social fabric.

Before embarking on all the detailed workings of these interlocking interest groups and their effect on immigration, Publius provides an excellent overview in the Introduction. It is an unequaled portrait

1

of the big picture of how the neoliberal establishment has operated since the 1970s. The main trends are clear: the transformation of the economy from a focus on manufacturing to finance, outsourcing of jobs to foreign countries, free trade, the decimation of labor unions, importing a new underclass from the Third World, and a decline in an ideology of economic or political nationalism.

This has had the effect of enriching those at the top of the economic pyramid—Wall Street and those who own or manage multinational corporations able to take advantage of these trends. But it has devasted the working class: Wages have stagnated beginning in the 1970s.

These changes have especially impacted the white working class. Not only have their wages stagnated, but they have less political power because of the decline of unions that had been a central constituency of the Democratic Party. The Democratic Party had been the party of the white working class but in the decades since the 1965 immigration law it became the party of diversity as intellectuals increasingly adopted the now-dominant "diversity is our greatest strength" stance that was clearly not in the interests of the white working class.

Whereas unions had staunchly opposed immigration because of its effects on jobs and wages, the Democrats welcomed immigration as the future of the party—as indeed it is given that non-whites vote overwhelmingly Democrat.

Without political representation at the national level, the white working class drifted to the Republican Party—the party that often gave lip service to immigration restriction but in fact welcomed immigration because it was the party of big business and cheap labor.

The political genius of Donald Trump was that he tapped into the political frustration of the white working class by adopting a populist, anti-immigration rhetoric that went beyond the moribund class basis of American politics by appealing to an implicit sense of whiteness and the interests of the working class in repatriating manufacturing and lowering immigration.

The Republican Party would be refashioned to be the party of white Americans, and the white working class became the largest constituency of the GOP. Of course, Trump's actions since becoming president have not lived up to his pre-election rhetoric—due at least partly to being stymied by investigations, threats of impeachment, a

2

unified and extremely hostile Democratic Party, and some Republicans who are not on board with his policy proposals.

A focus of my work, particularly my book, *The Culture of Critique*, is the rise of a new Jewish-dominated elite in America after a huge increase in the Jewish population resulting from immigration beginning in the late nineteenth century and continuing until immigration restriction was enacted in the 1920s.

The Jewish rise to power and influence was gradual but even in 1911 Jewish activism was responsible for abrogating the U.S.-Russia trade agreement despite opposition from President Taft. By the 1920s Jews had developed important strongholds in the media (Hollywood, *The New York Times*, CBS, NBC) and in academia (particularly in departments of anthropology because of the influence of Franz Boas).

Jewish influence increased markedly after World War II and anti-Semitism, which had been quite widespread in prior decades, declined dramatically. However, the 1960s was a watershed decade that saw the eclipse of the previously dominant White Anglo-Saxon Protestant elite with its power emanating from Ivy League universities and dominating business and professional societies. As Eric Kaufmann noted,

> By the 1960s, as if by magic, the centuries-old machinery of WASP America began to stall like the spacecraft of Martian invaders in the contemporary hit film, *War of the Worlds*. In 1960, the first non-Protestant president was elected. In 1965, the national origins quota regime for immigration was replaced by a "color-blind" system. Meanwhile, Anglo-Protestants faded from the class photos of the economic, political, and cultural elite— their numbers declining rapidly, year upon year, in the universities, boardrooms, cabinets, courts, and legislatures. At the mass level, the cords holding Anglo-Protestant Americans together began to unwind as secular associations and mainline churches lost millions of members while the first truly national, non-WASP cultural icons appeared.[1]

---

1 Eric Kaufmann, *The Rise and Fall of Anglo-America* (Cambridge: Harvard University Press, 2005), 2–3.

As Kaufmann notes, a key piece of legislation during the 1960s was the immigration law of 1965 that ended the national origins bias of U.S. immigration law that had favored northwest Europe. In retrospect this law should be seen as a sort of coming out party for the new Jewish elite.

Culture of Critique documents the role of Jewish activism in bringing about this sea change in American immigration policy. While the law did not immediately alter the demographic balance of the country, it did open the door, and in the ensuing decades activists, and, in particular, Jewish organizations, continued to press for greater numbers, with the result that the white population has declined from around 90 percent in the 1950s to less than 65 percent today.

These non-White immigrants and their children vote overwhelmingly for the Democratic Party which has championed immigration in recent years to the point that there is a very real possibility of one-party rule by a decidedly left-wing party.

Democrat presidential candidates called for an end to border enforcement, abolishing the Immigration and Customs enforcement, and making all immigrants—legal or illegal—eligible for medical care, voting rights, and driver's licenses. Any calls to limit immigration are greeted with cries of "racism," and attributions of Nazism are common.

Publius documents the continuing Jewish influence on immigration policy throughout, the interlocking network of NGOs, activists, media owners and producers, and wealthy donors.

With all that as background, Publius details the incredibly elaborate and incredibly well-funded pro-immigration infrastructure in the present. Immigration advocacy organizations are funded by a class of wealthy capitalists. For example,

> Pueblo Sin Fronteras is just one of a huge number of NGOs that are part of the vast refugee resettlement network. This network has virtually unlimited resources and is backed by some of the world's wealthiest individuals, not to mention multi-national corporations, banks, private equity firms, and national governments. Their synergy has produced the terrible globalist monstrosity known as "neo-liberalism" confronting us today.

He then describes how Pueblo Sin Fronteras is connected to a whole host of other non-profits and to donors like George Soros. And of course, Soros supports a wide range of leftist activist organizations and politicians.

The districts of politicians who are not completely on board with the immigration agenda are pinpointed for refugee resettlement. These are overwhelmingly white districts. The point is to destroy white enclaves and the high-trust societies that developed in traditional America.

Publius does an excellent job describing the costs of this onslaught. Crime: Somalis "are almost solely responsible—along with the Congolese—for all of the crime in the city" of Lewiston. There are also huge costs for welfare benefits and public housing, which push up property taxes.

Public housing is stretched to the point that there is an increase in homelessness for native Mainers, "yet the political class has prioritized the comfort of these migrants who have the backing of the entire globalist establishment." Most remain unemployed or in low-wage, part-time unskilled labor. Academic achievement is predictably poor.

Thus Maine is importing an underclass, but it's an underclass that will reliably vote for liberal politicians and provide cheap labor for Maine's businesses. All of this is justified by corrupt politicians bought and paid for by powerful economic and diversity-related interests who intone about Maine's "values"—the moral imperative that justifies this assault on the traditional population of Maine. Needless to say, these same processes are at work throughout the rest of the U.S.

The Way Life Should Be? provides a highly detailed picture of what is going on in Maine. It's really a reference source for those wishing to understand the interlocking, lavishly funded infrastructure that is destroying America. Its conclusion is exactly right:

> The many service providers and NGOs described in this book are absolutely essential to the vast matrix of "philanthropic capitalism," and it should be abundantly clear by now that all of these organizations from the "charitable" to the state- and corporate-sponsored are inter-connected and their machinery is geared toward first splintering and then eradicating the native populations

of the Western world, indeed all unique races, ethnicities, and cultures under the heel of the neo-liberal oligarchy. Understanding these mechanisms is absolutely essential in counter-acting the Establishment's destructive agenda.

Introduction

"As Maine goes, so goes the nation."—Popular saying

In the summer of 2019, Portland, Maine, of all places, was suddenly and seemingly inexplicably inundated with hundreds of central African migrants. The city was understandably unprepared, for as a matter of course, refugees are typically less concerned with plotting a perfect 12,000-mile journey with an indeterminate source of funds than with escaping persecution alive.

In what is surely one of the most peculiar odysseys of migrants of any era, these Angolans and Congolese had taken the circuitous route from central Africa to Brazil to Ecuador to Mexico to San Antonio, Texas and finally Portland, Maine. This amounts to a bare minimum of 11,264 miles traveled "as the crow flies," and as much of the route was by land, it was surely much more.

As ostensible refugees, this naturally begs a couple of questions, namely: how can they afford to travel such distances with no income and just the clothes on their backs? How are they able to plan such a logistically-demanding trip? Why do they have international media and legal contacts? I took it upon myself to attempt to answer these questions, and have discovered in an almost-perfect analog with the on-going situations in Europe, Canada, the Antipodes, and elsewhere in the United States an existing support system and network that appears to be funneling migrants to particular pre-determined locales for reasons that will be discussed in this book. The primary actors and organizations, and their connections to what at first blush appears to be an isolated incident yet is anything but, will be revealed.

Demography is destiny; our ruling class understands that very well, which is why Mark Potok, formerly of the Southern Poverty Law Center,[2] gleefully charted whites' declining share of the American

---

2 "Our aim is to destroy [the groups on the SPLC's Hatewatch List] completely…We're trying to wreck the groups. We're trying to destroy them. It's strictly ideological."

population on a chart in his office. Why, exactly, the Southern Poverty Law Center (SPLC) and organizations like the SPLC are concerned with racial demographics will become apparent by the end of this book, but suffice it to say for now that despite the media claims that sea-change migration is "natural" and "inevitable" is patently false and is only so much propaganda to mask what the ruling class is doing.

There is nothing natural or inevitable about people from central Africa having the expertise, connections, and financial wherewithal to plot a perfect 12,000-mile-plus journey across the better part of three continents to arrive in a thinly-populated outpost in the extreme Northeast of the United States.

This would be a stretch with a handful of people, let alone hundreds traveling together, especially if they are all fleeing immediate persecution and are financially destitute, as the narrative would have you believe.

The moral argument for endless Third World immigration is completely disingenuous and only serves to mask the real reasons for the mass importation of huge numbers of alien peoples. One of the most essential arms of the neo-liberal establishment is comprised of non-governmental organizations (NGOs) through which immigration and "refugee re-settlement" as it is euphemistically called can be cloaked in humanitarian terms.

This global network of NGOs has a variety of functions, from the propagandistic to the financial to the infrastructural; these are the groups ferrying African migrants across the Mediterranean and purchasing bus tickets to send migrants to preferred destinations, the latter of which is precisely what happened in the case of Portland.

The government is complicit in encouraging mass immigration as well, in addition to its enabling of the exploitation of workers, decimating entire industries and communities, and enshrining the asset-stripping method of "running" a country along the private equity model. From economics to basic common decency and morality to public health concerns, this is decidedly *not* the way a ruling class that cares about its people behaves.

As the border in the United States of America effectively does not exist, the risks become all the more pronounced; as just one example—and a potentially seriously lethal one—Brian Lonergan writes:

8

What would happen if we encouraged and accepted seemingly infinite numbers of asylum seekers into our communities? The results are coming in, and they're not pretty…The Democratic Republic of Congo is currently suffering through an Ebola epidemic so bad that the World Health Organization is considering declaring an international emergency there (note: they did in fact end up declaring it an international emergency). Normally, asylum seekers are subject to a health check and quarantine if necessary before entering the U.S. However, Acting Homeland Security Director Kevin McAleenan recently admitted that, because of the overflow at the border, thousands of border crossers and illegal immigrants are being released into the country every week without undergoing tests for diseases. Given these factors, a potentially deadly outbreak of Ebola in the United States seems almost inevitable.[3]

In other words, not only are you being pushed out of a job, reminded daily in the media and on college campuses that you're responsible for all the wrongs of the world, but you also now run the risk of dying from Ebola and a host of other exotic and terrible diseases now streaming into America. Cases of the *bubonic plague* have even cropped up along the southern border, and the mass outbreak of the Chinese coronavirus was enabled by a one-two punch of systemic unwillingness to sacrifice economics for health and deep fears of appearing "racist." Perhaps we need to work on what we define as "enriching," but one thing is for sure: for a very small coterie of individuals, the present state of affairs *is* enriching, and it comes at your expense.

Unfortunately, there are precious few voices advocating for responsible governance favoring regular Americans over foreigners and/or massive corporations, financial institutions, and vulture capitalists. This is because, as we shall see, the ruling class is irredeemably corrupt. We hear so much about compassion for "the other," for the immigrant, but so many hearts turn to stone when it comes to their neighbors. Instead of caring for their fellow countrymen, the

3 Lonergan, Brian, "Compassion for refugees can hurt US communities," June 21, 2019. *Fox News.*

extensive network of NGOs and various other religious and secular groups masquerading as charities spend their time and energy trying to import as many Third World peoples into the West as is humanly possible while simultaneously lecturing us on our privilege and haranguing us for perceived slights construed as "racism."

This word has lost all meaning in the hands of those who have weaponized it. They play on the emotionally-charged history of slavery and segregation in America's past and try to pretend as though the few functional detention centers along the southern border are concentration camps.

The rhetoric is so far out of control as to be reckless, and yet the race-baiting, the name-calling, and the hyperbole continue unabated, with those who most foam-mouthedly hurl insults and accusations at their opponents the guiltiest of the sins they project. The Anti-Defamation League defames people with impunity while sitting on an endowment built on a murderous lie and ill-gotten gains from organized crime connections. That doesn't stop them, though.

Many of these NGOs and globalist organizations operate in the shadows with questionable practices and sources of funding, others in the open under false pretenses, and still others are merely extensions of the government, "washing" taxpayer dollars in fraudulent humanitarianism, essentially acting as loopholes to bring in more people above and beyond legal limits.

Whether for ideological purposes, as a money-making scheme, or both, virtually none of these organizations is actually predicated on altruism or anything of the sort.

Then there is the erroneous historical claim of America's wealth being mostly generated by generous immigration, let alone slavery; the founding colonial stock has been almost exclusively responsible for the country's economic growth, and immigration, which is taken as sure as death and taxes these days, is by no means necessary; as we've seen post-1965, far from being beneficial, even slightly in a purely economic sense as was the case prior to the 1921 Emergency Quota Act and the 1924 Immigration Act, immigration has proven to be a major detriment to the country at large.

The social costs of a particular sub-set of that pre-1920s immigration group has proven catastrophic. Furthermore, the American economic juggernaut of the 1950s was the product of a confluence of factors, not least of which was the cultural and racial cohesion of the country following decades of immigration restriction and legally-enshrined protections to preserve the demographics of the nation.

Despite the fact that real wages declined in the UK by 0.7%, in Italy by 0.6%, and in Spain by 0.1% in 2018, for example, and in the United States, according to Pew Research, the $4.03-an-hour rate recorded in January 1973 had the same purchasing power that $23.68-an-hour has now, we incessantly hear about the need for immigration, and lots of it. We all know mass immigration is the only thing that can keep an economy humming since Poland, which has almost none, has seen its economy grow at a close to 4% clip, and Japan, which has almost none, has one of the largest and most dynamic economies in the world, and Hungary, which has almost none, saw real wage growth of close to 5% in 2018. The Visegrad Group (Hungary, Poland, Slovakia, Czech Republic) comprised four of the top seven nations in real wage growth for 2018—and they all have minimal immigration.

The rest, Latvia (in second), Slovenia (in fifth), Israel (in sixth), South Korea (in eighth), Estonia (in ninth), and Iceland (in tenth) also have minimal immigration, though Iceland has of late started to make noise about ramping up its immigration numbers, and Estonia is starting to concern me with comments like this from Head of the Citizenship and Migration Policy Department of the Ministry of Internal Affairs Ruth Annus: "We are working toward increased migration." Contrary to the narrative that we "need" immigration to bolster our economies and feed our bloated welfare states, importing the Third World has proven to be not only an intolerable burden, jeopardizing social capital and safety in the process, but it represents yet another unsustainable expense, compounding the cost of lavish benefits already in place.

The Swedish government, for example, was "forced" to raise the retirement age of native Swedes "due to longer life expectancies," but surely at least a contributing factor is the need to pay for the migrants' entitlements; one need look no further than the roughly 99.7% unemployment rate from the 2015 batch of migrants in Sweden measured the year after their influx. That is 494 employed asylum-seekers out of almost 163,000. Maybe more found work since, but given the reality on the ground, it could not have been in appreciable numbers. The 2015 migrant influx alone could cost the German government up to €1.5 trillion long term. That is beneficial how, exactly?

In the United States, according to the Center for Immigration Studies, in 2014, 63% of households headed by a non-citizen reported they used at least one welfare program, compared to 35% of native-headed households—and this is undifferentiated by race, as the percentages vary dramatically.

In California, 72% of non-citizen-headed households used one or more welfare programs. Of households headed by immigrants who have been in the country for more than two decades, 48% still receive welfare; households headed by immigrants from Central America and Mexico (73%), the Caribbean (51%), and Africa (48%) have the highest overall welfare use.[4] Since the year 2000, the US population living at or below 200% of the federal poverty level grown by twenty-five million—roughly coinciding with the numbers of non-Western immigrants that have been permitted to flood into this country and the pervasiveness of neo-liberalism.

The Federation for American Immigration Reform (FAIR) found that 21% of the foreign-born residents in the states of New Hampshire, Mississippi, Alaska, Maine, North Dakota, West Virginia, South Dakota, Vermont, Montana, and Wyoming were illegal aliens and that each alien carries a net tax deficit of between $4,000 to $6,500 annually; these aliens have given birth to tens of thousands of "anchor babies," who automatically become US citizens due to our nonsensical birthright citizenship.[5]

This obsession with mass immigration only makes sense in the context of an exponential growth model with gross domestic product as the sole or primary metric of economic health, but even then, it is flimsy at best.

A 2016 report entitled "Do Mature Economies Grow Exponentially?" by a trio of German researchers states: "Our findings cast doubts on the widespread belief of exponential growth," concluding

---

4 Camarota, Steven A., "Welfare Use by Immigrant and Native Households," September 10, 2015. Center for Immigration Studies.
5 O'Brien, Matt, Spencer Raley, and Casey Ryan, "Small Migrant Populations, Huge Impacts." February 2020. A Federation for American Immigration Reform Report. Fair Horizon Press.

that the basic assumption of open borders lackeys that "economic growth must always be exponential growth" is fundamentally wrong.[6] Additionally, as Edwin S. Rubenstein explains:

> Immigrant workers increase U.S. GDP, but the vast bulk of the gain goes to the immigrants themselves: only 2% goes to native-born Americans. By increasing the number of workers in the economy, immigration lowers the wages of native-born workers...If per capita GDP depended on a rising population, Africa, Latin America, Indonesia, and the Philippines would be rich...GDP does indeed rise when new immigrants enter the labor force. But living standards are best measured by per capita, not total, GDP. Per capita income falls if immigrants are less educated, productive, motivated—and earn less—than natives. This is the case in the U.S., as seen in the Bureau of Labor Statistics' (BLS) latest survey of the immigrant workforce... My own research...estimates that the foreign-born population cost the federal government $346 billion in FY2007. That translates to about 13% of that year's federal outlays—$9,100 per immigrant.[7]

On average, only 6.5% of legal immigrants have skills deemed "essential" to the US economy (in some years, such as 2009, that number has dipped below 6%). About 60% of immigrants to the United States come as a result of "family re-unification"—chain migration. As a consequence, according to the latest Census Bureau data, almost half of all residents in America's five largest cities do not speak English at home, with Los Angeles "leading" at 59% (and an astronomical 90% in East Los Angeles). 67 million people in this country do not speak English at home—a number almost triple that of 1980.

This amounts to over one-fifth of "Americans" who are estranged from one of the most basic of shared national bonds, that of

6 Lange, Steffen, Peter Putz, and Thomas Kopp, "Do Mature Economies Grow Exponentially?" January 15, 2016.
7 Rubenstein, Edwin S., "Expert analysis reveals the 'biggest losers' of mass immigration are America's poor and middle class," March 8, 2016. Negative Population Growth.

language. 44% of California's school-age children speak a foreign language at home. Unsurprisingly, as Spencer P. Morrison writes:

> Although California spends $88.3 billion on its K-12 public education system, its schools are among the worst in the country. Not only does California have one of the highest student-to-teacher ratios in America—35 percent above the national average—but per-pupil spending has been decreasing steadily.
>
> A recent study ranked California's K-12 public education system as the 37th worst in the Union in terms of educational quality, and 49th in terms of school safety. That is, California's schools not only provide students with middling educations in reading and arithmetic, but they're also dangerous, violent places. Many high schools are little more than publicly-funded gang-academies... Academics attribute the problems to a plethora of marginally relevant factors, like difficulties in raising taxes—which I assure you is not a problem—a lack of federal funding, and of course *racism*...
>
> Given the proportion of illegal aliens and anchor babies relative to the broader student body, we can conclude that illegal aliens and their children consume $17.4 billion in additional educational costs...[Further,] Texas spends $7.9 billion educating illegal immigrants annually.[8]

This is, unfortunately, just a drop in the bucket. Mass Third World immigration is costing Americans trillions of dollars over the course of their lifetimes[9] to say nothing of the deterioration of the social fabric of this country.

As Edwin S. Rubenstein explains, immigration restriction benefits both the average and the struggling American and reduces the extreme disparity between rich and poor the Left *used to* at least claim to care about:

---

8 Morrison, Spencer P., "Illegal Immigration Destroys American Schools, Hurts Kids the Most," January 24, 2018. *National Economics Editorial.*
9 Rector, Robert and Jamie Bryan Hall, "Trump-Endorsed Immigration Bill Would Save Taxpayers Trillions," August 14, 2017. The Heritage Foundation.

The Roaring Twenties marked the start of a forty-year period during which ordinary workers got richer while the rich got relatively poorer. After an early recession, unemployment dropped below 5% and stayed below that level for most of the decade.

Americans found themselves sharing broadly similar lifestyles in a way not seen since before the Civil War. Amazingly, only about 500,000 legal immigrants entered the U.S. during the whole of the 1930s. And only about a million entered in the 1940s — including World War II refugees. The post-war era saw a return to the 156,700 per year cap on legal immigration.[10]

According to a State Department report, from 2005-2014, the United States spent $96.6 billion on refugees, which rises to $126 billion when officials count the extra cost of paying for the refugees' spouses and children. Additionally, as Neil Munro writes:

The $126 billion bill is just for programs managed by the Department of Health and Human Services. It excludes additional taxpayers' spending via state programs, as well as federal spending on Social Security, education, and housing programs, plus tax credits…The huge cost adds up to $670 per working American, not counting the hard-to-assess costs of crowded schoolrooms, flooded labor markets, civic diversity, and shifts in political power away from Americans.

The massive spending will continue because the vast majority of the 606,000 refugees remain in the United States, mostly in low-skilled jobs, and will age into retirement.[11]

The Office of Refugee Resettlement revealed the following in their 2016 Annual Report to Congress covering refugee arrivals between 2011 and 2015:

---

10 Rubenstein, Edwin S., "The Negative Economic Impact of Immigration on American Workers," March 8, 2016. Negative Population Growth.
11 Munro, Neil, "Welfare for Refugees Cost Americans $123 Billion in 10 Years," September 27, 2018. *Breitbart.*

Among refugees age 18 or older who had lived in the United States between 4.5 and 6.5 years, 53 percent spoke English "not well" or "not at all," based on self-assessments…Respondents age 25 or older averaged 8.7 years of education before arrival; about half did not have a high school diploma upon arrival; and 29 percent of refugees age 25 or older listed their prior educational attainment as "none." Among respondents age 18 and older, 16 percent were pursuing a degree of some kind, with most seeking high school equivalency.

The claim that these migrants are the future of specialized labor and intellectually-demanding professions in the West and other developed nations is completely bogus; for example, according to Dr. Farrukh Salem, 60% of the Muslim world is illiterate. The Organization of Islamic Cooperation countries are home to 25% of the world's people, but as of 2012, they contributed just 1.6% of the world's patents, 6% of academic publications, and 2.4% of global research expenditures.

In the US, from the Office of Refugee Resettlement Annual Report to Congress Fiscal Year 2013, we know that 19.7% of Middle Eastern refugees received public housing, 68.3% received cash assistance, 73.1% received Medicaid or Refugee Medical Assistance (RMA), and 91.4% received food stamps.

On average, each Middle Eastern refugee resettled in the United States costs an estimated $64,370 in the first five years, or $257,481 per household.[12]

In case you were wondering, by the United Nations' own admission, for 2015: "548 individuals, or less than one per cent of the overall figure of 134,044, were submitted under the emergency priority." Further, as a percentage of total resettlement submissions by the UN High Commissioner for Refugees (UNHCR), emergency cases were 0.8% of all submissions for 2011, 1.4% for 2012, 1.2% for 2013, and 0.8% for 2014.[13] For 2017, "Some 869 individuals, or just over 1 per cent of all submissions, were submitted under the emergency priority,

---

12 Camarota, Steven A., "The High Cost of Resettling Middle Eastern Refugees," November 4, 2015. Center for Immigration Studies.
13 UNHCR Projected Global Resettlement Needs, 2017 Report.

an increase of 66 per cent compared to 2016."[14] According to the UNHCR, in Italy in 2016, only 2.65% of the record-level 181,436 persons arriving were actually deemed to have met the qualifications for refugee status.[15] In the US, at least 30% of asylum claims for religious persecution are fraudulent.[16]

The US Citizenship and Immigration Services' (USCIS) National Security and Records Verification Directorate's Fraud Detection and National Security Division completed a report in 2009 on asylum fraud in cases considered by asylum officers, studying a sample of asylum applications affirmatively filed between May and October 2005. A case was classified as fraudulent if reliable evidence pertaining to the applicant's asylum eligibility proved "a material misrepresentation and the evidence was more than just contradictory testimony given by the applicant."

If the indicators of fraud existed and pertained to the applicant's asylum eligibility but fraud could not be confirmed by evidence external to the applicant's testimony, the case was classified as possible fraud. 12% of these cases were found to be proven fraud and another 58% were possible fraud for a total 70% rate of proven or possible fraud. The Obama administration refused to make these findings public.[17] So these people aren't even refugees—it's a scam.

According to the World Economic Forum, ranked by the metrics of economic, social, and political freedom, legal protections, and safety and security, it's all the primary sources of these "refugees" that are the worst countries in the world for women:

1. Afghanistan
2. Syria
3. Yemen
4. Pakistan
5. The Central African Republic

---

14 UNHCR Projected Global Resettlement Needs, 2019 Report.

15 Williams, Thomas D., "Report: Only 2.65 Percent of Immigrants into Italy are Refugees," April 24, 2017. *Breitbart.*

16 Sessions, Jeff, Steven A. Camarota, Rosemary Jenks, and Michael Maxwell, "Panel Transcript: Implications of the Hagel-Martinez Amnesty Bill," June 15, 2006. Center for Immigration Studies.

17 House Judiciary Hearing before the Subcommittee on Immigration and Border Security, "Asylum Fraud: Abusing America's Compassion?" February 11, 2014.

6. The Democratic Republic of the Congo
7. Iraq
8. Mali
9. Sudan
10. Niger
11. Lebanon
12. Cameroon
13. Chad

The top twenty nations on the Fragile State Index (meaning least stable), in order, are as follows: South Sudan, Somalia, the Central African Republic, Yemen, Sudan, Syria, the Democratic Republic of the Congo, Chad, Afghanistan, Iraq, Haiti, Guinea, Nigeria, Zimbabwe, Ethiopia, Guinea-Bissau, Burundi, Pakistan, Eritrea, and Niger; the countries with the lowest life expectancy on earth are Swaziland, Angola, Zambia, Lesotho, and Mozambique. Six of the top eight countries for violent death rates per 100,000 people are in Latin America—El Salvador, Guatemala, Venezuela, Belize, Colombia, and Honduras—and one is in the Caribbean—Trinidad and Tobago. Haiti, Panama, Brazil, Guyana, Jamaica, and Mexico are all also in the top twenty most violent nations on earth.

So this is what we are importing. There is also the ever-present threat of disease such as that reported by Lonergan and experienced with the coronavirus, not to mention terrorism, crime of all kinds, pollution, corruption, the disintegration of social capital and infrastructure, and the fact that home just doesn't look and feel like home anymore.

Yet still the entire establishment is in unison that diversity is our strength, we need to take in all the world's "refugees," immigration is only ever a good thing, and that, to paraphrase Tucker Carlson, more investment banking is always the answer.

This isn't some strange coincidence. The entire system is deeply inter-connected, and virtually every country on earth is tied in to this global network to some degree. It is abetted by organizations such as the International Monetary Fund (IMF), the World Bank, and the World Trade Organization (WTO), the various NGOs and shadowy organizations, wealthy financiers, and the governments themselves. Not one single claim in support of the benefits of mass immigration holds up, so our governments resort to suppression, censorship, imprisonment, and the threat of state violence—not to protect us, but to hasten our dispossession. To the managerial class, we're just lambs to the slaughter, necessary casualties in the service of all this wonderful diversity.

The ever-shrinking middle class bears an ever-increasing share of the burden, and our tax dollars are used to subsidize mass Third World immigration to drive down labor costs and to finance deluxe football stadiums and Amazon's second headquarters—not to mention welfare for all of the Amazon and Uber employees who are unable to even earn a living wage.

In 2015, the middle class ceased being a majority in the United States for the first time, contrasted with 1971, when 67% of Americans lived in middle-income households according to Pew Research. This was before neo-liberalism had fully taken root in a country that had only just opened itself back up to mass immigration, and not from the European source of the pre-1921 restriction.

Not only did the middle class become a minority, but the median income of the American middle class in 2015 was down 4% from the year 2000.

In the United States, the Democrats are happy to let the Republicans do the heavy lifting on tax cuts for corporations and on capital gains, and both "sides" have enabled the burden of Left-wing vote-buying to fall on the loathed white middle- and working-classes. These cosmic scapegoats finance their own dispossession through onerous taxes and wealth re-distribution (while capital is taxed at just half the rate of labor) as they are assailed on all sides. The Uni-Party has honed its craft to devastating effectiveness. Tucker Carlson offers one illustrative example:

> Corporate tax cuts are also popular in Washington, and [Mitt] Romney is strongly on board with those, too. His piece throws a rare compliment to Trump for cutting the corporate rate a year ago. That's not surprising. Romney spent the bulk of his business career at a firm called Bain Capital. Bain Capital all but invented what is now a familiar business strategy: Take over an existing company for a short period of time, cut costs by firing employees, run up the debt, extract the wealth, and move

on, sometimes leaving retirees without their earned pensions. Romney became fantastically rich doing this.[18]

Romney is mimicking his betters: it's what the aliens do in *They Live*—they strip-mine entire planets and then move on the next to do it all over again, rootless as they are. In the meantime, they "pass" as human, but they are not. Of course David French and Ben Shapiro object to Carlson; their entire existence, in the former case, is to hold water for the neo-con wing of the Establishment, and in the latter case, to provide a nice, kosher "alternative" to the Left's "identity politics" while simultaneously affirming his own Jewish identity and pro-Zionism. Neither views America as anything but a GDP farm.

We are still in thrall to Bolshevism in a sense, particularly in terms of Cultural Marxism, though economically the "victors" over communism were not the victors. The victors were the globalists who had been playing both sides all along. The losers were those who went from living in a nation, to living in a country, to living in a society, to living in a market.

Business, politics, advertising, fashion trends, civil wars, foreign interventionism—at this point, what difference does it make? All are inextricable. It is abundantly clear that our governments no longer operate with the consent of the governed, and have not for a long time now. They are instead illegitimate occupation governments which are nothing more than extensions of the globalist neo-liberal oligarchic cabal: hand-in-glove—the invisible hand turned iron fist underneath the velvet glove of utopianism.

The marriage of the political and the corporate defines the modern era. Neo-liberalism is both an economic system and an ideology, but it masquerades as a vehicle of "social justice." This is not business as usual, and even the most basic claims of equality and empowerment fall apart with just a little scrutiny.

There's another shrewd tactic here: by "allying" with "social justice," corporations can then rhetorically attack the "nativist" Right and, with the Left now totally subverted, erode the final barrier to open borders. Their rhetoric is then internalized by consumers to TAKE ACTION, either in the form of purchasing more products like the

---

18 Carlson, Tucker, "Mitt Romney supports the status quo. But for everyone else, it's infuriating," January 3, 2019. *Fox News*.

Kaepernick Nikes for social approval or literal action, which also involves purchasing products, like milkshakes to hurl at anyone who isn't officially-sanctioned ideologically. Hell, Burger King UK will use its official Twitter account to encourage you to buy milkshakes from them in order to then throw them at people you don't agree with![19]

The smoke-and-mirrors is all meant to direct attention away from the profit motive, but it's profit motive with a twist. You get to be the customer of your own demise, paying people who despise you. Your destruction has the added benefit of removing you as an obstacle to greater profits. You would likely demand pesky nuisances like lunch breaks, weekends, and a livable wage. You wouldn't have an eighth child you couldn't afford to care for. You might question why, exactly, you should have to pay almost double your home's value by the end of a thirty-year mortgage.

By creating a snake oil "academic" framework through which to lend cultural credence and legitimacy to concepts such as "privilege," the private sphere is given carte blanche to dismantle the obstinate white population and scrap our nations for parts—with ample government assistance in the interim stage, as the state is run by and for the financial institutions and corporations until it, too, can be dismantled and discarded.

If you think the push for open borders has anything to do with humanitarianism, you're being naïve at best. The Central Bank of Ireland admitted in 2019 that the neo-liberal establishment needs a certain intake of people to keep wages from rising.[20] There are other reasons for the mass importation of alien peoples as well, but

---

19 "In May [2019], a day after it emerged that a McDonald's restaurant in Edinburgh had been asked by police not to sell milkshakes because it was located within 200 metres of where Farage was to hold a rally and protesters might throw them, Burger King tweeted: 'Dear people of Scotland. We're selling milkshakes all weekend. Have fun. Love BK. #justsaying'. Farage had previously been hit by a milkshake in Newcastle city centre, after a spate of similar incidents against far-right candidates in the European elections campaign, a form of protest known as 'milkshaking'. Farage was scheduled to make more public appearances in Scotland following the Burger King tweet." From Mark Sweney, "Watchdog bans Burger King tweet about 'milkshaking' Nigel Farage," October 1, 2019. *The Guardian.*

20 Chance, David, "Not enough migrants arriving to keep pay down—Central Bank," July 30, 2019. *Independent.ie.*

as regards wages, it's primarily considerations of supply-and-demand and collective bargaining, or lack thereof. As Piotr and Pawel Zuk explain, "Neoliberalisation and globalisation generate and utilise the mobility of both capital and labour.

Meanwhile, labour migration is presenting a challenge to the observance of labour rights. Present-day methods of capital accumulation rely on the search for cheap labour and the relocation of production to territories that do not protect workers' rights." Free trade is essential for wage suppression and out-sourcing, and for the erasure of national boundaries to facilitate the un-restricted movement of people and goods. Any impediment to this process is treated by the neo-liberal establishment as an obstacle to be destroyed. It is a process that is being replicated from Ireland to the ASEAN region in Southeast Asia to the great state of Maine.

In the antebellum South, indentured servants and slaves filled the labor needs of many major landholders, whereas in the North child labor was often prevalent. As the mid-19th century approached, increasing immigration padded the numbers of the Yankees laboring in factories and mills in the rapidly-industrializing Union. Freed blacks filled this role during the Great Migration after the immigration restrictions and quotas in 1921 and 1924, and around the same time women were "liberated" from their "burdens" of home-making and child-rearing to depress wages and provide a financial windfall of tax revenue to the federal government.

Immigrant populations arriving in the United States have typically come in waves, and these waves very often served to provide cheap, disposable labor for the expanding industrial economy as the 19th century progressed, and the de-industrialized service-sector economy post-1965. This model has been adopted across the West at various intervals in the immediate aftermath of World War II and has only accelerated, however if there are positives to be found from the Chinese coronavirus pandemic, it is that it exposed both how fragile the system is and how vital it is for a country to have full control of its own manufacturing and financial capabilities.

Immigrants, women, and now sexual identity groups (although the latter two are more white-collar phenomena) have been a boon to capitalists looking to keep wages as low as possible and to break the collective bargaining power of organized labor, which has also traditionally been the bulwark against mass immigration, not just in the United States but in many Western countries like Australia and others.

The specific context of Maine will be explored in great depth in this book as a microcosm of what is happening across the West, but before we get too deep into the details, it is important for the reader to understand this economic motivation on the part of Money Power in order to see the big picture. Without grasping the economics, much of what the "elites" are doing remains obscured.

What is vital to understand is that when we have the Democratic Socialists of America and the Libertarian Party essentially running on the same platform, the public-private binary reveals itself as a false dilemma. The spectrum of options for American voters is either cultural degeneration and racial erasure with a "social justice" paint job, or one that masquerades as "individual liberty." Though they may couch their ulterior motives in so much rhetoric, just as with the elephant and the jackass, the leadership's eyes might as well be represented by those cartoon dollar signs. The nexus of venture capital and big tech has proven profoundly damaging to any notions of nation, but for executives, major shareholders, the various "compliance" cottage industries, advocacy groups, and the like it has been a financial bonanza.

The financial sector in the United States has tripled since the 1980s, while the real economy has shrunk and labor's share of income has declined. This is not coincidental, as the American economy continues to be oriented along a FIRE (finance, insurance, real estate) axis, which includes rent, debt, and interest payments.

To quote Michael Hudson, "The financial sector has succeeded in depicting itself as part of the productive economy, yet for centuries banking was recognized as being parasitic. The essence of parasitism is not only to drain the host's nourishment, but also to dull the host's brain so that it does not recognize that the parasite is there." How right he is.

In a debt-driven economy, one predicated on an exponential growth model, extensive lines of credit, and the creation of new markets both in terms of consumers and goods and services, the entire apparatus is increasingly being built on a house of cards.

The economy is basically a Ponzi scheme, one where all of the benefits accrue to the top 1%. When we see things like the self-created housing shortage in Britain corresponding *exactly* to the number of immigrants who arrive every year, when "conservatives" scream about a 2% inflation rate from the Federal Reserve, when the entire globalist establishment decries tariffs and "nativism" in favor of "free trade" and open borders, it's not difficult to see what the angle is here.

Per Michael Hudson:

> When we say "people worry" about inflation, it's mainly bondholders that worry. The labor force benefitted from the inflation of the '50s, '60s and '70s (note: which is also why the populist movement of the late-19th century, led by William Jennings Bryan, advocated a move away from the gold standard). What was rising most rapidly were wages. Bond prices fell steadily during these decades. Stocks simply moved sideways. Inflation usually helps the economy at large, but not the 1% if wages rise. So the 1% says that it is terrible. They advocate austerity and permanent deflation. And the media say that anything that doesn't help the 1% is bad. But don't believe it. When they say inflation is bad, deflation is good, what they mean is, more money for us 1% is good; we're all for asset price inflation, we're all for housing prices going up, and we're all for our stock and bonds prices going up. We're just against you workers getting more income.[21]

Now obviously inflation is to be differentiated from hyper-inflation—the kind that occurs when you steal whites' land and drive them out of the country, as happened in Rhodesia, and which is now set to commence in South Africa and probably Namibia in the near future. White farmers still own 70% of commercial farmland in Namibia per the Namibia Statistics Agency.

This means that like Rhodesia, like South Africa soon, this gross inequity must be resolved with the whites getting short shrift, of course, for a "legacy of colonialism," with land expropriation high

---

21 Hudson, Michael and Bonnie Faulkner, "The Slow Crash. The Shrinking of the Real Economy," April 2016. Global Research.

on the agenda. Never mind that in South Africa, blacks already took monetary reparations instead of land—now they want the land, too.

In 2000, the former Rhodesia's government expropriated white farmers' land without compensation, triggering hyperinflation and food shortages. Agriculture represented a 21.8% share of Zimbabwe's GDP in 1998 and has been halved since the expropriations. Zimbabwe went from a food exporter to a food importer. In 2001, Zimbabwe was the world's sixth-largest producer of tobacco, but by 2008 was producing just 21% of the amount grown in 2000.

The country's trade surplus went from hundreds of millions of dollars before the expropriations were enacted to an $18 million deficit within two years. The economy has deteriorated significantly since then. Zimbabwe was once called "the bread basket of Africa," and it is now struggling to feed its own population, with nearly half of the population malnourished.

Zimbabwe is a microcosm of Africa, which imports $35 billion of food every year, a bill that is expected to swell to $110 billion by 2025, says Akinwumi Adesina of the African Development Bank (AfDB).

Cultivating Community in Portland tries to set up refugees from Africa with their own farms in Maine, which is a fool's errand, considering what we've just discussed as well as the fact that at least 60% of Africa's arable land lies uncultivated (one 2011 report put it at 79%); Africa has around 600 million hectares of uncultivated arable land, a whopping 60-65% of the global total.

More damning still, the Food and Agriculture Organisation estimates that by 2050, three-quarters of the land in use from 1960 will have had its soil depleted due to the fact that there are virtually no conservation measures in place.

To top that off, Maine has notoriously acidic and rocky soil, so only a local and/or a truly expert farmer is going to get much out of the land. Therein lies the rub with regards to that buzzword sustainability—despite the neo-liberal marketing campaign, only locals and/or people who are otherwise expert know their land or their oceans well enough to have good crop yields or catches that do not deplete resources and destroy the ecosystem.

Neo-liberalism does not allow for that. When everything becomes commodified, what happens to the environment is of little consequence;

disruption of the eco-system, mass die-offs, and environmental degradation and devastation are dismissed as "externalities." What we have is a government run by financial institutions and corporations for financial institutions and corporations; when the puppet government no longer serves its purpose, it will be discarded along with the country itself in the anarcho-capitalist wet dream of full privatization.

As the real injustices perpetrated by neo-liberalism go unremarked-upon, the exploited peoples of the world are spoon-fed nonsense about "white supremacy," "a legacy of colonialism and slavery," et cetera. Stoking resentments is part of the tried-and-true tactic of divide-and-conquer. While with any good lie there is always a nugget of truth, the intended effect is to project the crimes of the accuser on to the accused.

Thus, the catch-all of European colonialism neatly skirts over or distorts the worst injustices and ignores any potential positives. The treatment of the Congo at the hands of King Leopold of Belgium is one such example. Yes, the abuses of the people of the Congo were horrific, but what is "conveniently" neglected in the narrative is that the Congo was for decades a privately-held asset of King Leopold.

Privatization most certainly can be a problem—the atrocities committed against the labor force in the Congo were done in the name of profit. Our modern cultural commissars would like us to believe this was done by the Belgians acting out their version of white supremacy, but the Belgian government actually intervened and took the colony away from Leopold because the human rights abuses had gotten so egregious.

As with most things, from slavery to women's suffrage, it is the white impetus to commit resources, time, and energy to rectifying moral injustices only to eventually be blamed for them once the out-facing Cultural Bolshevists have sufficiently indoctrinated a population.

Even the use of charity and philanthropy have been co-opted by the neo-liberal machinery. It's a sad state of affairs when charity has been weaponized, but here we are. It certainly wasn't always this way—it was once an integral part of the old WASP establishment's noblesse oblige to those less fortunate than they.

As Alison Powell, Willa Seldon, and Nidhi Sahni write:

Throughout the 20th century, large US institutional foundations such as the multiple Carnegie foundations, the Ford Foundation, and The Rockefeller Foundation played an outsize role in philanthropy. By virtue of their large share of the philanthropic marketplace, these institutions were able to shape the thinking of policymakers, attract social innovators, and exert influence to bring together the private sector, government, and civil society. As a result, they played a vital role in underwriting social change: They helped to eradicate polio in the United States and then across most of the world; they provided 96 percent of Americans with easy access to free libraries; they helped to reduce smoking in the United States by more than 60 percent; and they promoted a "green revolution" that dramatically increased agricultural production.[22]

Certainly these magnates were not without fault by any stretch of the imagination, and a strong executive such as Teddy Roosevelt proved necessary to rein them in. There's a lesson in that, an essential one, in that strong and responsible governance on behalf of the people and the environment is an essential counter-point to the all-consuming profit motive and in-group cronyism.

Our current government hasn't the spine to curtail the cravenness and grotesque gluttony, the likes of which would've made the robber barons blush. To quote Tucker Carlson:

In January of 1914, Henry Ford more than doubled the prevailing factory to a then remarkable $5 for an eight-hour day. Ford didn't have to do that. But his company was succeeding, and he thought he should. Some historians trace the creation of the American middle class to that decision. Either way, it is nearly impossible to imagine a big company doing anything like that today. Attitudes are just too different. Your average finance mogul looks at workers merely as costs to be reduced or eliminated entirely. Private equity isn't

22 Powell, Alison, Willa Seldon, and Nidhi Sahni, "Reimagining Institutional Philanthropy," Spring 2019. *Stanford Social Innovation Review.*

building a lot of public libraries these days. Instead, the model is ruthless economic efficiency. Buy a distressed company, outsource the jobs, liquidate the valuable assets, fire middle management, and once the smoke is cleared dump what remains to the highest bidder, often in Asia. It's happened around the country. It has made a small number of people phenomenally rich.[23]

Incidentally, by 2030, two-thirds of all middle-class spending power is projected to be concentrated in Asia as a consequence of these decisions. As the Nielsen Research Group found in a recent survey, Asia-Pacific consumers felt the most optimistic about their financial situation, with 70% reporting that they are in a better position today compared with five years ago.

In places like Japan, South Korea, and Han China they don't have to worry about being ethnically replaced, either. At least not yet: the UN does have South Korea and Japan squarely in its crosshairs for future "enrichment."

Of the CEOs polled in "The Future of Foundation Philanthropy" (December 2016) sponsored by the Center for Effective Philanthropy, many stated that their philanthropic endeavors were necessary to circumvent the "political climate and structure that is hostile to advancement in our mission areas," and "political gridlock, especially at the federal level, which makes it almost impossible to address critical long-term issues in an informed manner." That would be all well and good if the causes being advanced were not terribly destructive and totally self-serving, but they are. And the government—at least in theory accountable to the people—is constrained in ways the private sector is not, despite its cooption. Other salient points included (and as always, you need to read between the lines):

> The majority of foundation CEOs interviewed— almost 60 percent—identify climate change or the environment as a pressing issue. Several comments stress the importance of climate change in particular…Several CEOs suggest that "federal government interference with philanthropy" or "governmental efforts to more

---

23 Carlson, Tucker, *Tucker Carlson Tonight*, December 3, 2019. *Fox News.*

tightly regulate foundations and endowments" may pose challenges and heighten restrictions for foundation philanthropy in the future.

Some CEOs specifically mention a "backlash against tax deductions" or "potential changes to IRS tax laws related to foundation giving."...On the topic of race, a number of CEOs contemplate what the future holds. Several believe that a "majority-minority shift in U.S. demographics" and "the browning of America" will have implications for foundation staffing and leadership—namely, in a needed "transition to multiethnic leadership" and a greater focus on "diversity in leadership."

Some note the importance of diverse staffing, governance, and leadership for foundations overall for "achieving better results."...

Others note that foundations can take risks and test ideas without the constraints or ramifications that business or government might have.[24]

As it stands, we have watched America become little more than an economic zone, a gigantic market, its founding stock the target of ultimate erasure through a mixture of malice and greed. Kerry Bolton extensively documents the bankrolling of feminism, "civil rights," and other causes that have proven corrosive to the moral foundations of this country by foundations such as the Ford Foundation and the Rockefeller Foundation as part of the global capitalist framework, which includes support of communism.

Regarding immigration, in 1983, the Ford Foundation initiated a greatly expanded immigration program, in the process becoming one of the leading funders in the field. The Ford Foundation established Grantmakers Concerned with Immigrant Rights and Refugees (GCIR) in 1991, which had swelled to over one hundred foundations by 2008. From the Louis Freedberg with assistance from Ted Wang report to the Ford Foundation, "The Role of Philanthropy in the US Immigrant Rights Movement," in the early 1980s:

---

24 Buteau, Ellie, Naomi Orensten, and Charis Loh, "The Future of Foundation Philanthropy: The CEO Perspective," December 2016. The Center for Effective Philanthropy.

Immigration was becoming a prominent political and social issue that Washington would attempt to control through major legislation. Polls showed public opinion running strongly against the admission of more than 100,000 Cuban and Haitian "boat people."... "Immigration was not an issue in the 1940s, 1950s and 1960s," said Demetrios Papademetriou, president of the Migration Policy Institute in Washington D.C. In fact, the proportion of the population that was foreign-born actually declined in the 1950s and 1960s... "It was only in the mid-1970s that the immigration pot began being stirred again," said Papademetriou. The reason: the sweeping changes wrought by the Immigration and Nationality Act of 1965 had significantly altered the racial and ethnic makeup of immigration flows to the United States by eliminating the "national origins quota system" which had been in place for 40 years...Within a decade of its passage, the Asian immigrant population in the United States had increased by 663 percent...

The number of immigrants who came to the United States without valid documents also increased exponentially... As the battles around immigration in Congress intensified, the Ford Foundation increased its support for immigration rights, including a grant of $300,000 to the Forum in 1984. Border apprehensions, almost non-existent in1960, started picking up momentum in 1975, and reached a peak of 1.8 million 1986.[25]

Instead of the democratic response, which is to listen to the people, organizations like the Ford Foundation, the German Marshall Fund, the MacArthur Foundation, the San Francisco Foundation, and the Rockefeller Foundation stepped in and began pouring money into expanding immigration and "refugee resettlement":

"This is something Ford has understood, that you have to stay with organizations for the long term," reflected

---

25 Freedberg, Louis with Ted Wang, "The Role of Philanthropy in the US Immigrant Rights Movement," Report to the Ford Foundation.

Diana Morris...who now directs the Baltimore office of the Open Society Institutes, had worked as a young attorney in the Office of the Legal Adviser in the State Department just before coming to Ford, working closely with the Refugee Bureau there. Her main assignment had been clarifying key elements of the recently passed Refugee Act of 1980, which had significantly expanded the number of refugees that would be allowed into the United States. In many ways, the Foundation's approach to the immigration rights field was a logical extension to its decades-long involvement in the civil rights movement, and its long-term support for key organizations that played a central role in it. It also was built on its ongoing support for prominent Latino organizations such as MALDEF and the National Council on La Raza...Morris, who described herself as a "frustrated anthropologist," also initiated another prominent Ford project, which looked at the "culture of immigration"...At the time, only a handful of smaller foundations were involved in immigration issues, mostly notably the Rosenberg Foundation in San Francisco... Most of the immigrant coalitions were brand new organizations, and Ford's grants to them had to be funneled through established non-profit organizations such as MALDEF or the United Way...In another major Ford research initiative...The Migration Policy Institute was founded in 2001 with a $2.5 million grant from the Ford Foundation...Ford continued to support organizations such as the Lawyers Committee for Human Rights, the Haitian Refugee Center and MALDEF...The ACLU Immigrants' Rights Project brought a range of lawsuits challenging the way the legalization process was implemented and enforced... Another of the early foundations to join with Ford was the Carnegie Corporation of New York...Philanthropy, like the movement itself, found itself in a defensive posture. The Ford Foundation provided grants to the National Immigration Forum, the National Council on La Raza, and the National Immigration Law Center, among others, who embarked on a unified campaign to undo some of the most punitive restrictions embedded in the welfare, immigration and anti-terrorism legislation… The welfare reform legislation also elicited one of the most dramatic philanthropic responses to date on behalf of immigrants.

In a widely publicized gesture, Hungarian immigrant and multi-billionaire [the Jewish] George Soros announced that he was setting up the Emma Lazarus Fund, a $50 million, three-year fund named after the [Jewish] poet who wrote the words inscribed on the Statue of Liberty. The fund, administered by Soros' Open Society Institute, was intended to help immigrants naturalize as a way to blunt the effects of the legislation restricting their eligibility for benefits. Soros recruited Antonio Maciel, an attorney who was in charge of the immigration portfolio at the Joyce Mertz-Gilmore Foundation. Before that, he had worked for the ACLU's Immigrants' Rights Project. Maciel convinced Soros that focusing too narrowly on naturalization would limit the effectiveness of the program, and that 10 percent of the fund, or $5 million, should go to advocacy organizations like the National Council of La Raza, the National Immigration Forum and Catholic Legal Immigration Network, Inc. (CLINIC)…[In the 1990s] with support from Ford, the Open Society Institute, Carnegie, Hagedorn and the Evelyn and Walter Haas Jr. Fund, over 200 local, grassroots organizations called for comprehensive immigration reform under several national networks.[26]

Following 9/11, representatives of the Ford Foundation, Carnegie, and the Open Society Foundations met to map out a strategy to ensure that their gains in transforming the country would not be undone by the frustrations and changing sentiment of the time, and in 2003, Ford began sponsoring so-called "freedom riders"—again attempting to evoke the Civil Rights Era—heading to Washington, DC to "protest" on behalf of illegal aliens. As the mid-2000s wore on:

---

26 Ibid.

Leading immigrant rights organizations, in collaboration with the SEIU, formed the "We Are America Alliance" to increase civic participation on the part of the newly-mobilized immigrants. Another new organization, Mi Familia Vota, along with organizations like National Association of Latino Elected Officials and National Council of La Raza, teamed up with Univision to launch a naturalization campaign called "Ya Es Ahora." In the first year of the program, some 1.3 million immigrants submitted their naturalization papers as a result of this effort.[27]

Some of the old guard Establishment magnates were essential in the process of colluding with the predominantly-Jewish interlopers in the late 19th and early 20th centuries in re-fashioning the ruling class and establishing an oligarchy, but others like Henry Ford were not.

That said, as with virtually all of the philanthropic charities established by America's old financial and industrial magnates, once the original benefactor had died, the foundation was co-opted and re-fashioned in order to undermine the communities and society it was ostensibly there to help. These foundations' traditional methodologies and operations are slowly becoming obsolete in the 21st century, however, with the predominance of private equity and the private equity model, though they still play a prominent role at present.

The private equity model has actually been adopted by philanthropies to some degree, but what is far more prevalent is the treatment of philanthropic organizations as investments. Lobbying is such a dirty business and has such negative PR, but charity and philanthropy…well, that's another story.

That's how big business can couch the importation of a new labor force in humanitarian terms. That's how big capital and multi-nationals can super-charge their efforts to knock down borders, socially re-engineer entire populations, and even ethnically cleanse those populations proving to be reluctant in getting on board with the program.

The rise of the private equity model is one way in which Big Capital's interlopers were able to effectively corral the old WASP

---

27 Ibid.

establishment; the growth potential of private equity and its relative complexity could rapidly out-strip the resources of the extant American ruling class and first enfold and then subsume them into the burgeoning neo-liberal system.

Not that the WASPs were entirely hoodwinked—they had plenty of willing collaborators to do their dirty work in the World Wars, transformative immigration, the erosion of civil liberties, et cetera. In terms of adapting to the new model, Jeffrey C. Walker catalogues:

> Over time, larger, more professional private equity businesses emerged, with whom the wealthy families couldn't compete. Instead, those families began to invest through the new PE funds. The PE industry then began offering funds specializing in particular industries (such as health care, tech, media, industrial, or consumer), geographies (including the United States, Europe, China, and Latin America), and deal sizes. Focused on pursuing higher rates of investment return, these specialized PE funds enjoyed [a] competitive advantage.[28]

Now here's where things get interesting; returning to Walker:

> Like PE funds, these philanthropic funds are focused on specific objectives—for example, the sustainable development goals (SDGs) established by the United Nations. Like PE funds, they are managed by experienced, knowledgeable leaders who can apply the most current knowledge of impactful program design to their investment decisions.
>
> And like PE funds, they allow wealthy families to channel their funds to a larger number of organizations than they could reach if they tried to seek out one well-run, effective nonprofit organization at a time.[29]

This is almost surely the primary reason that "social change" has accelerated so rapidly. Speaking at the 2017 Global Steering Group

28 Walker, Jeffrey C., "Attracting Greater Philanthropic Funding: The Private Equity Model," March 20, 2019. *Stanford Social Innovation Review.*
29 Ibid.

for Impact Investment Summit, Sir Ronald Cohen, an "impact investing innovator and advocate," believes that the field's rapid growth will reach a tipping point and "spark a chain reaction in impact creation," touching investors, big business, foundations, and social organizations.[30]

We are witnessing that already. Susan Wolf Ditkoff and Abe Grindle concur: "Many of today's emerging large-scale philanthropists aspire to…audacious successes…Steady, linear progress isn't enough; they demand disruptive, catalytic, systemic change—and in short order." From Bank of New York Mellon Wealth Management's paper "From Philanthropy to Social Investment" (2018):

> Demographic shifts are poised to bring about significant changes in the philanthropic market, and this evolution is being accelerated by the emergence of newer, more dynamic models for giving and changes to the U.S. tax code. It's imperative for both institutions and the individuals they serve to recognize how these changes will affect their philanthropic endeavors and learn how to navigate them in the most efficient manner possible… The continued evolution of the philanthropic market… will have a profound effect on how we view giving— less as charity, and more as a social investment…As philanthropists come to think of themselves as social investors, non-profits must also redefine themselves as "for-purpose" institutions. This must be more than a rebranding. An effective for-purpose institution must… aid in identifying opportunities across the investment spectrum…A "social investor" will endeavor to compile a portfolio of solutions that draws from both the non- and for-profit worlds…According to the Global Impact Investing Network, measurable investments in impact vehicles reached $228 billion in 2016, equal to 55% of the traditional philanthropic market. These vehicles, which fall under the umbrella of "social finance," do more than just pursue a positive societal or environmental impact;

---

30 Addy, Chris, Maya Chorengel, Mariah Collins, and Michael Etzel, "Calculating the Value of Impact Investing," January-February 2019. *Harvard Business Review.*

they also seek to offer a satisfactory financial return…To [younger givers], environmental, social and governance issues are intertwined with financial health and long-term, corporate sustainability.[31]

To some degree, this last point may be a "life imitating art or art imitating life" question, but most likely these "younger givers" have been conditioned to hold this view and are simply reflecting the neo-liberal architecture back at itself. Many others are legacies, and are merely carrying on the family tradition.

In any case, the ruling class has indeed made "environmental, social, and governance issues…intertwined with financial health and long-term, corporate sustainability." This is precisely the problem, and it goes way beyond "woke-washing" brands with the rainbow. It is social and political engineering on a global scale, where the ruling class has gone so far as to attempt to "elect a new people."

The ability to "seed" money/investments globally has allowed for a synergistic effect which, provided the present architecture remains unchanged or worse is built upon and expanded, can only amplify the stated aims of globalization.

Though Walker obviously believes this is a good thing, look past his glowing language to identify the strategy at play here, a strategy I will provide countless examples of regarding Maine in the body of this book:

> There are now philanthropic funds that focus on supporting great new ideas from top social and system entrepreneurs. This has been a core strategy of groups such as New Profit, Draper Richards Kaplan, Ashoka,[32] and Echoing Green. New Profit, in particular, has been investing in social change for 20 years, and has supported the growth of nonprofits like Teach for America, Kipp Schools, and City Year. Much like venture capital funds, philanthropic funds like New Profit install staff members on the boards of the organizations they support, where

---

31 Fontaine, Avery Tucker, "From Philanthropy to Social Investment: A New Way of Giving," 2018.
32 Ashoka has received funding from the Tides Foundation.

they spend three to five years adding value through the counsel, management insights, and useful connections they provide.[33]

This is the essential framework of philanthropic capitalism. The vast network of organizations are linked by personnel, history, ideology, and financial aims and ties. The various charities and philanthropies do not view their works as good for its own sake—there is *always* an ulterior motive, and it almost always involves an economic component. The highest "good" as it currently stands is creating social disharmony among whites, both from an ideological and economic standpoint.

Regarding the economics of "philanthropy," consider the Rise Fund's calculations on social investment; their charity is filtered through an economic lens of GDP and return on investment: "In the malaria world…organizations can measure the return on dollars invested in mosquito bed nets against lowering health costs and increasing a country's 10-year GDP. The result has been a 15-to-1 payback." Saving lives is a nice by-product, but those lives translate into more workers and more consumers. As Chris Addy, Maya Chorengel, Mariah Collins, and Michael Etzel explicate:

> The partnership between Rise Fund and Bridgespan Group has produced a forward-looking methodology to estimate…whether corporations or institutions can evaluate the projected return on an opportunity. We call our new metric the impact multiple of money (IMM). Once they have identified the target outcomes, social impact investors need to find an "anchor study" that robustly translates those outcomes into economic terms.[34]

This is not about "empowering women" or "marginalized communities," it's about training a semi-educated and compliant workforce who will readily buy from the company store. It is not hyperbolic to state that the neo-liberal establishment is looking to

---

33 Walker, Jeffrey C., "Attracting Greater Philanthropic Funding: The Private Equity Model," March 20, 2019. *Stanford Social Innovation Review.*
34 Addy, Chris, Maya Chorengel, Mariah Collins, and Michael Etzel, "Calculating the Value of Impact Investing," January-February 2019. *Harvard Business Review.*

create a globalized, mobile, deracinated, and compliant serf class. They are already well on their way. Whether or not they are ultimately successful is up to us, Dear Reader.

The small cabal who've become wealthy beyond any bounds previously-imaginable obviously don't want anything to change; sure the country is being scrapped for parts—they're the ones driving it— but things like civic duty and family are quaint notions of a by-gone era anyway. What really matters are things like GDP and *profit*. In their case, what's good for the goose is good for the gander. It just so happens to be devastating to the people who call this place *home*, but the ruling class doesn't like us much, anyway.

To combat the pernicious agenda of the globalist establishment, we must first understand it. We must know the what's, the when's, the where's, the who's, the why's, and the how's. This volume strives to make that plain as day using Maine as a microcosm.

Chapter One: Do Not Pass NGO, Do Not Collect $200

"The invisible line would have no meaning unless most people were on the wrong side of it. Exclusion is no accident: it is the essence."—C.S. Lewis

Any treatment of the conflagration of aliens spreading across the state of Maine must first start with a southern border so porous it might as well be non-existent. This is not a recent phenomenon, either, as Michelle Malkin wrote in 2003 about Organ Pipe National Monument in southern Arizona:

> As many as 1,000 illegal aliens a day trample across Organ Pipe—trashing our fences, ruining the environment, breaking our laws and endangering lives. It's a smugglers' paradise and a national security nightmare. "We have caught people from China, Pakistan and Yemen coming through," says Bo Stone, an Organ Pipe ranger and close friend of Eggle. "If 1,000 illegal immigrants can walk through the desert here, so can 1,000 terrorists." Some 200,000 illegal border-crossers and 700,000 pounds of drugs were intercepted at Organ Pipe last year alone. According to Border Patrol agents, foreign invaders are so brazen that they've actually cleared their own private roads through the park.[35]

Fast forward to mid-June 2019, and as Yogi Berra once said, "It's déjà vu all over again":

> The U.S. Border Patrol chief testified…that migrants from 52 countries have illegally crossed the border

---

35 Malkin, Michelle, "Immigration, the War on Terror and the Rule of Law," April, 2003. *Imprimis*, Vol. 32, No. 4.

this year as she described an agency "overwhelmed on a daily basis" by the escalating crisis. "While smugglers primarily target the Northern Triangle, family units from 52 countries have illegally crossed the southern border so far this year," U.S. Border Patrol Chief Carla Provost told the House Homeland Security Border Security, Facilitation and Operations Subcommittee…"In just two weeks, more than 740 individuals from African nations—primarily family units—have been apprehended in Del Rio sector alone, compared to only 108 who crossed the southern border in the first eight months of the fiscal year," she said…Earlier in her remarks, Provost said that she has had to move 40-60 percent of manpower away from the border to process and care for nearly 435,000 families and children who have traveled across the border this year.[36]

Nevertheless, the official line is that America had, has, and will always have eleven million "undocumented persons." There are several obvious questions here for any thinking person beyond why the number of illegal aliens has been fixed into perpetuity, not least of which is how in just this small half-a-month snapshot over 740 Africans wound up surging across just one small section of the US-Mexico border.

As mentioned in the introduction, a perfectly-planned 12,000-mile-plus journey with hundreds of people doesn't just happen as a matter of course, even if one does have the funds.

Even accepting the official line at face value—always a dubious proposition—it defies logic that genuine refugees under immediate fear of persecution in deeply impoverished conditions had the time, means, and expertise to plot this multi-stage journey on Travelocity and execute it to perfection, all while having access to international media outlets to give interviews along the way.

And it's not like these African migrants are alone, either, they're just among the most conspicuous given the logistics. On March 25th, 2018 (Palm Sunday) a caravan of at least 1,200-1,500 people began their

---

36 Shaw, Adam, "Illegal immigrants from 52 countries crossed US-Mexico border this year," June 20, 2019. *Fox News.*

trek north toward the United States through Mexico, banking on the fact that no one from customs would stop them, or at the very least, that they'd be granted asylum in the land of milk and honey. Mostly from Honduras, and calling themselves "Migrants in the Struggle," these were not refugees—they were fleeing no conflict and were not at risk of ethnic or religious persecution—but they represented the Latin American version of Jean Raspail's Last Chance Armada from *The Camp of the Saints*, spurred on by the volunteers of People Without Borders/Pueblo Sin Fronteras.

They marched for "dignity" and the "right to asylum," and the end of "violence against women and the LGBTQI community." Ironically, the homosexual members of the caravan arrived separately because they had been ostracized from the body of migrants due to their sexuality. Such is the price of progress, I suppose.

How exactly LGBTQI rights and dignity ties into demanding a foreign country accept these illegal aliens is not explicated, but in case you hadn't noticed, the thinking train left the station a long time ago when it comes to "matters of the heart." As Jean Raspail wrote, "The important thing about oppression, if you're going to keep it panting in the public eye without killing it outright, is to make sure there's plenty of variety." The "dream" of Pueblo Sin Fronteras is, "to build solidarity bridges among peoples and turndown (*sic*) border walls imposed by greed."

Starting on the 18th, the Armada began amassing in Tapachula, Mexico, after illegally crossing the border, and over the course of the next week, more people subsequently joined as the group of aliens and their sponsors celebrated this first victory "against" borders—"The Refugee Caravan knocking down borders yesterday in Huehuetan! Immigration agents abandoned the post when they saw us coming. The people celebrate this first small victory!"

BuzzFeed published a story of an immigration agent who saw the caravan coming and simply walked off her post to get a Coke at a local restaurant as she watched the Armada stream by.

On April 5th, some no doubt well-intentioned American lawyers joined up with the caravan in Pueblo, Mexico, and de-briefed its Christs on the intricacies of immigration law and asylum claims and the like, all in the service of tearing down the awful borders that divide the rich tapestry of humanity!

The ultimate destination was Tijuana and on to Jerry "Moonbeam" Brown's California (which, by the way, is up 842% in human trafficking in the last decade).

Under the banner "We Are All Native Americans" (recalling eerily "We Are All From the Ganges Now"), the caravan specifically timed their departure to coincide with Holy Week and Easter; their self-styled "Stations of the Cross" will surely recall the timing of the landing of the Last Chance Armada from *The Camp of the Saints*, though in this instance it is the launch, not the landing, of the Armada.

The symbolism should be eminently clear—not only did the caravan's journey take forty days, but its genesis on Palm Sunday and its first Holy Week was consciously done to imbue the caravan with a certain religio-mythical aura and divinity of purpose that, coupled with its ceaseless sentimentalization in the public space that only grew the nearer they got to the US border, made its refusal of entry the most egregious of crimes, a violation of our most basic humanity.

An alternate slogan of this Last Chance Armada was "Migrants in the Battle," and several media outlets framed the caravan as a "crusade." Not a single member of the caravan saw fit to apply for a visa. This is actually an extremely entitled way to conduct oneself; imagine for a minute you were hosting an event and a group of people simply showed up and *demanded* entry.

By all rights you would refuse them, and yet here we found ourselves with thousands of individuals marching on the United States border illegally through Mexico while that nation does nothing (which should tell you all you need to know about Mexico's stance regarding its northerly neighbor), and *expect* admittance despite not qualifying under any definition as refugees, despite no formal invitation, and despite the fact that the American public has always in the majority been staunchly opposed to Third World immigration. We would be complete monsters to refuse their entry, though, to hear the media, academia, and so many politicians tell it.

This Pueblo Sin Fronteras is just one of a huge number of NGOs that are part of the vast refugee resettlement network. This network has virtually unlimited resources and is backed by some of the world's wealthiest individuals, not to mention multi-national corporations, banks, private equity firms, national governments, and supra-national and international governing bodies. Their synergy has produced the terrible globalist monstrosity known as "neo-liberalism" confronting us today.

Pueblo Sin Fronteras is affiliated with La Familia Latina Unida, a Chicago, Illinois-based 501(c)(4) illegal immigration advocacy organization formed in 2001 by Elvira Arellano, and the Chicago-based 501(c)(3) pro-illegal immigration group Centro Sin Fronteras, founded in 1987 by Emma Lozano, formerly of Centro de Accion Social Autonomo ("Center for Autonomous Social Action," or CASA), "the self-proclaimed vanguard of an ethnic Mexican class-based revolution" following a Marxist-Leninist ideology.[37]

The Last Chance Armada caravan was organized by Pueblo Sin Fronteras in conjunction with the CARA Family Detention Pro Bono Project, which consists of the Catholic Legal Immigration Network, Inc., the American Immigration Council, the Refugee and Immigrant Center for Education and Legal Services, and the American Immigration Lawyers Association. All are in favor of more immigration and mass amnesty.[38,39]

According to WND, at least three of the CARA organizations derive funding from George Soros's Open Society Foundations; the John D. and Catherine T. MacArthur Foundation (often shortened to just the MacArthur Foundation), the Ford Foundation, and the Carnegie Corporation also provide funding.[40]

Further:

> Alex Mensing is one of the organizers of the Pueblo sin Fronteras group, serving as an official spokesman at the border. While identifying himself as a paralegal at the University of San Francisco's Immigration and Deportation Defense Law Clinic, he also works with CARA. He regularly briefs leftist website and magazine Mother Jones, also a major recipient of Soros grants... Earlier this month [April 2018], Oregon's Democratic

---

37 Ruiz, Vicki L., *Latinas in the United States: A Historical Encyclopedia.* Indiana University Press: Bloomington, IN. 2006.
38 "Viacrucis de Refugiados (Refugee Caravan 2017)." Pueblo Sin Fronteras.
39 "Who," CARA, 2018.
40 WND Staff, "Border Caravan? Call it the George Soros Express," April 29, 2018. *WND.*

Governor Kate Brown accepted a contribution to her re-election campaign from Soros...Three days later, Brown announced the Oregon National Guard would not be participating in President Trump's effort to get the Guard providing border security... Last fall, Soros transferred $18 billion to the Open Society Foundations, the network of non-profits Soros uses to advance his globalist, borderless ideology both in the U.S. and around the world...Inside Philanthropy reported in 2016 that Soros...has said that he considers himself to be "some kind of god"... In the U.S., his foundation has provided funding for the Black Lives Matter movement and open borders activists...Documents show U.S. Agency for International Development (USAID) funds were funneled through that agency's Civil Society Project to back Soros's left-wing Open Society Foundations in Albania...USAID reportedly gave $9 million in 2016 to the "Justice for All" campaign, which is overseen by Soros's "East West Management Institute." Soros is also funding programs to fund the entry of "refugees" into Italy [and] Hungary.[41]

In January 2019, the Catholic Legal Immigration Network, Inc. (CLINIC) founded by the US Conference of Catholic Bishops[42] and

---

41 Ibid.

42 According to their Wikipedia page, CLINIC's "Center for Immigrant Rights tackles problems faced by low-income immigrants and CLINIC member agencies that can only be resolved through advocacy, education, pro bono representation, litigation, and media. The Center identifies legal trends and issues affecting immigrants and pursues responsive solutions. The Center prioritizes its advocacy agenda in concert with its member agencies. It also collaborates with Migration and Refugee Services of the United States Conference of Catholic Bishops (USCCB). At the national level, the Center for Immigrant Rights focuses on administrative advocacy with officials at the Department of Homeland Security (DHS) and the Executive Office for Immigration Review (EOIR). At the local level, the Center supports the efforts of advocates working to combat state and local anti-immigrant measures. To increase representation to detained immigrants, the Center coordinates the Board of Immigration Appeals Pro Bono Project. Because documentation and media coverage of the human impact of U.S. immigration policies are crucial to advocacy efforts that seek to create a more just immigration system, the Center

part of the CARA Family Detention Pro Bono Project joined forces with the Southern Poverty Law Center and the Legal Aid Justice Center to sue the Trump administration over the detainment of illegal alien children.

Why is a legal immigration network getting involved with illegal aliens? The same reason the Southern Poverty Law Center gets involved with cases that have nothing to do with poverty, unless it's to target impoverished people who can't afford decent representation, or else leave them impoverished after slandering their careers into the graveyard and bankrupting them from legal fees.

CLINIC works with the US Conference of Catholic Bishops (USCCB) and Catholic Charities USA (CCUSA) as part of the "refugee resettlement" racket. The US Conference of Catholic Bishops is one of nine private US "voluntary agencies" (VOLAGs) that work with the US State Department to place refugees in locales around the United States.

Although technically not one of the VOLAGs, CCUSA and several other Catholic organizations such as CLINIC are in effect partners and should be taken in totality as one. CCUSA programs are funded by the United States Conference of Catholic Bishops Office of Migration and Refugee Services, the US State Department, the US Department of Health and Human Services' Office of Refugee Resettlement, Diocesan support, and various other sources including private donations. As Ann Corcoran explicates:

> [The UN High Commissioner for Refugees] "virtually calls the shots" for the US Refugee Admission Program (RAP)... The U.S. State Department brings in the refugees that the U.N. has largely chosen for us, and Homeland Security are supposed to screen them... Then, these are divvied up, literally, between nine major contractors (VOLAGs) that include groups such as the U.S. Conference of Catholic Bishops, World Lutheran Service and Hebrew Immigrant Aid Society. There are six of them that are supposedly religious charities...funded

---

documents and facilitates media coverage of the challenges facing immigrants served by its network. It also provides support to its member and colleague agencies engaged in media outreach."

by the U.S. taxpayer. They then divide up their allotment of refugees among 350 subcontractors in 190 U.S. cities. They literally compete with each other for these refugees, because money comes along with each refugee.[43]

The tripartite US RAP is officially administered by: the US Department of State, Bureau of Population Refugees and Migration (PRM) that admits and contracts with voluntary agencies to process refugees; the Department of Homeland Security (DHS) that allegedly screens refugees abroad and the US Citizenship and Immigration Services (USCIS); and the Office of Refugee Resettlement (ORR) of the US Department of Health and Human Services (HHS) that funds grants to program contractors and refugee ethnic groups for "community absorption."[44]

In practice, the VOLAGs' funding comes from a variety of governmental sources beyond the latter, including but not limited to the State Department directly, USAID, the DHS, and others.

They are supported by the UN and the International Organization for Migration (IOM) as well as several other major NGOs in addition to the VOLAGs and the subcontractors. PRM funds and the International Refugee Committee (IRC) runs the Cultural Orientation Resource Exchange (CORE), an NGO which basically just tells the "refugees" where to go to receive benefits and hand-outs. Refugees International (RI) is a "refugee advocacy organization" run by Eric P. Schwartz, formerly with the US State Department and the United Nations and current Board member of the Hebrew Immigrant Aid Society (HIAS) and the Jewish Community Relations Council of Minnesota and Dakota.

Refugees International and other partners successfully advocated for the passage of the Elie Wiesel Genocide and Atrocities Prevention Act of 2018, which made it US law to regard "the prevention of genocide and other atrocities" as a core national security interest and moral responsibility, meaning never-ending world policing and accepting infinite numbers of "refugees."

---

43 Gordon, Jerry and Mike Bates, "Trojan Horse Federal Refugee Program Brings Jihadi Threat to America: An Interview with Ann Corcoran," June, 2015. *New English Review.*
44 Ibid.

Refugees International was the facilitating organization that tried to get illegal aliens in Israel re-located to Western countries such as Canada. The Jewish George Soros is a Director Emeritus. They receive funding from, among other companies and organizations: Akin Gump Strauss Hauer & Feld LLP, Google, Pfizer, the NoVo Foundation, Gilead Sciences, the Annie E. Casey Foundation, the World Bank, Steven Rattner, JP Morgan Chase, the Blackstone Charitable Foundation, CBS, Visa, Intel, the Tides Foundation, Booz Allen Hamilton, Comcast, AT&T, and UPS. The reader will see these names recur time and again in these pages.

Another NGO/501(c)(3) is InterAction, whose members include: the American Jewish World Service, Catholic Relief Services, Heartland Alliance, the International Catholic Migration Commission, Islamic Relief USA, Clark University, Oxfam America, Refugees International, US Climate Action Network, US Fund for UNICEF, Church World Service, the Ethiopian Community Development Council, the Hebrew Immigrant Aid Society, the International Rescue Committee, Norwegian Refugee Council USA, the Pan American Development Foundation, and the US Committee for Refugees and Immigrants.

It is partnered with the World Bank, the United Nations, the European Commission, the government of the United States, the government of Sweden, FedEx, UPS, the Open Society Foundations, the Wellspring Philanthropic Fund, the Rockefeller Foundation, the New Venture Fund, the Annenberg Foundation Trust at Sunnylands, and the Bill and Melinda Gates Foundation among others. Major sources of funding include USAID, the Rockefeller Foundation, UPS, the Wellspring Philanthropic Fund, the Bill and Melinda Gates Foundation, the New Venture Fund, the Open Society Foundations, FedEx, the US State Department Bureau of Population Refugees and Migration (PRM), and more.

Lastly, we have Refugee Council USA, a coalition of refugee advocacy and resettlement NGOs, which includes all nine VOLAGs in addition to Amnesty International, Refugees International, Islamic Relief USA, the International Catholic Migration Commission, Oxfam, and others. The nine American VOLAGs are:

- Church World Service (CWS)
- Ethiopian Community Development Council (ECDC)

- Episcopal Migration Ministries (EMM)
- Hebrew Immigrant Aid Society (HIAS)
- International Rescue Committee (IRC)
- US Committee for Refugees and Immigrants (USCRI)
- Lutheran Immigration and Refugee Service (LIRS)
- The United States Conference of Catholic Bishops (USCCB)
- World Relief (WR)

As the Capital Research Center notes, "Because they are non-governmental organizations (NGOs), they can and do lobby for advantageous changes to immigration law and build allies in Congress and the bureaucracy."

Further, as Jerry Gordon and Mike Bates report:

> Congress has never exercised effective oversight of the Refugee Admissions Program (RAP) through hearings and recommendations. The US RAP has been used punitively against political critics. One example is the assignment of large numbers of Somali refugees to the Congressional District of former US Rep. Michelle Bachmann in St. Cloud, Minnesota. The US RAP has been fraught with fraud...20,000 fraudulently admitted Somali refugees were never pursued or ejected. Given the world's attention on the problem of illegal migrants crossing the Mediterranean, the State Department refugee program let in to the US hundreds of Somalis who fled to the Island of Malta without any clearances... [Growing numbers of refugees] will be "seeded" in American cities under the Fostering Community Engagement and Welcoming Communities Project of the ORR with the Soros-backed NGO, "Welcoming America."45

There is a saying, "Shit rolls downhill," and when considering the "refugee re-settlement" business—and it is in no small part a business—this saying is very apropos.

Starting with the United Nations at the top, the nine major contractors in the US then "farm out" these refugees (most of whom

---

45 Ibid.

are anything but) to approximately 350 sub-contractors to "seed" the refugees across the country.

Most are settled in overwhelmingly white areas with high trust and social cohesion under the auspices of humanitarianism and economic necessity. There is certainly an economic imperative for mass immigration on behalf of the Money Power, one which I will continue to illustrate, but there is also a very clear ideological motivation as well.

As immigrants largely cluster in major cities, migrants must be artificially pumped into rural and/or less-"sexy" destinations by NGOs, the government, businesses, or some combination thereof. Migrant labor has been one of the primary drivers of the demographic transformation of areas in states from Oregon to Kansas to Georgia, but the vast network of re-settlement organizations, often with ample governmental or extra-governmental assistance, are able to pin-point and target areas to be totally "re-made." These areas are *always* overwhelmingly white and generally unprepared for their diversity enema. Maine is, unfortunately, but one.

For perspective, one of the *smallest* of these VOLAGs, the Ethiopian Community Development Council (ECDC) and its subsidiaries received almost $21.9 million from federal, state, and local government grants in 2016 according to their own financial report on the condensed consolidated statement of activities. In fiscal year 2019, they received $16.844 million from USAID, $8.641 million from the US State Department, and $3.864 million from the Department of Health and Human Services.

They have also received recent donations from the United Way, IKEA, HSBC Bank USA, the Wells Fargo Foundation, Capital One, BB&T, SunTrust Bank, Whole Foods, TD Bank, Susan G. Komen, Ethiopian Airlines, the Church of Jesus Christ of Latter-Day Saints, E*Trade, Bed Bath and Beyond, PNC, and Golden & Cohen LLC. They've received Open Society and Tides money in the past; additionally:

> ECDC testified before Congress last year that the Unaccompanied Alien Children crisis could "lead to the demise of the refugee resettlement program as we know it." This was primarily a funding concern...

ECDC provides a wide variety of services to refugees, and is involved in other contractual services as well, for example Small Business Administration microloans for new minority businesses.[46]

Organizations like the ECDC and CASA de Maryland (which receives money from the Open Society Institute in Baltimore) partner with Citigroup to offer microloans to cover the fees for immigrants who apply for US citizenship:

In recent years, the banking company has given more than $1 million to CASA for its immigration work, including a $100,000 grant this year for the group's efforts to promote citizenship. For Citigroup, the program is a farsighted effort to curry favor with new Americans who might well become financial customers. One of every seven Marylanders is foreign-born; in New York, where Citi also sponsors citizenship programs, the proportion is one-in-three. Among immigrants who aren't citizens, 23 percent don't use a bank, according to a 2013 report by the Federal Deposit Insurance Corp., but the figure shrinks for naturalized citizens to just 5 percent. For a bank, more citizens means more business…"It's clearly not just building a national identity and becoming an American," [Bob Annibale, global director of Citi Community Development] explains. "They're building a financial identity." George Escobar, senior director of health and human services for CASA de Maryland, acknowledges Citi's business interest in helping immigrants gain access to credit…While the loans themselves are underwritten by two community development financial institutions, funds from Citi have been used to administer the program, including staffing for financial education, coordinating the loan program, and monitoring payments. The bank gets a branding boost, too: some program materials clearly state Citi's involvement as one of the backers, according to Escobar. Citi doesn't have branches in Maryland, but

---

46 CRC Staff, "Refugee Resettlement: The Lucrative Business of Serving Immigrants," July 28, 2015.

it has credit cards and other financial products available to consumers across the country. "Yes, there's an interest that a financial institution might see from folks that now have a more stable credit rating and they're able to apply for more products," Escobar said. "That's what this economy is built on."[47]

Based on 2012 IRS Form 990 submissions, the International Rescue Committee (IRC), received over $332 million in federal grants and contracts, and in 2018, per *Forbes*, its total revenues were $747 million, $442 million of which came from government sources. It has also received millions from the Ford Foundation and the Open Society Foundations, among others, and is active in facilitating migrants into Europe in addition to its subversive efforts in the United States. According to Influence Watch, the Vanguard Charitable Endowment Program provided over $22 million to the International Rescue Committee between 2005 and 2013. Vanguard:

> Offers customers donor-advised funds, which allow customers to channel donations to organizations of the donor's choosing, although in practice directors of donor-advised funds often recommend organizations and initiatives to support. Donor-advised funds are also often used by foundations that wish to mask their money flows to controversial grantees. Thus Vanguard has been the conduit for extensive support of immigration "reform" groups like Welcoming America (2014 net assets $4.5 billion).[48]

The IRC has a long and strange history; its German precursor—International Relief Association (IRA)—was founded by the Communist Party Opposition (KPO) and the Socialist Workers Party (SAP); its American faction was founded in 1933 by the Jewish Albert Einstein and the Jewish head of the American Communist Party Jay Lovestone (who had changed his name from Jacob Liebstein), among others, and their primary purpose was aiding Jews and communist

---

47 Hesson, Ted, "Citigroup's Investment in Soon-to-Be Citizens," July 6, 2015. *The Atlantic.*
48 "Vanguard Charitable Endowment Program," Influence Watch.

factions (often one and the same) in Germany, Spain, France, and Italy. By the 1950s under the leadership of the Jewish Leo Cherne it was a vital extension of CIA operations across the globe.

Large scale "refugee" re-settlements of mostly Jews were also central to their mission until later in the 1950s and into the 1960s when Vietnamese, Cuban, and Haitian "refugees" began to receive IRC assistance. It's now basically anyone and everyone who is not white.

The IRC is headquartered in New York but is active across the United States and in at least forty countries; it is run by the Jewish David Miliband, son of Marxist sociologist Ralph Miliband and former Labour MP, Foreign Secretary, and Environment Secretary to Tony Blair. "Climate change" became a priority during Miliband's tenure as Environment Secretary. His brother was the inaugural Secretary of State for Energy and Climate Change.

The IRC's Board of Directors is comprised of:

- Zeid Ra'ad Al Hussein (Former UN Human Rights Chief)
- Clifford S. Asness (Managing and Founding Principal, AQR Capital Management)
- George Biddle (Chairman, World Connect)
- Florence A. Davis (President, Starr Foundation)
- Susan Dentzer (Visiting Fellow, Duke-Margolis Center for Health Policy)
- Cheryl Cohen Effron (Founder, Conjunction Fund)
- Timothy F. Geithner (75th US Secretary of the Treasury; President, Warburg Pincus)
- Becca Heller (Executive Director, International Refugee Assistance Project)
- John Holmes (Co-Chair, Board of Directors, IRC-UK)
- Maria Hummer-Tuttle (Chair of the Board of Trustees, J. Paul Getty Trust; Member, Council on Foreign Relations; President, Hummer-Tuttle Foundation)
- Andrew Klaber (Partner, Paulson & Company)
- Steven Klinsky (Founder and CEO, New Mountain Capital)
- David A. Levine (Former Chief Economist, Sanford C. Bernstein)

- François-Xavier de Mallmann (Chairman of the Investment Banking Division, Goldman Sachs)
- Eduardo G. Mestre (Chairman of Global Advisory, Evercore Partners; Chair IRC Overseers)
- David Miliband (President and CEO, International Rescue Committee)
- Jillian Muller (wife of hedge fund manager Pete Muller)
- Thomas Nides (Vice Chairman, Morgan Stanley)
- Michael J. O'Neill (Executive Vice President, Corporate & External Affairs, American Express Company)
- Anjali Pant MD, MPH
- Dr. Kathleen Pike (Professor of Psychology, Departments of Psychiatry and Epidemiology, Columbia University Medical Center)
- Omar Saeed (Portfolio Manager, Millennium Management)
- Pamela Saunders-Albin (Co-Founding Investor, Goldman Sachs Social Impact Fund)
- Gillian Sorensen (Senior Advisor, United Nations Foundation)
- Joshua L. Steiner (Co-Chairman of the Board of Castleton Commodities, and Senior Adviser, Bloomberg, LP)
- Sally Susman (Executive Vice President, Corporate Affairs, Pfizer Inc.)
- Mona K. Sutphen (Senior Advisor, The Vistria Group)
- Tony Tamer (Founder and Co-CEO, H.I.G. Capital)
- Dr. Merryl H. Tisch (Former Chancellor of the New York State Board of Regents)
- E. Eric Tokat (Partner, Centerview Partners)
- Maureen White (Senior Fellow at the Foreign Policy Institute at the Paul H. Nitze School of Advanced International Studies, Johns Hopkins University)
- Leah Joy Zell (Founding Partner, Lizard Investors, LLC)

Additionally, the IRC has a Board of Overseers, which is comprised of:

- Morton I. Abramowitz (Senior Fellow, The Century Foundation and President Emeritus, Carnegie Endowment for International Peace)

- Madeleine K. Albright (Chair, Albright Stonebridge Group)
- Laurent Alpert (Senior Counsel, Cleary Gottlieb, Steen and Hamilton)
- F. William Barnett (Former Director, McKinsey & Company, Inc.)
- Alan R. Batkin (Chairman and CEO, Converse Associates, Inc.)
- Christoph Becker (Chief Executive Officer and Chief Creative Officer, gyro)
- Georgette F. Bennett (President, Tanenbaum Center for Inter-religious Understanding and Founder, Multifaith Alliance for Syrian Refugees)
- Vera Blinken (Chair, Primavera Mobil Mammography Program; Vice Chair, Foundation of Art Preservation in Embassies; Co-Chair, Blinken European Institute/Columbia University)
- Betsy Blumenthal (Senior Managing Director, Kroll Associates)
- W. Michael Blumenthal (Former Secretary of the US Treasury and Founding Director of Jewish Museum Berlin)
- Andrew H. Brimmer (Partner, Joele Frank, Wilkinson, Brimmer, Katcher)
- Jennifer Brokaw, MD (Associate Professor of Clinical Emergency Medicine, University of California, San Francisco)
- Tom Brokaw (Special Correspondent, NBC News)
- Glenda Burkhart (Director of Organizational Development, Exxon Chemical; Consultant, Bain and Company; Coordinator of the US-wide roll-out and subsequent effort to affect policy from the research of William G. Bowen and Derek Bok regarding race-sensitive admissions policies in colleges and universities, *The Shape of the River, Long-Term Consequences of Considering Race in College and University Admissions*)
- Frederick Burkle, MD (Senior International Public Policy; Scholar at Woodrow Wilson; International Center for Scholars)
- Néstor Carbonell (Former Vice President for International Public Affairs, PepsiCo)

- Robert M. Cotton (Staff Assistant at the White House in Washington, DC; Attorney-Advisor, the Agency of International Development at the Department of State in Washington, DC)
- Trinh D. Doan (Senior Vice President, Bank of America)
- Jodie Eastman (Member; Leadership Council, New York Stem Cell Foundation)
- Andra Ehrenkranz (wife of John Ehrenkranz, Chief Investment Officer, Ehrenkranz Partners; previously, John was a Managing Director at Morgan Stanley Capital Partners, the private equity investment group of Morgan Stanley)
- Laura Entwistle (Co-Founder and CEO, EmancipAction)
- Katherine Farley (Former Senior Managing Director Brazil, China & Global Corporate Marketing, Tishman Speyer)
- Princess Firyal of Jordan
- Vicki Foley (wife of investment banker David Foley)
- Kenneth R. French (Carl E. and Catherine M. Heidt, Professor of Finance at the Tuck School of Business at Dartmouth College)
- Jeffrey E. Garten (Dean Emeritus, Yale School of Management)
- Corydon J. Gilchrist (President/Owner, KCG Holdings I, LLC)
- Robin Gosnell (retired attorney)
- Evan G. Greenberg (Chairman and CEO, Chubb)
- Maurice R. Greenberg (Chairman and CEO, C.V. Starr & Co.)
- Sarah K. Griffin (Partner, Milbank LLP)
- Morton I. Hamburg (Professional Photographer)
- Philip Hammarskjold (CEO & Managing Director, Hellman & Friedman LLC)
- Leila Heckman (Managing Director, Lebenthal Asset Management)
- Karen Hein, MD (Former President of the William T. Grant Foundation)
- Lucile P. Herbert (Volunteer, International Rescue Committee)
- Bob Horne (President, ZS Fund LP)

- Aly S. Jeddy (Director, McKinsey & Company)
- Marvin Josephson (Founding Chairman, ICM Holdings, Inc.)
- Alton Kastner (Former Deputy Director, International Rescue Committee)
- M. Farooq Kathwari (Chairman, President and CEO, Ethan Allen Interiors, Inc.)
- Caroline Kennedy (the only surviving child of President John F. Kennedy and First Lady Jacqueline Bouvier Kennedy; former US Ambassador, Japan; married to Edwin Schlossberg, Jewish author and designer)
- Henry A. Kissinger (former US Secretary of State; Chairman, Kissinger Associates)
- Yong Kwok (Physician)
- Reynold Levy (Former President, Lincoln Center)
- Winston Lord (Former US Ambassador, China)
- John J. Mack (Chair Emeritus, Morgan Stanley)
- Vincent A. Mai (Chairman and CEO, Cranemere, Inc.)
- Robert E. Marks (President and Chairman, Marks Ventures, LLC)
- Roman Martinez IV (Former Managing Director, Lehman Brothers, Private Investor)
- Kati Marton (author and journalist)
- David Miliband (President and CEO, International Rescue Committee)
- W. Allen Moore (Distinguished Fellow, The Henry Stimson Center)
- Sara Moss (Executive Vice President and General Counsel, The Estée Lauder Companies)
- Indra Nooyi (Former Chairman and CEO, PepsiCo)
- Sarah O'Hagan (Former Co-Chair, International Rescue Committee Board; Consultant)
- Susan Patricof (wife of Alan Patricof, a Jewish pioneer of venture capital and private equity, founder of Apax Partners—based on a play on Patricof's name: Alan Patricof Associates Cross (x) Border—which today remains one of the largest private equity firms in the world)

- Scott Pelley (Anchor and Managing Editor, CBS Evening News and Correspondent, 60 Minutes)
- Dylan Pereira (Head of Strategic Solutions, GLG)
- David L. Phillips (Director of the Program on Peace-building and Rights at Columbia University's Institute for the Study of Human Rights)
- General Colin L. Powell (Former U.S. Secretary of State and Chairman of the Joint Chiefs of Staff)
- Her Majesty Queen Rania Al Abdullah of Jordan
- Milbrey Rennie (Consultant)
- Condoleezza Rice (Thomas and Barbara Stephenson Senior Fellow on Public Policy at the Hoover Institution, Stanford University)
- Andrew Robertson (President and Chief Executive Officer, BBDO Worldwide)
- Felix G. Rohatyn (Special Advisor to the Chairman and CEO, Lazard Freres)
- Gideon Rose (Editor, Foreign Affairs)
- George Rupp (Former President and CEO, International Rescue Committee)
- George Sarlo (Managing Director, Walden Venture Capital)
- Reshma Saujani (Founder and CEO, Girls Who Code)
- Tom Schick (Former Co-Chair, International Rescue Committee Board)
- Dr. Rajiv Shah (President, Rockefeller Foundation)
- James T. Sherwin (J.D. Hon LLD; Director, Hunter Douglas N.V.)
- James C. Strickler, M.D. (Emeritus Professor Medicine and Community Medicine, Emeritus Dean, Dartmouth Medical School)
- Arthur O. Sulzberger, Jr. (Chairman of the Board, The New York Times Company)
- Liv Ullmann (actress and director)
- William J. vanden Heuvel (Chairman, the Franklin and Eleanor Roosevelt Institute)
- Josh Weston (Honorary Chairman of the Board and former CEO, ADP)

- Jonathan L. Wiesner (Owner and CEO, Sustainable Apparel Group, LLC)
- William T. Winters (CEO, Standard Chartered)
- James D. Wolfensohn (Chairman of Wolfensohn Co., LLC, Chairman of Citi International Advisory and Former President of the World Bank)
- Tracy R. Wolstencroft (President & CEO, National Geographic)

The IRC-UK is funded by:

AS Roma; Bernard van Leer Foundation; Edelman; The Financial Times; J. Paul Getty, Jr. General Charitable Trust; RELX Group; the Sir James Reckitt Charity; Stavros Niarchos Foundation; the UK Mutual Steam Ship Assurance Association; UBS Optimus Foundation; Vitol Foundation; the Asfari Foundation; the Saïd Foundation; the British Embassy in South Sudan; Danish International Development Agency (DANIDA); Development Cooperation Division of the Department of Foreign Affairs of Ireland (Irish Aid); Dutch Ministry of Foreign Affairs (Dutch MFA); European Commission Directorate General for Development and Cooperation (EuropeAid); European Commission Directorate General Humanitarian Aid and Civil Protection (ECHO); European Development Fund; French Development Agency (AFD); German Development Bank (KfW); German Society for International Cooperation (GIZ); Humanitarian Innovation Fund (HIF); Start Fund; Swedish International Development Cooperation Agency (SIDA); Swiss Agency for Development and Cooperation (SDC); UK Department for International Development (DFID); Action Against Hunger / Children's Investment Fund Foundation; Christian Blind Mission; and the Ethical Tea Partnership, among others.

For 2018, the IRC-UK's principal funding sources were:

- ECHO: £51.1 million (2017: £54.2 million)
- DFID: £47.3 million (2017: £59.7 million)
- SIDA: £11.7 million (2017: £7.9 million)
- EuropeAid: £9 million (2017: £7.1 million)
- Dutch MFA: £3.7 million (2017: £0.6 million)
- Irish Aid: £2.3 million (2017: £1.5 million)

• DANIDA: £2.4 million (2017: £1.2 million)
• GIZ: £1.2 million (2017: £0.5 million)
• SDC: £1.2 million (2017: £1.7 million)
• Other: £7.3 million (2017: £2.2 million)

For fiscal year 2019, the IRC received over $100 million from USAID, $74.273 million from the US State Department, $28.12 million from the Department of Health and Human Services, $3.776 million from the Department of Justice, nearly $1 million from the Department of Homeland Security, nearly $500,000 from the Department of Agriculture, $150,000 from the Small Business Administration, nearly $50,000 from the Corporation for National and Community Service, and just over $44,000 from the Department of the Treasury. Their total revenue for their fiscal year ending on September 30th, 2018 per *Forbes* was $747 million.

Let's take a look at the other seven VOLAGs. The USCRI created the framework for the Obama administration's Central American Minors program, and its President and CEO, Lavinia Limón, served as the director of the Office of Refugee Resettlement during the Clinton administration before moving on to the National Immigration Forum. For fiscal year 2019, the Department of Health and Human Services granted the USCRI $23.145 million and the State Department granted the USCRI $2.812 million.

In fiscal year 2019, Church World Service received over $42 million from the US State Department, $7.292 million from the Department of Health and Human Services, and nearly $230,000 from the Department of Homeland Security. Church World Service is also funded by George Soros, the Ford Foundation, the Tides Foundation, and Vanguard, among others. The Ford Foundation:

> Financed creation of the open borders movement and multiculturalism in the 1960s. Funded creation and growth of the radical Mexican American Legal Defense and Education Fund (MALDEF), which spawned the DREAM Act concept, the National Council of La Raza (NCLR) and the Puerto Rican Legal Defense and Education Fund, which gave us Supreme Court Justice Sonya Sotomayor... Ford money created the "public interest" law movement, with tens of millions

going to organizations supporting minorities…as well as environmental legal groups such as the Environmental Defense Fund and Earthjustice…Walter Olson refers to Ford as "the Johnny Appleseed of litigation liberalism" and notes that funding activist lawyers has been a key theme of Ford's grantmaking for decades. For over half a century, the Ford Foundation has operated behind the scenes to flip American law schools into operatives of 1960s-style "social change." Other large organizations like Carnegie, Open Society, and MacArthur have followed the Ford Foundation's path, and the result can be seen in landmark Supreme Court decisions, the abundance of politicized "legal clinics" across college universities, and the courts' growing willingness to defer to "international law."…The foundation devoted tens of millions of dollars to organizations supporting President Barack Obama's choice for Supreme Court, Judge Merrick Garland, after the death of Justice Antonin Scalia…It is credited with turning the League of United Latin American Citizens (LULAC) from a conservative group that helped Hispanics assimilate into just another radical leftist Hispanic grievance group. Ford's impact on immigration activism cannot be overstated (2013 net assets, $12.1 billion).[49]

From 2008-2015, Episcopal Migration Ministries (EMM) received $105.2 million from the federal government, and continues to subsist primarily on government grants, but it has also received money from the Church of Jesus Christ of Latter-day Saints (LDS). They received $17.3 million in 2012 as reported by an independent auditor, but they don't publish any IRS documents and the numbers can be tough to track down. I was able to find a church statement from 2017 where the EMM said it anticipated $14.2 million from the US State Department and $6.2 million from the federal Department of Health and Human Services.

The EMM's "preferred communities" are: "Special Immigrant Visa holders (SIVs) who arrived with physical disabilities or medical

---

49 "Ford Foundation," Influence Watch.

conditions; refugees experiencing social or psychological conditions; single mothers; elderly refugees without family support; LGBTI refugees; HIV-positive refugees; refugees with a history of suicide factors; and youth and young adults without parental support."[50] Real cream of the crop there. The Domestic and Foreign Missionary Society (DFMS) is the corporate and legal entity of the national Episcopal Church.

World Relief, in addition to its government funding, receives funds from the Vanguard Charitable Endowment Program, the Mustard Seed Foundation, the Soros Fund Charitable Foundation, the Pfizer Foundation, and Global Impact among others. World Relief, officially World Relief Corporation of National Association of Evangelicals, had revenues in 2018 of over $65 million. For fiscal year 2019, they received $16.844 million from USAID, $8.641 million from the US State Department, and $3.864 million from the Department of Health and Human Services.

The Lutheran Immigration and Refugee Service (LIRS)—the VOLAG primarily responsible for re-settling so many Somalis in Minnesota—receives both federal grants ($57.3 million in fiscal year 2019) and private funding from the usual suspects, as well as revenue from its Lutheran Center Corporation, and it also *provides* grants to the Hebrew Immigrant Aid Society and Catholic Charities. On February 1st, 2020, the Department of Health and Human Services' Administration for Children and Families announced a $20 million grant to LIRS for "residential shelters and transitional foster care for unaccompanied alien children." LIRS works closely with the ACLU on behalf of "refugee rights" and:

> In 2017, LIRS collaborated with the Tent Partnership for Refugees to develop the U.S. Employers' Guide to Hiring Refugees. As a mobilizing force for the private sector to support refugees, the Tent Foundation sought LIRS's expertise on hiring just as many companies were offering strong public commitments to employing and investing in refugees and their communities. Leveraging LIRS's 20 years of experience providing employment assistance to national resettlement organizations, the

---

50 Episcopal Migration Ministries Annual Report, 2018.

Hiring Guide helps corporations better understand who refugees are, their journeys through the complicated resettlement process, the benefits of hiring refugees, and the solutions for overcoming workplace challenges.[51]

In the summer of 2015, LIRS arranged for migrants to accompany HIAS's interns to meet with legislators including Maine Senator Susan Collins "to discuss legislation that protects refugees." The Hebrew Immigrant Aid Society (HIAS)[52] describes itself as a "major implementing partner of the United Nations Refugee Agency and the U.S. Department of State." It provides pro bono legal services for asylum applications and removal hearings, including "filings with USCIS, representation at asylum interviews (Credible Fear Interviews, Reasonable Fear Interviews), representation before local immigration courts, representation before the Board of Immigration Appeals (BIA), and representation for federal court appeals."

HIAS places border fellows in NGOs along the southern border to provide legal representation to asylum seekers and border-crossers;

---

51 Lutheran Immigration and Refugee Service Annual Report, 2017.

52 "HIAS, the Hebrew Immigrant Aid Society, is the national and worldwide arm of the organized American Jewish community for the rescue, relocation and resettlement of refugees and migrants. HIAS works closely with Jewish Federations, Jewish Family Service and Jewish Vocational Service agencies across the nation to maintain an extensive cooperative network committed to providing the broadest possible spectrum of professionally staffed resettlement services. All HIAS affiliates receive Reception and Placement grant funds to assist in meeting the needs of refugees in their initial phase of resettlement. Many HIAS affiliates also elect to supplement these services with private funding and other resources, enabling them to participate in the ORR Voluntary Agency Matching Grant Program as a way of further enhancing their ability to assist refugees to attain economic and social self-sufficiency. Several HIAS sites have also been awarded ORR Preferred Communities funding to help HIAS diversify its caseload, an effort that has resulted in an increasingly large proportion of HIAS's refugee arrivals being from populations other than the former Soviet Union and Iran. In addition, HIAS has received funding from ORR to oversee marriage education activities conducted by affiliates in Tucson, San Diego, Atlanta, Chicago, and Bergen County (NJ) and to provide technical assistance to other ORR grantees. HIAS also has received funding to foster civic participation among emigres from the former Soviet Union (read: Jews) living across the United States." From the Office of Refugee Resettlement's 2005 Annual Report to Congress

they also run a program called the HIAS Border Response Team, which trains Spanish-speaking people to help those attempting to enter into the United States with the filling-out of forms, the translating of documents, and other tasks. HIAS helps the NGO Kids in Need of Defense (KIND) with the legal representation of "forcibly separated families."

Their leadership also does plenty of pro-open borders propaganda such as the TED Talk "Why Asylum is a Fundamental Right" by HIAS Senior Vice President for Public Affairs Melanie Nezer.

HIAS does all of this and more, and has gone one step further in profiting off mass migration into the US—HIAS has an agreement under which it collects on loans given out by the International Office of Migration (IOM) to refugees. HIAS keeps 25% of the total amounts collected, and recognizes it as migrant loan processing fees and repayments revenue in the accompanying consolidated statements of activities. HIAS's corporate partners include Airbnb, 3M, Starbucks, Marriott, and Sodexo.

Surely there is no vested interest in having cheap labor by these companies. HIAS also received nearly $20 million from the US State Department in fiscal year 2016 and over $4.3 million from the US Department of Health and Human Services; for fiscal year 2019, they received nearly $20 million from the US State Department, nearly $4.6 million from the US Department of Health and Human Services, and $250,000 from the Department of Homeland Security. Private donors include Vanguard and the Tides Foundation.

Claiming to have managed project and grantmaking activities of more than $2 billion since its creation, the Tides Foundation has supported hundreds of nonprofit projects in its quest to "accelerate toward a world of shared prosperity and social justice."[53] The Tides Foundation:

> Is a pass-through fund which launders money for wealthy donors who want to support radical causes without being identified. R.J. Reynolds' granddaughter, Nancy Jane Lehman, co-founded Tides in San Francisco along with New Left organizer Drummond Pike (2013 net assets, $142.3 million). Its sister organization, the Tides Center,

53 "History," Tides Foundation, February 9, 2017.

was directed for years by ACORN founder and director Wade Rathke (2013 nets assets, $68.2 million). Tides Center lists "support to resettle displaced Iraqi refugees" and to combat "inhumane immigration policy…" among its 2013 activities. Related organizations include the Tides Network (2013 revenues, $13.7 million), Tides, Inc. (2013 net assets, $432,000), and Tides Two Rivers Fund…Under tax law, the Tides Foundation is not obligated to report where it uses funds contributed by specific donors. One can discover many of donors to the Tides Foundation, and the Tides Foundation is obligated by law to disclose its grantees, but the link between the donor and the donee is washed away as the money passes through the Tides Foundation. The Tides Foundation maintains what are known as donor-advised funds (DAFs)…

Tides's global services division has helped manage more than $120 million in grants to over 150 countries, helping organizations with government compliance and overcoming regulatory burdens…It is difficult to know the full extent of the Tides Foundation's donor network. As a dark money operation, the Tides Foundation is not required to release this information, even if it does release some aggregate numbers.[54]

For the information available, we are able to find out that the Vanguard Charitable Endowment Program, Fidelity Investments Charitable Gift Fund, and Schwab Charitable Fund are commercial donor-advised fund providers.

A list of foundations that made donations to Tides from 1993-2003 was uncovered by Discover the Networks and includes: the W.K. Kellogg Foundation, the Richard and Rhoda Goldman Fund, the Vira I. Heinz Endowment, the Verizon Foundation, the Rockefeller Foundation, the Schumann Center for Media and Democracy, the Stern Family Fund, the Open Society Institute, the Vanguard Public Foundation, the John D. and Catherine T. MacArthur Foundation, the Ford Foundation, the Fannie Mae Foundation, the Carnegie

---

54 "Tides Foundation," Influence Watch.

Corporation of New York, the Bill and Melinda Gates Foundation, the Ben & Jerry's Foundation, the Andrew W. Mellon Foundation, the Annie E. Casey Foundation, the AT&T Foundation, the Barbara Streisand Foundation, the Arca Foundation, the ChevronTexaco Foundation, and the Bauman Family Foundation. We also learn that:

> It's not just private organizations and individuals who donate to the Tides Foundation. The Tides Foundation and affiliated Tides Center received $395,319 from the Department of Interior; $3,350,431 from the Environmental Protection Agency; $3,487,040 from the Department of Housing and Urban Development; $208,878 from the Department of Agriculture; $39,550 from the Department of Energy; $93,500 from the Small Business Administration; $10,986 from the Department of Health and Human Services; and $84,520 from the Centers for Disease Control U.S. Agency for International Development from 1997 to 2001 alone.[55]

Prominent members of the Tides Foundation's Board of Directors include Jacob Weldon, part of the Executive Management function at The Estée Lauder Companies, Inc., where he focuses on Global Public Affairs and Philanthropic Investments, and Steve Zuckerman, a Stanford MBA with a private investment firm background; from the Tides Center's Board we see Suzanne Nossel, architect of the first UN resolution on the rights of LGBTQ persons, CEO of PEN America, and former senior fellow for the Council on Foreign Relations (CFR), the Century Foundation, and the Center for American Progress (CAP), a think tank founded by John Podesta. She was also Vice President of US Business Development for Bertelsmann Media, associate in consumer and media practice at McKinsey & Company, and was the former Executive Director of Amnesty International. She is credited with co-coining the term "Smart Power" which furthers "liberal internationalism" through "soft power" and the US military. As a result of such views, Chris Hedges promptly announced he would no longer be participating in the PEN World Voices Festival upon hearing of her appointment to PEN, stating:

---

55 Ibid.

> Nossel's relentless championing of preemptive war—
> which under international law is illegal—as a State
> Department official along with her callous disregard for
> Israeli mistreatment of the Palestinians and her refusal as
> a government official to denounce the use of torture and
> use of extrajudicial killings, makes her utterly unfit to
> lead any human rights organization, especially one that
> has global concerns.[56]

For her part, Nossel, who traces her interest in human rights to her growing up Jewish in America, visits Israel frequently: "It's a place where I feel very comfortable and at home."

Contradicting their stance on immigration in Western countries, both Israeli Jews and diasporic Jews in the large majority favor walls, borders, and minimal to non-existent non-Jewish immigration into Israel, which in and of itself is a nation of immigrants and was founded under very dubious pretenses, though this is a topic for another time.

The following is the most recent available list of grantees and the amounts awarded (2015) by the Tides Foundation, although the list is far from complete, unfortunately, given the limited transparency of Tides and dark money organizations like them:

- #BlackLivesMatter ($5,000)
- 350.org ($81,815)
- Academy for the Love of learning ($5,300,000)
- ACLU Foundation ($38,176)
- Center for American Progress Action Fund ($20,000)
- Color of Democracy Project ($280,000)
- Democracy Now! ($302,373)
- Earthjustice ($370,250)
- General Assembly Space, Inc. ($765,344)
- Initiatives for Medicines Access and Knowledge ($1,105,000)
- International Gay and Lesbian Human Rights Commission ($21,622)
- J Street Education Fund ($1,404,000)

---

56 Hedges, Chris, "Statement to PEN," re-printed with permission by *Truth-dig*, April 2, 2013.

- Massachusetts Institute of Technology ($680,000)
- Media Matters for America ($225,000)
- Mind and Life Institute ($2,500,000)
- Multidisciplinary Association for Psychedelic Studies ($1,500,500)
- The Opportunity Institute ($1,499,144)
- Planned Parenthood Action Fund, Federation, and Affiliated ($146,415)
- Sierra Club Foundation ($56,500)
- Tides Canada Foundation ($74,000)
- Tides Network ($643,581)
- Working Families Organization ($213,800)[57]

We do know some of grantees from Tides' past, which include the Southern Poverty Law Center (SPLC), the Council of American-Islamic Relations (CAIR), the Rockefeller Family Fund, the New Israel Fund, the Israel Policy Forum, the New World Foundation, the People for the Ethical Treatment of Animals (PETA), the League of Women Voters, the NAACP, MALDEF, Oxfam, the Mexico Solidarity Network, the American Immigration Law Foundation, Greenpeace, the ACORN Institute, the Border Action Network, the Feminist Majority Foundation, and the National Resources Defense Council.

The National Resources Defense Council and the Sierra Club have also received large donations in the past from Jewish hedge fund billionaire S. Donald Sussman, who we will become *very* familiar with by the end of this book. Sussman is on the Board at the Center for American Progress, where Suzanne Nossel was a senior fellow.

The Sierra Club and the National Resources Defense Council sound like great charities for people who care about nature and the environment to donate to, but the reality is that they have merely become ideological weapons.

The Sierra Club's mission has been grossly perverted following its effective takeover and weaponization as an open borders advocacy group following a massive financial infusion by Jewish benefactor David Gelbaum, who made it known that the money came with strings attached: "I did tell [Sierra Club President] Carl Pope in 1994

---

57 "Tides Foundation," Influence Watch.

or 1995 that if they ever came out anti-immigration, they would never get a dollar from me." Also, from the *Los Angeles Times* in 2004:

> Gelbaum, who reads the Spanish-language newspaper *La Opinión* and is married to a Mexican American, said his views on immigration were shaped long ago by his grandfather, Abraham, a watchmaker who had come to America to escape persecution of Jews in Ukraine before World War I. "I asked, 'Abe, what do you think about all of these Mexicans coming here?'" Gelbaum said.
>
> "Abe didn't speak English that well. He said, 'I came here. How can I tell them not to come?' "I cannot support an organization that is anti-immigration. It would dishonor the memory of my grandparents."[58]

As Kevin MacDonald writes:

> It turns out that Gelbaum is also a major donor to the ACLU — more than $20 million annually. The *New York Times reports* that Gelbaum will not be making his donation this year [2009].
>
> But the gap will be at least partially filled: "Donors like the Leon Levy Foundation, the Open Society Institute [funded by George Soros], Peter B. Lewis and John Sperling had stepped up with pledges totaling $23 million spread over the next three years."[59]

Remember, Tides has donated to both the ACLU and the Sierra Club. Additionally, the *Washington Free Beacon* discovered that a "Klein Ltd.," a company incorporated in Bermuda that exists solely on paper, donated millions of dollars to the Sea Change Foundation, which donated $5.45 million to the Sierra Club just in the year 2012; Sea Change also donated to the Tides Foundation. The Sierra Club received a huge $50 million donation from the Jewish Michael Bloomberg as well.

---

58 Weiss, Kenneth R., "The Man Behind the Land," October 27, 2004. *Los Angeles Times.*
59 MacDonald, Kevin, "Jews are the financial engine of the left," December 10, 2009. *The Occidental Observer.*

The Natural Resources Defense Council (NRDC), like the Sierra Club, has received donations from S. Donald Sussman, and has received at least $10 million from this Sea Change Foundation.

Other sources of funding for the NRDC include the Energy Foundation (at least $14.7 million),[60] the Schwab Charitable Fund, George Soros's Open Society Foundations, the William and Flora Hewlett Foundation, the Wasserman Foundation, the Turner Foundation, the Sulzberger Foundation,[61] the Steven and Michele Kirsch Foundation, the Stephen M. Silberstein Foundation, the Schumann Center for Media and Democracy, the Scherman Foundation, the Rockefeller Foundation, the Robert A. and Renee E. Belfer Foundation, the Richard and Rhonda Goldman Fund, the Richard and Hinda Rosenthal Foundation, the Pfizer Foundation, Pew Charitable Trusts, the New York Times Company Foundation, the Morris and Gwendolyn Cafritz Foundation, the Marilyn and Jeffrey Katzenberg Foundation, the Laurence D. Belfer Family Foundation, the Lisa and Douglas Goldman Fund, the Leonardo DiCaprio Foundation, the Katz Family Foundation, the Joseph Rosen Foundation, the John D. and Catherine T. MacArthur Foundation, the James and Judith Dimon Foundation, JP Morgan Charitable Trust, the JM Kaplan Fund, the Horace W. Goldsmith Foundation, the Harold K. Hochschild Foundation, the Helena Rubenstein Foundation, the Harold Rubenstein Family Charitable Foundation, the FAO Schwarz Family Foundation, the Epstein/Roth Foundation, the David Geffen Foundation, the David and Lucile Packard Foundation, the Carnegie Corporation, the ARIA Foundation, the Bauman Family Foundation, the Arca Foundation, the AT&T Foundation, the Barbara Streisand Foundation, the Sandler Foundation, and the Public Welfare Foundation. A huge percentage of those organizations are Jewish or Jewish-run.

Finally, we turn to the last of the VOLAGs, the US Conference of Catholic Bishops. Per an internal document, the USCCB had total assets of over $427 million in 2017 and over $365 million in

---

60 The Jewish Tom Steyer has been a major donor in the past; in 1991, the Energy Foundation began as a $20 million collaboration between the Rockefeller Foundation, the MacArthur Foundation, and Pew Charitable Trusts.
61 The Jewish Ochs-Sulzberger family runs The New York Times Company through a dual class share "super-voting" structure.

2018. Their government contracts and grants revenue in 2018 was just under $48.5 million, and for 2017 it was over $72.3 million. USCCB also works with and provides funding to Catholic Legal Immigration Network, Inc. (CLINIC),[62] Parishes Organized to Welcome Refugees (POWR)—"this program is designed to provide assistance to refugee agencies in order to engage and mobilize parishes to welcome refugees"—and Preferred Communities, a program funded by USCCB via DHS and "designed to assist programs that are high-impact sites where specific populations or needs occur. In our case, this means providing additional medical case management and support to families."

Affiliated organization Catholic Relief Services, a 501(c)(3) headquartered in Baltimore, founded by the US Conference of Catholic Bishops, has annual revenues of just under $1 billion. In fiscal year 2019, USAID granted Catholic Relief Services nearly $296 million, the Department of Health and Human Services granted just over $53 million, the Department of Agriculture granted over $41.7 million, and the State Department granted $4.73 million.

In close partnership with the USCCB and of particular concern to us regarding the state of Maine as "the only game in town," Catholic Charities is a tax-exempt 501(c)(3) headquartered in Alexandria, Virginia. Officially, Catholic Charities functions as a subcontractor for the USCCB, which takes advantage of its infrastructure and large geographical footprint, but its resources and role are such that it really should be considered alongside the USCCB as part of a Catholic consortium also extending to Catholic Relief Services and others. It's all rather convoluted from the outside and complicating things, as Ann Corcoran relates, a 2012 GAO study revealed that the VOLAGs were not holding regular stakeholder meetings to consult with local agencies and elected officials. They pretty much operate with impunity and are essentially unaccountable.

Forbes ranked Catholic Charities the thirteenth-largest charity in the United States by private donation amount with a total revenue of approximately $3.7 billion for fiscal year 2017, $1.27 billion of which came from government funding. For *Forbes*, it was the 21st-largest charity ranked by private donation on their 2019 list with total revenues of $4.45 billion; $1.875 billion came from government

---

62 They have received Open Society Foundations funding.

funding. In 2010, Catholic Charities had even greater revenues of around \$4.7 billion, with just over \$554 million coming from federal funds, per the Catholic Charities USA's Annual Survey. Total government funding to CCUSA exceeded \$2.9 billion, however, if we include state, local, and "unspecified" government revenue.

Though overall revenues are down slightly from 2010, CCUSA increasingly derives its funding from private sources. Roughly 62% of its funds in 2010 came from the government, whereas that number was around 34% in 2017 and just over 42% in 2019. Revenue from the private sector increased around \$600 million in the time frame 2010–2017. CCUSA, like so many of these organizations, also has its own donor-advised fund (DAF).

These 501(c)(3)s serve a vital role in subversion under the guise of charity, among their many other functions, as we've seen. Additionally, many of these 501(c)(3)s such as HIAS have diverse investment portfolios that include mutual funds (HIAS also invests in the State of Israel government bonds). As Wesley B. Truitt informs, "A number of mutual funds feature investments that are socially responsible according to criteria advertised by the fund...The Timothy Plan fund avoids investing in companies whose practices are considered contrary to Judeo-Christian principles."

The 501(c)(3)s are often a valuable conduit and/or cover for major profit-making ventures. The ability of the 501(c)(3)s to then invest tax-deductible money or other assets in donor-advised funds (DAFs) as tax-sheltered investment income for the donors is one major reason for their increasing popularity among investors. From the Ropes & Gray LLP document, "Beyond the Private Foundation" (March 2018):

> With the passage of the Tax Reform Act of 1969, private foundations were required to contend with many new regulatory requirements and restrictions...Subsequent rulings...confirmed the advantages of the DAF model. In 1987, the Internal Revenue Service lost its attempt to deny tax-exempt status to a public charity that existed almost exclusively to maintain DAFs and other donor-recommended charitable projects. Several years later, the Internal Revenue Service granted tax-exempt status to

a non-profit organization established to maintain DAFs and affiliated with Fidelity Investments, namely, the Fidelity Charitable Gift Fund. Since then, DAFs have flourished. In 2016, there were reported to be almost 285,000 DAF accounts holding assets worth nearly $85 billion.

Grants from donor-advised funds to charities increased almost 20% from 2016 to 2017, with the number of individual donor-advised funds growing a whopping 60.2%. Charitable assets increased 27.3%. The Standard & Poor's 500 (S&P Index) rose by 18.4%, or over 400 points, in 2017.[63] Scholars have found that the "strongest predictor [of individual giving] is the S&P Index…a 100 point increase in the index is associated with a $1.7 billion increase in charitable deductions." Roughly 60% of the contributions to donor-advised funds are non-cash assets such as publicly traded securities, closely held stock, real estate, and personal property.[64]

Donor-advised funds are fast becoming the preferred method of choice for investors, though not the only one. More capital and other assets are also flowing through a variety of linked structures, such as LLCs and 501(c)(4)s in an increasingly inter-connected fashion. Alison Powell, Willa Seldon, and Nidhi Sahni explain:

> Living donors are also increasingly willing to forgo the tax benefit of putting funds into a foundation and are embracing alternative legal structures that enable both for-profit investing and nonprofit giving, or giving to political donations and advocacy. These structures include limited-liability companies (LLCs, which allow for greater control of funds and stocks, diversity of investment options, and more privacy than a foundation) and the 501(c)(4) structure (which allows social welfare organizations to participate in political campaigns and lobbying while maintaining their nonprofit status). For example, the Chan Zuckerberg Initiative, the Omidyar Network, and the Emerson Collective (run by Laurene Powell Jobs) have all set up LLCs to allow for advocacy

---

63 "The 2019 DAF Report," 2019. National Philanthropic Trust.
64 Ibid.

or impact investing. Even a more traditional institution, the Walton Family Foundation, has set up multiple 501(c)(4)s to support its focus areas.[65]

The modern concept of DAFs can be traced back to the late nineteenth century, when the first federated charity, the Jewish Federation, was established in Boston.

By the mid-1930s, donor-advised funds began to proliferate within the Jewish community and were usually housed at local Community Foundations and Jewish Federations. This remains central to the disbursal of funds today. These Jewish Community Foundations are massively profitable in their own right, as Alyssa Ochs reports:

> The year 2017 was yet another record-breaking year for the Jewish Community Foundation of Los Angeles (JCFLA) because it gave the highest dollar amount in grants in the funder's history—$100 million. Back in 2016, the funder gave $81 million, so this was a 23 percent increase. In 2015, the foundation and its donors made $96 million in grants, a 35 percent increase over $71 million the year before…We've said it before and we'll say it again: Jewish giving is going strong and getting even stronger by the year. At the end of 2017, the foundation's total charitable assets under management was $1.25 billion, which is a 14 percent increase from 2016. JCFLA opened 58 new donor advised funds just last year as well. Overall, the Jewish Community Foundation of Los Angeles manages assets for over 1,300 families…Jewish donors who work through community foundations like this often have a very global perspective and give a lot of money to Israel and Jewish outreach areas in other parts of the world…Another trend that we've been noticing lately among Jewish foundations is an increasing willingness to support non-Jewish groups.[66]

---

65 Powell, Alison, Willa Seldon, and Nidhi Sahni, "Reimagining Institutional Philanthropy," Spring, 2019. *Stanford Social Innovation Review.*
66 Ochs, Alyssa, "Why We Pay Attention to This Top Jewish Community Foundation—And Why You Should, Too," September 14, 2018. *Inside Philanthropy.*

The Jewish Federation of Metropolitan Chicago, as another example, has net assets of $1.736 billion according to *Forbes*, the American Jewish Joint Distribution Committee (JDC) has net assets of $381 million, and the United Jewish Appeal (UJA)-Federation of New York has net assets approaching $1.5 billion.

Of particular note here is the substantial amount of funding Catholic Charities derives from Jewish sources. Combined Jewish Philanthropies' Legal Aid Fund for Immigrants raised more than $600,000 for Catholic Charities of Boston within the first half of 2018. Combined Jewish Philanthropies (CJP), Boston's Jewish Federation, and Catholic Charities of the Archdiocese of Boston launched the CJP Legal Aid Fund for Immigrants in order to "enable Catholic Charities to meet the growing demand for legal assistance to those in the Greater Boston area facing immigration-related legal challenges."

> Through the CJP Legal Aid Fund for Immigrants, CJP will help broaden the reach of these services, providing additional support to the hundreds of people who are currently waiting to receive legal guidance, often at the risk of being deported or separated from their families with each passing day. Many of these families receive other services from CJP's partner agencies, particularly Jewish Vocational Service (JVS), who refer them to Catholic Charities for legal assistance...
>
> CJP will raise funds to support the well-respected and faith-based work in this area performed by Catholic Charities, one of the largest providers of legal aid to immigrants in the Commonwealth..."As Jews, and as immigrants and the children of immigrants, we have a responsibility to help preserve the rights of those who have come to America to create a better life for themselves and their families," said Barry Shrage, CJP's president. "We believe this is a critical time for our two prominent faith communities to demonstrate that we can stand and work together to assist immigrant families and individuals who are in urgent need of our help."...
> Catholic Charities raised over $1 million at Spring

Celebration to support its numerous programs. Catholic Charities also presented CJP's President Barry Shrage with the 2018 Justice and Compassion Award at the event, paying tribute to his inspirational leadership and unwavering support of the two groups' shared mission.[67,68]

Catholic Charities works closely with a variety of Jewish organizations. The United Way, the Boston Foundation, and Catholic Charities were provided funding by CJP for the Fund to Aid Children and End Separation (FACES) initiative in June 2018.

Combined Jewish Philanthropies in Boston has total revenues of $390 million and net assets of $1.53 billion, some of which, in addition to Catholic Charities and associated projects, they donate to organizations such as the Anti-Defamation League (ADL) and the Hebrew Immigrant Aid Society (HIAS). The CJP also funnels money to other Jewish Federations, including: Palm Beach; Miami; Washington, DC; and Portland, Maine.

Catholic Charities has deep ties with many Jewish Federations from these locales to Cleveland to San Diego to Atlanta to Chicago to Portland, Oregon.

Catholic Charities in South Jersey works with the region's three Jewish Federations: Jewish Federation of Cumberland, Gloucester & Salem Counties; Jewish Federation of Atlantic and Cape May Counties; and Jewish Federation of Southern New Jersey (serving Camden, Gloucester and Burlington Counties). But as stated above, Jewish support for Catholic Charities is not limited to just the local Jewish Federation.

In addition to Boston's CJP as just one example, we can consider several others. These are essentially randomly selected, but the point is you could repeat this exercise virtually anywhere in the United States and find similar results.

Catholic Charities in Southwest Ohio works closely with the Jewish Community Relations Council (JCRC), the American Jewish

---

67 "CJP Legal Aid Fund for Immigrants," BostonCatholic.org, Archdiocese of Boston.
68 "Combined Jewish Philanthropies' Legal Aid Fund for Immigrants raises more than $600,000 for Catholic Charities of Boston," May 15, 2018. Catholic Charities, Archdiocese of Boston.

Congress (AJC), Adath Israel Congregation, Congregation Beth Adam, Congregation Etz Chaim, Immigrant and Refugee Law Center, Isaac M. Wise Temple, Jewish Federation of Cincinnati, JustLove, Mayerson JCC, Northern Hills Synagogue, Refugee Connect, Rockdale Temple, and Temple Sholom.

In Palm Beach, Catholic Charities are provided support by the Walter and Adi Blum Foundation, Inc. and Temple Beth Shalom (in addition to Walmart, the United Way, Wells Fargo, and other usual suspects, as we shall see the pattern repeat). One of the major financiers of not just Catholic Charities but the Catholic school system in Baltimore is the Harry and Jeanette Weinberg Foundation:

> "Now, there's a very simple reason why a foundation with a definite Jewish background—you might even call it a Jewish foundation—gives to Catholic schools," says Donn Weinberg, chairman of the Baltimore-area Harry and Jeanette Weinberg Foundation. "It's that the Catholic schools in Baltimore and across the country take all comers. They're educating poor kids in Baltimore— predominantly from black families. In other American cities, they serve mostly Latino families. Either way, these are usually kids from very low-income families…There is another, somewhat intangible, benefit to Catholic schools. Part of their mission is to impart American civic norms and values to their students. Of course, they're not the only schools that do this. But they definitely focus on the character, as well as the minds, of their students." The Harry and Jeanette Weinberg Foundation ranks among the 20 largest foundations in the country, with assets of nearly $2.5 billion and annual giving of almost $100 million. It is dedicated to assisting the poor by funding direct service organizations; within its mission, an emphasis is placed on supporting the elderly and the Jewish community.[69]

Bloomberg LP also plays a role with their Inner-City Scholarship Fund.

---

69 Levenick, Christopher, "An Episcopalian, an Atheist, and a Jew Walk Into a Catholic School…," 2019. *Philanthropy.*

The United Way is a major supporter of Catholic Charities (and Caritas Internationalis, of which Catholic Charities USA was a founding member) and like Catholic Charities it also has its headquarters in Alexandria, Virginia. It should also not surprise you that, yes, the Weinberg Foundation donates annually to the United Way (total revenue of $3.66 billion in fiscal year 2019), as do a host of other Jewish groups, organizations, and foundations. The United Way, in turn, donates money to Jewish groups in a kind of circular money-washing scheme. In fiscal year 2019, they donated $500,000 to CJP-Boston, for example. These schemes are anything but straightforward, which is partly why they have been so effective. The United Way:

> Has roots in Denver, Colorado, where in 1887 Frances Wisebart Jacobs, along with other religious leaders, began the Charity Organization Society, which coordinated services between Jewish and Christian charities and fundraising for 22 agencies. Many Community Chest organizations, which were founded in the first half of the twentieth century to jointly collect and allocate money, joined the American Association for Community Organizations in 1918. The first Community Chest was founded in 1913 in Cleveland, Ohio after the example of the Jewish Federation in Cleveland—which served as an exemplary model for "federated giving."[70]

The purpose of this particular kind of "giving" is framed as altruistic, but it is in reality totally self-serving. Larry Kaplan writes:

> Traditionally, US Jewish philanthropy has been focused on Jewish communal organizations such as Jewish federations, the regional nonprofit "middlemen" that distribute funds to causes in the US and abroad... Typically, Jewish federations emphasize the ethnic and cultural, non-religious expressions of Judaism, and reinforce the Jewish community's tradition of charitable giving as a group effort as an approach to social action.[71]

---

70 "United Way of America," Wikipedia entry.
71 Kaplan, Larry, "America's Jewish Community Leads in Per Capita Giving," December 19, 2017. *Non-Profit Quarterly*.

That seems fairly innocuous unless you've read *The Culture of Critique*, but for succinctness's sake, the following quote is illustrative, from a *New York Times Magazine* feature published in 2018 written by Michael Steinberger:

> Alex Soros said his father, "had always 'identified firstly as a Jew,' and his philanthropy was ultimately an expression of his Jewish identity, in that he felt a solidarity with other minority groups and also because he recognized that a Jew could only truly be safe in a world in which all minorities were protected. Explaining his father's motives, he said, 'The reason you fight for an open society is because that's the only society that you can live in, as a Jew — unless you become a nationalist and only fight for your own rights in your own state.'"[72]

Speaking of which, CJP-Boston, like HIAS, invests in bonds from the State of Israel, and contributed nearly $9 million last year to "empower people to advocate for Israel [and] create strong connections with Israel." You'll find a close relationship between CJP and organizations such as Friends of the IDF and others. One of the hallmarks of neo-liberalism is its "namelessness," that is to say that it largely operates anonymously, in the shadows, or by not calling something by its real name: "human rights," "liberal democracy," et cetera. It is power for cowards. To quote George Monbiot:

> The rentiers and inheritors style themselves entrepreneurs. They claim to have earned their unearned income. These anonymities and confusions mesh with the namelessness and placelessness of modern capitalism: the franchise model which ensures that workers do not know for whom they toil; the companies registered through a network of offshore secrecy regimes so complex that even the police cannot discover the beneficial owners; the tax arrangements that bamboozle governments; the financial products no one understands.[73]

---

72 Steinberger, Michael, "George Soros Bet Big on Liber Democracy. Now He Fears He Is Losing.," July 17, 2018. *The New York Times Magazine.*
73 Monbiot, George, "The Zombie Doctrine," April 16, 2016. *The Guardian.*

When it comes to electoral politics, money talks, which enables BS to walk. We are going to get into the byzantine gears of the neo-liberal machine here a little bit to see a prime example of how liberalism functions without calling something by its real name.

Under the Internal Revenue Code, all section 501(c)(3) organizations are absolutely prohibited from directly or indirectly participating in, or intervening in, any political campaign on behalf of (or in opposition to) any candidate for elective public office and that only "an insubstantial amount of a 501(c)(3)'s activities [may] constitute lobbying," however this does not stop them and there are numerous ways around this prohibition. One is that, as Erin Bradrick writes:

> We unfortunately do not have a clear definition of "insubstantial" in this context...[and] many 501(c)(3) organizations have the option of making the election under IRC Section 501(h) to have their lobbying activities measured based solely on expenditures. Section 501(h) also offers fairly generous thresholds for permissible lobbying expenditures by an electing organization.[74]

The following Catholic Charities donations sourced from the Center for Responsive Politics for example represent individuals within or affiliated with the organization donating to a specific candidate or specific candidates at a technical remove from Catholic Charities, but in such a way that would still represent CCUSA's interests and indicate the focus and priorities of Catholic Charities.

Contributions from Catholic Charities sources went almost exclusively to Democratic candidates—most of whom are abortion advocates, which doesn't seem very Christian—in the 2018 election cycle. Many of the names will be familiar to you, including: Richard Blumenthal, Al Franken, Bob Menendez, Adam Schiff, Kirsten Gillibrand, Elizabeth Warren, Beto O'Rourke, Bernie Sanders, Keith Ellison, Amy Klobuchar, and Kamala Harris.

Contributions also went to the campaign of House Representative Jared Golden of Maine during the 2018 election cycle. Catholic

---

74 Bradrick, Erin, "When Should a 501(c)(3) Consider Creating an Affiliated 501(c)(4)?" November 28, 2016. *Nonprofit Law Blog.*

Charities has publicly endorsed the DREAM Act and naturalizing DACA recipients, and supports a "just immigration process" which effectively means the kinds of open borders policies explicitly advocated for by Democrat Party leadership, including illegal immigration advocate and California politician Kevin De Leon, another recipient of Catholic Charities campaign donations in 2018.

Many 501(c)(3)s also establish their own 501(c)(4)s ("social welfare" organizations), which can engage in issue advocacy, though that all too often ends up as political advocacy. Their weighing-in during elections has been permitted as long as their primary activity is the "promotion of social welfare and related to the organization's purpose." According to the Center for Responsive Politics, 501(c)(4)s:

> May engage in political activities, as long as these activities do not become their primary purpose. The IRS has never defined what "primary" means, or how a percentage should be calculated, so the current de facto rule is 49.9 percent of overall expenditures, a limit that some groups have found easy to circumvent. Donations to these groups are not tax-deductible [as opposed to those to 501(c)(3)s].

Planned Parenthood and the Sierra Club are examples of 501(c)(4)s. 501(c)(4)s often function as "dark money" fronts because they are not required to disclose their donors. The "dark money" groups such as social welfare groups are allowed to raise and spend unlimited amounts however they see fit. Both dark money groups and SuperPACs can raise and spend unlimited amounts of money, but SuperPACs are required to disclose their donors. That said, SuperPACs may in some cases also function as "dark money" groups because they can accept unlimited contributions from political non-profits and "shell" corporations who may not themselves have disclosed their donors. Per the Center for Responsive Politics:

> In 2007, Wisconsin Right to Life v. FEC freed nonprofit 501(c) organizations to spend directly from their treasuries to make "issue ads" mentioning a candidate in the weeks immediately before an election or a political

convention—as long as they didn't exhort voters to cast their ballots one way or another. That was new, and in the 2008 presidential election, nondisclosed spending hit a record $78.8 million. The other case was 2010's Citizens United v. FEC, which made it possible for corporations, unions, nonprofit "social welfare" organizations and trade associations to take things a step farther by directly spending their treasury funds on advocacy expressly calling for the election or defeat of a candidate; these ads (or phone banks, or billboards, or opposition research, etc...) are known as "independent expenditures." The result has been an upsurge in political spending by nonprofit 501(c) (4) "social welfare" organizations—which aren't overseen by the FEC, but by the IRS...Occasionally, information comes to light that illustrates the kind of thing that could be happening on a larger scale—though there's no way to know. The health insurer Aetna, for example, made public pronouncements that showed support for President Obama's health care overhaul agenda in 2010, but it was later discovered that Aetna had contributed millions of dollars to two dark money organizations—the Chamber of Commerce and American Action Network—that engaged in a costly and sustained attack on the changes to the system that would become the Affordable Care Act. Many of the politically active nonprofits appear to coordinate their efforts, passing large amounts of money to one another. In doing this, they claim to be fulfilling their "social welfare" mandate... The lack of specific information that groups disclose on their IRS tax returns is one of the principal stumbling blocks faced by citizens and watchdogs who want to check the activities of politically active nonprofits. No detailed breakdown is required when groups report spending chunks of money on things like "issue advocacy," "grassroots issue advocacy," "media production/buys" or whatever general category they want to invent—all of which could contain political spending.[75]

---

75 The Center for Responsive Politics, "The 10 Things They Won't Tell You About Money-In-Politics."

Many of the loopholes and donation strategies we will cover in this book follow these lines and others, with campaign donations also taking different forms and from different sources.

To make things even more convoluted, many 501(c)(4)s often establish 501(c)(3)s, such as J Street and its J Street Education Fund Inc.; J Street also has a PAC to boot. Regarding candidates' campaigns, leadership PACs function at a technical remove but are basically designed to funnel additional money to campaigns, funding otherwise "impermissible spending." For the purposes of this book, I treat contributions to leadership PACs which find their way to or otherwise aid a campaign as contributions to that campaign.

Corporations are often less circuitous at the state level because unlike the prohibitions from directly contributing money to candidates at the federal level, many US states permit direct contributions to candidates at the state level, albeit usually capped. There are, obviously, ways around this, too. One way or another, the money is either going to the candidate's campaign or it is being spent in support of or in opposition to a certain candidate or candidates.

The use of bundlers is another "gray area" in campaign finance. Bundlers gather contributions from many individuals in an organization or community and present the sum to the campaign; as the Center for Responsive Politics notes:

> The Obama campaign created its own definition of a "volunteer fundraiser," which may not coincide with a common-sense understanding of what a bundler is. For example, celebrities George Clooney and Sarah Jessica Parker each raised millions by promising to have dinner with a certain number of people who donated to Obama. However, their names are nowhere to be found on the list…The amount raised by bundlers for winning presidential candidates has also grown: In 2000, it was at least $55.8 million; in 2004, at least $79 million; in 2008, a minimum of $76.25 million; and in 2012, the floor was $186.5 million… Hand-in-hand with the increasing sophistication of and reliance on bundlers is the heightened rate of return for those who bundle. According to Public Citizen, during his eight years in

office, George W. Bush appointed about 200 bundlers to posts in his administration. An iWatch News investigation uncovered that President Obama had already appointed 184 bundlers to his administration in his first term alone. Further, it is clear that bigger bundlers get more recognition, as nearly 80 percent of those collecting more than $500,000 for the Obama campaign took "key administration posts" as defined by the White House. Similarly, the Center has identified 35 of Obama's ambassador-level appointments as former bundlers for his campaign. The ambassadorships to France, the United Kingdom, and the European Union all went to campaign bundlers...There's no law requiring disclosure of campaign bundlers, as long as the fundraisers are not currently active, federally registered lobbyists.[76]

Nevertheless, lobbyists also often work "off the record" for congressional campaigns by arranging fundraisers, assembling PACs, and seeking donations from other clients, and many lobbyists in practice do not register and instead function as "advisors" and "government relations specialists."

Brendan Fischer has correctly identified the state of play as "effectively a legalized form of money laundering." Soft money has been generally enabled by the Supreme Court's decision in 2014 to eliminate some important campaign contribution limits in *McCutcheon v. Federal Election Commission*; this followed another major blow to election integrity from 2010, with *Citizens United*, when the Supreme Court ruled that the Free Speech clause of the First Amendment allows corporations to spend unlimited amounts of money on "political communications," though apparently the tech giants can censor your free speech rights on their platforms with impunity. Funny how that works. Generally the whole process can be extremely convoluted; as Elaine Godfrey wrote in 2018:

Across the country, dozens of Democratic candidates, from the democratic socialist Alexandria Ocasio-Cortez to the more moderate Conor Lamb, have proclaimed that

---

76 Ibid.

they won't accept campaign donations from corporate political-action committees… But that pledge, for many candidates, is mostly symbolic… Candidates can still accept donations from individual employees or owners of corporations, and those contributions can add up… Beto O'Rourke's Senate campaign offers another example of how messy this PAC business can get…The J StreetPAC, which supports Democrats favoring a two-state solution to the Israeli-Palestinian conflict, has collected more than $170,000 from its members to be donated to O'Rourke's campaign individually. In other words, the contributions were facilitated by a PAC, but didn't come from it.[77]

For our purposes and as a logical human being, I will treat this donation and donations of a similar kind as coming from J Street. There are, though, plenty of single-candidate SuperPACs, which are often themselves recipients of donations from corporate PACs, and can spend in support of or against a candidate (running advertisements for example) but cannot donate directly to a campaign. With corporations, it is senior management and ownership donating "as individuals" to advance their corporation's interests, in addition to employees who are donating or pooling resources to donate, and the corporation itself can sponsor its own PAC.

As Gregory Hamel writes, "Corporations can organize PACs to raise voluntary contributions for a select class of individuals, such as corporate managers and shareholders. A corporate sponsored PAC can then use those funds to contribute to political candidates." Additionally, as Hamel expands, "Corporate employees can make contributions to political campaigns through corporate drawing accounts which draw personal funds against salary, profits or other compensation."

In this book, I will typically be using larger donations and larger aggregate donation amounts as a kind of filter, albeit an imperfect one. Individual donations in the context we are discussing are seldom so straight-forward and innocent as a programmer for Google who wants to support Tulsi Gabbard and sends her campaign twenty bucks.

---

77 Godfrey, Elaine, "Why So Many Democratic Candidates Are Dissing Corporate PACs," August 23, 2018. *The Atlantic.*

The scale that concerns us here is far larger and with much more significant implications. When the organization chooses to obscure its donations through various means or using these individual donations as opposed to a PAC as a kind of built-in plausible deniability, in effect they are most certainly still donating to candidates on behalf of the organization, and this is before considering lobbying and all of the other various methods to influence elections and policies.

If twenty candidates have received individual donations, even smaller ones, from an organization or corporation, and eighteen are to Democrats, we can see the ideological position of the organization in question. Despite the campaign contributions originating from multiple individual sources within or affiliated with Catholic Charities, its ideological bent is obvious and anything but heterodox, so these donations evidence a pattern and as such and in light of everything else we've discussed so far, we can consider these donations to come from Catholic Charities even if it is not necessarily an "official" donation that tracks from Catholic Charities "proper" at Point A to Candidate X at Point B. Rarely in neo-liberalism is anything quite so simple and straightforward. That is a major component of its success. On the corporate side, what this looks like is:

> Based on Federal Election Commission data through the third quarter of 2019, includ[ing] money from the companies, their owners and employees and immediate families, as well as their PACs...Facebook, Google, Amazon and Apple...have given over $5.3 million collectively in campaign contributions... Alphabet, the parent company of Google, and its employees have donated more than $2.1 million so far...and 81 percent of that—more than $1.7 million—has gone to Democrats...Amazon and its employees have given more than $1.7 million in the 2020 cycle, and 74 percent of that to Democrats...Apple and its employees have contributed...96 percent for Democrats... Facebook and its employees have donated $824,600 so far in the 2020 cycle, and 70 percent of that has gone to Democrats... High-profile Silicon Valley fundraisers [include] events co-hosted by top Facebook and Google executives for

South Bend, Ind., Mayor Pete Buttigieg (D) and trips to the tech hub by Sen. Cory Booker (D-N.J.), *The New York Times* reported in June [2019].[78]

99.9% of YouTube campaign donations in the 2020 election cycle went to Democrats.

When we take a finer-toothed comb to the Facebook campaign contributions in the 2020 election cycle, we see that they take a variety of forms; fast-forwarding to a mid-April 2020 snapshot, we see $350,000 in "soft" money, $300,000 to PACs, and over $1.2 million in "individual donations" coming from Facebook as an institution, 85.8% to Democratic federal candidates and 81.7% to Democratic Congressional candidates.

Jewish representatives Adam Schiff and Jerrold Nadler received the maximum amount allowed from Facebook's PAC for direct donations in the 2020 election cycle (as did Nancy Pelosi), but Nadler only received $5 from "individual donations" (probably just one), which speaks to his genuine versus corporate support, whereas Bernie Sanders received over $109,000, all from "individual donations."

54.2% of Sanders's 2020 donations came from donation amounts of less than $200 according to the Center for Responsive Politics, which seems to suggest genuine popular support, however consistent support for Sanders by big tech as an institution, rank-and-file and management alike, also speaks to his alignment with neo-liberalism despite the tough talk. In point of contrast, almost 62% of Joe Biden's campaign contributions in the 2020 election cycle came from large contributions.

We can therefore begin to see who the Establishment prefers: the ready-made Establishment vessel over the coopted faux-revolutionary. For 2020, almost half of Donald Trump's donations were of the less than $200 variety; in the 2016 election, almost 20% of Trump's money came from his own coffers, and a paltry 14% of his campaign donations were large contributions, which shows just how extreme the Establishment's disfavor for him was in the midst of that election. With all of this considered, the donations to candidates coming from the organization in the context of elections which I will discuss and

---

78 Gangitano, Alex, "Tech industry cash flows to Democrats despite 2020 scrutiny," December 19, 2019. *The Hill.*

have discussed them therefore encompasses both the organization itself, as well as its subsidiaries, affiliates, ownership and primarily management but also the general body of employees along routes both relatively straightforward and circuitous insofar as they can be determined.

The individual contributions from rank-and-file employees are clearly not going to be as much of a factor as those of senior management and/or ownership, though again may be reflective of an "activist" culture of a Google or a Facebook. As the Center for Responsive Politics notes:

> The patterns of contributions provide critical information for voters, researchers and others. That is why Congress mandated that candidates and political parties request employer information from contributors and publicly report it when the contributor provides it. In some cases, a cluster of contributions from the same organization may indicate a concerted effort by that organization to "bundle" contributions to the candidate…
>
> Showing these clusters of contributions from people associated with particular organizations provides a valuable—and unique—way of understanding where a candidate is getting his or her financial support. Knowing those groups is also useful after the election, as issues come before Congress and the administration that may affect those organizations and their industries.

Logically we should be treating a donation from the CEO as one from the corporation or firm as their interests are in essence synonymous. For example, at least 90% of Elliott Management's campaign donations in the 2020 election cycle were made by Paul Singer.

Where relevant and either definitively or very strongly suggested, I will treat the campaign donations as coming from the organization or business directly ("Google donated to…" for example) because once we cut through all the noise, that is essentially where these donations originate and the interests they will further, just by necessity at a remove or through more indirect means.

I will therefore disregard the obscurantism and call a spade a spade, especially when it is clear that policy decisions are being influenced by these donations.

The benefits to these "outsourced" donations are many, not least of which, as the Center for Responsive Politics states, is the ability to "mask the true nature of a highly political organization through non-disclosure and to take donations from individuals and corporations that may not want shareholders or customers to know they're taking a stand on a controversial topic." Some don't care. We see the same phenomenon repeated as reflective of the interests and "corporate culture" or ideological orientation of the organization(s) in question.

With that in mind, in the 2020 election cycle, per the Center for Responsive Politics, we see Catholic Charities' institutional support for the neo-liberal system through donations to Bernie Sanders, Elizabeth Warren, Pete Buttigieg, Joe Biden, Kamala Harris, Julian Castro, Andrew Yang, Susan Collins, John James, Cory Booker, Amy Klobuchar, Beto O'Rourke, Joe Kennedy III, Kirsten Gillibrand, Adam Schiff, Alexandria Ocasio-Cortez, Maxine Waters, Nancy Pelosi, Ilhan Omar, Jared Golden, Cristina Tzintzun Ramirez, John Lewis, Rashida Tlaib, Richard Blumenthal, Eric Swalwell, Ayanna Pressley, and Donald Trump. With three exceptions, we see all Democrats, and there will be revelations in this book that do not paint Maine Senator Collins in a favorable light. John James is a Republican of the Turning Point USA variety, in other words an "as long as they come here legally even if it's the entirety of India" Republican.

Regarding lobbying, let's consider the Hebrew Immigrant Aid Society (HIAS); in 2010, their lobbyists were focused on the passing of the following, per the Center for Responsive Politics:

- Comprehensive Immigration Reform DOS Reauthorization CIR ASAP (HR 4321) Supplemental Security Income for Refugees Haitian TPS Increase of Reception and Placement (R&P) funding for refugees Resume HIV testing for refugees Repeal the "shout test" for Haitians Humanitarian parole for Haitians Reuniting Families Act (S 1085/ HR 2709) HELP Act (HR 4616; S 2998) Increase appropriations for the Office of Refugee Resettlement (ORR) Increase appropriations for Health and Human Services (HHS) Increase appropriations for Migration and Refugee Assistance (MRA) account Increase appropriations for State and Foreign Ops Increase appropriations for Department of Homeland Security (DHS) Family reunification for Somali refugees Refugee Protection Act of 2010 (S 3113)

- Refugee Protection Act (S.3113) Appropriations for MRA, ORR, IDA, and ERMA Comprehensive Immigration Reform Supplemental Security Income for Refugees Haitian Immigration Domestic Refugee Reform LGBTI Refugees HELP Act DREAM Act

- Refugee Protection Act State and Foreign Ops Appropriations Extending SSI Benefits Haitian Migration Comprehensive Immigration Reform Leahy Bill on Expedited Processing and Group Referrals DREAM Act (S. 3827) Colombian Refugee Resettlement

- Refugee Protection Act State and Foreign Ops Appropriations Extending SSI Benefits Comprehensive Immigration Reform DREAM Act (S. 3992) Leahy Bill on Expedited Processing and Group Referrals Darfuri Refugee Resettlement Immigration Reform

For Google, their 2013-4 lobbying along immigration lines looks like support for the following:

- Immigration Innovation Act of 2013 or the I-Squared Act of 2013 - Amends the Immigration and Nationality Act to establish an annual cap on H-1B visas…at between 115,000 and 300,000 visas depending upon market conditions and existing demand [would be an increase from the standard quota of H-1B visas of 65,000, which was temporarily increased to 115,000 for fiscal years 1999 and 2000 only; The first 20,000 petitions filed on behalf of beneficiaries with a U.S. master's degree or higher are exempt from the cap]; Directs the Secretary of Homeland Security (DHS) to: (1) authorize the accompanying spouse of an H-1B alien to work in the United States, and (2) provide such spouse with an appropriate work permit; Provides for the recapture of unused employment-based immigrant visas from FY1992 through the current fiscal year; Eliminates the per country numerical limitation for employment-based immigrants and increases the per country family category limit. Applies such provisions beginning with FY2014; Prohibits the Secretary of Homeland Security from denying a petition to extend the status of an H-1B or L-visa (intra-company transferee) nonimmigrant involving the same alien and petitioner unless the Secretary determines that: (1) there was a material error in the previous petition approval, (2) a substantial change in circumstances has taken place that renders the nonimmigrant ineligible for such status, or (3) new information has been discovered that adversely impacts the eligibility of the employer or the nonimmigrant; Directs the Secretary of State to authorize a qualifying alien admitted under an E-visa (treaty traders and investors), H-visa (temporary workers), L-visa (intracompany transferees), O-visa (extraordinary ability in the sciences, education, business, athletics, or the arts or films or television), or P-visa (athletes, artists, and entertainers) to renew his or her nonimmigrant visa in the United States; Eliminates the foreign student visa requirement that an individual has no intention of abandoning his or her foreign residence; Excludes from employment based immigrant limitations aliens: (1) who are the spouse or child of an employment-based immigrant; (2) who have a master's or higher degree in a STEM field (science, technology, engineering, and math) from a school qualified under the Higher Education Act of 1965; and (3) for whom a priority worker petition for an employment-based immigrant visa has been approved.

- A Chuck Schumer-sponsored bill which includes provisions like: "Makes 5,000 immigrant visas available in FY2014-FY2016 for individuals who were born in Tibet and have been continuously residing in India or Nepal prior to enactment of this Act. Considers a person to be a native of Tibet if such person was born in Tibet or is the son, daughter, grandson, or granddaughter of an individual born in Tibet"; "Increases the number of annual U-visas"; "Authorizes the spouse or child of a refugee or asylee to bring his or her accompanying or joining child into the United States as a refugee or asylee"; "Directs the Secretary of Labor to establish an H-1B recruitment website"; and which would raise the H-1B visa cap as well.

For Catholic Charities, pretty much every year they're lobbying for "comprehensive immigration reform," and we all know what that means. These are the priorities of the ruling class.

Catholic Charities is the organization responsible for sending hundreds of Angolans and Congolese to Portland, Maine from San Antonio, Texas, paying for their bus fare and providing specific instructions on what to do and where to go to claim benefits. Since 1975, Catholic Charities Maine Refugee and Immigration Services (RIS) has been the primary provider of resettlement services to refugees in Maine. In 2013, about 400 to 700 refugees arrived in the state through the Office of Resettlement at Catholic Charities, according to the *Portland Press Herald*.

These new groups of refugees coming from Burundi, Syria, and Angola joined the older immigrant communities from Somalia, Iraq, and Sudan, among others. A large number of Congolese, along with more Angolans, have arrived more recently still, and still more Somalis, Iraqis, and Sudanese arrive.

Though many of these "charitable organizations," such as Catholic Charities, do in fact receive substantial government (ie-taxpayer) funding and are thus beholden to the government as a kind of shareholder, this is only in principle. The Six Degrees of Separation between the federal consortium of agencies and the private voluntary agencies (VOLAGs) and subcontractors provides tremendous latitude for "discretionary" re-settlement should the government, as it has under President Donald Trump, decide to lower the refugee cap. This provides for a sort of humanitarian end-around where the Vatican or other globalist groups can wire money to groups on the Mexican side of the US border and facilitate refugees' or, even better, "asylum-seekers'" passage to the American side, where the VOLAGs and subcontractors then provide transport to places like Maine.

The asylum loophole is especially insidious. According to the US State Department, "In FY 2019, the United States expects to resettle up to 30,000 refugees, as well as processing more than 280,000 asylum seekers. They will join the over 800,000 asylum seekers who are already inside the United States and who are awaiting adjudication of their claims." The vast majority of those people never show up for their hearings and simply disappear within the country joining the ranks of the Eleven Million. Asylum claims and the refugee resettlement racket are each just one aspect of the global flood pouring into America, as the Capital Research Group Reports:

> A plethora of special programs allow persons into America outside the usual immigration process, including "diversity" visas, the refugee program, asylum seekers (asylees) and their families ("follow to join"). Refugees from Iraq and Afghanistan have their own special program, Special Immigrant Visas (SIV)... Additionally, special programs allow about 20,000 Cubans and Haitians to emigrate to the U.S. annually, with the same benefits received by refugees and asylees. There is even a "Rainbow Welcome Initiative" that funds a nonprofit contractor (Heartland Alliance International, LLC) to meet the special needs of lesbian, gay, bisexual, and transgendered (LGBT) refugees and asylees. Government funds 87 percent of the $10 million nonprofit. CEO Sid Mohn makes $330,000 per year in pay and benefits according to Heartland's 2014 tax return... Finally, in 1991, the government created "Temporary Protected Status" to grant legal status in the U.S. to Salvadoran illegal aliens and others fleeing war or natural disaster in Central America. Currently, over 300,000 TPS aliens in the U.S. are entitled to all the benefits of other legal permanent residents. While they are supposed to be "temporary," TPS enrollees simply re-enroll when their status expires. Most have been here since the 1990s.[79]

There are also the many work visas provided to foreign nationals to facilitate their entrance into the United States. These will be explored more fully later on in this book.

Catholic Charities of Maine operates several programs dedicated to helping refugees and other immigrants settle in the state, including job counseling, mentorship, and interpretation services. Additionally,

---

79 CRC Staff, "Refugee Resettlement: The Lucrative Business of Serving Immigrants," July 28, 2015.

they provide legal services to migrants, as well as refer them to immigration attorneys to help with asylum claims and deportation defense. Catholic Charities of Maine also runs a corporate training "'In Their Shoes' Refugee Experience" whereby whites will be browbeaten and guilted by the organization, their corporate overlords, and hand-picked deified brown people.

From their website:

> How can you welcome refugees to "The Way Life Should Be" in their new Maine communities? This interactive exercise engages participants with Catholic Charities Refugee & Immigrant Services staff to actively learn about the refugee process, the populations currently settled in Maine, the services available, and the challenges faced by Maine's newest arrivals.

Four key expected training outcomes:

1. Help people to understand and generate empathy for the arduous path that refugees take in arriving to the United States
2. Provide awareness of the various types of refugees and how this may influence their acculturation here in the United States, as well as which benefits they may be able to receive
3. Explain the services offered to refugees who arrive in the United States
4. Explain the legal and ethical use of professional interpreters when serving individuals who do not speak English well or at all.

Catholic Charities and the USCCB are also involved in a number of culturally- and morally-subversive projects outside the refugee racket, such as the grant-making vehicle the Catholic Campaign for Human Development (CCHD), founded in Chicago in 1969 to fund Saul Alinsky's Industrial Areas Foundation. According to the Capital Research Group:

> CCHD has been a radical leftist funding vehicle ever since, giving millions to ACORN, the radical training

school Midwest Academy, and others. The Industrial Areas Foundation, where a young Barack Obama was trained in "community organizing"with financial support from the Chicago Archdiocese, receives the largest percentage of CCHD grants of any CCHD grantee.[80]

On top of its other sources of income, Catholic Charities also derives substantial funding from large corporations and financial institutions, such as SC Johnson, Costco, US Bank, General Electric, Wells Fargo, UPS, JP Morgan Chase, FedEx, Apple, 3M, Office Depot, and First Bank. We will return to this particular "corporatized" aspect of the drive for open borders in much greater depth later in this book, as we continue to explore how the public-private binary has become a false dichotomy, one set up by the ruling class to keep people arguing over distinctions that do not exist.

Given the degree of inter-connectedness—or more accurately, perhaps, collusion—between these organizations, governing bodies, big businesses, financial institutions and banks, and the like already evidenced, the reader should have a pretty good idea at this juncture that this is the case, but sadly it gets much, much worse, as we will see.

In addition to those already introduced, there are multitudinous other NGOs that fund the VOLAGs and other similar organizations, and there is a sprawling yet deeply intertwined international network designed specifically to funnel migrants into the United States (and many other Western countries) along pre-established routes.

Both the Last Chance Armada and the Catholic Charities-funded Africans in Maine traveled along what has become known as the "Underground Railroad" of migrant safe houses that extends from Central America and beyond through Mexico into the United States. As Michelle Malkin relates in her excellent book *Open Borders, Inc.:*

> This sprawling network of aid stations has been in place for years, bolstered by global interests, left-wing activists, and religious institutions that advocate for illegal aliens… In 2012, for example, the United Nations' International Organization for Migration (IOM) in Mexico signed

---

80 CRC Staff, "Refugee Resettlement: The Lucrative Business of Serving Immigrants," July 28, 2015.

"cooperation agreements" with three migrant shelters along Mexico's southern border to support their work assisting "irregulars" traveling through the Mexican states of Chiapas and Oaxaca on their way to the US…IOM extended similar aid to nine other migrant shelters in the northern and central parts of Mexico…On the southern border of Mexico in Chiapas, the city of Tapachula is the first entry point for Central Americans headed to the U.S. There, the Fray Matías de Córdova Human Rights Center provides "comprehensive support" to illegal alien travelers, including legal consultations, monitoring detention centers, and offering "online resources, art and social activities, job training, and basic social services to migrants."…Also in Tapachula, the Jesuit Refugee Service (JRS) opens its churches and pastoral centers to provide shelter, monetary aid, voluntary aid, and emergency assistance. Its team of lawyers, psychologists, social workers, and Jesuit clergy spread from Tapachula to Comalapa and Mexico City. JRS staff served as Sherpas for the 2018 caravan marchers and liaisons with the U.N. High Commissioner for Refugees (UNCHR)…Along with JRS, the partners who provide "direct humanitarian assistance and accompaniment" with migrants on the trespassing path are: the California Province of the Society of Jesus, the Missionary Sisters of the Eucharist, the Mexican Province of the Society of Jesus, the Diocese of Tucson and the Diocese of Nogales…The Mexico City region hosts a multitude of *casas de migrantes*. The El Samaritano migrant house provides meals, baths, medical care, and phone services. It is conveniently located along the train tracks, and has become an inevitable magnet for narcotics and human trafficking…Casa del Migrante de Saltillo is gated and has "stunning" mountain views and close proximity to the train tracks. It provides three free meals a day and sells additional snacks and calling cards. Canada, the Netherlands, and the European Union provide donations to the migrant shelter.[81]

81 Malkin, Michelle, *Open Borders, Inc.: Who's Funding America's Destruction?* Regnery Publishing: Washington, DC. 2019.

Where the migrants' journeys are not paid for in full by these "generous" NGOs, governments, governing bodies, and affiliated organizations, an array of microfinance institutions (MFIs) have blossomed in the past few decades. It is now a multi-billion-dollar industry, and is only still in its infancy. The possible effects are profound. Microfinancing allows for small loans to be extended to migrants and enable their mobility in a variety of ways, as the Migration Policy Institute reports:

> MFIs (sometimes with the support of development institutions) are targeting migrant households for a variety of microfinance services, including loan products... Some households use microcredit as an advance on expected remittances from family members abroad; others use loans to finance the costs of migration. There is also evidence that migration is used as a coping mechanism to manage debt when microenterprises fail, pushing loan recipients abroad in search of better economic opportunity...In 2012, anthropologist David Stoll published an extensive ethnographic account of how microcredit has supported clandestine migration from Guatemala to the United States.[82]

While microfinancing dates back into the 1800s and perhaps even earlier, its institutionalization did not really begin until the 1970s. It has since expanded rapidly to the point where MFIs proliferate all over the world. As just one example, USAID helped establish Guatemala's largest MFI and works with a number of local banks in providing loans to migrants.

According to Bishal Kasu of South Dakota State University, "Literature shows that access to microfinance enhances both internal and international out–migration."[83] Maryann Bylander and Erin R. Hamilton's paper for *Population Research and Policy Review* looked at microfinancing in Cambodia and found that:

---

82 Bylander, Maryann, "The Growing Linkages Between Migration and Microfinance," June 13, 2013. *Migration Policy Institute.*
83 Kasu, Bishal, "How does microfinance affect out-migration?" November 12, 2018. *Sociology International Journal,* Vol. 2, Issue 6.

Over the past decade, developing countries, including Cambodia, have seen a marked increase in remittances received from migrants abroad. Estimates from the World Bank suggest that the level of remittance flows to developing countries (upwards of $400 billion dollars in 2012) is almost as large as foreign direct investment and more than twice the size of aid flows to developing countries. This tremendous growth, coupled with the dominance of neoliberal ideas, has led to renewed policy interest around the idea of leveraging migration for development.[84]

At the 2004 Special Summit of the Americas, President George W. Bush, along with other leaders of the hemisphere, committed to reduce the transaction costs associated with sending remittances by 50% by 2008.[85] At this summit, "hemispheric leaders committed to promote competition between providers of remittance transfers [and] eliminate regulatory obstacles and other restrictive measures that affect the cost of sending." Also in 2004, USAID announced:

Through a joint working group formed by the Global Development Alliance (GDA) Secretariat, the Bureau for Economic Growth, Agriculture and Trade (EGAT) and the Bureau for Latin America and the Caribbean (LAC), USAID is exploring the options for prudent involvement in improving remittance markets...The working group is financing a mix of pilot activities in Central and South America, Uganda and Rwanda to better understand remittance markets. USAID also participates in an inter-agency task force on remittances. Designed by participants of the 2003 international Conference on Migrant Remittances, the task force includes the World Bank, the Department for International Development (DFID), the Inter-American Development Bank (IADB), the International Monetary Fund (IMF) and the US Treasury. The European Commission, Canada, the

---

84 Bylander, Maryann, "The Growing Linkages Between Migration and Microfinance," June 13, 2013. *Migration Policy Institute.*
85 "White House Fact Sheet on Remittances," January 13, 2004.

German development consulting firm Gesellschaft für Technische Zusammenarbeit (GTZ), the International Labor Organisation (ILO) and the Asian and African Development Banks will soon join.[86]

USAID states that it aims to "bank the unbanked," and has also partnered with the World Council of Credit Unions (WOCCU) and VIGO (a money transfer operator) to facilitate these remittance flows. They also work with the Caja Popular Mexicana, the largest credit union in Mexico, to engage in remittance transfers from the United States. In their words, USAID/Mexico:

> Provides technical assistance on remittances and related financial service innovations. This is within a larger microfinance contract. The program seeks to help "bank the unbanked" by fostering innovative financial services and promoting alliances to enhance competition in the remittance market...USAID has helped to foster linkages between WOCCU, U.S. credit unions, and Caja Popular Mexicana to transfer funds at less than half the cost of Western Union. Since 1999, the cost of sending remittances from the United States to Mexico has fallen by 58 percent. USAID has also supported WOCCU's International Remittance Network (IRNet), which has facilitated transfers through credit unions in six Latin American countries.[87]

Following is a partial summary of USAID programming "designed to improve access to financial services":

- USAID/Jamaica provides support for a partnership program with the Jamaica National Bank (JNB) to encourage Jamaica nationals residing in the U.S. to open accounts at their local JNB bank. JNB will make funds available to relatives in Jamaica via ATMs.
- USAID (CAM and GDA), FINCA International (the Foundation for International Community Assistance), and

86 "Remittances at USAID," August 26, 2004.
87 Ibid.

VISA International have embarked on a two-year public-private partnership to improve the delivery of financial services to entrepreneurial women in developing countries through streamlining FINCA's operations and value-added services. This will enable cost effective transfer services as well as introduce remittance beneficiaries to banking products such as ATM cards, loans and saving accounts.

- USAID/LAC Regional and USAID/Colombia are supporting five microfinance institutions of the ACCION International network in Bolivia, Colombia, Haiti, Nicaragua, and Peru in the remittances market. The technical assistance program will help analyze MFI's potential to handle remittances, draft business plans, acquire the necessary technological infrastructure, and develop new financial products, technologies and services for their entrepreneurial clients. USAID will assist these MFIs in establishing agreements with money-transfer companies and in building ties with migrant communities and hometown associations in the United States.

- In Uganda, USAID/EGAT and the GDA Secretariat are co-financing a partnership between Hewlett Packard and three microfinance organizations to develop a remote transaction device and smart card technology that may permit those organizations to engage in in-country remittance transfers.

- In 2001, Banco de Brasil completed a $300 million bond issue securitized with future Yen remittance flows from Brazilian workers in Japan. The bond rating was significantly better than the country's sovereign debt rating. El Salvador, Mexico, Panama and Turkey have also used remittance-backed flows to secure financing. In addition, the Armenian Diaspora community created an SME Investment Fund sponsored by the IFC. Remittances and secured lending provide a useful example of leveraging fin services. Remittances are starting to be considered as a form of collateral for loan securitization and bond issues. Collateral-based loans are difficult to secure for those outside the formal banking process. This is the new area of exploration where donors together with partners in various countries are exploring ways to create new products that allow for remittances to serve as collateral.

1. Supporting Hometown Associations:

Hometown associations are small philanthropic groups of migrants that support a wide range of social and economic projects in the communities of their origin. These community investments, though a minor percentage of all remittances, are adding up to significant levels of money. USAID-supported research indicates that in 2002, Mexican hometown associations alone sent an estimated $30 million to their communities in support of local projects.

These associations leverage broader change and deepen the impact of development assistance while engaging in efforts complementary to USAID's. USAID is engaging these hometown associations in innovative partnership opportunities to leverage even more impact:

- LAC/RSD awarded a grant to the Pan American Development Foundation (PADF) for their project in helping hometown associations make productive investments in their home communities. Current projects are underway in Mexico, Haiti and El Salvador. Much of the work involves establishing methods to leverage remittances for employment generating activities. Examples include supporting the production, processing and marketing of nostalgic agricultural products to migrants, and providing technical assistance to increase the production of other high value crops.

- USAID/El Salvador, together with the Minister of Education launched ALCANCE (Alianza de Comunidades Apoyando la Niñez y su continuación en la educación), an innovative partnership to promote remittances for education in El Salvador. The program seeks to better identify the reasons that rural schoolchildren drop out of school and partially remedies those causes through a scholarship program supported by Salvadoran immigrant communities in the United States and the Salvadoran private sector. The program is managed by PADF, working with Salvadoran home town communities in the US, World Vision, the Salvadoran Foundation for Educational Development (FEPADE), and Banco Agrícola. The twelve month program provides up to 2,000 small scholarships consisting of school materials and other necessities for attending school for children most in need and will provide training and other support to local schools to improve student retention in 40 rural communities in four departments.

- USAID/Haiti is supporting a partnership program with PADF and Unitransfer that would result in a $1.00 donation for each remittance transfer fee collected by Unitransfer from a New York City pilot area. The donations would help support projects in Haiti with technical assistance provided by PADF. The program would also allow remitters to make additional donations when sending money. Last year, this partnership facilitated the reconstruction of a school in an economically depressed area. The school, located in a target area for USAID education programs, will also receive a package of USAID services to improve educational quality inside the classroom. The mission plans to expand this kind of activity and has a target of seven school reconstruction projects.

- The USAID/Haiti, PADF and Unitransfer program will use some of the proceeds from expanded remittance transfers to support health and education activities in Jamaica. USAID/Jamaica is also working with the Jamaica National Building Society Remittances program 'building bridges' to link hometown communities in US back to development projects in Jamaica. Western Union also contributes to this program.

- USAID/Colombia is supporting a local NGO in its creation of a mechanism for Colombians abroad to contribute funds to support grants for development projects in Colombia.

    2.   Supporting Research and Dissemination

- LAC/RSD has funded research by Dr. Manuel Orozco on the role Home Town Associations play in their home country, what activities are working best and on the role of governments in stimulating investment and supporting Home Town Associations. Reports were submitted on Mexico, Guyana and Nicaragua.

- USAID/Mexico funded a feasibility study by ACCION on opportunities for building further linkages between Mexican microfinance institutions and remittance transfer companies.

Both ACCION and WOCCU are examining the demand for financial products such as savings, mortgages, insurance and debit cards.

- USAID/Guyana intends to support workshops in Guyana to explore ways of channeling remittances into productive ventures, based on the research characterizing remittances and their senders and receivers.

- USAID/EGAT, with its BASIS CRSP mechanism, is working with the USAID/Moldova Mission on a program (similar to USAID/Guyana's) that channels remittances into productive ventures.

- USAID/EGAT Central Bureau supports research on approaches to expanding remittance-related financial products and on legal and regulatory issues.

- The World Bank and the Inter-American Development Bank have designed diagnostic tools to assist central banks in understanding the issue of remittances as it relates to them.[88]

Additionally:

US federal banking regulators have agreed that financial institutions should receive Community Reinvestment Act credit for offering international remittance services. CRA requires federal banking agencies to evaluate how regulated institutions meet the credit needs of their entire communities, including low and moderate income neighborhoods. In a letter dated June 3, 2004, the Federal Reserve Board of Governors (the Fed), the Federal Deposit Insurance Corporation (FDIC), the Office of the Comptroller of the Currency and the Office of Thrift Supervision said institutions would receive favorable consideration during CRA evaluation for providing this service.[89]

MFIs also play a vital role in aiding the movement of seasonal laborers, per Kasu: "Microfinance could be helpful in generating

---

88 Ibid.
89 Ibid.

sufficient household income that supports the cost of seasonal migration in the time when business suffers."[90]

The role of seasonal and migrant labor in the demographic transformation of formerly homogeneous, high-trust areas into crime-ridden and impoverished ones with low to no social capital will also be explored later in this book. Now, though, we turn to why exactly demographic transformation is such a concern in the first place.

90 Kasu, Bishal, "How does microfinance affect out-migration?" November 12, 2018. *Sociology International Journal*, Vol. 2, Issue 6.

Chapter Two: With Arms Wide Open

"We have been overwhelmed and have responded valiantly. Now we need breathing room. Our city is maxed out financially, physically, and emotionally."—Former Lewiston Mayor Larry Raymond

Senior FBI counter-terrorism official Michael Steinbach recently testified before the House of Representatives that the US presently lacks the capability to properly screen out terrorists from the ranks of the UN refugee program—to say nothing of those who come on various visas, sneak across the southern border, or even immigrate *legally*. So many tragedies could've been prevented, as Michelle Malkin writes:

> September 11 hijackers Hani Hanjour and Khalid Almihdhar were able to obtain fake photo IDs from illegal alien day laborers hanging out at a 7-11 in Falls Church, Virginia, a stone's throw from the Pentagon. It was in this same environment of disrespect for the rule of law that 1993 World Trade Center bomber Mahmud Abouhalima brazenly filed a bogus application for amnesty – under a federal program for illegal alien farmworkers – and won legal permanent residence; in which the September 11 terrorists got away with filing incomplete visa applications in clear violation of the law; and in which 21 Islamic radicals entered our country illegally during the past decade to carry out terrorist plots, from the 1993 WTC bombing, to the NYC subway bombing conspiracy, to the Los Angeles International Airport Millennium plot, to the September 11 attacks.[91]

---

91 Malkin, Michelle, "Immigration, the War on Terror and the Rule of Law," April, 2003. *Imprimis*, Vol. 32, No. 4.

The terror aspect is bad enough, yet for every spectacular tragedy perpetrated by the likes of Nidal Hassan (the Fort Hood shooter), there are thousands of "isolated" incidents like Kate Steinle's murder at the hands of José Inez García Zárate. That so many escape justice just shows how deep the rot has set in.

Of particular concern to Mainers has been the proliferation of Somalis since 2001, who regardless of context have been responsible for crime rates well in excess of their proportion of the population. For example, Somalis are almost four times more likely than native Norwegians and seven-and-a-half times more likely than native Finns to commit violent crime.

According to the official statistics from 2010-2014, we know that in that time period Somalis were almost thirty-six times more likely than native Danes to commit rape. Victoria police in Australia found that Somalis are five times more likely to commit crimes than native Australians.

Additionally, as Brian Lonergan writes:

> In the Minneapolis neighborhood of Cedar-Riverside, dubbed "Little Mogadishu," violent crimes increased by more than 50 percent in 2018. Law enforcement attributed the spike to Somali gang activity there. This is just one of many unpleasant statistics of growing criminal activity in the Minneapolis area. The Somali community in Minneapolis has also become a hotbed of terrorist recruitment in the U.S. The FBI reported that 45 Somalis left Minnesota to join al-Shabab or ISIS, both Islamic terrorist groups.
>
> In 2018 a dozen more were arrested attempting to join ISIS. The experiments in [Maine and Minnesota] not only have produced uninspiring results, they violate the "without risk to the rest of the country" component of Justice Brandeis' theory. Bad immigration policies cannot be contained within a city or state's boundaries. Their effects can touch all of us, as the noxious "sanctuary" trend demonstrates.[92]

92 Lonergan, Brian, "Compassion for refugees can hurt US communities," June 21, 2019. *Fox News*.

Minnesota Congresswoman Ilhan Omar—another Somali, and perpetrator of immigration fraud by marrying her brother[93]—intervened on the would-be terrorists' behalf and asked for their pardon.

It is more than fair to question where, exactly, Omar's loyalties lie, though one must expect to be shouted down by accusations of "Racism!" should they ask them aloud.

Lewiston, now Maine's second-largest city:

> Became a secondary migration destination for Somalis after social service agencies relocated a few families there in February 2001. Between 1982 and 2000, resettlement agencies placed refugees, including 315 Somalis, in the Portland, Maine area. High rates of rental housing occupancy in Portland led to the first relocations to Lewiston. Somalis have a history of nomadism and maintain contact, often via cell phone, with a large network of extended family, clan members, and friends. More Somalis learned about Lewiston and were attracted by the quality of life there, the low housing costs, good schools, safety and greater social control of their children in the smaller town. Between February 2001 and August 2002 over 1,000 Somalis moved to Lewiston. Most of these early secondary migrants came from Clarkston, Georgia, a suburb just outside Atlanta. By 2007, Somalis were 6.5% of the population of Lewiston and had come to the city from all over the United States and at least three other countries.[94,95,96]

93 "Ilhan Omar DID marry her brother and said she would 'do what she had to do to get him "papers" to keep him in U.S.', reveals Somali community leader." *Daily Mail,* 10 March 2020.

94 Mott, Tamara E., "African refugee resettlement in the US: the role and significance of voluntary agencies," February, 2010. *Journal of Cultural Geography,* 27 (1).

95 Nadeau, Phil, "The New Mainers: State and local agencies form partnerships to help Somali immigrants," Summer 2007. *National Civic Review,* 96 (2).

96 Huisman, Kimberly A.; Hough, Mazie; Langellier, Kristin M.; Toner, Carol Nordstrom (eds.). *Somalis in Maine: Crossing Cultural Currents.* North Atlantic Books: Berkley, CA. 2011.

One-in-six Lewiston residents are now Somali and the consequences have been predictably disastrous, just as they have been in other formerly high-trust cities across the country. Remember: there is no connection between increased crime in Lewiston and Somalis, the media reminds us. This is partially due to judicial activism suppressing the real numbers, and partially due to who owns Maine's media outlets and what their agenda is.

As regards the former, as Attorney General, current Governor Janet Mills repeatedly either declined to prosecute or delayed investigations of African migrants in Lewiston accused of violent crimes, including one brutal assault in June 2018 near Kennedy Park which ultimately resulted in the white victim's death. In an absolutely grotesque display, Mills led a rally the following year in the very same Kennedy Park called Standing Up Against Hate, where "intolerance" was condemned—but not the violent intolerance of the African imports toward their white neighbors, but that of the mosque shooting half a world away in New Zealand. South Portland City Council member Deqa Dhalac echoed Mills's condemnations of "white supremacy" in stating, "I am asking my non-Muslim brothers and sisters to stand with us in solidarity, and support us with your love and strong words to condemn white supremacy and Islamophobia." Naomi Mayer of Portland represented March Forth, a social justice group based in Portland. She asked pointedly, "Fifty people (gathered) where they thought they were safe? How would you like it if you were having a party with your friends, and someone came in and killed all of you?" Hmmm…more on this in a second.

Former Portland Mayor Ethan Strimling was there as well, and he was quick with the typical bromides: "We know better in the state of Maine about the importance of diversity and the importance of immigration," he said. "Probably what I am most proud of is how we do stand up and say we do not tolerate intolerance every time it occurs." Strimling, "proud of his city for standing against hate," joined Mayer at a 2017 rally in Portland "against white supremacy, neo-Nazism, the Ku Klux Klan, and President Trump."

Naomi Mayer told the crowd at that rally: "I'm not here because I'm Jewish. I'm here, and all of you are here, because we are human. None of you were born to hate. It wasn't in our DNA." All of this grand-standing must be little consolation to the family of the deceased Donald Giusti, the man who died three days after being savagely beaten by a gang of Somalis and Congolese in June 2018:

> In the days after the fight, several people insisted the attack on Giusti and his friends had been racially motivated, the result of tensions that had existed in and around the park since the end of winter…One witness, who videotaped part of the fight, told police a "white guy" had been running backward and had stumbled. After righting himself, "he was struck in the head with a brick, which caused him to fall to the ground."…
>
> "After he fell, the Somali and Congolese group 'stomped' him for about 10 seconds, before they took off running," Maine State Police Detective John L. Kyle II wrote in an affidavit. That witness said several people were armed with sticks, BB guns and a bat…Witnesses said the groups began fighting on Knox Street after teens in a car drove past the park and shot pellets and BBs at a group gathered there, striking several people…
>
> Police had said the investigation took longer than some because of the sheer number of people involved and because many were juveniles.[97]

That last claim is absolutely untrue, as I have on good authority the police were ordered to table the investigation until after Mills's election, but I cannot disclose my source.

Since her election, Mills has busied herself making criminally irresponsible decisions such as pardoning known drug traffickers like Lexius Saint Martin, deported by US Immigration and Customs Enforcement (ICE) officials in February 2018:

> That pardon comes almost a year after former Gov. Paul LePage, a Republican, denied a request from the family of Lexius Saint Martin, 36, to grant him a pardon for a 2008 drug conviction…Martin was married to Mindy Saint Martin, with whom he had three children…U.S.

---

97 Williams, Christopher, "State seeks to try Lewiston teen as adult on manslaughter charge," April 24, 2019. *Lewiston Sun Journal*.

immigration officials on Jan. 2, 2018, arrested Martin, who came to the U.S. from Haiti in 1994 as a refugee, outside his home for violating his immigration status. That violation was related to a 2008 felony drug conviction after police in 2007 arrested him after finding cocaine and $4,800 in his car. Martin pleaded guilty to a Class B count of drug trafficking and the state dismissed a more serious Class A charge of trafficking 112 grams or more of powder cocaine or 32 grams or more of base cocaine. He served seven months in prison and lost his refugee status. But his deportation was halted after a devastating earthquake struck Haiti in 2010, and he continued to live in Maine under conditions that he restrict his travel to the Northeast and regularly check in with U.S. Immigration and Customs Enforcement…In denying a pardon for Martin in 2018, LePage said at the time that Martin "completely ignored our laws until they caught up with him."[98]

Regarding Mills's interference in the investigation of the murder of Donald Giusti—and the source of criminality and violence in Lewiston and beyond—once again we see the obscuring of the true sources of racial tension and violence, a tried-and-true tactic practiced by the authorities from Sweden to Germany to the UK to Maine.

The media is also complicit in refusing to cover that which does not fit their narrative, from the fact that rape is up 1,666% in Sweden since that country opened itself up to mass immigration in 1975 to the thousands of German women sexually assaulted on one New Year's Eve alone across Germany by gangs of Middle Eastern and North African men to the UK grooming gangs, 70% of whom are Pakistani-Muslim, 84% "South Asian," and still others Somali.

Drug trafficker and illegal alien Mekonnen Berhe and his compatriot Abdirizak Farah were apprehended near the Maine Mall in September 2018 with eighteen grams of crack and $2,500 in cash, but to read it in the papers (other than the now-defunct Maine First Media, which provided all of the facts), you'd simply think Berhe was

---

98 Burns, Christopher, "Mills pardons Waterville man who was deported to Haiti in 2018," September 4, 2019. *Bangor Daily News.*

a "Westbrook man" in the same way Saint Martin is a "Waterville man." No mug shots were provided by police, probably for the same reason that for years Somali gangs used the Portland Public Library as a hub to deal drugs but the police did nothing because they didn't want to be accused of racial profiling.

Berhe already had a record but wasn't deported (with Mills in charge he'd probably be pardoned anyway) and Farah was charged with Operating after Suspension and Refusing to Submit to Arrest or Detention. Mouamed A. Mouamed was arrested that same month for cracking a man's skull open during a robbery, but is, apparently, just a "Lewiston man." Freddy Akoa was beaten to death during a break-in by three "Portland men"—illegal aliens with a combined *sixty-eight prior arrests.*

In 1980, there were 640 Somalis in the entire country. Now, there are at minimum 6,000 in Lewiston alone, and they are almost solely responsible—along with the Congolese—for all of the crime in the city. That said, from the "Immigrant and Refugee Integration and Policy Development Working Group Final Report" for the City of Lewiston, December 2017, "Immigrant and refugee youth of color can experience repeat encounters with the American juvenile justice system due in part to a lack of understanding around the way the system works."

So in other words, the thirty Africans who shot at and assaulted a group of whites outnumbered two-to-one didn't understand the legal complexities of not beating someone to death on purely racial grounds, so they should be absolved of any wrongdoing. Either that's a bald-faced lie, or these are *really* not the kind of people you want to be importing, probably both. A hate crime—or a crime at all—this apparently is not. But wanting to not have this done to you and your friends and family, to your fellow citizens—that is very hateful indeed. Apparently even those charged with upholding the law do not understand it: Maine's first Somali police officer, Zahra Munye Abu, was arrested at a Ja Rule and Ashanti concert and was charged with assault, battery, resisting arrest, disorderly conduct, disturbing the peace, and trespassing.

The rhetoric is at this point well-understood, and as we enter what the ruling class believes is the end-stage in their consolidation of permanent power, they have become more brazen, in many instances not even bothering to hide their true intentions. One example is in Lewiston, Maine, where city officials explicitly state that their importation of Somalis is in no small part to become cogs in the service sector economy. They provide English classes to these imports "in order to improve their chances for employment. The goal is to compress the usual multi-generational English-acquisition process to one generation so that the Somalis can get jobs in the service economy." Somalis serve the dual purpose of working at McDonald's and destroying social cohesion with violence and sheer alienness. But there's just one little hitch in the whole Somalis as the work force of future: foreign-born residents account for most of Lewiston's welfare costs.

The Federation for American Immigration Reform (FAIR) expands:

> City officials said the influx strained social services such as welfare, job training, and language classes. Somalis make up a third of all tenants at the city's largest public housing complex. More than a quarter of the families on the waiting list for public housing are Somali...The city has doubled its general assistance budget (which provides food, housing, utilities, and medicine), has earmarked about one percent of its budget for services for the Somalis, and has cobbled together federal and state grants. Lewiston's assistant city administrator said that the property tax rate has now grown so high that every dollar spent must receive careful scrutiny. Some recent press coverage has taken a more positive stance toward the influx of Somali immigrants that is not justified by economic data. Most notable is a Newsweek article that highlights the dramatic increase in English language learners and the emergence of Somali-oriented businesses as evidence that immigration had "saved" the town. A broader look at Lewiston's economic situation demonstrates that this is clearly not the case. In April 2008, the Maine Department of Labor issued a report finding that less than 10 percent of Somali immigrants to the town had stable employment, and that most

earned extremely low wages. About 30 percent find part-time employment, leaving the majority without any type of job. The massive influx of cheap, unutilized workers creates a golden opportunity for corporations that thirst for opportunities to lower wages and exploit cheap labor, something that Newsweek failed to mention in highlighting a business-oriented magazine's designation of Lewiston as a good place to do business. The drain on public coffers by Somali immigrants in Lewiston is not a new issue in the state. Indeed, a study conducted at Bates College reports that the influx of Somalis arriving in Lewiston started because "Portland's public housing... could not meet demand from the newcomers." Even by 2003, before the largest influxes, Somali immigrants made up two-thirds of the Hillview public housing complex, Lewiston's largest. Somali immigration peaked in 2005, when Somali Bantu immigrants who tend to be even less educated than their predecessors began settling in Lewiston.[99]

These Bantu received blanket permission from the American government to re-locate from camps in Kenya to the United States. Most wound up in Georgia, but because of few social programs and little in the way of welfare, plus a perception that their offspring were "assimilating too fast," they moved north.

One misleading statistic immigration advocates often use is that immigrants are more well-educated than the native population. In the context of Maine, despite the influx of non-Western immigrants in recent decades, a large share of immigrants to Maine still come from Canada—19.6% of its foreign-born population hails from Canada. Another 24.6% come from Europe.[100] This is in stark contrast to the United States as a whole, where only around 13% of immigrants hail from Europe and Canada. This was a conscious decision to re-make the demographics of the country on the part of the ruling class post-1965.

---

99 Federation for American Immigration Reform, "Maine," January 2012.
100 Migration Policy Institute tabulations of the US Census Bureau American Community Survey (ACS) and Decennial Census, 2017 data.

The Jewish Myer Feldman ghost-wrote John F. Kennedy's *A Nation of Immigrants*, published by the Anti-Defamation League of B'nai B'rith. The Jewish Emma Lazarus wrote the wretched "wretched refuse" sonnet "The New Colossus" mounted inside the pedestal of the Statue of Liberty.

The Jewish Ben Wattenberg formulated the idea of America as a "proposition nation." The notion of America as a "melting pot" comes from a play by the Jewish Israel Zangwill. The Jewish economist Bryan Caplan believes in "unrestricted immigration," most recently articulated in his book *Open Borders: The Science and Ethics of Immigration* (2019); he was given a very favorable interview by a member of the so-called "Intellectual Dark Web" and fellow Jew Dave Rubin.

The Jewish Senator Chuck Schumer supports a wall for Israel but not one for the United States; the $3.8 billion annual aid to Israel must continue, but those funds cannot be allocated to secure the southern border of this country. The Immigration Act of 1965, which has changed the demographics of the United States so dramatically, was supported by the Jewish Jacob Javits in the Senate, introduced to the House of Representatives by the Jewish Emanuel Celler, and written by the Jewish Norbert Schlei. Hugh Davis Graham expands:

> Most important for the content of immigration reform, the driving force at the core of the movement, reaching back to the 1920s, were Jewish organizations long active in opposing racial and ethnic quotas. These included the American Jewish Congress, the American Jewish Committee, the Anti-Defamation League of B'nai B'rith, and the American Federation of Jews from Eastern Europe. Jewish members of the Congress, particularly representatives from New York and Chicago, had maintained steady but largely ineffective pressure against the national origins quotas since the 1920s... Following the shock of the Holocaust, Jewish leaders had been especially active in Washington in furthering immigration reform. To the public, the most visible evidence of the immigration reform drive was played by Jewish legislative leaders, such as Representative

Celler and Senator Jacob Javits of New York. Less visible, but equally important, were the efforts of key advisers on presidential and agency staffs. These included senior policy advisers such as Julius Edelson and Harry Rosenfield in the Truman administration, Maxwell Rabb in the Eisenhower White House, and presidential aide Myer Feldman, assistant secretary of state Abba Schwartz, and deputy attorney general Norbert Schlei in the Kennedy-Johnson administration.[101]

The Jews have both historically and in contemporary society had a dramatically outsized role in immigration and "refugee re-settlement." "Elite" whites' interests are inextricable from globalism, which makes perfect sense especially when considering both the financialization of our society and the practice of Jewish inter-marriage into the "elites," most pronounced in the United Kingdom from the mid-19th century and the United States from the early- to mid-20th.

Furthermore, the interests of the money power and the state are inextricable from and/or coincide with those of powerful Jewish interests to a remarkable degree. In fact, in the countries occupied by the neo-liberal regime, there is almost total convergence.

Returning to Maine, in January 2017, the Federal Reserve Bank of Boston's *Communities & Banking* published a paper by Dickstein, et al. echoing the same "findings" of their Coastal Enterprises, Inc. paper from the year previous. The paper, entitled "Immigrants: An Important Part of Maine's Economic Development Strategy," concluded: "An increasingly diverse population in Maine will enhance the state's ability to attract talent and do business with the rest of the nation and the world" because immigrants to Maine are "young, well-educated, and motivated."[102] The numbers regarding the latter two claims contradict the authors' assertions—non-citizens and "naturalized citizens" have a lower workforce participation rate than native Mainers, and immigrants are almost twice as likely as Mainers to have less than a high school diploma. If we were to take a

---

101 Graham, Hugh Davis. *Collision Course.* Oxford University Press: Oxford. 2002.

102 Dickstein, Carla, John Dorrer, Elizabeth Love, and Tae Chong, "Immigrants: An Important Part of Maine's Economic Development Strategy," Winter 2017. Federal Reserve Bank of Boston.

finer-toothed comb to those numbers, since approaching half of the immigrants to Maine are still of Western origin, the disparity is more likely to resemble a chasm. Immigrants to Maine, then, slot cleanly into two strata: the highly-educated Canadians and Europeans, and the would-be cheap labor and ready votes imported from Somalia, Congo, Sudan, and elsewhere. The failure to differentiate between the two is a tried-and-true tactic employed to deliberately mislead the people. According to Rachel Desgrosseilliers, Lewiston's Somali influx has been a good thing because—like the French-Canadians and Irish before them—they are filling an urgent labor need.

What, precisely, that is we do not know, considering all the mills are closing or are closed. She then contradicts her kumbaya narrative by pointing out that, "It wasn't easy when the French Canadians arrived and the Irish had been here first. They felt that we were coming to take their jobs and there were big battles on the Main Street bridge and they threw each other in the river."

Interesting—different ethnicities pitted in economic competition coming to blows. Who could've foreseen that? Nevertheless, the state's leadership continues to double-down on the "necessity" of importing thousands of sub-Saharan Africans for both the economy and as a reflection of "our values."

Congresswoman Chellie Pingree released the following statement in response to Governor Janet Mills' announcement that the state will allow an influx of hundreds of African asylum-seekers who've flooded into Portland to apply for General Assistance (GA):

> Governor Mills' decision to expand general assistance funds statewide is pragmatic and a reflection of Maine's values. She has shown tremendous leadership in the face of this humanitarian crisis—as have City of Portland officials and Mainers themselves. When hundreds of people fleeing conflict arrived in Portland, the community responded by opening their doors and donating thousands of dollars to support their needs. With the oldest workforce in the nation and record low unemployment, Maine cannot afford to turn away people who want to make a fresh start here.[103]

---

103 Pingree, Chellie, "Press Release: Pingree Statement on Governor Mills'

What we cannot afford is to support the entire world's population run-off. Isn't it odd that the supposed boon to the economy these migrants represent needs such substantial funding and taxpayer largesse? And with record-low unemployment, why does Maine need to import workers as so many politicians, think tanks, and media outlets claim?

Congresswoman Pingree also announced the House Appropriations Committee released an "emergency supplemental spending package," which includes $60 million to support communities, like Portland, which have "experienced a significant influx of asylum seekers." None of these issues are treated with any concern by the ruling class, however. Old, white Maine *needs* migrants as the media states again and again, never interrogating the economic conditions that have produced this self-fulfilling prophecy of sorts.

Ostensibly driven by former Portland Mayor Ethan Strimling's siren song and with bus fare paid for by Catholic Charities, the summer of 2019 found hundreds of Angolans and Congolese winding their way north to an already over-burdened Portland and its ample social services and benefits.

Strimling specifically called for the migrants on social media taunting President Donald Trump, but without any proper plan in place and without notifying city officials. As *Portland Press Herald* reporter Randy Billings found, "Some of the migrants have said that word had spread…through Latin America of a welcoming attitude in Maine's largest city, along with available social services and an existing African community."[104]

From the *New York Times* we learn:

> Gloire Kikweta, 24, who came from Congo with his wife and two children — the younger of whom was born in Brazil on their way here…said he did not have a plan of where to go in the United States, but when he was in San Antonio, African immigrants there advised him to go to Portland, telling him that it was an aging city

---

Decision to Make GA Funds Available to Prospective Asylum Seekers," July 18, 2019.

104 Billings, Randy, "Several Portland councilors say mayor misinformed asylum seekers about housing options," July 24, 2019. *Portland Press Herald.*

that needed more people, and that it was safe. Vincent Mbala, 32, who is also from Congo, and came with his wife and three children, said that he learned through internet research that Maine provided financial support for asylum seekers.

Maine is unusual in providing general assistance, for up to two years, to immigrants who have valid visas or who have applied for asylum…Portland also has what local officials believe is the only municipal fund in the country that provides support to asylum seekers before they submit their applications.[105]

This is conjecture, but Kikweta sounds very much like he's been coached and is reciting a script; this passage provides us with much more insight than might at first appear, provided we read between the lines a bit. It hints at a much larger infrastructure—which as we have seen indications of and as will continue to be evidenced is definitely the case—and outlines that the migrants arriving in Maine followed at least one pre-established migratory route out of Africa to and through the Americas. The migration may be in fits and starts, but it appears that there are hubs at which the migrants re-consolidate or coalesce before continuing onward to the next hub or to their final destination.

When we combine these insights with those provided earlier by Michelle Malkin, the general path starts to become roughly apparent. There are certainly points at either extremity and in the center of Mexico, and in Brazil and Ecuador. Secondary migration within the United States is also a very common occurrence, with the awareness of greener pastures spreading by word of mouth, online resources, or "activist" organizations' assistance. Government agencies and corporations also have a not-insignificant role. States like Maine are a magnet for bogus asylum claims, "refugees," and migrants of all stripes with their generous hand-outs and craven, bought-off politicians clamoring for more, more, more!

Despite Strimling's public proclamations about accommodating any and all people who can make the trek to spite Donald Trump, when

---

105 Taylor, Kate, "Maine Needed New, Young Residents. African Migrants Began Arriving by the Dozens." June 23, 2019. *The New York Times*.

hundreds of these African migrants showed up, the city of Portland was nonetheless caught flat-footed, infrastructure was strained to the breaking point, and the city's minor league basketball stadium at the Portland Expo had to be converted into a giant homeless shelter.

Strimling apparently told migrants contradictory things, and at one point City Councilor Belinda Ray threatened to censure Strimling for spreading misinformation. A July meeting about what to do with the hundreds of migrants in the Expo with it needing to be emptied by August 15th disintegrated into a shouting match. As Billings reported in late July 2019:

> The state opened General Assistance to the asylum seekers, creating more housing options for the families. But many are refusing to accept housing outside of Portland, even though the state would help pay the rent and buy other necessities. "It's very frustrating and upsetting for staff to work this hard to find housing for these families and have it turned down over and over," said Kristen Dow, director of the city's Health and Human Services Department. Councilors said the city needs to close the temporary shelter at the Portland Expo by Aug. 15 and they endorsed a longstanding city policy that anyone in a shelter who refuses a housing offer made by their caseworker can no longer stay at the shelter. Councilors and staff placed the blame for the migrant families' refusal to be housed outside of Portland at the feet of Mayor Ethan Strimling, who said he's gone to the Portland Expo nearly every day to talk to families since it was designated as a temporary shelter...
>
> "We have a member of this body that has been spreading misinformation about the city policy and it is putting people in peril of becoming homeless," Ray said. "I don't think we can ignore this issue."
>
> Interim Social Services Director Aaron Geyer said 379 people have checked into the Expo since June 9. On Monday night, 229 individuals were staying there, he said. So far, 38 families, totaling 106 individuals, have been placed in housing in Portland, Westbrook,

Brunswick, Buxton, Yarmouth and Bath, Geyer said. But in recent weeks, families have refused housing outside of Portland, leading to the loss of available units, including some north of Augusta.[106]

Whether or not Strimling was indeed the root of all of the confusion at the Expo is not really the issue here, though. I am reminded of the old adage, "Beggars can't be choosers," but apparently that no longer applies—that or these migrants are not really beggars at all but opportunists. Furthermore, these other cities and towns are having to take the run-off from the Strimling debacle whether they want them or not—which is par for the immigration/refugee/asylee course in the West, really.

Elsewhere, as Joe Lawlor wrote in an August 31st, 2019 article in the *Portland Press Herald*, Mainers like David Pippin, Ashley Livingston, and their children, ages five and three, have been kicked out of homeless shelters to make room for these migrants. This particular young family was forced to pitch a tent to keep a roof over their heads as the children prepared for a new school year. Homelessness is surging in Greater Portland (imagine a scaled-down version of San Francisco) and yet the political class has prioritized the comfort of these migrants who have the backing of the entire globalist establishment instead.

Strimling bears plenty of blame, to be sure, but this surge of migrants isn't a one-off, and still they come: nearly two hundred arrived in the month after Strimling lost his re-election bid in November 2019. Plus, the pipeline of migrants into Maine has been open for decades, though appreciable numbers did not really begin to arrive until February 2001.

Portland has been hemorrhaging money for years as a result of the largely-African influx. Two-thirds of the 1,000 people receiving general assistance in Portland in January 2019 were asylum seekers. In just the month of September 2018, Portland paid over $125,000 in General Assistance aid to 273 asylum seekers.

For Maine, a report published by the Center for Immigration Studies (CIS) estimated that the state and local governments spent

---

106 Billings, Randy, "Several Portland councilors say mayor misinformed asylum seekers about housing options," July 24, 2019. *Portland Press Herald.*

$41 million on services for individuals residing in the state without legal permission.

As reported in the *Portland Press Herald*, for the first eleven months of fiscal year 2014, Portland provided roughly $3 million in General Assistance to 522 households whose asylum applications were still pending. That figure is an increase from 312 households and $1.8 million in General Assistance expenditures in fiscal year 2013—and nearly triple fiscal year 2011.

Maine taxpayers spend more than $19 million a year for ESL (English as a second language) instruction, an increase of more than 100% in just ten years. Portland estimated a cost of approximately $1.4 million to provide housing vouchers and other types of support to the migrants in the Expo as of July 2019—and this was before more arrived. At the end of June, Portland city councilors already had to re-appropriate $2.6 million in funds to provide General Assistance benefits for asylum seekers throughout the city. Asylum seekers primarily from African countries constitute 90% of the people living in city-run family and overflow shelters.

Immigrants accounted for three-fourths of Portland's recent population growth, the vast majority of whom hailed from sub-Saharan Africa, though some came from the Middle East and Eastern Europe. In 2013, Portland had the largest concentration of immigrants in the state— nearly 10,000 or 15% of the population representing 80 nationalities. That number has risen dramatically in just six short years. Currently, 42% of Portland's and 40% of nearby Lewiston's public school students are non-white, as are almost half of both cities' children under the age five. Lewiston's neighbor, Auburn, experienced a 400% growth in their English Language Learner student population from 2000–2010. Lewiston's immigrant and refugee population has grown by over 330% since 2004. In Lewiston schools, according to FAIR:

> Over the past 15 years, more than 7,500 migrants – most of whom are refugees from dozens of different countries – have resettled in the town, which has a population of less than 40,000. As is often the case, residents and city officials had no say in the resettlement process and little warning that these migrants were going to be placed in

their community... The public school system in Lewiston crumbled as a result. In 2004, roughly 95 percent of all students were considered "proficient" in the English language. But by 2017, nearly 30 percent of the students were designated as LEP [Limited English Proficiency] – three times more than the national average. And teachers have been forced to find a way to instruct a student body that speaks 34 different languages. In order to adequately educate the growing number of migrants moving to the state, Maine will need to increase its number of LEP-qualified teachers by as much as 110 percent... The unseen tragedy behind this mad dash to accommodate illegal aliens, refugees and legal immigrants is that despite all the money spent, there is little to show for it. LEP students consistently demonstrate dismal progress in all subject areas, and the fallout is affecting other students... Lewiston High School is ranked 458 out of 525 high schools in Maine and consistently underperforms on standardized tests.[107]

35% of students in Portland public schools speak a language other than English at home, according to the school district. Difficulties with integration and finding translators for often-obscure languages are just part of the problem. Driven primarily by African immigration, the public school system of not just Portland but those of other communities throughout the state must grapple with the ubiquitous behavioral issues the ACLU of Maine, naturally, blames on racism. Nevertheless, despite blacks comprising just 3.1% of all Maine public school students, they represent 6.2% of in-school expulsions, 6.3% out-of-school suspensions, 6.5% of referrals to law enforcement, 8% of expulsions under zero tolerance policies, and 18% of corporal punishments in school.[108] There are other costs as well. According to the FBI's National Gang Threat Assessment, Southern Maine now has at least 4,000 gang members, up from "no detectable presence"

107 O'Brien, Matt, Spencer Raley, and Casey Ryan, "Small Migrant Populations, Huge Impacts." February 2020. A Federation for American Immigration Reform Report. Fair Horizon Press.
108 LeBlanc, Emma Findlen, "We Belong Here," September, 2017. American Civil Liberties Union of Maine.

not long before a 2010 sweep of Greater Portland by ICE netted two dozen aliens from the Asian Boyz and two factions of the Bloods, the True Sudanese Bloods and the True Somali Bloods.

According to officials, Maine is being treated as an "open market" by a number of nationally-recognized gangs. As we shall see in the next chapter, however, it's not just gangs of the Bloods and Asian Boyz variety that have declared Dirigo an "open market."

Local and state officials say that Maine will look very different by 2050. Southern Maine, according to the State Planning Office, will become so urbanized that it will essentially be an extension of Boston. 27% of the state's major roads are in poor or mediocre condition, and 33% of its bridges are considered structurally deficient or functionally obsolete.

In spite of these serious issues and others such as the homelessness and opioid epidemics, Governor Mills decided to further relax restrictions on General Assistance to allow more asylum-seekers to claim benefits from the over-burdened state and a populace which already has the third-highest tax burden in the country.

Finally, regarding Portland's metamorphosis into San Francisco East, there's this, from a 2016 *Salon* piece:

> Portland, Maine had the second largest rise in rental rates in the U.S. Rents rose 17.4%, the median rent in Portland rising to $1582, more than much larger Philadelphia and Chicago.
>
> With many hundreds of new families relocating to the city every year, a housing shortage has worsened, and the rent increases have driven the working class out of town in droves. Portland's vacancy rate is near zero.
>
> Meanwhile shelters for the homeless are overflowing with citizens unable to compete with newcomers who consider the $1600 rents cheap by their former standards. The city has been struggling to come up with workable options to increase affordable housing without impacting Portland's "livability." Meanwhile, as rents have increased 40% in the past five years, Mayor Ethan Strimling has acknowledged that there was a $500 gap between what

people make in Portland and what they can afford to pay for housing.[109]

In lieu of addressing the real problems affecting the people of Portland, however, people like Strimling decided to exacerbate those problems by fully committing to the globalist agenda, a decision backed and aided by Governor Mills and Congresswoman Pingree and cloaked by the usual platitudes extoling diversity, appealing to "our values," and claiming "economic necessity."

This goes much deeper than just a few state officials or the odd virtue-signaling do-gooder organization, however—this is the work of a powerful global matrix of venture capitalists and financial institutions, corporations, NGOs, media conglomerates, politicians, academicians, law firms and assorted legal organizations and advocacy groups, foreign governments, and ethnic lobbies all collaborating to further the neo-liberal project.

---

109 Schwartz, Larry, "5 surprising cities where gentrification is displacing the poor," June 17, 2016. *Salon.*

Chapter Three: The Price of Doing Business

"Again the Roman customs and principles regarding money transactions are better than those of the Carthaginians. In the view of the latter nothing is disgraceful that makes for gain; with the former nothing is more disgraceful than to receive bribes and to make profit by improper means."—Polybius

Politicians largely serve at the pleasure of major corporate and financial interests and their wealthy backers. Maine politicians are no exception, and many are deeply corrupt. As Mike Bond expands:

> Some of America's most corrupt politicians can be found in the windswept wilds of Maine. The Pine Tree State rates next-to-last in citizens' trust of their legislators according to the Gallup Poll (April 4, 2014), and the Center for Public Integrity gives the state an F for corruption. Maine politicians appropriate taxpayer funds for their own companies, while governors pass legislation for huge energy projects which they then create companies to run. And energy companies write laws protecting their projects, laws that are obligingly passed verbatim by politicians who receive major payoffs from these companies. The Maine Center for Public Interest Reporting recently revealed that former state Senate President Justin Alfond introduced bills in the Senate written entirely by energy industry lawyers, after the industry awarded him with major donations to his Political Action Committee, funds which he then used to pay other Democrats so they would vote for him as state Senate President.[110]

---

110 Bond, Mike, "Killing Maine," August 21, 2015. Wind Task Force.

The Maine Center for Public Interest Reporting found in August 2010 that a major wind energy bill was passed unanimously and with no discussion. Not long after, transmission rates went up for Central Maine Power (CMP) customers by 19.6% on July 1ˢᵗ, 2012. The "Maine Power Reliability Project" (MPRP) represented a $1.5 billion CMP upgrade after its approval by the Maine Public Utilities Commission (MPUC); despite the fact that MPUC staff said that the upgrade could be accomplished for $667 million as opposed to $1.5 billion, Kurt Adams, MPUC Chairman, ignored the report and went ahead with the $1.5 billion upgrade. Come to find out, Adams had been interviewing for several months with a wind company, First Wind, where he was named Director of Transmission.

While still MPUC Chairman, Adams received over $1 million in stock options from First Wind, the largest "wind developer" in the state. Their chief outside counsel, Verrill Dana's Juliet Browne, is married to Maine State Representative Jon Hinck, who sits on the Energy and Utilities Committee that struck down *thirteen* citizen-sponsored bills in one year alone that would've regulated wind power. Eventually what is sarcastically called the "Fitts Amendment"—named after Energy and Utilities Committee Co-Chair Stacey Fitts whose company's website boasted, "we have been very active in the development of state regulations in Maine where one of Kleinschmidt's engineers is a member of the Governor's Ocean Energy Task Force"—was passed.[111]

Returning to Mike Bond, we learn of some other major players—whose names will be quite familiar by the end of this book—who made out like bandits:

> Hedge fund billionaire Donald Sussman, until recently the owner of most Maine newspapers, and the recipient of $200 million in taxpayer bailouts, was a major funder of an energy company now destroying Maine's mountains, and whose previous Italian partners have been jailed in the largest Mafia bust in Italian history. His ex-wife, Maine Congresswoman Chellie Pingree, helped former Maine governor Angus King get a fraudulent $102

---

111 Turkel, Tux, "Inadequate transmission lines keeping some Maine wind power off the grid," August 4, 2013. *Portland Press Herald.*

million taxpayer loan for energy projects he then made millions on, some of which he then used to buy his current seat in the US Senate.[112]

Senator Angus King has an atrocious record on immigration: Numbers USA gives him a career grade of F, and an F-minus for the 116th Congress. His peers Senator Susan Collins and Representative Chellie Pingree are similarly terrible: both also carry marks of F-minus for the 116th Congress, and Collins carries a career grade of F, no small feat given how long she's been a Senator. Representative Jared Golden has a C-minus, but give him time, he's a fresh face. It might be worth looking into who pays their campaign bills. Let's start with King.

In 2012, Angus King held a fundraising event with Michael Bloomberg, and he has also received substantial funding from S. Donald Sussman's Paloma Partners LLC. Some other top donors throughout King's career per the Center for Responsive Politics include PACs representing and/or individuals affiliated with: Verrill Dana, J Street (the "pro-Israel" PAC which, "advocate[s] for policies that advance shared US and Israeli interests as well as Jewish and democratic values, leading to a two-state solution to the Israeli-Palestinian conflict"), Bernstein Shur, Unum, Bowdoin College, Northrop Grumman, Drummond Woodsum, Texas Instruments, Raytheon, Geiger, Jackson Labs, Lockheed Martin, Boeing, T-Mobile, Harvard University, Microsoft, TD Bank, Comcast, Google, LL Bean, Podesta Group, Bain Capital, Time Warner, Walmart, the Rosenthal Foundation, McKesson, Liberty Mutual, Alphabet Inc., and Eliot Cutler LLC. The Jewish Eliot Cutler is very pro-immigration and is a former candidate for Maine's governorship.

Cutler is President of the Board of Directors of the Emanuel and Pauline Lerner Foundation, which is focused on "youth development programming." If said programming is anything like that of the state's governmental counterparts in TRIO, this means essentially indoctrinating children. Unfortunately I cannot reproduce the conversation I had with a former employee who reached out to me to discuss the abuses within the program witnessed over the course of several years, for they had anonymity concerns, but I was given the

---

112 Bond, Mike, "Killing Maine," August 21, 2015. Wind Task Force.

greenlight to provide a rough outline of the tactics employed and the operant ideology. Effectively, disadvantaged and low-income students are isolated from their school friends and forbidden from speaking with them over the duration of seasonal "camps," held at a physical remove, where the threat of expulsion and ostracism from their new "friends" in the group looms if they are found to be in violation of any of the myriad rules and/or ideological transgressions.

Ideologically, the program is designed to facilitate the transmission of anti-white programming and various other Cultural Marxist permutations—including the glorification of African migrants and pushing a pro-mass migration stance, incentivizing identification with "queerness" and gender fluidity, etc.—under the guise of advance collegiate preparatory scholarship (which, depressingly, it sounds like). There is no outside oversight.

The Lerner Foundation has also made the following organizations funding priorities: the Holocaust & Human Rights Center of Maine; Justin Alfond's Maine chapter of the League of Young Voters (the League of Young Voters US is a national advocacy organization which organizes progressive voter guides and voter blocs nationwide, particularly geared towards the 18–34 age group); EqualityMaine; Mano en Mano; Opportunity Alliance; Somali Bantu Youth Association; African Diaspora Institute; Portland Adult Education, which has reoriented itself as essentially a jobs- and language-training program for migrants; Immigrant Legal Advocacy Project (ILAP); Maine Women's Policy Center; the University of Maine Law School Justice for Women Lecture Series; Community Financial Literacy (described as: financial literacy programs for immigrant/refugee communities); Coastal Enterprises, Inc. (CEI); the United Way; Out! As I Want to Be (for the "expansion of the Gay-Straight-Trans Alliance presence in Midcoast schools"); Maine Initiatives (described as: ethnic community-based organization learning community project); Maine Access Immigrant Network (MAIN); and the Franco American Heritage Center, which seems innocuous until you understand that this organization is no longer designed to preserve the Acadian-French culture but rather use the Francophone "heritage" as a justification for settling Congolese in central Maine.

Cutler's former post-merger firm Akin Gump Strauss Hauer & Feld LLP is deeply embedded in the network of immigration law firms that make significant money undermining federal immigration enforcement and representing the interests of the many large corporations seeking to import workers to undercut American workers' wages and/or displace said workers. From their site:

> With the largest public law and policy practice in the country, Akin Gump often represents clients in matters relating to immigration policy. We conduct analyses of legislative and regulatory proposals, and advocate on behalf of our clients in all areas of immigration policy... In every U.S. Akin Gump office, our lawyers represent clients seeking asylum in the United States. Asylum applications are adjudicated by the USCIS Asylum Office and/or the immigration courts. In either forum, access to a lawyer is key... Since 2007, nearly every Akin Gump summer associate, supervised by Akin Gump lawyers, has represented undocumented women who have been victims of domestic violence and need to "self-petition" for legal residency in the United States.
>
> Through this program, more than 150 women have secured permanent residency in the U.S. for themselves and their children...according to a study by the U.S. Commission on International Religious Freedom, asylum seekers represented by an attorney are 12 times more likely to be granted asylum than those without attorney representation....
>
> Our experienced team of lawyers is deeply rooted in the immigration law community and is involved with various immigration-related organizations, such as the American Immigration Lawyers Association...Akin Gump's pro bono work in the area of immigration has been recognized on multiple occasions. An early leader in conducting Deferred Action for Childhood Arrivals (DACA) employment authorization clinics, our firm has been involved in hundreds of immigration cases in the last decade. Through corporate and pro bono immigration work, our lawyers have obtained a thorough understanding of the process required to

obtain employment authorization, Social Security cards, Individual Taxpayer Identification Numbers (ITINs), and the process necessary for foreign nationals to travel abroad and obtain visas at U.S. consulates. We have worked with multiple families ensuring entry of dependents into the United States, filed applications for Employment Authorization Documents and "advance parole," and communicated with U.S. consulates and ports of entry to ensure the safe return of our clients to the United States…Our immigration practice group provides a broad range of immigration services for business organizations and individual clients in need of assistance. Our lawyers have knowledge and experience in the following areas of immigration law:

- business immigration
- employment-based temporary work visas
- permanent resident ("green") cards
- company executive transfers
- EB-5 Immigrant Investor Program
- immigration compliance
- waivers of inadmissibility
- employee training programs
- foreign national hiring practices
- immigration-related internal investigations
- H-1B visa enforcement issues
- E-Verify Program
- policy and lobbying
- legislative proposals
- advocacy before executive branch agencies
- family-based immigration
- student visas
- visa issuance abroad
- travel to and from the United States
- naturalization[113]

Cutler is senior advisor to the Chairman and CEO of Thornburg Investment Management, and is now a member of the Board of

---

113 Akin Gump Strauss Hauer & Feld LLP, "Immigration Law and Policy," 2019.

Directors. For the 2020 election cycle, the largest donation amount of over $17,000 in "individual donations" originating from Thornburg went to homosexual Democratic candidate for New Mexico's Third District John Blair, who as the Department of the Interior's Director of Intergovernmental and External Affairs during the Obama Administration "helped with the creation of the Paris Climate Accords and was on the team that helped make the Stonewall Inn the nation's first LGBTQ National Monument," favors mass immigration, and makes numerous overtures to the "rich Hispanic tradition" of New Mexico and blathers on about "Native Americans." We also see from the Center for Responsive Politics's database significant donations to Xochitl Torres Small, Krishna Bansal, Beto O'Rourke, and Ben Ray Luján.

In 2016, donations of thousands of dollars went to both Hillary Clinton and Bernie Sanders from Thornburg sources. This would be defined as significant and reflective of Thornburg's interests and ideological position; a $1 individual donation in the 2020 election cycle to Tulsi Gabbard is not significant, although the near-uniformity of Democrat recipients (91.2%) does reflect their corporate culture. Finally, we can also see from 2012 campaign money flowing to Angus King, who we are very familiar with at this point. Given both Cutler's and Thornburg's investment in the Chinese market and its prominent place in the company's investment portfolios, it's little surprise the official line on populism is that it is "divisive," and that tariffs as an impediment to free trade are viewed as a bad thing. This is not unusual among the neo-liberal establishment. In fact, it defines it.

Perhaps most disconcerting is the close relationship between the state of New Mexico, its census, the "progressive" and open-borders policies of politicians like Small, and backers like Thornburg, but that is a story for another time.

Cutler's MaineAsia LLC has received ample subsidies to explore the uses of "renewable energies," greenhouse gases, and solar technology in year-round crop production in cold climates, such as Maine's. Incidentally, Cutler is also a principal investor in ArchSolar, a company "developing more efficient solar electric technologies for sustainable year-round agriculture in northern latitudes." Interesting. His Maine Seafood Ventures LLC is working to continue to expand the Asian market for Maine's seafood industry, which will of course need more cheap labor to fish the waters into maritime fauna extinction.

Over her career, Senator Susan Collins's major donors include, per the Center for Responsive Politics, PACs representing and/or individuals affiliated with: Goldman Sachs, the Blackstone Group, Marriott, Lockheed Martin, Raytheon, FedEx, Unum, Blue Cross/ Blue Shield, the Cohen Group, Verizon, Kleinberg Kaplan et al, Lions Gate Entertainment, Liberty Mutual, New Balance, Boeing, Pfizer, Warner Media Group, MGM Resorts, Morgan Stanley, UPS, Bank of America, Aetna, AT&T, Walmart, Home Depot, AFLAC, General Electric, Hewlett-Packard, Northrop Grumman, General Dynamics, Berkshire Hathaway, Exxon Mobil, Microsoft, Visa, American Bankers Association, New York Life Insurance, MetLife, Citigroup, Cisco Systems, JP Morgan Chase, Target, Elliott Management, DLA Piper, Blank Rome LLP, MBNA Corp., Fidelity, and McDonald's. Susan Collins has also, like Angus King, received campaign contributions from Michael Bloomberg. In fact, Michael Bloomberg's fingerprints are all over the state of Maine.

Since 2016, 54 communities, including Portland, Maine, have been selected for the Gateways for Growth Challenge, designed by the Partnership for a New American Economy and Welcoming America, which aims to "develop multi-sector strategic plans for attracting, retaining, and integrating immigrants and international talent."

Though it is a cliché to mention George Soros, it's a cliché in the same way the Rothschilds are—deservedly so. Welcoming America is, in fact, backed by Soros money.

Their companion organization in the Gateways for Growth Challenge, the Partnership for a New American Economy (NAE), was founded by the Jewish billionaire Michael Bloomberg and is helmed by Bloomberg's chief policy advisor and "gun control" lobbying organization Everytown for Gun Safety president John Feinblatt (also Jewish). Its primary purpose is to use its media influence to artificially create "support" for their anti-American policies and to lobby for increased immigration from the Third World and for more H-1B visas, thereby securing cheap labor for its members and ready consumers for their products.

NAE also lobbies Congress and the White House to enact legislation which will "create a path to legal status for all undocumented immigrants now in the United States." In addition to cheap labor and a higher-time-preference population/market, new ethnic lobbies can be counted on to increase political clout for certain beneficiaries and Jewish interests get a multi-cultural shield with which to operate behind and manipulate for their purposes.

In light of this information, it's little surprise NAE counts the following individuals among its members:

- Disney CEO Bob Iger
- Democratic Presidential Candidate Julian Castro
- Democratic Presidential Candidate Cory Booker
- Silver Lake Partners co-founder Glenn H. Hutchins
- Oracle CEO Mark Hurd
- Boeing Chairman Jim McNerney
- News Corporation Chairman, CEO, and founder Rupert Murdoch
- Marriott Chairman and CEO JW Marriott, Jr.
- Former Philadelphia Mayor Michael Nutter
- Former Los Angeles Mayor Antonio Villaraigosa
- AOL Chairman and CEO Tim Armstrong
- Interstate Hotels & Resorts CEO Jim Abrahamson
- Immigration Solutions Group PLLC Managing Partner Peter Asaad
- Facebook CEO Mark Zuckerberg
- Chairman and Senior Executive of IAC/InterActiveCorp and Expedia Group Barry Diller
- President and CEO of the United States-Mexico Chamber of Commerce Al Zapanta
- H. Rodgin Cohen, Senior Chairman of Sullivan & Cromwell LLP
- Yahoo co-founder Jerry Yang
- Richard W. Edelman, President and CEO, Edelman
- Brad Feld, Managing Director, Foundry Group
- President and CEO of the California Chamber of Commerce Allan Zaremberg
- Michael I. Roth, Chairman and CEO, Interpublic Group
- Former Goldman Sachs Chairman and CEO and current Senior Chairman Lloyd C. Blankfein

- President and CEO of the San Antonio Chamber of Commerce Ramiro Cavazos
- Jamie Dimon, Chairman and CEO of JP Morgan Chase
- Dallas Mavericks NBA franchise owner Mark Cuban
- Former Chicago mayor Rahm Emanuel
- Alan H. Fishman, Chairman of Ladder Capital Finance LLC
- BlackRock Chairman and CEO Laurence Fink
- Mort Zuckerman, co-founder, Executive Chairman, and former CEO of Boston Properties and owner of *US News & World Report*
- Minneapolis Regional Chamber of Commerce President and CEO Todd Klingel
- St. Paul Area Chamber of Commerce President and CEO Matt Kramer
- Mitch Landrieu, former mayor of New Orleans
- Charles Weinstein, Chief Executive Officer, EisnerAmper LLP
- Martin Lipton, Senior Partner at Wachtell, Lipton, Rosen & Katz
- Former New York Stock Exchange CEO Duncan Niederauer
- RT Rybak, former mayor of Minneapolis
- Haim Saban, Chairman and CEO of Saban Capital Group
- Stephen Schwarzman, Chairman, CEO, and co-founder of the Blackstone Group
- New York Mets baseball franchise owner Fred Wilpon
- Steven A. Ballmer, former CEO of Microsoft and owner of the Los Angeles Clippers basketball franchise

You might have noticed that some of the communities most impacted by "refugee resettlement," such as Minneapolis-St. Paul, are also present on that list. That is, unfortunately, just a small sampling. You may have also noticed that approximately half of those individuals are Jewish.

Also represented, among a slew of politicians, are current and former CEOs of companies and organizations such as JetBlue, Hewlett-Packard, Delta Airlines, Freeland Construction, Cabrera Capital Markets, Xerox, Barber Foods, Allstate Insurance, CW Biofuels, Time Warner, A Second Chance Immigration Services, Maverick Capital, Grooveshark, the Jones Group, Challa Immigration

Law Offices, American Express, Chipotle, Western Union, PetSmart, Quicken Loans, Geiger, the Rockefeller Group, Continental Grains, Overstock, MetLife, LinkedIn, Weight Watchers, Eli Lilly, Esteé Lauder, Macy's, Liz Claiborne, McGraw-Hill, Quest Diagnostic, Liberty-Mutual, Mi Ranchito Tortilla Chip Company, Adobe, Citigroup, General Mills, Zagat, Gaylord Entertainment, Rose Immigration Law Firm, Foursquare, Saks Fifth Avenue, Cummins, Fairchild Semiconductor, and Starwood Hotels and Resorts. Still thinking a boycott is going to work?

Oh, and in case you were wondering, Dana Connors, President of the Maine Chamber of Commerce, is a member of the Partnership for a New American Economy as well. You may be interested to learn that the Maine Chamber of Commerce counts among its board representatives from Jackson Labs, TD Bank, Tyson Foods, IDEXX Labs, LL Bean, Nestlé Waters (more on them later), Purdue University Global, United Insurance, AT&T, Pratt & Whitney, Bank of America, Unum, and Texas Instruments.

Also present are Bernstein Shur and Verrill Dana, represented by the Jewish James I. Cohen. Now to be fair, not everyone on the Board is going to be an immigration advocate, or even aware of what's going on, but for the major players, at least, we see their names recurring constantly.

It may also interest you to know that many of the major beneficiaries of taxpayer subsidies to the tune of hundreds of millions of dollars each include: Goldman Sachs, JP Morgan Chase, Google, Apple, Silver Lake, Disney, Morgan Stanley, Cabela's, Eli Lilly, the Blackstone Group, Comcast, Prudential, Amazon, Pfizer, ConAgra Foods, Bank of America, Jackson Labs, Citigroup, and Nestlé.[114]

Although NAE and Welcoming America are the principal partners in the Gateways for Growth Challenge, Unbound Philanthropy and the JM Kaplan Fund have also lent financial support. The JM Kaplan Fund is named after its founder, the Jewish "philanthropist, merchant, and self-made financier" Jacob Merrill Kaplan. In his day he was a major financier of the NAACP and various other "civil rights" causes. Kaplan's fund was used as a front by the CIA, which is such a strange saga it warrants its own book, or at least article.

---

114 Mattera, Philip, "Subsidizing the Corporate One Percent," February 2014. Good Jobs First.

Today, however, the fund is primarily concerned with "combatting climate change" (which as we know is just a euphemism for the consolidation of resource control and speculation) and "mitigating the impact of the criminal justice system on youth, people of color, and immigrant communities."

Whether it is still used by the CIA to de-stabilize regimes in Latin America and the Caribbean is classified. Unbound Philanthropy "is an independent private grantmaking foundation that invests in leaders and organizations in the US and UK working to build a vibrant, welcoming society and just immigration system…We work on behalf of refugees and migrants." Unbound:

> Claims it is dedicated to "Welcoming newcomers. Strengthening communities." Its mission is to "transform long-standing but solvable barriers to the human rights of migrants and refugees and their integration into host societies.…" Grant recipients include the National Immigration Forum, National Immigration Law Center, American Immigration Council, Tennessee Immigrant and Refugee Rights Coalition, Media Matters, Tides Foundation, the radical-left Southern Poverty Law Center, and Hillary Clinton's favorite think tank: the Center for American Progress.
>
> Unbound financed the pro-refugee propaganda film Welcome to Shelbyville. Since 2008, Unbound has provided at least $2.4 million to the International Rescue Committee (IRC), and its net assets in 2013 were $141 million.[115]

They also partner with the Open Society Foundations, the NoVo Foundation, the Ford Foundation, the W.K. Kellogg Foundation, and others on the Pop Culture Collaborative, "a multi-year, multi-million dollar hub for high-impact partnerships and grants designed to leverage the reach and power of pop culture in service to social change goals."

Pop Culture Collaborative Senior Fellow Ryan Senser "has consulted and led projects for a range of private, non-profit and

115 "Unbound Philanthropy," Influence Watch.

advocacy organizations including Consumer Reports, 32BJ-SEIU, Color Of Change, Planned Parenthood Federation, Ford Foundation, Open Society Foundations, IBM, Starbucks, Microsoft, Johnson & Johnson, PepsiCo and the American Heart Association."

Unbound's 2019 grantees in the UK included the Paul Hamlyn Foundation,[116] Joint Council for the Welfare of Immigrants, Immigration Law Practitioners' Association, Refugee Action, Migration Museum Project, and the Runnymede Trust. 2019 grantees in the US included Church World Service, the Migration Policy Institute, Funders' Collaborative on Youth Organizing—a project of Bend the Arc: A Jewish Partnership for Justice, and several NEO Philanthropy projects. Per their website:

> Taryn Higashi is the Executive Director of Unbound Philanthropy. Prior to working at Unbound, from 1997 to 2008, Taryn managed the migrant and refugee rights portfolio at the Ford Foundation and served as Deputy Director of the human rights unit from 2001-2008. Previously, Taryn was a Program Officer at The New York Community Trust... She is a former Chair of the Advisory Board of the International Migration Initiative at the Open Society Foundations and former Co-Chair of the Board of Grantmakers Concerned with Immigrants and Refugees.

Unbound's Board members also have ties to the American Jewish World Service, the Migration Policy Institute,[117] the Rockefeller Foundation, the National Bank of Ukraine, and PEN International. Michael Bloomberg was also a donor to long-time Maine Senator Olympia Snowe. Per the Center for Responsive Politics we learn that Snowe's other major donors included: the Blackstone Group, Verizon Communications, Unum, Berkshire Hathaway, AT&T, the National Football League, Major League Baseball Commissioner's

---

116 It was named after its founder publishing magnate Paul Hamlyn who "was a migrant, fleeing persecution in Nazi Germany."
117 Which has itself received funding from the Open Society Foundations, producing such reports as Judith Kumin's December 2015 "Welcoming Engagement: How Private Sponsorship Can Strengthen Refugee Resettlement in the European Union."

Office, Raytheon, International Paper, Blue Cross/Blue Shield, Sprint Communications, Microsoft, Planned Parenthood, Goldman Sachs, Boeing, Morgan Stanley, Bank of America, Home Depot, Northrop Grumman, Google, DLA Piper, Barclays, TD Bank, Aetna, New York Life Insurance, General Dynamics, Lockheed Martin, Comcast, WarnerMedia, General Electric, the Carlyle Group, FedEx, Genesis Healthcare, Sallie Mae, Women's Alliance for Israel, Women's Pro-Israel National PAC, Eli Lilly, JP Morgan Chase, FleetBoston Financial, Walmart, iHeartCommunications Inc., American Airlines, and GlaxoSmithKline, plus "individual donations" from figures from IDEXX, Verrill Dana, Elliott Management, Oaktree Capital, Bear Sterns, and Pingree Associates.

We turn now to the Democratic Representative and vociferous supporter of the Green New Deal Jared Golden's sources of funding, once again per the indispensable Center for Responsive Politics. Golden, who joined Congresswoman Chellie Pingree in voting in favor of amnesty for illegal alien "Dreamers," has received almost $85,000 from Alphabet, Inc. including "individual donations."

Visa has donated to Jared Golden's Golden Leadership Fund PAC, and major Golden donors in the 2020 election cycle included donations from PACs representing and/or individuals affiliated with the Council on Foreign Relations, J Street, the Carlyle Group, the League of Conservation Voters, BlackRock, the Federal Reserve System, and Fannie Mae. Some of his top donations in the 2018 election cycle were from PACs representing and/or individuals affiliated with Google, Apple, J Street, Catholic Charities, Facebook, Twitter, Cisco Systems, Rachael Weinstein Alfond, Harvard University, Stanford University, End Citizens United PAC, Bates College, Wicklow Capital, the University of Maine, Berwind Corp., Berman & Simmons, and Drummond Woodsum. Drummond Woodsum Attorneys at Law's immigration team:

> Represents businesses, individuals and families on all aspects of immigration law and procedures throughout New England and the country. We assist businesses with immigration filings in all non-immigrant visa categories, labor certification, permanent residence status for key alien employees, and employment compliance

including I-9 compliance reviews, trainings and defense in ICE enforcement matters. We also have experience in the complex area of export control licensing and its interaction with immigration law – an area of heightened scrutiny by the federal government. We also represent scores of individuals and families seeking marriage-based permanent residence, naturalization or family reunification.[118]

They also work on employment visa processing, corporate compliance, and various other immigration-related services, including representing high school students who can't compete in local poetry contests because they don't have a green card.

Also from their site:

Our clients include companies in the following industries:
- Information Technology
- Software Development
- Health Care
- Colleges, Universities and Schools
- Construction and Engineering
- Supply Chain Management
- Manufacturing
- Financial Services Consulting
- Multi-National Corporations
- Religious Organizations
- Trade Groups[119]

Many attorneys at the firm provide pro bono legal services for the Volunteer Lawyers Project and the Immigrant Legal Advocacy Project. Drummond Woodsum received the Immigrant Legal Advocacy Project (ILAP) award for "excellence in providing pro bono representation to asylum seekers and other noncitizens" in 2009, 2010, and 2011.[120]

Berman & Simmons has entered into a partnership with ILAP

---

118 Movafaghi, Mona T. and Christina R. Simpson de Reyes, "Immigration." Drummond Woodsum Attorneys at Law.
119 Ibid.
120 Drummond Woodsum Attorneys at Law, "About."

and aided in their endeavor to open a new office in Lewiston with financial support and pro bono assistance. Bates College has also partnered with ILAP. ILAP provides free legal services to immigrants, including obtaining green cards or work visas, citizenship, and asylum claims.[121] ILAP is a 501(c)(3) with support from the United Way and Maine Women's Fund, which dispensed $132,550 to "social justice causes" in 2018 and an aggregate of over $2.4 million in its existence.

There are a slew of refugee/immigrant grants in the state of Maine, many of which are tied to Jewish or Israeli organizations: "Grants to US and Israel organizations for programs and projects that promote social justice and human rights…grassroots organizations for programs to strengthen minority communities against social injustice. Funding is intended to support organizations serving immigrant, Arab-American, Muslim, and Black communities, and all people of color, LGBTQ, etc."

There were at least twenty-five grants under the auspices of the "People of Color Fund" for 2019, which included:

- Somali Bantu Community of Lewiston, Maine, to help create a sustainable goat farming and halal slaughtering operation which meets the cultural, dietary, and employment needs of the community.

- Maine Access Immigrant Network, to improve access to, and use of, health and social services for refugee and immigrant communities in a culturally and linguistically appropriate way: $10,000.

- Hand in Hand / Mano en Mano, to build community and organizational capacity around racial and multilingual justice: $6,000.

- University of Southern Maine, to pilot a community engagement and leadership fellowship for young adult emerging leaders who are immigrants or other racial/ethnic minorities: $6,000.

- Maine Community Integration, to expand cultural competency training for educators in the Lewiston schools

---

121 Berman Simmons, "Immigrant Legal Advocacy Project opens new Lewiston office with support from Berman & Simmons," September 20, 2018. Berman & Simmons Trial Attorneys.

and close the cultural gaps between white educators and students of color: $5,000.

- Gateway Community Service Maine, to expand youth leadership programs to help young people from immigrant, refugee, and asylee families learn new skills, gain opportunities, and grow into community leaders: $10,000.

- Indigo Arts Alliance, to host a symposium with scholars, activists, artists, and the public to explore the cultural traditions of the African diaspora and indigenous peoples: $5,000.[122]

Chellie Pingree, educated at the College of the Atlantic and the University of Southern Maine, has received substantial campaign donations, as reported by the Center for Responsive Politics, from PACs representing and/or individuals affiliated with: Goldman Sachs, General Dynamics, Unum, Harvard University, Berman & Simmons, the Rosenthal Group, Raytheon, Lockheed Martin, Boeing, Nancy Pelosi for Congress, the Sierra Club, Planned Parenthood, Diversified Communications, Farm Aid, Inc., Tishman Construction, Harvard University, Drummond Woodsum, the University of Maine, UPS, Texas Instruments, Prudential, Bernstein Shur, Joe Bornstein, Pfizer, Caremi Partners, the Tides Foundation, and MoveOn.org.

MoveOn.org is a notorious far-Left organization funded by people like George Soros and Asana CEO and Facebook co-founder Dustin Moskovitz.

Interestingly, according to the *Jewish News of Northern California*, in 2016:

The top five donors to Hillary Clinton's presidential bid are Jewish: They are Donald Sussman, a hedge fund manager; J.B. Pritzker, a venture capitalist, and his wife, M.K.; Haim Saban, the Israeli-American entertainment mogul, and his wife, Cheryl; George Soros, another hedge funder and a major backer of liberal causes, and Daniel Abraham, a backer of liberal pro-Israel causes and the founder of SlimFast… Facebook co-founder Dustin Moskovitz, who is Jewish, donated $35 million

122 People of Color Fund, "2019 Grants."

to political groups supporting Hillary Clinton and other progressive causes, adding him to the top ranks of Clinton's financial backers. Moskovitz and his wife, Cari Tuna, made two donations in the past six weeks — the most recent contribution amounting to $15 million and an earlier one totaling $20 million — according to Politico.[123]

A recent explosive report by the International Consortium of Investigative Journalists chronicled a number of rich and powerful people's illicit dealings involving HSBC—a list including al-Qaeda members, Jewish billionaire and Victoria's Secret owner Les Wexner, and Jewish financier S. Donald Sussman, ex-husband of Maine Democratic Congresswoman Chellie Pingree.

Sussman's Paloma Partners LLC has donated over $236,000 to Pingree's political campaigns and Pingree allegedly used Sussman's private jet to attend campaign fundraisers, which is illegal. Pingree has also received over $100,000 from EMILY's List, a pro-abortion PAC founded by the Jewish Ellen Malcolm, and over $41,000 from J Street.

Sussman has also donated large sums of money to EMILY's List, where he is on the Board of Directors. In fact, he donated over $1.5 million to EMILY's List in the 2018 election cycle alone. Angus King received $37,900 from Paloma Partners (on top of his almost $89,000 from J Street), putting him in such company as Debbie Wasserman Schultz, Chuck Schumer, Kirsten Gillibrand, and...Chellie Pingree. Despite no longer being wed, Sussman seems to continue to be able to open the purse strings for the "progressive" Pingree. You may find it interesting that Pingree's daughter, Hannah, was appointed to the newly-created post of Head of the Office of Innovation by Governor Janet Mills—the same Mills whose campaign both Hannah and Chellie Pingree donated to in 2018.

Mills, widow of the late real estate developer Stanley Kuklinski, like Portland Mayor Ethan Strimling and Congresswoman Pingree, received funding from EMILY's List. Other Mills donors from the 2018 election cycle and to her subsequent inaugural and transition

---

123 J. Correspondent, "5 top donors to Clinton election bid reportedly are Jewish," October 28, 2016. *The Jewish News of Northern California.*

efforts in addition to EMILY's List and the Pingrees include Tom Steyer and S. Donald Sussman directly, Marilyn Moss Rockefeller, LL Bean, Tabitha and Stephen King, Drummond Woodsum, attorney Joe Bornstein, Clayton Rockefeller, Justin Alfond, Ira Waldman of Cox Castle & Nicholson LLP, Bernstein Shur, several marijuana dispensaries, Equality Maine, Henry van Ameringen, Rachael Alfond, former National Football League Commissioner Paul Tagliabue, James Hormel, Larry Rockefeller, League of Conservation Voters, Charles Koch, Judith Glickman Lauder, John Baldacci, the Human Rights Campaign, George J. Mitchell, Verrill Dana LLP, Verizon Communications, Oliver Platt, Feminist Majority, and James I. Cohen.

Strimling, it may surprise you to learn, was not the city's first Jewish mayor. "Coincidentally" James I. Cohen, attorney specializing in banking and financial services, oversaw Portland becoming the home to the largest community of Sudanese in the United States in his brief stint as mayor of the city.

Strimling has ties to the Democratic Socialists of America (DSA) party, and just 22% of his re-election campaign donations in 2019 came from Portland residents and businesses. Major Strimling donors in that campaign cycle include:

- The Jewish Jeffrey "Sleazy" Solomon, Democratic candidate for the Florida State House of Representatives—Miami-Dade County, lobbyist, and tax evader

- The Jewish Marc I. Gross, senior counsel at Pomerantz LLP in New York, board member of T'ruah: The Rabbinic Call for Human Rights, and President-Elect of the Institute for Law and Economic Policy (ILEP), a 501(c)(3)

- Jewish psychiatrist Marc Shinderman

- The Jewish Marc Cohen, Executive Chairman of C4 Therapeutic, co-founder and Chief Executive Officer of Bublup, Inc. and COBRO Ventures, Inc., co-founder and Chairman of Acetylon Pharmaceuticals, Inc. and ONCOPEP, Inc., and co-founder, Chief Executive Officer, and Chairman of OPNET Technologies, Inc.

- Roberta Lipsman, Project Coordinator of the United Way of Greater Portland

- Jewish attorney Joe Bornstein
- Kenneth Lewis, Senior Director of MaineHealth
- Yusuf Yusuf and Abdullahi Ali of Gateway Community Services
- Amod Damle, Senior Recruiter for MTS Systems, a company that relies heavily on H-1B visas
- Tae Chong of Coastal Enterprises, Inc. (CEI) and Catholic Charities
- L'Africana Market LLC
- Notorious political consultant Rich Schlackman
- Tim Shannon, attorney at Verrill Dana LLP
- Suzanne Botana, wife of Xavier Botana, who is on the Board of Directors for the United Way of Greater Portland and is the Superintendent of Portland's Public Schools ("as a Cuban refugee, Botana is proud of his district's diversity")
- Linda Larkin, voice of Princess Jasmine in Disney's *Aladdin* (1992)
- Immanuel Herrmann, director of online fundraising and digital strategist for MoneOn.org, formerly of the ACLU and Grassroots Campaigns, Inc.

Grassroots and MoveOn often work with each other to "increase visibility and expand the membership base for a number of progressive groups, issues, and campaigns." Grassroots, headquartered in Boston, is a controversial for-profit consultation and canvassing corporation enlisted at various times by organizations such as Oxfam, the ACLU, the Sierra Club, the SPLC, the League of Conservation Voters, ACORN, Save the Children, Equality Maine (a nationally-affiliated LGBTQ advocacy group with corporate partners such as IDEXX Labs and WEX Inc.), the National LGBTQ Task Force, Doctors Without Borders, the Democratic National Committee, Amnesty International, Planned Parenthood, and the Center for American Progress. Despite its "progressive" bona fides, Grassroots has had unfair labor practice grievances filed against it related to coercion, intimidation, illegal surveillance, illegal office closures, and retaliatory layoffs.

Immanuel Herrmann is also an advisor to New Media Mentors, which runs training programs for "progressive" NGOs. New Media Mentors is headed by the Jewish Elana Levin and Liza Pike, formerly with the Natural Resources Defense Council. Other advisors include:

- The Jewish Berit Ashla, Rockefeller Philanthropy Advisors; formerly Senior Advisor for Special Projects at Tides

- The Jewish Jane Levikow, Rockefeller Philanthropy Advisors, formerly Senior Vice President of Tides

- The Jewish Anna Lefer Kuhn, Arca Foundation, formerly Program Officer at George Soros's Open Society Institute (OSI)

- Martin Collier, Glaser Progress Foundation (established by the Jewish Rob Glaser), member of the Global Fund private foundation constituency group, an advisory board member of the UCSF Global Health Group, and an advisory board member of the University of Washington Evans School of Public Affairs

Ethan Strimling is quite the piece of work. While first running for office, Strimling was carrying on an affair with his campaign manager Stephanie Clifford, spending his nights at the Hyatt Place in Portland.

It gets better, as Chris Busby reports:

> Clifford is a partner and president of Baldacci Communications, a public relations and lobbying firm (note: they donated heavily to Strimling's reelection bid campaign). One of her two co-partners is Bob Baldacci, the former governor's brother and a real estate developer who previously led a high-profile effort to redevelop the publicly owned Maine State Pier.
>
> The firm's lengthy client list includes Cate Street Capital, Central Maine Power, the National Resources Council of Maine, and numerous political figures of the past and present. Baldacci Communications continues to do work for Strimling, but the mayor said their role is now limited to filing campaign finance reports. Strimling

recently raised the issue of revisiting development of the Maine State Pier. Up till now, his discussions about this inside or outside City Hall have taken place without the participants' knowledge that Strimling has a romantic relationship with the business partner of one of the prime movers behind the previous effort to privatize this public asset.[124]

Strimling's co-ethno-religionist James I. Cohen, briefly mayor of Portland in the mid-2000s, is a partner at Verrill Dana LLP. Verrill Dana has a robust infrastructure for immigration law, supporting the obtainment of green cards and H-1B visas, corporate Petitions for Immigrant Workers (I-140 petitions) with USCIS to sponsor beneficiaries for US permanent resident status, and the like. It is unsurprising they would have a vested interest in the presence of more immigrants and refugees in Maine.

Verrill Dana donates large sums of money to pro-immigration groups such as the United Way, LearningWorks, the Campaign for Justice, Immigrant Legal Advocacy Project (ILAP), the Maine Civil Liberties Union, and the Maine Women's Fund. Many of Verrill Dana's attorneys serve on the board of directors or are trustees for organizations such as ILAP, Jackson Labs, MaineHealth, Pine Tree Legal Assistance (PTLA), the Maine Chamber of Commerce, and the United Way. PTLA is:

> A non-profit law organization dedicated to 'providing high quality, free, civil legal assistance to low-income people in Maine.' Committed to the principle that 'all Mainers have access to justice,' PTLA aims to ensure 'that state and federal laws affecting poor people are enforced while also addressing the systemic barriers to justice that low-income Mainers face.[125]

A major organization to which Ethan Strimling financier Marc I. Gross belongs is T'ruah: The Rabbinic Call for Human Rights, whose mission statement is unanimously-echoed in some form by all of the

---

124 Busby, Chris, "The Strimling Affair," February 24, 2016. *The Bollard.*
125 City of Lewiston, "Immigrant and Refugee Integration and Policy Development Working Group," December, 2017.

Jewish organizations or affiliated organizations we've covered or will cover in-depth in this book:

> The Torah teaches the obligation to love and care for the immigrant, just as God does... The ancient rabbis taught that the city of Sodom was considered the epitome of evil because the residents made laws prohibiting kindness to strangers. Welcoming immigrants and strangers remains a core Jewish value, as well as an American one...Too many Jews died after being trapped in Europe after the U.S. borders closed in 1924 to Jews and members of other ethnic groups.
>
> We know that immigration policy can be a matter of life or death. T'ruah takes an immigrant-led, human-rights-based, and Jewishly-informed approach to immigration issues. We support comprehensive immigration reform in the United States that will provide a path to citizenship for our country's 11 million undocumented immigrants...[We] oppose the use of the criminal justice system as a means of immigration enforcement...
>
> Campaign decisions are influenced by the direction of the movement from those most affected by immigration and refugee policies; we strive to ensure that our actions align with and further the goals of immigrant-led organizations. Doing so strengthens the fabric of our interfaith, interracial, interclass society, and close collaboration demonstrates an understanding of immigrant communities as neighbors and friends — not as "others." T'ruah works as part of an interfaith network to mobilize synagogues and other communities to protect those facing deportation or other immigration challenges. Through our Mikdash (Sanctuary) Network, communities pledge to take concrete actions, which may include legal support, housing, financial help, and other assistance for immigrants at risk of deportation. We connect congregations to local sanctuary networks, so that our communities can be in relationship with immigrant communities and with other communities

of faith, and can provide the most effective support for neighbors facing immigration challenges.

Returning to the influence of S. Donald Sussman, his Paloma Partners has also donated to Shenna Bellows, state senator and Executive Director of The Holocaust and Human Rights Center. Sussman and Paloma Partners also fund Emerge Maine, an organization dedicated to "increase the number of Democratic women leaders from diverse backgrounds in public office through recruitment, training and providing a powerful network."

Emerge Maine also receives funding from the Maine Education Association, Berman & Simmons, Drummond Woodsum, Bernstein Shur, Justin Alfond, the Maine Democratic Party, Janet Mills, Chellie Pingree, Hannah Pingree, Shenna Bellows, Mike Michaud, Time Warner Cable, and Susan Feiner. Feiner, a former professor of women's studies, is barred from teaching in the University of Maine system for offering an unauthorized one-credit course to participate in a protest against Senator Susan Collins for her support of then-Supreme Court nominee Brett Kavanaugh.

Sussman disburses funds widely over the state; in addition to the people and organizations we've just covered, he also finances or co-finances: the Maine People's Alliance, along with George Soros; the pro-amnesty, pro-open borders Maine Center for Economic Policy (which also receives funding from the Ford Foundation and Fidelity Investments Charitable Gift Fund); the Maine Democratic Party; Maine Equal Justice Partners (MEJP), notorious for suing the LePage administration because it stopped the flow of welfare to illegal aliens; State Victory Action, along with fellow Jewish billionaires Soros and Tom Steyer through his NextGen America; and Maine Women Together. State Victory Action has given hundreds of thousands of dollars to Rebuild Maine, which in turn has allocated nearly $300,000 in "independent spending" in support of Mills.

Planned Parenthood of Maine has spent over $85,000 in support of Mills; Rebuild Maine is affiliated with both Planned Parenthood and the Maine People's Alliance (MPA), which has received hundreds of thousands of dollars from Soros's Open Society Foundations. Maine Women Together has spent over $77,000 in support of Mills and Priorities USA Action PAC—supported by a whole lot of wealthy

Jews like Seth Klarman, Joshua Bekenstein, Steven Spielberg, Jeffrey Katzenberg, Irwin M. Jacobs, J.B. Pritzker, and, yes, S. Donald Sussman—has spent nearly $182,000 in support of Mills.

These are not considered donations since they are "independent" of the Mills campaign despite being on her behalf.

Sussman is the largest donor to the Working for Us PAC, along with Patricia Bauman of the Bauman Family Foundation. Working for Us:

> Is an independent political committee that seeks to influence the outcome of federal elections in favor of Democrats…The president is Steve Rosenthal, the founder and president of two other political entities: The Organizing Group (TOG) and the Atlas Project… Rosenthal has been known as a particularly aggressive campaign operative. In 2004, Donna Brazile, who would become chair of the DNC during the 2016 U.S. Presidential election, complimented him for being "as mean and vicious as they come" and the "last great hope of the Democratic Party."…
>
> Rosenthal was also a co-founder and CEO of America Coming Together (ACT), a liberal 527 political action committee with a budget of $142 million, offices in 17 states, and 3000 canvassers, that claimed to have made 16 million door-to-door contacts prior to Election Day 2004. In 2007, the Federal Election Commission (FEC) unanimously ruled that most of ACT's 2004 campaign cycle donations had violated federal election law, and assessed a $775,000 fine – then the third-largest fine ever imposed by the FEC.[126]

The Bauman Family Foundation (BFF):

> Financially supports the full-range of far-left agenda items, such as open borders amnesty, doing away with any sort of Voter ID and ballot integrity laws, doing away with the secret ballot when workers vote whether to

---

126 "Working for Us PAC," Influence Watch.

unionize ("card check"), and the extreme environmental demand to eliminate the "fossil fuels" industry...The BFF has donated $6,265,000 since 2004 to the Tides Foundation and $2,665,000 since 2006 to Rockefeller Philanthropy Advisors... The BFF donated $5,060,000 since 2001 to the Natural Resources Defense Council (NRDC)...Other Bauman Foundation grantees include National Council of La Raza ($275,000 in 2012)...

Since 2004 the BFF has donated $150,000 to the Gamaliel Foundation, a radical community organizing group that "worms its way into church congregations and uses the 'in-your-face' tactics espoused by community organizing guru Saul Alinsky to incite church members to agitate for socialism," according to a Capital Research Center profile.

"Worse, Gamaliel indoctrinates its own community organizers in creepy cult-like teachings and deceives church congregations about its real motives." Gamaliel is also famous for its ties to Obama's early days as a community organizer in Chicago in the early 1980s...The BFF has donated $500,000 since 2010 to the Brennan Center for Justice. The BCJ subscribes to an extreme activist jurisprudence that first came to prominence in President Woodrow Wilson's "What is Progress?" speech that elaborated the concept of "the living constitution."...

The BFF has donated $1,915,000 since 2005 to the Center for Community Change. CCC is a flagship far-left activist group. Founded in 1968 as the first grant recipient of the RFK Memorial Foundation, it boasts of having had a hand in implementing the Community Reinvestment Act of 1974 that used the coercive power of government to strong-arm banks into lending to applicants with substandard credit scores. CRA legislation set the precedent for U.S. Attorney General Janet Reno's lawsuits in the 1990s against banks that denied as few as three minority applicants with insufficient credit. The CRA helped to encourage the mass origination of billions of dollars in bad mortgages and mortgage-backed securities that were primary drivers of the financial collapse of 2007.[127]

The BFF was founded by Lionel R. Bauman, lawyer, real estate investor, and "proud New Yorker." According to the *Jewish Telegraphic Agency*, on September 13th, 1963, Bauman was "elected national president of the American Friends of the Hebrew University by the board of directors of the organization."

The BFF's Board includes:

- David Brock of Media Matters
- Gerald Torres, a professor at the University of Texas Law School "and a leading figure in critical race theory" as well as "an expert in agricultural and environmental law"; he was "honored with the 2004 Legal Service Award from the Mexican American Legal Defense and Educational Fund (MALDEF)" and is "Chair of the Advancement Project and a Trustee of the Natural Resources Defense Council"
- John Landrum Bryant, Patricia Bauman's husband; oversees the foundation's investments and "is a polymath designer of jewelry, furniture, lighting and bath and home accessories"; in 2012 he was sued for $6 million over sexual harassment allegations made by a 24-year-old immigrant maid, who said he was ordered to strip to his underwear and give Bryant a massage)
- Patricia Bauman, Vice Chair of Democracy Alliance, Co-Chair of the Brennan Center for Justice, Vice Chair of the Natural Resources Defense Council, Co-Chair of Catalist, and founding donor and advisory council member of J Street[128]

Bauman is also on the Board of NEO Philanthropy:

Formerly called Public Interest Projects, NEO spent $15.7 million in 2013 to "promote strongly aligned and effective immigrant rights organizations working to

---

127 Hanen, Jonathan M., "The Bauman Family Foundation: Funding community organizers for a progressive paradise," December 1, 2014. *Foundation Watch.*
128 Ibid.

advance immigration policy and reform; immigrant civil engagement and integration; and defense of immigrant rights." This includes Alabama Appleseed ($50,000), Arab Community Center ($100,000), Border Action Network ($125,000), Border Network for Human Rights ($390,000), CASA de Maryland ($270,000), Colorado Immigrant Rights Coalition ($360,725), Comunidades Unidas ($15,000), Welcoming America ($89,000), TIRRC ($469,000), Massachusetts Immigrant and Refugee Advocacy Coalition ($210,000) and many others.[129]

NEO Philanthropy receives funding from George Soros's Open Society Foundations, the Ford Foundation, the Gill Foundation, the MacArthur Foundation, the Pew Trusts, the Carnegie Corporation, and others. NEO bankrolled the Shout Your Abortion campaign and the Federal Agencies Project (FAP), an LGBTQ advocacy organization. NEO also helped sponsor the propagandistic campus sexual assault "documentary" called *The Hunting Ground*, which was, in a dark irony, distributed by The Weinstein Company of the notorious Harvey Weinstein.

S. Donald Sussman is on the Board for the Center for American Progress (CAP) think tank, along with John Podesta, Stacey Abrams, Glenn H. Hutchins, and others. Tom Steyer is an alumnus. Suzanne Nossel was a former senior fellow, as was Van Jones. Sources of funding include the Open Society Foundations, the Sandler Foundation (over $22 million), the Tides Foundation, Comcast, Walmart, General Motors, Pacific Gas and Electric, General Electric, Boeing, Lockheed Martin, Goldman Sachs, Blue Shield of California, Johnson & Johnson, T-Mobile, Wells Fargo, Quest Diagnostics, Novo Nordisk, the Blackstone Group, Citigroup, Joan and Irwin Jacobs, Apple, Google, Microsoft, CVS, Samsung, Northrop Grumman, American Beverage Association, BMW, Visa, Toyota, Coca-Cola, the Stephen M. Silberstein Foundation, the Bill and Melinda Gates Foundation, the Rockefeller Foundation, Schwab Charitable Trust, Akin Gump Strauss Hauer & Feld LLP, the Sea Change Foundation, Bank of America, the Carnegie Corporation, the Wyss Foundation, the Glaser

---

129 "NEO Philanthropy," Influence Watch.

Progress Foundation, DRS Technologies, Eli Lilly, Time Warner, PepsiCo, DISH Network, Discovery, Daimler, DeVry Education Group, Kohlberg Kravis Roberts, Dewey Square Group, the Albright Stonebridge Group, Harold Ickes, the Annie E. Casey Foundation, and the Federal Home Loan Bank of Dallas. The Center for American Progress also receives funding from Unbound Philanthropy. They also have a lobbying arm called CAP Action, which has received funding from the Motion Picture Association of America (MPAA), Google, and Blue Shield of California. Some of its Board Members include Peter Edelman, Greg Rosenbaum, Hilary Rosen, Anna Burger, and Ronald Klain, described by *The Forward* as a "top Jewish lawyer" and former "Ebola czar" in the Obama Administration.

While married to Congresswoman Chellie Pingree, S. Donald Sussman, through his Maine Values LLC, acquired a 75% ownership stake in MaineToday Media—the newspaper group that owns the *Portland Press Herald*, the *Maine Sunday Telegram*, the *Kennebec Journal*, the *Coastal Journal*, and the *Morning Sentinel*—meaning Sussman now had a controlling interest in most of Maine's largest newspapers. The Jewish Cliff Schechtman is the editor of the *Portland Press Herald*, which has published naked propaganda supporting former Portland Mayor Ethan Strimling's call for any and all "migrants" to come to the city. The *Press Herald* and *Sunday Telegram* editorial board has endorsed Eliot Cutler (childhood friend of former owner Richard L. Connor) for governor—Maine's six largest newspapers all endorsed the Jewish Cutler in his gubernatorial bid, in fact—and in Portland's 2015 Mayoral election, the newspaper endorsed Strimling.

Despite the rare moments of truth delivered by the few objective voices remaining, such as those cited in this book, the paper has a long history of neglecting to report on essential facts—such as violent felons' immigration status—and favoring biased hit pieces. In other words, it is lock-step with its national counterparts. What better way to control the narrative than to control the media?

In 2015, Sussman sold the controlling interest in MaineToday Media to another Jewish man named Reade Brower. In 2017, Brower bought Sun Media Group, parent company of the *Sun Journal*, in Lewiston. Brower now owns six of Maine's seven daily newspapers and prints its seventh, the *Bangor Daily News*. He also owns twenty-one of Maine's thirty weeklies and a number of other specialty publications (Brower has also expanded into Vermont, purchasing the Rutland[130] *Herald* and the Barre-Montpelier *Times Argus*). From Brower's profile in the *New York Times* (itself adamant that Maine and neighboring New Hampshire are too white and too old and... you know the rest):

> "Mr. Brower's hold on the newspaper industry of a single state stands out...Maine's emergence as a national political hot spot...adds to the influence Mr. Brower could have over the public discourse through his properties."[131]

Who needs state-run media when the unaccountable private sector exerts monopolistic control? So we have a situation in Maine where nearly the entire media apparatus is owned by one man, its refugee re-settlement program has been largely privatized, and its financial and business interests—fully committed to importing an entirely new population—control its politics.

If indeed the old saying is true, "As Maine goes, so goes the nation," then we are in serious trouble.

---

130 Regarding the small Vermont city, Adam Federman reports its targeting and the opaque nature of the "refugee re-settlement" racket with this 2016 article from *The Vermont Digger*: "Some residents and elected officials in Rutland County say they're frustrated they've been unable to obtain the full 126-page application for local refugee resettlement that the U.S. State Department is weighing...Rutland First has challenged the plan to bring refugees to Rutland and the process by which the decision was made...It said residents and members of the Board of Aldermen have made Freedom of Information Act requests for a copy of the application from the State Department and other agencies involved but have been rebuffed...[Rutland County Senator Kevin] Mullin said he has made his own requests, to no avail... 'I would love to look at it,' said Dean Mudgett, public records officer for the [Agency of Human Services], 'but we don't have it here.'...Asked if she would consider making it public, Amila Merdzanovic, director of the Vermont Refugee Resettlement Program, said that was a decision for the U.S. Committee for Refugees and Immigrants president and CEO, Lavinia Limon. Limon is on vacation until the middle of next week... The organization has a policy of not sharing the full application with the public, according to Stacie Blake, the group's director of government and community relations." Liberal democracy, folks.
131 Carpenter, Murray, "Meet the Media Mogul of Maine," November 26, 2017. *The New York Times*.

Chapter Four: There's Always a Catch

"Our inheritance is turned to strangers, our houses to aliens."
— Lamentations 5:2

The State of Tennessee filed a lawsuit against the federal government in March 2017 claiming that the refugee resettlement program represents federal overreach as these powers are not specifically delegated to the federal government by the Tenth Amendment. Unfortunately, even if they win, this would change little. In fact, it would likely make things worse for Tennessee, as we will see in the case of Maine. Under former Governor Paul LePage, Maine actually withdrew from the federal refugee re-settlement program, which should have ended the flow of refugees to the state, but—libertarians rejoice!—with the increasing privatization of "refugee re-settlement," the well-intentioned decision has actually been counter-productive, which we'll get to in a second. Canada's provision for privatized refugee sponsorship, which is in addition to (read: above and beyond) governmental policy, has resulted in the highest rate of refugee re-settlement per capita in Canada of any Western country, presently *over seven times* that of the United States according to official figures. In Canada:

> Provisions for the Private Sponsorship Program were introduced as part of the Immigration Act of 1976. It was recognized at that time that in addition to a planned government effort to help refugees, Canada would benefit from a mechanism that would allow private citizens and corporations to become involved in refugee resettlement. [What was originally viewed as a very incidental part of the system of refugee intake, if it were ever to be utilized, quickly became the most imaginative innovation in refugee resettlement with the massive intake of Indochinese refugees beginning in 1979 and

154

1980 in which, during an 18-month period, 32,000 refugees were sponsored by the private sector.][132]

This is of course nowhere near enough for the anti-white ideologues or for the special interests who want it fully privatized. The US and other countries are being pressured by the private sector to move closer to, and ultimately beyond, the Canadian model, although we are already in many ways in a state of de facto privatization. In the present American model, according to the Office of Refugee Resettlement (ORR): "If a State chooses to withdraw from the Program...ORR may select one or more other grantees, typically private non-profit organizations, to administer federal funding for cash and medical assistance and social services provided to eligible refugee populations in that State." In Maine, Catholic Charities has become that organization:

In 2017, after the withdrawal of the State of Maine from the administration of the federal Refugee Resettlement Program, Catholic Charities of Maine (CCM) established the Office of Maine Refugee Services (OMRS), which is distinct from RIS, to coordinate statewide infrastructure related to refugee resettlement and administer federal funds to subgrantees throughout the state...In March 2017, Catholic Charities assumed the administrative roles related to refugee resettlement that had previously been held at the state level. Upon establishing OMRS, the roles of State Refugee Coordinator, State Refugee Health Coordinator, and a data and contract analyst, were created to administer the federal fiscal resources and responsibilities associated with refugee resettlement... OMRS is responsible for infrastructure related to refugee resettlement on a statewide basis, including education, health, employment, and working with federal, state, and local officials. In this capacity, OMRS administers funding to RIS, to school departments with significant numbers of refugee students (including Lewiston, Portland, and Westbrook), and to the adult education

132 "Private Sponsorship of Refugees Program" Discussion Paper, *Refuge*, Vol. 12, No. 3 (September 1992).

programs, among others. OMRS coordinates planning for resettlement across the state, hosting the quarterly State Refugee Advisory Council meeting, at which upcoming resettlement is discussed with state, local, and community partners.[133]

Given what we've discussed about Catholic Charities, it is little surprise the demographic transformation of the state has only accelerated. The number of refugees in Portland alone has exploded since 2013, much of that number coming since LePage's withdrawal of Maine from the federal re-settlement program.

As many migrants arrived in June 2019 as in the entirety of 2013. 51% of the refugees admitted to the United States are from Africa, but a near-totality of refugees and asylum-seekers arriving in Maine are from sub-Saharan Africa, with a sprinkling of Middle Easterners. Regarding the Refugee Re-Settlement Industrial Complex, insert "Hotel California" joke here. As Don Barnett writes:

> States that withdraw from the program find the program continues in the state with the potential to operate on a larger scale than before withdrawal and with no state participation…No state has ever been allowed to exit the program completely, though that was clearly the intent of the state of Maine…it is the 1994 regulation (45 CFR 400.301), not the statutory 1984 Wilson/Fish Amendment that allows for the federal government to bring in a private contractor to run the program when the state has exited the program. The Wilson/Fish statutory amendment does not grant authority to either HHS or ORR to fund an alternative program as a way to establish or continue an initial resettlement program in a state when that state has withdrawn from the federal program. It unintentionally provided a framework and funding that is more advantageous to the contractors. That is why it is the preferred mode of contractor operations when a state has withdrawn from the program. Ironically, what was meant to reduce costs and ensure accountability

---

133 City of Lewiston, "Immigrant and Refugee Integration and Policy Development Working Group," December, 2017.

became a boon to the contractors, which together with regulation 45 CFR 400.301, allowed them to bypass any state influence and impose even more costs on the states where they operate…It was instrumentalized to the advantage of the very entities it was meant to control.[134]

In other words, it functions exactly as it's supposed to. It should be clear why it is advantageous for law firms, corporations, banks and other financial institutions, big agra, and other businesses to partner with these refugee re-settlement organizations; this "economic impetus" to humanitarianism is central to what is colloquially called the "Woke Capital" model.

This more than just a branding exercise, although "woke washing" is certainly a lucrative marketing tactic—it's about curating a particular kind of consumer base, ensuring a steady supply of cheap, disposable labor (with private citizens often unwittingly padding the bottom line through confiscatory taxation, further aided by government corporate tax cuts or tax breaks), and a pliable, easily-"sold" population. You can't ask questions if you don't know what to ask.

This is not to say that the state isn't at least partially involved—it is, more as a conduit than anything else, though. Labor is taxed at twice the rate of capital, which accelerates the accrual of capital to the top 1% and steepens the divide between haves and have-nots. It's part of the reason someone like Alexandria Ocasio-Cortez has a base—they're dimly aware that they're being exploited, but given their paucity of critical thinking faculties and the sheer amount of programming—they simply regurgitate what they're told: "White people." Therein lies another benefit of trading whites for Woke Golems who will screech about "white supremacy" while the real supremacists act with impunity.

As you can see, these things are all interrelated even if they aren't always working in direct conjunction. We'll get more into asset privatization specifically in the Nestlé/Poland Springs context in the next chapter, but for our purposes here, I'll simply state that the deleterious effect non-whites have on their surroundings then "necessitates" privatization as corporations have preemptively

---

134 Barnett, Don, "Do States Have a Say in the Refugee Resettlement Program?" January 24, 2018. Center for Immigration Studies.

consolidated resource control and may then mark it up for major profit. Consider the conditions of public drinking water in places like Flint, Michigan, and then consider the newly-created need for bottled water.

There's another bonus here, too. When an area has become sufficiently "diversified," elevated crime, ruined social capital, driven down property values, and caused White Flight, the process of gentrification may begin, and enterprising developers stand to make a killing re-selling whites and "model minorities" a facsimile of what they had before diversity.

You may even have a situation like that in Detroit with Jewish billionaire Dan Gilbert (Quicken Loans/Rock Ventures/Cleveland Cavaliers) and his Bedrock Detroit project—the anarcho-capitalist fantasy. As an added bonus, local taxpayers will contribute $618 million to be eventually priced-out of their own homes. But as always—think of the GDP! The role of capital in this process is essential.

Additionally, the much-vaunted "investment" in diversity is really just a positive-PR spin on the training of the new, semi-literate, semi-skilled cheap and compliant workforce/serf class of the future. Capital Impact Partners provides an illustrative example, in their own words:

> Capital Impact Partners has continued to invest in shared prosperity, equity, and inclusion for its communities nationwide. With income inequality, mass incarceration, wealth stripping, and other forms of structural discrimination continuing unabated, breaking barriers to success for underinvested communities has become ever more important.
>
> Capital Impact announced…financing and investment efforts…to serve more than 14,500 beneficiaries and create more than 515 permanent and construction-related jobs… Transforming marginalized communities into places of opportunity comes from disrupting structural racism and discrimination in order to expand economic and social justice…Capital Impact also took a leadership role in exploring how financial institutions can be more inclusive of individuals with criminal records… Capital Impact's…financing…create[s] new educational oppor-

tunities and…safe spaces for immigrants to live in communities across the United States.[135]

Specific examples include:

- In Bridgeport, CT, Great Oaks Charter School is bringing high-quality education to a census tract with a 71 percent poverty rate. Eighty-six percent of the students who will attend the school qualify for free and reduced-price lunch… Capital Impact supported the construction of a 70,000 sq. ft. facility that will become the permanent home of Great Oaks Charter School…The school will scale up from serving 400 students in grades 6-9 to 750 students in grades 6-12, 15 percent of whom are English language learners and 20 percent of whom have disabilities. Great Oaks has…a focus on professional development for local students.
- Brooklyn Laboratory Charter Schools is creating a high school in Dumbo…The majority of the students are expected to be African American, 85 percent of whom will be eligible for free and reduced-price lunch, and 32 percent of the student population are going to receive special education at the school. Because of its proximity to technology companies in Dumbo, the school curriculum focuses heavily on technology.
- Creating schools that intentionally reflect the socioeconomic, racial, and cultural diversity of the communities in which they operate—diverse by design—is a promising practice within education that is showing results. Citizens of the World Charter Schools (CWC) is the first national school network to follow a diverse by design model, creating an environment in which all students thrive no matter their background, precisely because they are integrated. Diversity is a cornerstone of school leadership as well, with minorities making up 60 percent of the leadership team and 40 percent of the board.
- Tacoma Community House (TCH) in Tacoma, Washington… has seen an increasing number of farmworkers and refugees,

---

135 Capital Impact Partners, "Capital Impact Focuses on Equity, Justice in Third Quarter," December 11, 2018. Capital Impact Partners.

resulting in a significant need for social and legal services... TCH is the only center providing comprehensive services to immigrants and refugees in the region. TCH serves immigrants from 105 countries – approximately 4,000 individuals each year. The majority of their clients are of Latino and Asian descent, with the remainder hailing from Eastern Europe, the Middle East, and Africa. Through partnerships with regional community colleges, businesses, housing providers, local health centers, and government offices, the center provides access to education programs for children and adults and job placement, internships, and training for job seekers. TCH also offers immigration services and advocacy.[136]

Dovetailing with capital and "social justice" are the supports for the architecture of philanthropic capitalism, from the advocacy groups to the law firms. Add to the multitudinous alphabet soup of advocacy organizations the Alliance for Justice (AFJ); Edward Labaton, co-founder and President of the Institute for Law and Economic Policy (ILEP), was honored by the AFJ as its 2015 Champion of Justice; what said "justice" looks like is the usual sentimentalized dreck the reader will no doubt be well-familiar with at this point:

"Immigration is baked into our DNA as a country. People from all over the world seek refuge and opportunity in America, and how we treat those who are new to our country says a lot about us as humans."

In conjunction with AFJ, a number of organizations co-signed a 2018 letter protesting several judicial appointments of judges who believe a non-Israeli country should have the right to police its borders. Included on the list of co-signing organizations were: the NAACP, Bend the Arc Jewish Action, MoveOn.org, CAIR, the Rwandese Community Association of Maine, Immigrant Legal Advocacy Project (ILAP), Maine Business Immigration Coalition, the National Council of Jewish Women, and the National Immigration Law Center (NILC), whose mission is:

To protect and promote the rights and opportunities of low income immigrants and their family members. NILC staff specialize in immigration law, and the employment and public benefits rights of immigrants. The Center

---

136 Ibid.

conducts policy analysis and impact litigation and provides publications, technical advice, and trainings to a broad constituency of legal aid agencies, community groups, and pro bono attorneys.

NILC has ties to Democracy Alliance, the San Francisco Foundation, the Open Society Foundations, the US Department of Commerce, the Muslim Ban Outreach and Legal Fellow for Advancing Justice-Asian Law Caucus, CAIR San Francisco Bay Area, the Protecting Immigrant Families Campaign, the NoVo Foundation, the Broad Center, the Central American Refugee Center (CARECEN) in Los Angeles, the Indivisible Project, and El Rescate, a legal and social services agency serving immigrants in Los Angeles.

The NoVo Foundation is Warren Buffet's son Peter's pet project, and it has dispensed funds to the Center for Popular Democracy, NEO Philanthropy, Demos, the Rockefeller Family Fund, the pro-reparations Movement for Black Lives for the Electoral Justice Project, the New Venture Fund, and the New World Foundation, and it has a large donor-advised fund with the Tides Foundation. Hillary Clinton spent the better part of the 1980s involved with the New World Foundation (NWF), which has assets approaching $95 million.

Not quite as impressive as NoVo's $528 million, but still pretty substantial. NWF President Colin Greer was in the employ of Hillary Clinton while she was First Lady. The New Venture Fund (NVF) is part of a network of "non-profits" run by Arabella Advisors, founded by Clinton administration alum Eric Kessler:

> In 2018, Arabella's four nonprofits reported combined revenues of $635 million...These non-profits [the New Venture Fund, the Sixteen Thirty Fund, the Hopewell Fund, and the Windward Fund] have collectively hosted hundreds of left-wing policy and advocacy organizations (referred to by critics as "pop-up groups" because they are little more than websites)... Arabella claims to have carried out more than 150 domestic and international projects for clients with combined assets worth more than $100 billion.[137]

---

137 "Arabella Advisors," Influence Watch.

All of this infrastructure is designed to ensure that the influx of foreigners is not impeded; among their many uses to the neo-liberal order, Third World immigrants are a huge investment opportunity. Mission Investors Exchange says as much: "Venture capitalist investors, philanthropists, and businesses are looking at immigrants and refugees as opportunities for investment." They then list some of the major players:

- Nuveen: Nuveen is a private investment manager that recently made an investment in an online-based remittance provider that focuses on channels in sub-Saharan Africa and Southeast Asia. The goal is to invest in technology to lower the cost of remittance for migrant populations.

- NeedsList: NeedsList addresses the need for massive innovation in the humanitarian sector with a marketplace connecting local NGOs with individual and corporate donors.

- Refugee Investment Network (RIN): The RIN moves private capital from commitment to active investment by sourcing, structuring, and supporting the financing of projects and companies that benefit refugees and host communities. They are creating an investor-centered knowledge hub targeting business opportunities that support refugee self-reliance; building a pipeline of deals that will speed and scale private investment in communities of displaced people; and articulating investor needs to funders, governments, and the development community.

- Tent Foundation, or The Tent Partnership for Refugees: This foundation was established by Hamdi Ulukaya, founder and CEO of Chobani. The initiative, a partnership of over 80 businesses in over 30 countries, grew out of the Obama Administration's appeal for the business community to engage more deeply with global refugee crises. In addition to sparking a $500 million investment commitment from George Soros, the appeal built a coalition of businesses expressing measurable commitments.

- George Soros and Open Society Foundations: Open Society Foundations founder and chair George Soros announced a pledge to invest up to $500 million in startups, established companies, and other businesses founded by migrants and refugees. The assets will be managed by Open Society Foundation and is in addition to its existing grant and program-related investments of the Foundations.

- Community Enterprise Development Services (CEDS): A nonprofit lender that provides business startup training and micro loans to immigrant and refugee entrepreneurs, as well as entrepreneurs who face barriers accessing traditional sources of capital.

- OpenInvest: This financial analysis and investing platform developed an investment screen allowing its customers to invest in the companies helping refugees. The company's #WithRefugees Impact Investment Screen identified 21 public American companies making significant contributions to refugee survival and welfare.[138]

Mission Investors Exchange is a massive network of community foundations, public charities, private foundations, "impact investors," law firms, investment advisors, asset managers, consultants, and community development financial institutions (CDFIs). Their aim is "to build an infrastructure that assures the sustainability of impact investing and expands [its] ecosystem." Partnering or affiliate organizations include: the Boston Foundation, the AARP Foundation, the Ford Foundation, the Rockefeller Foundation, Deutsche Bank, the Bill and Melinda Gates Foundation, the Walton Family Foundation, the Conrad N. Hilton Foundation, the John T. Gorman Foundation, the MetLife Foundation, the W.K. Kellogg Foundation, Silicon Valley Community Foundation, the Prudential Foundation, Nutter McClennan & Fish LLP, Community Development and Investment Group at Northern Trust, the MacArthur Foundation, US Trust—Bank of America Private Wealth Management, Graystone Consulting, the Climate Trust, Bank of the West BNP Paribas Wealth Management, TD Bank, Solomon Hess Capital Management, Maycomb Capital, National Association for Latino Community Asset Builders, the Omidyar Network, Coastal Enterprises, Inc. (CEI), and Cornerstone Capital.

---

138 Mission Investors Exchange, "Foundations and Others Investing in Immigrants, Migrants, and Refugees," June, 2018. Mission Investors Exchange.

Self-described "Jewish lesbian" founder and CEO of Cornerstone Capital Erika Karp penned an op-ed for *Forbes* in 2012 where she explicitly ties capitalism, globalism, "social justice," and her ventures to Judaism, opening with a quote from Hillel and using it as a through-line, along with her Jewish identity—two themes which are echoed in another article by Karp from 2016, this time featured on Cornerstone's own website. She states:

> As we once again approach the Jewish High Holidays — "The Days of Awe" — we return to a theme we have touched upon before: the importance of amplifying the voices of progress... "The Days of Awe" could bring lessons to leverage the power of capitalism towards its best and highest purpose...In reflecting on the future of capitalism, we draw from wisdom of the great scholar Hillel..."If I am not for myself, then who will be for me? And if I am only for myself, then what am I? And if not now, then when?" These questions posed at around 50 BC are incredibly timely in the context of today's struggling global economy and threats to our system of capitalism...All the pieces are in place to move forward and leverage the extraordinary power of capitalism on behalf of the entire world. We have everything we need across the broad realms of technology, science, academia, economics, government and finance... There are one thousand asset management firms representing $30 trillion in assets...These firms [are] all signatories of the Principles for Responsible Investment.[139]

The Principles for Responsible Investment (PRI) was set in motion by then-United Nations Secretary General Kofi Annan, the same Annan whose:

> Real legacy was to continue the trend of morphing the secretary-general's administrative responsibilities into a symbolic role to justify jet-setting across the globe. He continued that in his retirement, flailing hopelessly

---

139 Karp, Erika, "Hillel's Voice," September 28, 2016. *Journal of Sustainable Finance and Banking.*

in Syria (despite his organization's huge budget), and bankrupting his own Global Humanitarian Forum through gross mismanagement. His son Kojo first used his father's credentials to make a quick buck, and then took corruption to a new level, as his prominent feature in the Panama Papers [shows].[140]

The PRI is an official UN-supported network of global capital, "based on the notion that environmental, social and governance (ESG) issues, such as climate change and human rights, can affect the performance of investment portfolios and should therefore be considered alongside more traditional financial factors if investors are to properly fulfill their fiduciary duty. The six Principles provide a global framework for mainstream investors to consider these ESG issues."

Just two years after Karp's second piece, the PRI had swollen to almost $90 trillion in assets under management and rising.[141] For perspective, the annual global gross domestic product (GDP) is estimated to be approximately $80 trillion, and the collective global wealth is about $300 trillion. In other words, closing in on one-third of the entire planet's wealth is under the control of this particular international network of neo-liberal capitalists who are facilitating resource consolidation and speculation, mass migration into and erasure of white nations, moral and environmental degradation, and clandestine in-group supremacy. And by the way, global debt is now estimated to be $257 trillion according to the Institute of International Finance. Karp has also been involved with the World Economic Forum (WEF), the International Organization for Public-Private Cooperation "strengthened by a strategic partnership framework agreement with the United Nations." David Wallace-Wells describes its annual summit as "an orgy of plutocratic comity."

Comprised of NGOs, supra-governmental organizations, venture capital firms, multi-national companies and banks, diplomats, academic institutions, and media figures, WEF is essentially the last word in neo-liberal globalism.

---

140 Rubin, Michael, "Kofi Annan represented all that is wrong about the United Nations," August 20, 2018. *The Washington Examiner.*
141 United Nations Principles for Responsible Investment, "Annual Report 2018."

Partner and affiliated organizations include: Nestlé, Soros Fund Management, Hong Kong Exchanges and Clearing, Hess, Walmart, Visa, Verizon, Hewlett Packard, Deloitte, ING, Western Union, Tyson Foods, TD Bank, the Rise Fund, Toshiba, Coca-Cola, Silver Lake Partners, Pepsi, Prudential, Pfizer, S&P Global, Nasdaq, Nielsen, the *New York Times*, Polo Ralph Lauren, Procter & Gamble, NBC, the New York Stock Exchange, Novo Nordisk, Morgan Stanley, Nokia, MasterCard, Allianz, AIG, Alibaba, AT&T, Microsoft, Marriott International, the Bill and Melinda Gates Foundation, Mitsubishi, Toyota, Goldman Sachs, Adobe, Advantage Partners, African Rainbow Minerals, Merck, Lloyds Banking Group, Kaiser Permanente, Liberty Global, State Grid Corporation of China, Saudi Telecom Group, Johnson & Johnson, Lockheed Martin, JP Morgan Chase, LinkedIn, Hyundai, IBM, Infosys, Guggenheim Partners, Gulf International Bank, Hydro Quebec, Huawei Technologies, HSBC, Google, Facebook, Heineken, General Electric, Hitachi, London-Heathrow Airport, Humana, HP, Ericsson, eBay, Dow, the Emirates Group, Deutsche Bank, the European Investment Bank, the European Bank for Reconstruction and Development, Dell, Discovery, Chevron, BP, BBVA, Citi, Cisco, Barclays, Bayer, the American Heart Association, Amazon, Bank of America, BlackRock, the Blackstone Group, Santander, Boeing, Booking.com, Credit Suisse, McKinsey, LUKOIL, PayPal, Thomson Reuters, UPS, Unilever, Anglo American, Investment Corporation of Dubai, Industrial Development Corporation of South Africa, Bank Leumi Le-Israel, Dubai Electricity and Water Authority, Bloomberg LP, the LEGO Company, Volvo, Anheuser-Busch, Volkswagen, Airbus Defense and Space, AARP, the African Development Bank Group, Bain & Company, Expedia, Development Bank of Southern Africa, Iron Mountain, Investec, Ingka Group (includes IKEA), Levi Strauss, the Mayo Clinic, Scotiabank, Royal Dutch Shell, Royal Bank of Scotland, Stanley Black & Decker, Swarovski, African Export-Import Bank, Banco do Brasil, Prudential, Discovery, Ontario Teachers' Pension Plan, the State Bank of India, and Quest Diagnostics.

The future these entities are planning for us in what WEF calls the Fourth Industrial Revolution / Globalization 4.0 is one of unlimited mobility—ie, the mass movements of cheap labor/consumers and goods in the service of the neo-liberal economy. Ultimately, WEF and its affiliates such as the World Trade Organization (WTO) and the International Centre for Trade and Sustainable Development (ICTSD) desire to "maximize…foreign direct investment on the economy, society and the environment" and increase "global economic interdependence."

These are central planks of its E15 Initiative, a partnership between the WEF, the ICTSD, the WTO, the UN, the OECD, the Center for International Development at Harvard University, the Inter-American Development Bank, the Evian Group, the Brussels European and Global Economic Laboratory (BRUEGEL), Chatham House, Climate Strategies, the Global Governance Programme, the European University Institute, the Graduate Institute of Geneva Centre for Trade and Economic Integration, the World Trade Institute, Friedrich Ebert Stiftung (named after the first president of Germany's Weimar Republic),[142] the International Food and Agricultural Trade Policy Council, the Peking University National School of Development, the International Institute for Sustainable Development, the International Institute for Management Development (IMD) International Business School, Kommerskollegium National Board of Trade (a government agency in Sweden that answers to the Ministry for Foreign Affairs), Southern Voice (a network of over fifty think tanks from the Global South that actively supports the UN's Agenda 2030), and the governments of Sweden, the UK, the Netherlands, Denmark, Finland, Canada, and Switzerland. Major features of the E15 Initiative include:

- An emphasis on multi-lateral trade agreements styled after the Trans-Pacific Partnership that undermine national sovereignty and enforce a kind of "trade egalitarianism"

---

142 "The FES was a section of the Social Democratic Education and Culture Organisation, and was banned along with the party itself in 1933 by the Nazis. In 1946, the FES was reinstituted at the founding assembly of the Socialist German Student Federation. In 1954, the FES was restructured into a charitable organisation 'for the advancement of democratic education.' This established the FES as an independent, self-contained institute. In addition to education programmes, the FES has also worked in the area of development aid since the 1960s. In this effort, it has supported democracy and freedom movements, for instance in the African National Congress (ANC), and played an important role in overcoming dictatorial regimes in Greece, Spain, and Portugal." FES Wikipedia entry.

- An international appeals process to undermine existing bilateral trade agreements
- The removal of all tariffs by "developed countries" for imports from the Third World; near-removal of all other tariffs
- "Scale technical assistance from the International Monetary Fund or multilateral development banks to LDC sovereign debt issuers"
- Increase foreign aid from "developed countries" to the Third World
- "Mandate within the WTO the disclosure and phased prohibition of fossil fuel subsidies, according special and differential treatment to poorer developing countries"
- Create a system of global food stamps
- Emphasize blended finance or hybrid-model capitalism as the preferred method of development
- "Streamline processes and procedures related to visas and work permits and establish a plurilateral but open 'innovation zone'…within which skilled researchers and technical personnel would be able to migrate freely for up to ten years"
- "Establish an Advisory Centre on International Investment Law to level the playing field for developing country governments that lack the legal expertise to defend themselves adequately in disputes, based on the model of the Advisory Centre on WTO Law" (read: standardize all economic systems to neo-liberalism)
- "Enhance local capacity to conform to global standards"
- "Develop norms for making regional and plurilateral agreements more inclusive"
- "Combining improvements in infrastructure, investment climate institutions and workforce skills with openness to foreign direct investment…Emphasize the facilitation rather than restriction of imports and inward foreign investment"
- Establish a global supply chain
- Mandate compliance with the Paris Climate Accord[143]

---

143 Melendez-Ortiz, Ricardo and Richard Samans, "The E15 Initiative: Strengthening the Global Trade and Investment System in the 21st Century," 2016. World Economic Forum and The International Centre for Trade and Sustainable Development.

Despite using the usual wet cardboard euphemisms such as "sustainability" and "equity," Karp's brand of "social impact investing" is not predicated on making a positive impact or anything of the sort— it is about crippling the West, exploiting the Third World, enforcing globalism, and putting a rainbow paintjob on the contemporary vehicle of plutocratic domination while generating previously-unfathomable profits for a small coterie of these oligarchs. Amy Bennett relates Karp's rough outline of the Shape of Globalization to Come:

> Far from simply catering to progressive individuals looking to "invest their values," environmental, social and governance (ESG) factors provide critical insight into a company's viability and long-term economic performance. It's not ancillary analysis, it's critical fundamentals. This realization...was a pivotal moment for Erika Karp and a key to success in developing a truly integrated research framework..."Economics is a wonderful way to think about, and put a framework around, social constructs," says Erika...[Karp] established relationships in different areas of the capital markets—including corporations, non-governmental organizations, regulatory agencies, exchanges, wealth asset managers, investment banks, accountants and others (including the United Nations and the Clinton Global Initiative)... It all involves having a macro capital markets view. Erika notes it's not about moving millions or even billions, but trillions of dollars towards impact, especially when considering ESG imperatives like climate change, women's economic empowerment, animal welfare, education, ocean pollution, potable water and increasing broadband access. "To give you a sense, in 2017 maybe $400 billion of venture money was moved towards alternative energy. We need to move $1.5 trillion a year if we're going to achieve anything like the COP 21 [United Nations Framework Convention on Climate Change] objectives. And that's just for alternative energy. If you can't get the capital markets working and having money flow towards progress, we won't be able to do it...We don't think of ESG or impact investing as an asset class. We think it

169

should be completely integral to the investing process.". . . Donor advised funds and similar philanthropy-focused investment vehicles are critically important "portals" for wealth management clients to access impact investing, Karp adds. "We are seeing a transformation of traditional philanthropy strategies towards impact investing."[144]

This transformation is all-encompassing and signals a full integration of disparate modes of investment with philanthropic endeavors and different modes of lobbying.

The American Bar Association is keenly aware of the need to provide services—and reap the financial windfall—navigating the complex international framework of labor laws and corporate restructuring, especially as private equity firms have increasingly become involved in mergers and acquisitions—described by Market Realist as "a frenzy." Tali Orner writes:

> For companies that employ foreign nationals, that task is even more complicated as there are significant immigration-related consequences that must be addressed prior to sealing the deal on a merger or acquisition. Because most work visas are employer-specific, changes in a company's structure could affect the validity of a foreign national employee's nonimmigrant visa status or pending green card application. . .
>
> It is critical for in-house counsel to be aware of immigration-related issues that may arise as a result of a restructuring between companies that employ foreign nationals. Companies should work with competent and experienced immigration counsel early on in any transaction to ensure that they are in compliance with immigration regulations and to ensure that foreign national employees remain authorized to work in the United States.[145]

---

144 Bennett, Amy, "The Economics of Sustainable and Impact Investing," May 7, 2018. *Real Leaders.*

145 Orner, Tali, "The Impact of Corporate Restructuring on Foreign National Employees," April 30, 2013. The American Bar Association.

While parasitic in nature, these parasitic entities have their own kind of symbiosis that allows them to flourish and generally escape scrutiny while they scrap our nations for parts.

They are all deeply dependent on each other, and their enmeshing—often collusion—provides for mutual benefit. It is vital to understand that this is how the neo-liberal model continues to perpetuate itself and accelerate the accrual of capital and resources to its beneficiaries at the expense of the many through its predication on exponential growth and its maintenance of a mutually-reinforcing network of inextricably intertwined universities, NGOs, think tanks, various media outlets, governing bodies, corporate boards, law firms, financiers, and the like.

One example of this type of relationship is exhibited by Ropes & Gray LLP, advisors to Kohlberg & Co. in connection with obtaining financing for the acquisition of CIBT Global, Inc., a provider of travel visa and immigration services to corporations, travel management companies, and individuals. They also make big money advising charitable foundations, and they work closely with Silver Lake Partners. Ropes & Gray also works closely with Bain Capital, which is very much invested in this particular model.

On October 20th, 2016, Greg A. Shell, managing director of Bain Capital Double Impact Fund, gave the keynote speech at the Leading by Example conference hosted by The Boston Foundation, Boston College, and Ropes & Gray.

This conference is one of the premier conferences of its kind where leading figures in this burgeoning industry—and yes, it should be abundantly clear by now it *is* an industry—compare notes and network. The 2018 edition featured a lot of kvetching about diversity, which will surely be reflected where you live and work and not where these people do. One major point of discussion was the nexus of "civic engagement" in "inner city communities" with economic output—so here you get the perfect twofer of Democrat votes and Chamber of Commerce GDP!

Another point of discussion was why it is much more advantageous to lobby under the pretense of philanthropy as opposed to direct lobbying, and that is for several reasons, not least of which are avoiding "registration and disclosure requirements" and "restrictions imposed by sources of funding."

Confiscatory taxation of the middle class transfers wealth predominantly to the imported Americans of Tomorrow (trademarked), who exhibit all of the ideal characteristics of great consumers. Then, quoting George Monbiot, "Interest payments, overwhelmingly, are a transfer of money from the poor to the rich."

Everything funnels upward to the 1% who then get their nice, tidy tax breaks courtesy of the neo-conservatives. The state is more intermediary, a guarantor of continuous funding and enforcer of compliance than anything else; nations are reduced to subsidiaries—HR departments with an extensive network of intelligence agencies and a lethal globalized security force. Not interested in playing the game? Sorry, but that's not an option. As Charles Eisenstein writes in *Sacred Economics:*

> Debt repudiation is not much of an option for private citizens. For sovereign nations it would seem to be a different matter entirely. In theory, countries with a resilient domestic economy and resources to barter with neighbors can simply default on their sovereign debts. In practice, they rarely do. Rulers, democratic or otherwise, usually ally themselves with the global financial establishment and receive rich rewards for doing so. If they defy it, they face all kinds of hostility. The press turns against them; the bond markets turn against them; they get labeled as "irresponsible," "leftist," or "undemocratic"; their political opposition receives support from the global powers that be; they might even find themselves the target of a coup or invasion. Any government that resists the conversion of its social and natural capital into money is pressured and punished. That is what happened in Haiti when Aristide resisted neoliberal policies and was overthrown in a coup in 1991 and again in 2004; it happened in Honduras in 2009; it has happened all over the world, hundreds and hundreds of times. (It failed in Cuba and more recently in Venezuela, which has so far escaped the invasion stage.)…In October 2010 a coup barely failed in Ecuador as well—Ecuador, the country that repudiated $3.9 billion in 2008 and subsequently

restructured it at 35 cents on the dollar. Such is the fate of any nation that resists the debt regime.[146]

The integrative approach promises mutual support and amplified profits, in addition to the financial interests and incentives already present in each sphere. For example, the VOLAGs (refugee re-settlement agencies) have already monetized migration through per-head payouts. The VOLAGs are reinforced by the plethora of law firms, advocacy groups, and other charities that either profit directly from their services or indirectly as covert lobbying organizations, fronts or conduits for illicit financial dealings, and/or social engineering vehicles.

ILEP is a perfect case-in-point (incidentally, all five of ILEP's principal figures are Jews, including former Portland Mayor Ethan Strimling donor Marc Gross). While this 501(c)(3) generally stays within the lines of symposia on class action lawsuits and the like, its innocuousness camouflages a deeply subversive agenda. Consider that in 2018, ILEP partnered with Loyola University-Chicago for a symposium on consumer protection that featured the nipples-protruding Jewish *Barney Frank*, of all people, as its keynote speaker. Yes, that would be the same disgraced Barney Frank who:

> Accept[ed] as a gift a round trip fight on a luxury jet from S. Donald Sussman of Paloma Partners, a hedge-fund manager who had previously received a $200 million federal bailout as a subsidiary of AIG. As chairman of the House Financial Services Committee, Frank oversaw the dispersion of the bailout funds. Frank reported the cost of the 2009 flight from Maine to the Virgin Islands, estimated to be worth $30,000 each way, to Congress as worth only $1,500…Scandal is nothing new to Barney Frank. The Boston Globe asked him to resign in 1989 after it was revealed that he had fixed parking tickets for a male prostitute who was running a brothel out of his Dupont Circle condominium…While serving on the House Financial Services Committee, Frank consistently supported the expansion of questionable mortgage

---

146 Eisenstein, Charles, *Sacred Economics*, Chapter Six. North Atlantic Books. 2011.

173

loans through Fannie Mae and Freddie Mac while his partner, Herb Moses, was an assistant director of Fannie Mae responsible for relaxing mortgage standards. This policy, of which Frank was a prime mover, led to the largest credit implosion in the history of civilization... Frank, who continued to promote dangerous credit expansionary policies throughout the Bush years, subsequently partnered with Sergio Pombo, who was an employee of the World Bank...Frank consistently reaped campaign money from Fannie Mae and Freddie Mac as well as from various banks...As chairman of the House Financial Services Committee, Frank inserted a special provision into bailout legislation to grant $12 million in TARP funds for One United Bank, a bank connected to the husband of Rep. Maxine Waters.[147]

I've used the adjective "incestuous" to describe the ruling class before, and clearly with good reason. Essentially, traditional notions of public versus private are out the window, with governments themselves part of the investment portfolio, so long as they serve as profitable vehicles and/or useful intermediaries.

As it is, funneling huge funds through various philanthropic loopholes pads profits through tax exemptions and amplifies the ability of investors and Big Capital to influence the political process. The goal, as stated by Cornerstone Capital, is for "partnerships, integration of philanthropy into business strategies, and innovative types of investments, including impact-focused investments, [to] transform the traditional economy." What was so wrong with the traditional economy that it needed transforming?

For all the talk of sustainability by the corporate and financial class and their functionaries, the transformative, globalist model is decidedly *not* sustainable. Nothing that relies on presumptions of exponential growth on a planet with finite space and resources ever is. It sounds nice, sure, but all this "sustainability" talk is only so much empty rhetoric masking what's really going on, and that is resource consolidation, privatization, and speculation.

---

147 Morse, Chuck, "Barney Frank's pattern of disgrace and corruption," October 20, 2010. *WND.*

Chapter Five: Consolidation, Privatization, Speculation

"By [accumulation by dispossession] I mean the continuation and proliferation of accumulation practices which Marx had treated of as 'primitive' or 'original' during the rise of capitalism. These include the commodification and privatization of land and the forceful expulsion of peasant populations...; conversion of various forms of property rights into exclusive private property rights...; suppression of rights to the commons; commodification of labor power and the suppression of alternative (indigenous) forms of production and consumption; colonial, neocolonial, and imperial processes of appropriation of assets (including natural resources); monetization of exchange and taxation, particularly of land; the slave trade (which continues particularly in the sex industry); and usury, the national debt and, most devastating of all the use of the credit system as a radical means of accumulation by dispossession."—David Harvey

The rhetoric of climate change has become millenarian and hysterical, uncoupled from any genuine environmental concerns, of which there are many. If a picture is worth a thousand words, let the image of Greta Thunberg, the teenaged Swedish environmental activist's arrival in New York on a former Rothschild family racing yacht—and the numerous flights that made the journey possible in the first place—serve as example number one.

It is in the climate of Establishment-generated climate change hysteria that the contradictions of, say, an Ayanna Pressley—vocal supporter of the fellow self-styled "Squad" Member Alexandria Ocasio-Cortez's Green New Deal—and the sources of her financial backing—such as Global Partners LP (whose "operations focus on the importing of petroleum products and marketing them in

North America"), a slew of real estate developers, and Blue Haven Initiative—become all the more grotesque. Blue Haven Initiative, by the way, is another one of these "impact investment" organizations; its co-founder and principal investor is none other than Liesel Pritzker Simmons, of the Jewish Pritzker family. Blue Haven will make another appearance later.

The Green New Deal resolutions in the US House of Representatives and the Senate were sponsored by Alexandria Ocasio-Cortez and Ed Markey, respectively. It is always worth looking into where politicians derive their campaign finances from, as this gives us a window into the interests that they represent. It is worth emphasizing that the Center for Responsive Politics states, "Our research over more than 20 years shows enough of a correlation between individuals' contributions and their employers' political interests that we feel comfortable with our methodology." Employers and senior management also find many ways to spend lavishly on the candidates they want to control beyond their own individual "hard money" and corporate PAC donations, but the money we can trace gives us a good picture.

For Markey, in the 2020 election cycle, that would be PACs representing and/or individuals affiliated with: Akin Gump et al., DLA Piper, Bain Capital, Blackstone Group, Tufts University (alma mater of Anti-Defamation League CEO Jonathan Greenblatt), Harvard University, Google, Immigrant Learning Center, DISH Network, iHeart Media, Estee Lauder, the National Basketball Association, Verizon, Brownstein Hyatt et al., WilmerHale LLP, T-Mobile, Sunovion Pharmaceuticals, Vertex Pharmaceuticals, Sprint, Hilton, Morgan Stanley, Dell, Bristol-Myers Squibb, Twitter, and Oracle. Many of these organizations are a part of Michael Bloomberg's New American Economy and/or are helmed by Jewish CEOs (or commissioners in the NBA's case), such as Oracle's Safra Catz. Markey has received money from Bernie Madoff and S. Donald Sussman's Paloma Partners in the past. Also, Markey's wife, it should be noted, is the Jewish Susan Blumenthal, whose resumé includes a number of high governmental positions, professorships at Georgetown, Brandeis, and Tufts, and a column for the *Huffington Post*.

In gearing up for her 2020 re-election campaign, Ocasio-Cortez's primary donors included PACs representing and/or individuals affiliated with: Google, Facebook, Amazon, Apple, Alphabet Inc., Delta, Kaiser Permanente, "majority women-owned" law firm Selendy & Gay, and WilmerHale LLP. Robert Mueller is a partner at WilmerHale's Washington office, and the firm is notorious for shady dealings and representing the unscrupulous, including Jewish insider trader Ivan "Greed is Good" Boesky.

In recent elections, donations from WilmerHale went not just to Markey and AOC, but Elijah Cummings (now deceased), Kirsten Gillibrand, Kamala Harris, Pete Buttigieg, Amy Klobuchar, Joe Biden, Julian Castro, John Hickenlooper, Elizabeth Warren, Adam Schiff, Mitch McConnell, Jerrold Nadler, Beto O'Rourke, Bernie Sanders, Tim Ryan, Ben Sasse, Ted Lieu, Joe Kennedy III, Lindsey Graham, Maxine Waters, Tulsi Gabbard, Cristina Tzintzun Ramirez, Mike Levin, and Cory Booker. Ayanna Pressley also received donations from WilmerHale and Alphabet Inc. in her initial election bid.[148]

While we've discussed half of "The Squad," we should not neglect to look into who helped finance Ilhan Omar and Rashida Tlaib's re-election bids as well. For Omar, her top donors in the 2020 election cycle included PACs representing and/or individuals affiliated with: Google, Apple, Alphabet Inc., Creatis Capital, Evercore Partners, Dana Investment, Paradigm Global Group, Tiger Global Management, and Patagonia, Inc. (which is also a Pressley donor—maybe that's why they're all so *fashionable*).

For Tlaib: Fedex, Boeing, AT&T, Evercore, the End Citizens United PAC, East Bridge Capital, Microsoft, and the commercial real estate IDS Real Estate Group. Indeed, irrespective of their "wokeness" or sass quotient, it appears the saucy Congresswomen are, as we expected, nothing but mouthpieces for multi-nationals and global capital. Insert "color-blind" joke here. Donald Trump, however, is *not*. From the *Times of Israel*:

> Democratic presidential candidate Beto O'Rourke, a former congressman from Texas, tweeted: "When he calls 6 members of Congress — all women of color or Jewish — 'savages,' he wants you to think of them as

---

148 In 2019, Alphabet Inc. spent $12.66 million on lobbying costs in addition to the company and its employees' almost $4.7 million in campaign contributions; 82.5% of Alphabet Inc.'s lobbyists previously held government jobs.

less than human. Like when he calls immigrants an 'infestation' and says 'no human being' would want to live in Baltimore.' We can't be surprised when violence follows."

Thank you, Robert Francis. Thank also his donors from Sanchez Oil & Gas (O'Rourke has publicly supported the Green New Deal), Microsoft, Dell, IBM, Apple, AT&T, Cisco Systems, the Blackstone Group, Amazon, Alphabet Inc., and the University of Texas.

Adam Schiff, recipient of WilmerHale campaign donations (as is Maine Senator Susan Collins), has also received money from Quinn Emanuel Urquhart & Sullivan, which spawned Cortez donor Selendy & Gay, as well as from PACs representing and/or individuals affiliated with Paloma Partners, Soros Fund Management, Raytheon, DLA Piper, Georgetown University, Cisco Systems, Disney, Saban Capital Group, the University of California-Berkeley, Chelsea Handler Inc., Lauder Partners, the Federal Reserve System, Stanford University, Warburg Pincus, Lockheed Martin, the Council on Foreign Relations, Northrop Grumman, Point72 Asset Management (the Jewish Steven A. Cohen's Point72 was founded in 2014 as the successor to SAC Capital the year after the firm pleaded guilty to federal insider trading charges, paid a $1.8 billion fine, was given a five-year probation, was required to hire an outside monitor, and was ordered to terminate managing money for outside investors), Google, Amazon, WarnerMedia, and AT&T. Another Schiff donor is the Sandler Foundation, founded by the Jewish Marion Osher Sandler (born in Biddeford, Maine) and her husband Herb. The Sandlers:

> Were the billionaire owners of Golden West, a savings and loans bank. The Sandler family is often noted for instituting and pioneering the aggressive lending practices that lead to the housing crisis of the late 2000s. Golden West was sold by the Sandlers to Wachovia for $24 billion in 2006, prior to the 2008 financial crisis.[149]

As reported earlier in this book, the Sandler Foundation has provided in excess of $22 million to the Center for American Progress as well as donations to the Natural Resources Defense Council.

---

149 "Susan Sandler," Influence Watch.

They've also disbursed funds to the ACLU, the Rocky Mountain Institute, J Street, Media Matters, Sierra Club, the Tides Foundation, and the German Marshall Fund of the United States.

The Sandlers' daughter, Susan, is a Board trustee. She has donated extensively to the campaigns of Barack Obama, Cory Booker, and Kamala Harris and is a prominent member of Democracy Alliance, one of the most influential and well-endowed NGOs in the world, with which her parents were involved in its early stages. As Kenneth Vogel reports, the "middle man" organization has "steer[ed] more than $600 million. . . to a portfolio of carefully selected groups, including pillars of the Clinton-aligned establishment like the think tank Center for American Progress and...Media Matters."[150]

Media Matters for America was founded by David Brock, a neo-conservative "discovered" by the Jewish John Podhoretz turned Left-wing mouthpiece and functionary. In the early 2000s, Brock "switched allegiances" (I say this sarcastically as neo-cons and neo-liberals are two sides of the same coin) and aligned with Clinton advisor and confidant the Jewish Sidney Blumenthal. Brock asserted in his 2002 book *Blinded by the Right: The Conscience of an Ex-Conservative* that he had been "a Jew in Hitler's army" and a "witting cog in the Republican sleaze machine."

Brock launched Media Matters in 2004 with substantial assistance from the Center for American Progress, Democracy Alliance, and major telecommunications executive, Stanford MBA, and Council on Foreign Relations member Leo Hindery. Also with prominent roles were James Hormel, the first gay man to represent the US as a foreign ambassador and the grandson of George A. Hormel, founder of Hormel Foods and creators of Spam, and Susie Tompkins Buell, co-founder of Esprit clothing and the North Face. Buell held a fundraiser for Brock's Media Matters at her San Francisco home and is close friends with Hillary Clinton. She has also worked closely with George Soros, Drummond Pike, and Pat Stryker. George Soros is a major donor to Media Matters.

According to Influence Watch, other major donors have included a number of Jewish communal funds and philanthropies including Combined Jewish Philanthropies of Greater Boston and

---

150 Vogel, Kenneth, "'The 'Resistance,' Raising Big Money, Upends Liberal Politics," October 7, 2017. *The New York Times.* October 7, 2017.

the Community Foundation of the United Jewish Federation of San Diego, as well as the Glaser Progress Foundation, the Fidelity Investments Charitable Gift Fund, the Vanguard Charitable Endowment Program, and the New York Community Trust. Media Matters researcher Talia Lavin previously worked at *The New Yorker*, where she resigned in June 2018 after falsely labeling an ICE agent's US Marines tattoo a "neo-Nazi symbol." Lavin also had a journalism course she was scheduled to teach at NYU canceled. She claims that any criticism of George Soros is "an anti-Semitic dog whistle." The National Council of Jewish Women (NCJW) similarly worries about "anti-Semitism," stating that "Congress should pass the Khalid Jabara and Heather Heyer NO HATE Act (S 2043 / HR 3545), which would tie hate crime reporting and training to federal grants."

Using the "our shared values" clap-trap, firmly believes that, "The truest way to honor the lives impacted by hate in the United States is to come together to actively fight anti-Semitism, racism, transphobia, xenophobia, and other systems of oppression." What is this "hate" and what is its barometer? Is "hate" simply anything inconvenient or in opposition to the ruling class's agenda? In light of everything we've seen there really can't be any other conclusion.

In 2014, a leaked document revealed Democracy Alliance's "Aligned Network" and "dynamic investments" funding organizations, to which they had pledged nearly $40 million for that year alone, including the Center for American Progress, Media Matters, the Black Civic Engagement Fund, Progressive Majority, the Latino Engagement Fund, the Brennan Center for Justice, and more.

Also included in their "Progressive Infrastructure Map" were: J Street, Movement Advancement Project (MAP), Bend the Arc: A Jewish Partnership for Justice, Color of Change, the Center for Media and Democracy, Hip Hop Caucus, the Southern Poverty Law Center, the Roosevelt Institute, the NAACP (who have also received Tides Foundation funding), Mother Jones, NARAL (who have also received Tides Foundation funding), Main Street Alliance, Mi Familia Vota, National Democratic Redistricting Trust, Sunlight Foundation, Vote Latino, National Immigration Forum, the National Gay and Lesbian Task Force (now the National LGBTQ Task Force, who have also received Tides Foundation funding), Race Forward, Rock the Vote (who have also received Tides Foundation funding),

Project New America, Planned Parenthood (who have also received Tides Foundation funding), EMILY's List, La Raza, and the Sierra Club (who have also received Tides Foundation funding).[151] Other affiliated organizations include MoveOn.org, the ACLU (with its net assets of $491 million), the Women's March, GiveGreen, the National Immigration Law Center, and PICO. In April 2005:

> Democracy Alliance held its first three-day conference for fifty "partners" in Phoenix, Arizona. Among that first group of partners were billionaires George Soros, Peter Lewis and Herb and Marion Sandler; major Clinton fundraisers Mark and Susie Buell and Bernard Schwartz; New York venture capitalist and longtime Clinton supporter Alan Patricof; Hollywood celebrities Rob Reiner and Norman Lear; wealthy high-tech Californians such as Working Assets founder Michael Kieschnick; and the AFL-CIO and the SEIU…In June 2006, a group of partners from the Alliance's progressive wing were elected to the board, this group included a number of notable names. They included then-Open Society Institute official Gara LaMarche; Anna Burger, then of the Service Employees International Union (SEIU); Drummond Pike of the Tides Foundation; and Rob McKay, Taco Bell heir and president of the McKay Family Foundation.[152]

The reader may notice a preponderance of Jewish names on that list, and that of the following.

The five credited founders of Democracy Alliance are Rob Stein, Steven Gluckstern, Mike McCurry, Andrew Rappaport, and Simon Rosenberg, although Democrat political operative Erica Payne of the Agenda Project[153] stakes a claim as a co-founder; other prominent members past and present include Tom Steyer, Paul Egerman

---

151 "Democracy Alliance Portfolio Snapshot," April 2014.
152 Berman, Ari, "Big $$ for Progressive Politics," September 28, 2006. *The Nation.*
153 Donor organizations include the Lebowitz-Aberly Family Foundation and the Stephen M. Silberstein Foundation; featured speakers at previous events include Chuck Schumer, Paul Krugman, Van Jones, and Kirsten Gillibrand.

(finance chair for Elizabeth Warren and member of the Board for J Street and the New Israel Fund), Julie Kohler, Randi Weingarten, Anna Burger, Jonathan Rosen, Patricia Bauman, Anna Lefer Kuhn, and Kim Anderson.

Returning to campaign financing, Jews Adam Schiff and Jerrold Nadler also receive funds from Alphabet Inc. Alphabet Inc.'s fingerprints are everywhere; they were "Mayor Pete" Buttigieg's primary donor in his presidential bid, along with PACs representing and/or individuals affiliated with AT&T, Microsoft, Disney, Comcast, Amazon, Wells Fargo, Kaiser Permanente, McKinsey, Harvard University, Facebook, Apple, and the Blackstone Group.

Alphabet Inc. is an American multinational created through a corporate restructuring of Google and is now the parent company of Google and several former Google subsidiaries. As evidenced above, Alphabet Inc. is a primary donor to Alexandria Ocasio-Cortez and Ilhan Omar, and small donations from Alphabet found their way into the coffers of Rashida Tlaib and Ayanna Pressley in the 2020 election cycle as well. In addition to providing funds to "The Squad" and Buttigieg, Alphabet Inc. and its employees, subsidiaries, and affiliates also donated over $200,000 to Elizabeth Warren, over $160,000 to Bernie Sanders, $120,000 to Kamala Harris, $60,000 to Andrew Yang, nearly $60,000 to the Democratic Congressional Campaign Committee, $37,000 to Cory Booker, over $34,000 to Joe Biden, over $24,000 to Beto O'Rourke, and over $23,000 to the Democratic Senatorial Campaign Committee in the 2020 election cycle; Alphabet Inc. and its subsidiaries and employees have also disbursed funds to the following: Tulsi Gabbard, Nancy Pelosi, Ro Khanna, Mike Levin, Jay Inslee, Kirsten Gillibrand, Eric Swalwell (who proposed using nuclear weapons on those unwilling to turn their guns over to the federal government), Amy Klobuchar, Julian Castro, John Hickenlooper, Tim Ryan, Ted Lieu, Jared Golden, John Lewis, Hank Johnson, Xochitl Torres Small, Cristina Tzintzun Ramirez, Debbie Wasserman Schultz, Joe Kennedy III, Jon Ossoff, Aisha Wahab, Nabilah Islam (it should be noted Islam is a Program Associate for the Land, Water, and Climate Justice team for the American Jewish World Service organization), and a slew of PACs, per the Center for Responsive Politics.

The American Jewish World Service is:

> The only American Jewish organization solely dedicated to ending poverty and advocating for human rights in the developing world, AJWS partners with Jewish leaders to shape policies that will help people in the developing world... In our current political climate, many U.S. policies have harmful effects on millions of people who live far beyond our national borders. For example, the recent expansion of the 'Global Gag Rule'—a policy that blocks U.S. federal funding to international organizations that provide abortions or abortion-related services to their patients—is an assault on the human rights of women, girls and LGBTI people.

While hewing heavily Left, Alphabet and its employees also donated to the National Republican Congressional and Senatorial Committees in the 2020 election cycle, as well as individual candidates Chuck Grassley, Ben Sasse, Mike Lee, Mitch McConnell, Steve Scalise, Tim Scott, David Perdue, Liz Cheney, Lindsey Graham, Justin Amash (now "Independent"), and...Donald Trump. The sprinkling of funds to these mostly Establishment mainstays is also important in its own right to the maintenance of the status quo, i.e.—allowing Alphabet and the other tech companies to do whatever they want.

Alphabet Inc. and its employees dispensed over $8.2 million in the 2018 election cycle, 82.3% of which went to Democrats, including almost $85,000 to Maine Congressional candidate Jared Golden, another vociferous supporter of the Green New Deal. They also gave nearly $16,000 to Maine Senatorial incumbent Angus King and almost a quarter of a million dollars to Beto O'Rourke in his unsuccessful bid to unseat Ted Cruz in Texas. This is before considering the almost $21.8 million in lobbying expenditures for the year of 2018 alone, most of which was spent by Google.

Alphabet Inc. also has deep ties to numerous Jewish organizations, not least of which is the Anti-Defamation League (ADL). Facebook, Google, Microsoft, Twitter, and other technology companies work with the ADL on the "Cyberhate Problem-Solving Lab" and the Best Practices for Challenging Cyberhate guidelines. Google subsidiary YouTube has tasked the ADL with filtering out and banning "extremist content" from its platform. Further, as Corinne Weaver writes:

George Soros, Google, and the ADL all have something in common: they all take interest in "white nationalism" online. Google sent an interesting representative to the hearing on "Hate Crimes and the Rise of White Nationalism" on April 9. Alexandria Walden, Google's Counsel on Free Expression and Human Rights, was introduced by the House Judiciary Committee Chairman as a former Center for American Progress employee. The center is a liberal non-profit that was founded by President Clinton's former chief of staff John Podesta, and funded by liberal billionaire George Soros…

Google already had a friend at the hearing, however. Chairman Jerry Nadler (D-New York) tweeted on April 8 that he was "Honored to join #GrowwithGoogle for its launch with partners @GoodwillNYNJ @HudsonGuild @galeabrewer & others."

According to OpenSecrets.org, Nadler's top donor for his 2018 campaign was Alphabet, Google's parent company, which donated $26,000. Google is a major landlord and employer in Nadler's district…

The spokesperson for the Anti-Defamation League, Eileen Hershenov, blamed platforms like Gab and 8chan for being "recruiting grounds for terrorists" and "round the clock white supremacist rallies." She also stated that the rhetoric of "elected officials and candidates" was encouraging white nationalist crime.[154]

Hershenov's bona fides include a stint as a law clerk for Jack B. Weinstein in New York's Eastern District, a Karpatkin Fellow with the ACLU focusing primarily on "women's rights" and immigration, and as general counsel for George Soros's Open Society Foundations as well as his Central European University. ADL CEO Jonathan Greenblatt served as the Director of the Impact Economy Initiative project at the Aspen Institute, which has received more than $500,000 from George Soros' Open Society Foundations. The Aspen Institute

---

154 Weaver, Corinne, "Google Sends Former Soros-Funded Employee to White Nationalism Hearing," April 9, 2019. *MRC NewsBusters.*

is also involved with the World Economic Forum (WEF).

Since 1985, when it began tracking "hate groups'" use of online bulletin boards, the ADL has dedicated resources to censoring the internet, espionage, and sharing intelligence with law enforcement and the government (which includes Israel).

Who can forget the infamous "HateFilter" the ADL sent to market in 1998? From a November 2017 Omidyar Network press release on the ADL's Center for Technology and Society:

> The ADL...announced new funding for the center from Omidyar Network, the philanthropic investment firm created by eBay founder Pierre Omidyar...
>
> Earlier this year at the South by Southwest conference, ADL CEO Jonathan Greenblatt announced that the organization was establishing the CTS with a $250,000 seed grant from Omidyar Network. Now up and running, CTS will lead ADL's efforts to fulfill its civil rights mission in the digital space... Omidyar Network has committed additional funding and will provide $1.5 million to support the Center's work...
>
> The board members are: Danielle Citron, a law professor at the University of Maryland and author of Hate Crimes in Cyberspace; Brad Hamm, dean of the Medill School of Journalism at Northwestern University; Shawn Henry, former FBI executive assistant director; Reddit founder and CEO Steve Huffman; James Joaquin, co-founder and managing director of Obvious Ventures; Aileen Lee, Cowboy Ventures; Matt Rogers, Nest founder and chief product officer; Facebook VP of Product Guy Rosen; Jeffrey Rosen, president of the National Constitution Center and professor of law at George Washington University; Jeffrey Saper, vice chair of the global tech law firm Wilson Sonsini (note: Saper is also a national commissioner for the ADL);
>
> Snapchat's head of public policy, Micah Shaffer; former Twitter executive Katie Jacobs Stanton, Color Genomics' chief marketing officer; Anne Washington, a public policy professor at George Mason University who focuses on

the social dynamics of information; and Whitney Wolfe, CEO of the dating app Bumble.[155]

What you might find interesting is that Greenblatt and Omidyar have a working relationship that extends back to the early 2000s when Omidyar invested in Greenblatt's Ethos Water; they eventually sold the company to Starbucks and Greenblatt worked for the Jewish Howard Schultz as the Vice President for Global Consumer Products. Remember how the ADL was going to do the anti-bias training for Starbucks in 2018 before the Black Lives Matter leadership turned on them? Rather ironic all things considered.

The ADL's CTS also has entered into a fellowship program sponsored by the Robert A. and Renee E. Belfer Family Foundation. The Belfer fortune is from "an oil empire that is now in its third generation." Inside Philanthropy expands on the Jewish Belfers:

> In 1992, Robert founded Belco Oil & Gas Corp., a leading independent producer of domestic oil and gas. Belfer is currently chairman of Belfer Management LLC, a private investment firm. Belfer took a big financial hit a while back, losing somewhere in the neighborhood of $700 million because of shares he held in Enron…Albert Einstein College of Medicine at Yeshiva University also received more than $120,000 from the foundation in the past.
>
> The foundation is also passionate about Jewish causes. They've given more than $86,000 recently to the American Jewish Committee. Central Synagogue, the UJA Federation of New York and Columbia Barnard Hilel have all received funds from in recent years… [The Belfers] have recently shown a major concern with cybersecurity.
>
> To that end, they recently gave a $15 million gift to the Belfer Center for Science and International Affairs at the Harvard Kennedy School to establish the Cyber Security

---

155 Omidyar Network, "Leading Tech Platforms and Cyber Experts Join New ADL Advisory Board to Clamp Down on Online Hate," November 13, 2017. Omidyar Network.

Project, which "seeks to help create the conceptual arsenal" for strategists to confront cyber threats.[156]

One of the three inaugural fellows is Samuel Woolley of the Oxford Internet Institute at the University of Oxford, who works with Jigsaw, a Google subsidiary whose CEO is the Jewish Jared Cohen.[157]

---

156 *Inside Philanthropy* entry.

157 Cohen was a former advisor to Condoleezza Rice and Hillary Clinton and was revealed to have used his position within Google Ideas, the Jigsaw precursor, to help foment regime change in Syria and other covert activity in the Middle East. As Yazan al-Saadi wrote in "StratforLeaks: Google Ideas Director Involved in 'Regime Change,'": "Stratfor's staff make reference to a *Huffington Post* article which highlighted Cohen's role in 'delaying the scheduled maintenance on Twitter so the Iranian revolution could keep going' and a *Foreign Policy* article that noted that Cohen 'was a Rhodes scholar, spent time in Iran, [and] hung out in Iraq during the war.' These casual discovers further perked Stratfor's curiosity about Cohen. The following day, [Stratfor's vice-president of counter-terrorism Fred] Burton forwarded a message to the secure email list from 'a very good Google source' who claimed that Cohen '[was] off to Gaza next week'. Burton added, 'Cohen, a Jew, is bound to get himself whacked....Google is not clear if Cohen is operating [with a] State Dept [or] WH [White House] license, or [is] a hippie activist.' Korena Zucha, another senior analyst on the list, queried, 'Why hasn't Google cut ties to Cohen yet? Or is Cohen's activity being endorsed by those higher up in the [company] than your contact?' In turn, Burton replied, 'Cohen's rabbi is Eric Schmidt and (sic) Obama lackey. My source is trying to find out if the billionaire owners are backing Cohen's efforts for regime change.' Later on, Burton forwarded information from the 'Google source' of Cohen's links in establishing Movements.org. The source added, 'A site created to help online organization of groups and individuals to move democracy in stubborn nations. Funded through public-private partnerships.' Burton pointed out that the US State Department is the organization's public sponsor...Burton responded, 'GOOGLE is getting WH [White House] and State Dept. support and air cover. In reality, they are doing things the CIA cannot do. But, I agree with you. He's going to get himself kidnapped or killed. Might be the best thing to happen to expose GOOGLE's covert role in foaming up-risings, to be blunt. The US Gov't can then disavow knowledge and GOOGLE is left holding the shit bag.'" Julian Assange corroborates: "Only a few months before he met with me, Cohen was planning a trip to the edge of Iran in Azerbaijan to 'engage the Iranian communities closer to the border,' as part of a Google Ideas' project on 'repressive societies.'...Cohen flew to Ireland to direct the Save Summit, an event co-sponsored by Google Ideas and the Council on Foreign Relations...The event aimed to workshop technological solutions to the problem of 'violent extremism.'... Cohen's Save Summit went on to seed

From the ADL press release: "[Woolley's] fellowship project will work to understand how political bots and algorithms have been leveraged to target the Jewish community and use this understanding to find ways to counter this bias."

The Center also has joined forces with UC Berkeley's D-Lab to create the Online Hate Index. Per the ADL's website:

> The ADL (the Anti-Defamation League), Moonshot CVE, and the Gen Next Foundation…announced a partnership to counter white supremacist and jihadist activity online. The program, dubbed the Redirect Method, will use advertising to redirect individuals who search online for violent extremist material to content that exposes the falsehoods of extremist narratives and directs searchers to non-violent content. This new effort borrows from best practices Moonshot CVE developed with Google for ISIS-related searches, and builds on the previous deployment of the Redirect Method USA – which the RAND Corporation found showed promise – in partnership with the Gen Next Foundation.[158]

Yasmin Green works with the ADL and is the Director of Research and Development for Jigsaw and was previously Head of Strategy and Operations for Google Ideas. Green launched the Redirect Method, born out of a partnership in 2016 between Jigsaw, the Google-backed London-based Moonshot start-up, and the Gen Next Foundation (see Jared Cohen footnote). Edward C. Baig reports what the project will look like in practice:

> If a person on the fringe, or in some pre-radicalization mode, enters a search query asking, "Is it true that the

AVE, or AgainstViolentExtremism.org, a long-term project whose principal backer besides Google Ideas is the Gen Next Foundation. This foundation's website says it is an 'exclusive membership organization and platform for successful individuals' that aims to bring about 'social change' driven by venture capital funding. Gen Next's 'private sector and non-profit foundation support avoids some of the potential perceived conflicts of interest faced by initiatives funded by governments.' Jared Cohen is an executive member."

158 "'Redirect Method' Yields Invaluable Insights for Countering Online Extremism," January 16, 2020. Anti-Defamation League.

Mossad took down the World Trade Center?" the counternarrative reflected in a top search result would direct the person to a place that would make it clear that that was just an unfounded conspiracy theory. A search on "I want to join the KKK" could lead to a search result and link that says that "No race should be superior. Make up your own mind. Browse our playlist to find out more."[159]

Incidentally, *every single Democratic candidate for president* who has received funds originating from Alphabet Inc. has also endorsed the Green New Deal, notable—beyond its infeasibility and general ridiculousness—for its preoccupation with "carbon emissions." If carbon emissions were a problem, the solutions are actually rather straightforward: curtail mass migration, focus on localized trade and sustainability and re-structure the economy so productive people don't have to commute (gulp!), and simply *plant more trees!*

There's no money in that in the current system, obviously, but it does beg the question: why carbon, especially when fossil fuels produce such massive revenues?

Fossil fuels are a finite resource, and the alternatives so far have been wildly inefficient and sorely lacking. As with the whole "climate change" manufactured hysteria in general, this is about resource consolidation and speculation first and foremost, but there are other key reasons as well, ranging from the propagandistic—fewer white babies to save climate while guilty Western nations must also accept millions of African "climate change refugees"—to the "proprietary." "Carbon will be the world's biggest commodity market, and it could become the world's biggest market overall," said Louis Redshaw, head of environmental markets at Barclays Capital and former power trader at Enron. The carbon-trading market, masquerading as "environmentalism," does nothing positive for the environment *nor* does it even address the "problem" of carbon emissions. From Bank Track, "Carbon trading, especially through banks' proprietary trading desks, is a way for banks to make money from money, without contributing new capital towards solving climate change."

---

159 Baig, Edward C., "Redirecting hate: ADL hopes Googling for KKK or jihad will take you down a different path," June 24, 2019. *USA Today.*

The pretensions of our ruling class are purely in the realm of abstraction. Essentially, the "elites'" vague concerns over things like carbon emissions are totally disconnected from the onerous tax burden placed on the middle class to: a) adhere to a Paris Accord all developing nations, including India and China ignore; and b) pursue a quixotic "environmentalist" agenda based on faulty and dubious research whilst ignoring real issues like over-population, pollution, and environmental degradation.

These policies have compounded the economic malaise of the middle- and working-classes and continued to adversely affect many other Western nations while they simultaneously receive a massive influx of foreign nationals in the millions, bringing with them all of the attitudes and behaviors feminists attribute to the demonized white male patriarchy. The carbon-trading market, masquerading as "environmentalism," is illustrative of the twin engines of social control and economic gain working in tandem; it does nothing positive for the environment *nor* does it even address the "problem"— totally manufactured for reasons related to false scarcity and resource consolidation—of carbon emissions. Per Rowena Mason:

> It's not just speculative profiteering and outright fraud that have caused outrage. There is also concern that industry is going to get huge windfall profits from the sale of carbon allowances accumulated during lower activity in the recession. One of the main problems highlighted by bodies such as the Committee on Climate Change is that there are too many free credits floating around. This means it is often cheaper for companies to just pay and pollute than invest in energy efficiency.[160]

The meat of the problem affecting the average people and the working class in Europe (and the rest of the West) is that, in the same vein as the gas tax, again quoting Mason, "It pushes up household bills and the price of manufactured goods in return for the wider social good of falling carbon emissions." But is it a social good or just a way to make money from money at proprietary trading desks? Furthermore, Mason expands:

160 Mason, Rowena, "The great carbon trading scandal," January 30, 2011. *The Telegraph.*

The European Commission admits that around half of Europe's registries are not protected against fraud... Some, like Friends of the Earth, prefer the concept of a flat tax on carbon, fighting against the idea that millionaire offset investors such as Vincent Tchenguiz and Al Gore, or the proprietary trading desk at Citigroup, are likely to end up with sizeable financial proceeds from a system that adds to household energy bills...The worst offender has been "industrial gas credits"...[now-banned] allowances for destroying dangerous greenhouse gases used as refrigerants called hydrofluorocarbons. It costs 7p to eradicate gases equivalent to one tonne of carbon dioxide and the resulting offsets could be sold on the market for about €11, giving a total return of more than 99pc. Developers found this so lucrative they were creating the gases purely to be destroyed and adding to other dangerous by-products in the atmosphere. In the end, industrial gas credits made up 85pc of the market. Critics say this is awarding free money to Chinese and Indian developers straight from the utility bills of European consumers with no environmental gain. In fact, Michael Wara of Stanford University estimates it unnecessarily cost billpayers $6bn.[161]

Jewish vulture capitalist Dan Loeb owns a 200-foot yacht, once named *April Fool*, which he bought for $52 million from Sandy Weill, the Jewish financier behind the creation of Citigroup. These people are making out like bandits and playing us for fools, which explains why former Rothschild employee Emmanuel Macron is perfectly happy to introduce yet more fuel taxes that would effectively be the nail in the coffin of the country's middle class in the interest of "reducing carbon emissions"—almost as big a scam as the UN Migration Pact, which, along with UNICEF, claims that "climate change" is a primary driver of equatorial "refugees" who, of course, must be imported into the West en masse to up their consumption and thus increase their carbon footprint.

Makes sense.

161 Ibid.

Meanwhile, in Brazil:

> The Amazon recedes at a rate of 325,000 hectares each year in favour of Soya crop, according to NASA (note: a perfect image of modern neo-liberalism?)…Replanting a hectare of forest removes 175 cubic tons of carbon from the atmosphere compared to a maximum saving of 56 tons when bioethanol replaces fossil fuel. But clearing one hectare of rainforest releases an immediate one-off 200 cubic tons of carbon into the atmosphere and also destroying nature's mechanism for trapping carbon.[162]

Thus, even if we were to accept for argument's sake every line about "climate change" and its human causes, the alternatives are ineffective or worse, like clear-cutting the rainforest to grow soy or crippling the middle class to make gas more expensive. There are real, tangible consequences, but these do not concern the Davos set. Their "concern" is making money and playing God; the environmental aspect is just a route to resource consolidation and speculation and a means to build up a social cache by signaling support.

Meanwhile real pollution, environmental degradation, and species and sub-species endangerment are totally fine, so long as it looks like "change." If our self-styled "betters" were concerned about carbon emissions, then the solution is easy and obvious: more trees, less globalism.

The faux-Right has no answer but to de-regulate, which in select contexts isn't bad, especially in the face of some of the more bizarre and irrational Leftist-driven policies, but taken in totality—especially the way the neo-cons want to do it—most certainly is. If the Left, or anyone for that matter, truly cared about the environment, they'd find a way to pressure their governments into introducing harsh economic sanctions on nations that did not practice sustainability regarding fragile eco-systems such as the rainforest, or on those that introduced excessive pollutants into the atmosphere or discarded huge volumes of effluvium into the world's rivers and oceans.

Additionally, there are over 90,000 cargo ships crisscrossing the world's oceans facilitating global trade; each one emits *fifty million*

---

162 "Biofuels menace rainforests," April 17, 2007. *The Guardian.*

times more pollution than a car annually. Remember "Buy Local"? The Left doesn't. From behind the wheels of their Priuses or the walls of their gated communities, Leftists fervently spout the officially-sanctioned superficial platitudes that have no real-world applicability and even less intellectual weight behind them.

Whatever happened to campaiging for an end to the destruction of the rainforest? If Leftists are so concerned about global warming, why have they ceased discussing the de-forestation and environmental devastation of this fragile ecosystem? To say nothing of the DIVERSITY of the rainforest, trees need carbon dioxide the same way we need oxygen; an acre of trees can store 2.6 tons of carbon dioxide and produce enough oxygen for eighteen people per year!

Instead of making it impossible for middle- and working-class people to live to stay in accordance with the Paris Accord, why not continue to push for conservation, and even put international aid to good use by helping impoverished equatorial countries so they don't have to engage in massive de-forestation to grow more crops or create grazing pastures for cattle as in Brazil? Why not create bilateral trade deals with different countries for the medicines and herbs that can be harvested from the forest? Per the Growing Air Foundation, if we can convince farmers to harvest the sustainable products of the rainforest such as nuts, fruits, medicinal extracts, and essential oils, they would reap an average of $2,400 per acre, as opposed to $60 for cattle and $400 for timber. What about clean drinking water? Trees act as a natural filter of rainwater and help shield aquifers from pollutants. Trees also stave off soil erosion and have been proven to trap other harmful gasses such as carbon monoxide and sulfur dioxide. What about the environmental cost of exponential population growth?

The global population in many Third World countries is set to triple or quadruple by the end of the century, and legitimate conservation attempts have gone the way of Free Tibet bumper stickers. Concerned about carbon emissions? Protect the forests we have, practice sustainable logging and farming, and hell, maybe even grow *more* trees!

Per North Carolina State University's Trees of Strength website: "The evaporation from a single tree can produce the cooling effect of 10 room size air conditioners operating 20 hours a day." That's too simple, though, and there's no money in it.

The term "Green New Deal" was first used by the Jewish Thomas Friedman in January 2007 and the United Nations Environment Program began to promote the concept in 2008. Apple, Facebook, Microsoft, Google, IKEA, Coca-Cola, and GM have publicly backed the "renewable" plank of the Green New Deal.

But what are the specifics? They're sorely lacking. This is called *greenwashing*, the term activists developed to describe the corporate practice of claiming that self-serving policies and harmful products are environmentally-friendly. As with "equality," "inclusion," and the other plethora of Cultural Bolshevist concepts, most of this rhetoric regarding "sustainability" and the like is a smoke-screen for power and profit, most of which tends to accrue to the inside dealers and their sycophants. Regarding "greenwashing," Katharine Schwab writes:

> The International Monetary Fund estimates the collective worth of Apple, Google, Amazon, Facebook, and Microsoft at $3.5 trillion, more than the GDP of the United Kingdom…Google and Apple claim to be completely carbon neutral: Apple says all its facilities are powered entirely by renewable energy, while Google has become the world's largest buyer of renewable energy to offset its energy costs…A story in Gizmodo in February 2019 revealed how Microsoft, Google, and Amazon are helping to "automate" the climate crisis by providing big oil companies with the technological tools to streamline their operations and help them find even more oil.[163]

Not exactly "sustainable," but if these major companies are set on a "zero emissions" US economy by 2030, they'll need a whole lot of solar panels, and that will require a massive energy expenditure. As Jasper Bernes writes:

> From space, the Bayan Obo mine in China, where 70 percent of the world's rare earth minerals are extracted and refined, almost looks like a painting. The paisleys of the radioactive tailings ponds, miles long, concentrate the

---

163 Schwab, Katharine, "Apple, Amazon, and the rest of Big Tech have a lot to learn from the Green New Deal," June 27, 2019. *Fast Company*.

hidden colors of the earth: mineral aquamarines and ochres of the sort a painter might employ to flatter the rulers of a dying empire... Dotted with "death villages" where crops will not fruit, the region of Inner Mongolia where the Bayan Obo mine is located displays Chernobylesque cancer rates...To meet the demands of the Green New Deal, which proposes to convert the US economy to zero emissions, renewable power by 2030, there will be a lot more of these mines gouged into the crust of the earth. That's because nearly every renewable energy source depends upon non-renewable and frequently hard-to-access minerals: solar panels use indium, turbines use neodymium, batteries use lithium, and all require kilotons of steel, tin, silver, and copper. The renewable-energy supply chain is a complicated hopscotch around the periodic table and around the world. To make a high-capacity solar panel, one might need copper (atomic number 29) from Chile, indium (49) from Australia, gallium (31) from China, and selenium (34) from Germany. Many of the most efficient, direct-drive wind turbines require a couple pounds of the rare-earth metal neodymium, and there's 140 pounds of lithium in each Tesla...It takes energy to get those minerals out of the ground, energy to shape them into batteries and photovoltaic solar panels and giant rotors for windmills, energy to dispose of them when they wear out. Mines are worked, primarily, by gas-burning vehicles. The container ships that cross the world's seas bearing the good freight of renewables burn so much fuel they are responsible for 3 percent of planetary emissions...Mines require a massive outlay of investment up front, and they typically feature low return on investment, except during the sort of commodity boom we can expect a Green New Deal to produce.[164]

Ah, there it is. There will be a commodity boom and there will need to be more cheap labor to manufacture and distribute the commodities. One of the primary goals of the World Economic Forum (WEF) to

164 Bernes, Jasper, "Between the Devil and the Green New Deal," April 25, 2019. *Commune.*

"combat climate change" is to "prevent labour market exclusion" and "ensure…openness," meaning no impediments to the movement of labor across international boundaries, which is obviously at odds with lowering humans' carbon footprint.

This will naturally keep labor costs low and destroy social cohesion, which is essential to the maintenance and expansion of neo-liberalism. From the European Union to the Association of Southeast Asian Nations (ASEAN), it starts with "intra-regional labor mobility" and ends with mass migrations, particularly from the Middle East and sub-Saharan Africa, where the population is expected by some measures to quadruple by the end of the century. 70,000 arrived in Malaysia—*Malaysia*—alone in 2012: "Malaysia is now a country of asylum for forced migrants originating from Angola, Burundi, Bhutan, Central African Republic, Cameroon, Democratic Republic of Congo, Algeria, Guinea, Ethiopia, Iran, Iraq, Kenya, Kuwait, Rwanda and Senegal."[165]

Beyond the need for cheap labor, there will need to be more markets beyond just the United States to purchase these products as the United Nations and the complicit globalist establishment hammers us with propaganda about the need for "global solutions in an increasingly global world"—*which is precisely the root of the problem.*

In terms of catering to these "new markets," the Omidyar Network has facilitated partnerships between oil companies like Shell looking to diversify with their New Energies division and d.light, a solar energy company launched at Stanford University aimed at opening up the "developing world" market:

> Shell's New Energies business was created in 2016 and focuses on two main areas: new fuels for transport, such as advanced biofuels and hydrogen; and power, which includes low-carbon sources such as wind and solar. Within the power portfolio, Shell is also actively pursuing commercial opportunities to invest in energy access solutions in Africa and Asia. The New Energies business is supported by Shell Ventures B.V., the corporate venture capital arm of Royal Dutch Shell PLC ("Shell")…

---

165 Wahab, Andika Ab, "The Future of Forced Migrants in ASEAN," August 2, 2017. *Heinrich Boll Stiftung.*

Shell Vice President Energy Solutions Brian Davis said, "We are impressed by d.light's track record in meeting evolving customer needs for access to electricity across both Africa and Asia. Their experienced team has developed efficient sales and distribution channels in these markets and continues to expand their product range. We look forward to supporting d.light to realize its growth ambitions. With this latest investment, Shell takes a step closer to meeting its ambition to provide a reliable electricity supply to 100 million people in the developing world by 2030."[166]

Blue Haven Initiatives is pursuing a similar strategy. Blue Haven Senior Advisor Chad Larson is the co-founder of M-Kopa, a pay-as-you-go solar company based in Kenya. As an answer to the deep corruption and unreliable electrical grid in Kenya, M-Kopa profits off of selling the panels to the rural poor and extending lines of credit to them in order to afford the attendant kit of batteries, bulbs, et cetera. The kit also includes a SIM card that "can communicate with M-Kopa headquarters in Nairobi. When a customer has made a payment via mobile phone, the SIM card sends a signal to activate the battery, which is powered by the panels."[167] This inter-connectedness is central to the profit-multiplying effect of these companies, firms, and organizations working in tandem. As Stephan Faris writes:

> In 2007 the Kenyan mobile operator Safaricom launched a service called M-Pesa, allowing customers to use a phone to send cash. Originally intended as a way to help microfinance borrowers make and repay loans, M-Pesa was rapidly adopted for everything from salaries to taxi rides, bringing banking to people who were miles from physical bank branches. Today about a third of the Kenyan economy flits across Safaricom's airwaves, and 82 percent of Kenyan adults have a mobile phone...Slogans hand-painted on concrete buildings hawk the power of the

---

166 d.light, "d.light welcomes investment from Shell on its journey to impact 100 million lives."
167 Faris, Stephan, "The Solar Company Making a Profit on Poor Africans," December 2, 2015. *Bloomberg Businessweek*.

> Internet in the service of selling smartphones: "Take
> Google With You" and "You Are Not on Facebook?"...
> It was [M-Kopa co-founder Nick] Hughes, when he
> was an executive at Vodafone—which owns 40 percent
> of Safaricom—who first came up with the idea that
> would become M-Pesa. M-Kopa's director of operations,
> Pauline Vaughan, was in charge of the mobile-money
> service during its early years.[168]

As M-Kopa grows its market, it will need more employees, and
another senior advisor, Paul Breloff is there as CEO of Shortlist,
"a recruiting technology startup transforming how talent meets
opportunity in emerging markets...Shortlist is on a mission...source
and screen great job-seekers for growing, purposeful companies across
India and East Africa." The market growth is intended to be inter-
connected, multi-faceted, and exponential:

> "If you take the long-term view and if you treat low-
> income people as customers...you can change the
> world," [co-founder Jesse] Moore says...Once M-Kopa
> has a customer, it works hard to sell him more products
> on installment. "Your anchor product is clean energy, and
> then you build a finance relationship," Hughes says...M-
> Kopa also sells Samsung smartphones and offers loans to
> pay for school fees...The interest M-Kopa charges is high
> by U.S. or European standards. The cash price of one of its
> products is about 20 percent less than the installment price.
> But in the markets where the company's working—so far,
> Kenya, Tanzania, and Uganda—the rates are competitive.
> Traditional microfinance companies typically charge
> about 20 percent interest on their loans...In November
> [2015], M-Kopa received a clear vote of confidence when
> it completed a $19 million investment round, including
> $10 million from Generation Investment Management,
> a fund co-founded by former U.S. Vice President Al
> Gore that's also invested in SolarCity, the biggest U.S.
> rooftop solar installer, and digital thermostat maker
> Nest Labs (note: Nest Labs was acquired by Google

---

168 Ibid.

in January 2014). "We think they have the potential of being a multibillion-dollar African success story," says Colin le Duc, GIM's head of research. Other investors in the round included Virgin's Richard Branson and AOL co-founder Steve Case.[169]

Superficially it all sounds great—feel virtuous, make money, and save the planet, but the reality, as is virtually always the case with any ruling-class-hatched scheme, is the opposite: not just grim and ugly, but deadly. Returning to Jasper Bernes:

> The problem with the Green New Deal is that it promises to change everything while keeping everything the same… The appeal is obvious but the combination impossible…The Green New Deal…thinks you can keep capitalism, keep growth, but remove the deleterious consequences. The death villages are here to tell you that you can't. No roses will bloom on that bush.[170]

Every rose doesn't even get the chance to have its thorn. As declining infrastructure and environmental degradation are part and parcel of neo-liberalism's infinite growth model, it stands to reason that one of the most fundamental elements of life—water—should eventually become commodified and privatized. This has already occurred to a frightening degree, though the process is not yet complete. We would do well to understand precisely what this entails and what methods are being used to achieve these ends.

With a market in excess of $19 billion in the US alone and a price point that's nearly 2,000 times more expensive than tap water and four times more expensive than regular-grade gasoline, the market for bottled water is enormous, and its potential, if you'll pardon the pun, is as of yet still largely untapped. It will not stay that way for long, though. According to a 2017 OECD policy paper, plans are already underway to create "a global public–private platform for knowledge exchange and effective engagement, collaboration, and action across governments and regulators in developed, emerging

---

169 Ibid.
170 Bernes, Jasper, "Between the Devil and the Green New Deal," April 25, 2019. *Commune.*

and developing economies, institutional investors, the private sector, international organisations, philanthropies, academia and civil society organisations."[171]

This kind of hybrid action is not limited to just the OECD and its partners. According to the United Nations' Agenda for Sustainable Development, the aim is for major multi-nationals to "collaborate with governments, UN bodies, NGOs, industry associations and other businesses to create more effective, enabling environments for achieving the Millennium Development Goals, on both international and national levels." In addition to an accelerated wealth transfer from the First to the Third World to "bridge the infrastructure gap" and "combat climate change," so-called "impediments to private investment in infrastructure" will be removed and "blended finance" will allow for public funds to underwrite projects where the profits will naturally accrue to the private sector.[172]

---

171 OECD Policy Paper No. 11, "Financing water: Investing in sustainable growth," 2018. *OECD Policy Perspectives.*

172 Ibid. From the OECD policy paper: "Blended finance is not an asset class, rather it uses a range of instruments to calibrate the risk-return profile of projects and to address other barriers to private investment...Challenges related to blending include the need for a good enabling investment environment, ensuring that development finance does not crowd out private finance and that the desired development outcomes are realised...Investments in water security compete with other sectors for financiers' attention, driven primarily by the attractiveness of the risk-return profile. This depends on two factors: i) a stable revenue stream; and ii) how the range of risks related to water security investments are shared between public and private actors. Mobilising commercial finance, in particular domestic sources, need to be based on policy reforms of the water sector to promote efficiency gains, cost reduction and cost recovery, as well as improving the balance of tariffs and taxes as sources of finance." Also from said paper, and of particular note to how the globalist entities view the project to commodify water and ultimately completely privatize it, with the state only useful in an interim stage as facilitator: "[To date] water services are often under-priced, resulting in a poor record of cost recovery for water investments...Valuing water means recognising and considering all the diverse benefits derived from improvements in water management in terms of valued goods and services... It creates opportunities for converting the benefits from investments in water management into revenue streams, potentially improving the financial case for investment...Financial flows may benefit projects which are bankable, but may not maximise benefits for communities and the environment...Mapping the flow of finance to water security investments can identify the ultimate sources of capital...The 'Infrastructure Data Initiative' was recently launched to address

In "neo-liberalese":

> Both public and private investment have key roles to play in
> infrastructure financing, including through development
> banks, development finance institutions and tools and
> mechanisms such as public-private partnerships, blended
> finance, which combines concessional public finance with
> non-concessional private finance and expertise from the
> public and private sector, special-purpose vehicles, non-
> recourse project financing, risk mitigation instruments and
> pooled funding structures. Blended finance instruments
> including public-private partnerships serve to lower
> investment-specific risks and incentivize additional
> private sector finance across key development sectors
> led by regional, national and subnational government
> policies and priorities for sustainable development...
> We encourage the use of innovative mechanisms and
> partnerships to encourage greater international private
> financial participation.[173]

As we've explored in other contexts, this vast matrix of
organizations works in tandem or at least toward common ends
through mutually-ensured profit-maximization schemes and social,
political, and demographic transformation in whatever form will be
most expedient. It is truly a global phenomenon:

> Philanthropic funds often foster healthy information-
> sharing and cooperation among the organizations they
> support. They also often work on common problem-

this need and support efforts to establish infrastructure as an asset class. This
is a joint initiative by the OECD, the European Investment Bank, Global
Infrastructure Hub, Long-term Infrastructure Investors Association and the
Club of Long-Term Investors, which aims to create a centralised repository on
historical long-term data on infrastructure (including water) at an asset level...
This methodology should also explore the potential benefits from synergies
emerging from interrelated projects and their impact on water resources. It
would inform project preparation and selection by governments, development
finance institutions and other partners."
173 United Nations, "Addis Ababa Action Agenda of the Third International
Conference on Financing for Development," July 2015.

solving strategies with other kinds of donors. These include multilaterals such as the World Bank, the Global Fund, or the World Health Organization; bilaterals such as USAID and the UK's Department for International Development (DFID); and large foundations, corporations, and significant individual donors.[174]

To provide a clearer picture of the over-lap here, the following is a sample of the attending organizations at the 2012 Secretary's Global Diaspora Forum in Washington, DC, supported by USAID, the Migration Policy Institute, and the US Trade and Development Agency:

- US State Department
- The Aspen Institute
- BMA Capital
- The Brookings Institution
- National Endowment for Democracy
- The World Bank-IMF African Society
- Ashoka
- York University (Canada)
- US Department of Defense
- United Way
- Government of Canada
- Embassy of Ireland
- Peace Corps
- International Rescue Committee
- US Department of Commerce
- American Jewish Committee
- US Department of Justice
- Clinton Bush Haiti Fund
- The QED Group LLC
- Echoing Green
- Woodrow Wilson Center
- Islamic Society of North America
- Harvard Kennedy School
- Mexican-American Coalition

---

174 Powell, Alison, Willa Seldon, and Nidhi Sahni, "Reimagining Institutional Philanthropy," Spring, 2019. *Stanford Social Innovation Review.*

- Government of Haiti
- World Bank
- Baltimore City Health Department
- National Institutes of Health (NIH)
- Accenture
- Office of Refugee Resettlement
- Inter-American Development Bank
- UNCF
- American Jewish Joint Distribution Committee
- Microsoft
- Oxfam America
- Harvard Business School
- USC
- United Nations Foundation
- US Department of Health and Human Services
- The White House
- Simon Fraser University (Canada)
- Dublin City University
- Western Union
- Council on Foreign Relations (CFR)
- Citigroup
- US Department of Labor
- 7-Eleven

Many of the new philanthropic funds are funded by private equity and venture capitalists. New Profit, as just one example, is housed in the offices of Bain Capital and receives its funding from private equity professionals affiliated with Greylock, JP Morgan Chase, and others in addition to Bain Capital.

These groups and individuals apply the private equity model to their philanthropy, which is reflected in a variety of ways. In 2017, charitable assets in donor-advised funds reached an all-time high of $110 billion. Donor-advised assets have a growth rate of nearly 20% annually. In practical terms, let's see what the profit-maximizing chain of events looks like with "charitable nonprofits" as the tip of the spear:

Splash, a relatively small nonprofit with revenues of about $3 million in 2017, that in 2018 received a green light for an investment of $20 million from the Children's Investment Fund Foundation (CIFF), with a match of more than $12 million from city and state governments in Ethiopia and India, to dramatically expand its efforts to bring clean water to millions across the globe. Splash… was tackling an enormous problem (lack of clean water for people around the world); it was approaching that problem innovatively, using off-the-shelf technology employed by the most sophisticated corporations, such as McDonalds. For Splash, the big bet was designed to build something that local actors would then sustain. Eric Stowe, Splash's founder and director, and his team pivoted to that longer-term vision and developed an investment concept with a clear and compelling goal: to provide clean water, sanitation, and hygiene to all public schools in two of the biggest megacities in the developing world. At the end of five years, Splash's work in Kolkata, India, and Addis Ababa, Ethiopia, is expected to reach the point where local government and local private-sector actors, already well-established in those places, take it over.[175]

Now what happens when inevitable mismanagement from the local government causes regression to the mean? Well, those private sector actors are there to assume full control, and there are certainly plenty of bottled water companies out there to "supplement" cities suffering clean water crises with their products. We have seen the dire consequences here in the United States as a result of the demographic transformation of cities such as Flint, Michigan and Camden, New Jersey, and the consequent neglect, gross mismanagement, and corruption. These are reflections of a wider trend; since peaking in 1977 inflation-adjusted federal funding for water infrastructure has been cut 74%. In 1977, the federal government spent almost $77 per person (in 2014 dollars) on water infrastructure, but by 2014 that support had fallen to slightly more than $14 per person.[176]

175 Foster, William, Gail Perrault, and Bradley Seeman, "Becoming Big Bettable," Spring, 2019. *Stanford Social Innovation Review.*
176 Food & Water Watch, "Take Back the Tap: The Big Business Hustle of Bottled Water," February, 2018. Food & Water Watch.

As Alexis Bonogofsky reports:

> According to the Environmental Protection Agency, the nation's drinking water utilities need $384.2 billion in infrastructure investments over the next 20 years for thousands of miles of pipe as well as thousands of treatment plants and storage tanks to ensure the public health. Consequences of this inadequate investment have been seen in recent high-profile public health crises in Flint, Michigan, and the New Jersey public schools. Internationally, the UN finds that investment in public water systems and infrastructure is at an all-time low.[177]

The Trump administration has advanced plans to make it easier for private companies to control public water systems, including further cuts to federal funding for water protection; the administration's plan "relies on a $100 billion fund incentivizing private sector involvement in public utilities to address aging pipes, aqueducts, and other critical pieces of hardware essential to the provision of drinking water."[178]

We already know what this looks like, and it is not pretty. From a 2018 exposé penned by Sharon Lerner and Leana Hosea:

> Flint and Pittsburgh have many unfortunate parallels. Residents of both cities unknowingly drank water with high levels of the potent neurotoxin [lead], which has long-term health consequences…The two lead crises have another important thing in common: a private water company named Veolia.
>
> The world's largest supplier of water services, Veolia had contracts with both Flint and Pittsburgh around the time that lead levels rose in their drinking water. And in both places, Veolia wound up in legal disputes over its role in the crises… The promise of saving money has been central to Veolia's appeal to cash-strapped cities and

---

177 Bonogofsky, Alexis, "Nestlé Is Trying to Break Us": A Pennsylvania Town Fights Predatory Water Extraction," April 25, 2016. *Truthout*.

178 Lerner, Sharon and Leana Hosea, "From Pittsburgh to Flint, the Dire Consequences of Giving Private Companies Responsibility for Ailing Public Water Systems," May 20, 2018. *The Intercept*.

towns struggling with water provision. That was certainly the case in Pittsburgh, where the water authority was facing more than $720 million in debt when it decided to contract with Veolia in 2012. The contract was based on Veolia's "peer performance solutions" model, in which the company is paid based in part on how much it cuts costs.[179]

This has proven very lucrative for Veolia, which now has in excess of $30 billion in revenue and its stock price has more than doubled over the past half-decade. We also learn from Lerner and Hosea's piece that, "At least some of those profits may be stowed in an offshore company Veolia set up in the Bahamas, according the Paradise Papers database." Under Veolia's oversight, residents' water bills have steadily risen while the water quality has continued to decline. Controversy seems to follow Veolia wherever they've been contracted:

> The company's methods have also come under scrutiny outside the U.S., with controversies in Canada, France, and Gabon. In 2015, Romania's anti-corruption agency launched an investigation into Veolia's Romanian subsidiary, Apa Nova Bucuresti, and individual executives for allegedly running a multiyear, multimillion-euro bribery scheme in order to dramatically raise water rates.[180]

Though the crises caused by municipal degradation in Flint, Camden, and to a lesser extent Pittsburgh are in no small part the consequence of their demographic transformation, these kinds of systemic failures are not confined to cities and communities hammered by "diversity"—though that is certainly why they receive more media coverage than Martin County, Kentucky, for example. At nearly 94% white and entirely rural, Martin County is indicative of the deep neglect our non-metropolitan and –cosmopolitan communities suffer at the hands of a ruling class that hates them and wants them extinguished. Residents in Martin County have had to grapple with what has been described as "a catastrophically failing water system" compounded by

179 Ibid.
180 Ibid.

water rates rising close to 50%, even though many residents have to purchase bottled water because the tap water is often undrinkable. The continued failure—by design—at the municipal level dovetails rather nicely with the privatization schemes of companies such as Nestlé that benefit from public disinvestment in water infrastructure, as the Chairman of Nestlé Waters stated in 2009: "We believe tap infrastructure in the U.S. will continue to decline...people will turn to filtration and bottled water for pure water needs."

A recent study predicts over a third of Americans could be priced out of their municipal water supplies within the next half-decade as costs triple while the infrastructure continues to break down.[181]

The only alternatives will then be to turn to bottled water or find local natural springs that aren't owned by these companies or other possible water sources; as 83% of Americans live in metropolitan areas and their suburbs and exurbs, finding clean natural sources of water will not be an easy task, to put it mildly. According to the United Nations, up to two-thirds of the world's exploding population could be living under "stressed water conditions" by the mid-2020s. Returning to Alexis Bonogofsky:

> Internationally, bottled water consumption is estimated to have neared 70.4 billion gallons in 2013, according to data from the latest edition of Beverage Marketing's report "The Global Bottled Water Market." Consumption increased 6 percent in one year and is projected to grow. In fact, the International Bottled Water Association predicts the largest growth in bottled water to be in poor countries, where access to safe and clean water is not necessarily a given, and public water infrastructure is severely underfunded.[182]

Providing one case-in-point, Caroline Winter reports:

> Failing infrastructure has already led to a near-total reliance on bottled water in parts of the world. Nestlé

181 Mack, Elizabeth A. and Sarah Wrase, "A Burgeoning Crisis? A Nationwide Assessment of the Geography of Water Affordability in the United States," January 11, 2017. *PLOS ONE* 12(4).
182 Bonogofsky, Alexis, "Nestlé Is Trying to Break Us": A Pennsylvania Town Fights Predatory Water Extraction," April 25, 2016. *Truthout*.

started selling Pure Life in Lahore, Pakistan, in 1998 to "provide a safe, quality water solution," the company says. But locals wonder if the Swiss multinational is exacerbating the problem. "Twenty years ago, you could go anywhere in Lahore and get a glass of clean tap water for free," says Ahmad Rafay Alam, an environmental lawyer in the country. "Now, everyone drinks bottled water...What Nestlé did is use a good marketing scheme to make tap water uncool and dangerous. It's ubiquitous, like Kleenex. People will say, 'Give me a bottle of Nestlé.'"...He adds that this change has taken the pressure off the government to fix its utilities, degrading the quality of Lahore's supply.[183]

Nestlé has been anticipating and increasingly exploiting this situation for decades, controlling local springs and aquifers for their exclusive use. Other bottled water companies do the same. While people are literally dying from the water in Flint, a mere two hours down the road, Nestlé pays just $200 a year in municipal extraction fees to pump clean water and sell it at dramatically marked-up prices. Nestlé's California water use increased by 19% during the driest period in state history from 2011 to 2014. The company paid only $524 annually in permit fees to pump water from the San Bernardino National Forest—on a permit that was nearly thirty years expired, no less.

Nestlé generally seeks out areas with weak or antiquated water laws and regulations. In states like Maine and Texas, a law from the 1800s called "absolute capture" is still in effect. Absolute capture allows for landowners to use unlimited amounts of groundwater "captured" from said property. Nestlé will then appeal zoning resolutions and other restrictions to build massive facilities to extract the water, as in Fryeburg, Maine, where Nestlé's Poland Spring line now has the means and the rights to extract water for the next twenty to forty-five years, perhaps longer.

Nestlé has sought to influence the political process at the state level in Maine as well, donating to such PACs as [Susan] Collins for

183 Winter, Caroline, "Nestlé Makes Billions Bottling Water It Pays Nearly Nothing For," September 21, 2017. *Bloomberg Businessweek.*

Senator, Angus King for US Senate, Leading to a Balanced Maine, and the Alfond Business Community and Development.

The Alfond Family are an extraordinarily wealthy Jewish family—the wealthiest family in Maine, in fact—working to transform Maine both through their involvement in politics and through their many "philanthropic endeavors." Nestlé/Poland Springs effectively has carte blanche in the state to buy up as many springs and aquifers as they can, privatizing what was once publicly-accessible and what for many Mainers was their primary or secondary water source.

Water independence is part of the deeply self-reliant culture found in the state of Maine; 40% of Mainers drink private, unregulated well water as opposed to 86% of Americans who drink municipal water treated with fluoride, chlorine, and other chemicals. Furthermore, writes Winter:

> Despite the Safe Drinking Water Act of 1974, compliance with harmful chemical restrictions isn't monitored carefully, and most wastewater-treatment systems aren't designed to remove hormones, antidepressants, and other drugs...77 million Americans are served by water systems that violate testing requirements or rules about contamination in drinking water, according to the Natural Resources Defense Council...[Bottled water] outpaced soda sales for the first time as drinkers continue to seek convenience and healthier options and worry about the safety of tap water after the high-profile contamination in Flint, Michigan...Nestlé has come to dominate a controversial industry, spring by spring, often going into economically depressed municipalities with the promise of jobs and new infrastructure in exchange for tax breaks and access to a resource that's scarce for millions. Where Nestlé encounters grass-roots resistance against its industrial-strength guzzling, it deploys lawyers; where it's welcome, it can push the limits of that hospitality, sometimes with the acquiescence of state and local governments that are too cash-strapped or inept to say no.[184]

---

184 Ibid.

Nestlé will also sometimes buy water straight from a municipality with clean water, such as Fryeburg, and as Katy Kelleher writes, "sell it under its private labels, meaning that the same water flowing through faucets in Fryeburg for free is distributed in convenience and grocery stores throughout the country for around $1.99 a liter. One of those private labels is Poland Spring."[185] If neither springs nor compliant municipalities with clean water are available, Nestlé is content to use common ground water from populated areas and pass it off as "fresh"; a recent lawsuit alleges Poland Spring bottles much of its water from ground water near petroleum pits, landfills, and densely-populated areas. In fact, per Kelleher, "Multiple lawsuits alleging mislabeling of water have been brought against Poland Spring over the past 20 years. A 2017 class-action lawsuit argued that 'not one drop of Poland Spring Water emanates from a water source that complies with the FDA's definition of spring water.'"[186]

Not that any of this comes as a surprise from a Nestlé that in the 1970s and 80s pressed a misinformation campaign on women across the Third World and aggressively marketed their infant formula—to be mixed with local water, which as we know is likely to be impure and/ or polluted—as a superior alternative to breastfeeding. Nevertheless, the United Nations High Commissioner for Refugees (UNHCR) saw nothing wrong with entering into a partnership with Nestlé. In fact, in a darkly ironic turn:

> In 2003, Nestlé began a partnership with the U.N. High Commissioner for Refugees (UNHCR) to address the water needs of 210,000 Somali refugees and local people in Eastern Ethiopia. The partnership was both financial and practical, including on-going technical assistance in the form of a Nestlé Waters hydrogeologist and water resources manager... During 2005, the process of handing over the long-term operation and maintenance of the system to local water authorities was commenced...In November 2005, Nestlé became a founding member of BAFF, a coalition working to reduce vitamin and mineral deficiencies through food fortification. Nestlé is the world's largest producer of manufactured foods fortified

185 Kelleher, Katy, "Wet 'N Wild," April, 2019. *Topic Magazine*, Issue 22.
186 Ibid.

with micronutrients. Nestlé collaborated with NGOs, ENDA Tiers Monde, and the International Association for Maternal and Neonatal Health in Senegal to establish a number of local centers "to improve nutritional and hygiene status of mothers and their infants under 5 years of age."[187]

The Nestlé Nutrition Duchess Club markets Nestlé products to children in countries such as Nigeria under the guise of humanitarian outreach in order to, "Meet basic needs such as nutrition, healthcare, water...through affordable products and services. Food and beverage companies can develop new products that combat nutritional deficiencies and are affordable to low-income families."[188]

Nestlé works with NGOs and governmental organizations in countries such as Turkey, Egypt, South Africa, and Malaysia to do something similar.

Nestlé, in conjunction with Project Head Start in townships around Pretoria, South Africa, "trains adult caregivers in adequate pre-school education to stimulate children, age 6 and under. Teaching materials as well as health and nutrition education are given to overcome negative effects of poor nutrition. Workshops and weekly training at the University include appropriate handling of HIV/AIDS cases in the pre-school environment and treating of cuts and wounds."[189] Nestlé also provides funding for a dietician to give nutrition advice and help to "inner-city" HIV/AIDS patients in France.

As we might expect, the unethical and probably lethal practices of Nestlé have not disqualified the company from "educating" Senegalese mothers on the very infant formula they'll be purchasing in bulk—or subsidized to purchase in bulk in any case—for their average close to five children per mother. With its dysfunction, dearth of education, and high birth rate, Senegal makes for the perfect market.

In another instance of the neo-liberal establishment using biological predispositions and particular sets of circumstances to their benefit, a corporation named Bridge International Academies

---

187 Nestlé Public Affairs, "Nestlé, the community and the United Nations Millennium Development Goals," January, 2006. Nestlé SA.
188 Ibid.
189 Ibid.

(BIA) is opening for-profit schools across the Third World, where instructors in the Bridge schools teach a pre-scripted curriculum from a computer. Liberia is considering outsourcing its entire elementary program to BIA, which is funded by Bill Gates, Mark Zuckerberg, and a number of prominent interests from Wall Street.

Recalling the marketing strategies used in Pakistan discussed earlier and understanding the just-aforementioned factors of the Senegalese and Third World peoples in general, Nestlé has endeavored to position itself as a major beneficiary of America's continued demographic transformation and municipal services degradation:

> According to a 2014 market research report, adults that consume large volumes of bottled water are more likely than average to be African American, and Latinos make up the key customer base for bottled water. Researchers from the Medical College of Wisconsin and the University of Wisconsin found that Latino and African-American parents were more likely to buy bottled water than white parents, and they are dishing out more money on bottled water primarily because of perceived health benefits.
>
> The bottled water industry markets to Latino immigrants…in part by exploiting bottled water as part of the immigrant "heritage" of coming from places with less access to clean drinking water. Nestlé Pure Life's target audience is recent Latin-American immigrants, particularly mothers. In 2014, Nestlé spent over $5 million advertising Pure Life… and three-quarters of this spending ($3.8 million) went to Spanish-language television advertising.[190]

A recent Penn State study found that black and Hispanic adults in the United States are half as likely as whites to drink tap water and more than twice as likely to drink bottled water. Much of this is attributable to the state of municipal tap water in more "diverse" and urban environs, but the ability to market to these population groups more successfully is also a major factor.

---

190 Food & Water Watch, "Take Back the Tap: The Big Business Hustle of Bottled Water," February, 2018. Food & Water Watch.

This may seem harsh, but there are also particular pathologies, disparities, and predispositions at the population level that do make blacks and browns better consumers than whites, and other cognitive factors make these populations easier to manipulate and thus control. Despite the fluffy egalitarian propaganda that would force us to think otherwise, the ruling class understands this well—so well they're party to mass genocide in order to produce a new hyper-consumerist, easily-controlled global serf class.

It truly is a numbers game for them, and you can scarcely find anything more dehumanizing than that.

Chapter Six: Cheap Labor is the Opiate of Dying Nations

"Next up: Yelp ratings and TripAdvisor reviews for illegal alien shelters? (I say this only half tongue in cheek. There is already a site called Contratados.org, which is billed as a Yelp or TripAdvisor-style tool that "lets migrant workers rate their experience of recruiters or employers online, by voicemail or by text message.")"—Michelle Malkin

It is a well-documented but much-ignored phenomenon that parts of the rural Midwest have been totally transformed due to meatpacking companies' employment of almost exclusively Hispanic migrant labor to drive down labor costs. The effects were already stark in the early stages of America's "browning":

> Meatpacking wages fell sharply after peaking in 1980. In Iowa, the average hourly earnings of meatpackers in 1981 was $11.33, 50 cents less than the US average $11.83. Wallace Huffman of Iowa State University noted that real meatpacking earnings fluctuated between 1963 and 1988, but were lower in 1988 than in 1963...An INS agent in 1995 estimated that almost 25 percent of the workers in 222 meatpacking plants in Nebraska and Iowa were illegally in the US...
>
> According to meatpackers, there is very high turnover among 10 to 30 percent of the work force, so that a plant with 500 employees may issue 1,000 to 1,200 W-2 statements at the end of the year. Some critics of the meatpacking industry argue that the companies encourage high turnover to keep most workers at the low end of the wage scale...In Albert Lea, Minnesota, city officials were not sure that they wanted a meat packing

plant employing 700 that was closed for a year reopened. According to one official, "a meatpacking plant can butcher public budgets as well as hogs." One study found that, despite new payrolls, per capita income declines in some small communities that attract meatpacking plants.[191]

From 1990 to 1996, many Midwestern localities witnessed their Hispanic populations grow anywhere from 200% to 500%, largely at the behest of major meatpackers and other corporate interests facilitating their new labor force's re-settlement, though not without substantial assistance from the government, social advocacy groups and law firms, and religious charities.

The movement of huge numbers of alien peoples into formerly high-trust, tight-knit communities might help companies' bottom lines in terms of labor costs and general product consumption, but it splinters and ravages these communities—which is also by design.

The Democrat Party benefits from a bumper crop of new voters, the religious charities get to feel righteous, the Chamber of Commerce gets its profits, and the assorted "social advocacy groups" get to act out particular ethnic grievances—often via the witting or unwitting accomplices in the Christian charities—under the guise of humanitarianism. The list of winners definitely does not include the locals:

> Given their small populations, rural towns can be transformed almost overnight by immigration, leading to issues that range from an inability to communicate with public authorities to non-English speaking children in school. Lexington, Nebraska went from a population that was five percent Latino in the 1990 Census to nearly 45 percent Latino in 1994, on a Census re-check.
>
> The growth of the Latino population is attributed to IBP, a meat packer that employs 2,500 workers, and has a $58 million annual payroll, in a town of 9,000. The transformation of Lexington has drawn mixed reviews.

---

191 "Latinos Surge in Midwest," July, 1996. The University of California-Davis *Rural Migration News*, Vol. 2, No. 3.

On the one hand, business, especially in the downtown area, is up. However, some established residents complain that Spanish-speaking meatpackers and their families drive old cars without licenses and insurance, and that the needs of their children lower the quality of the schools.

The crime rate in Lexington has doubled... According to one Nebraska police chief, "where you have the meatpacking plants, you have an immigration of Hispanics, and you are seeing an increase of gangs."[192]

This phenomenon has been replicated across the country in different industries, such as Wisconsin's dairy industry:

Some Wisconsin dairy farmers, claiming that 40 percent of hired workers on dairies are immigrants, were quoted as saying: 'If E-Verify passes, it will kill the dairy industry in Wisconsin.'

John Rosenow of Rosenholm-Wolfe Dairy asserted that '60 percent of the milk that's harvested is harvested by immigrants, and the vast majority are probably undocumented.'[193]

Georgian poultry is another example:

The *Washington Post* on April 3, 2006 profiled immigration to Gainsville, Georgia, the self-proclaimed 'poultry capital of the world.' Between 1990 and 2005, the city's population almost doubled to 32,000, while the number of Hispanics quadrupled, so that the town is now 50 percent Hispanic. Gainsville's demographic change was induced by poultry processors such as Fieldale Farms, Koch Foods and Pilgrim's Pride. About 3,000 of Fieldale's 4,700 workers are Hispanic and earn $10 an hour. About 70 percent of the pupils in Gainesville Elementary are Hispanic, and 90 percent qualify for subsidized meals.[194]

---

192 Ibid.
193 Ibid.
194 Ibid.

In Maine, it is the blueberry, broccoli, forestry, egg, seafood, and apple industries. Let us consider tiny Milbridge, Maine, home to the Mano en Mano organization. Mano en Mano / Hand in Hand is an organization created specifically to provide big agra with inexpensive unskilled farm labor, primarily from Latin America and Haiti.

Based out of Milbridge, Maine, the organization's recent efforts have been to use funding from the USDA to build subsidized apartments specifically to house migrant farm and aquaculture workers. Due to this influx of cheap farm labor, 24% of the elementary school students in Milbridge in Washington County are now Hispanic or mestizo, in a state that is 94-95% white.

Migrant workers patch together seasonal jobs picking blueberries, harvesting and processing sea cucumbers, and processing lobsters. Immigrants from Lewiston recently relocated to Skowhegan in Somerset County in order to work at Backyard Farms, a hydroponic farm in Madison that "has had difficulty filling its job openings," according to the Federal Reserve Bank of Boston.

The function, as is so often the case, is both economic and ideological, but not in the way that groups like Mano en Mano frame their mission; rather, instead of serving as a vehicle to destroy cohesive and high-trust white societies, provide mega-corporations and their executives with cheap help and ready consumers, and an 80% vote share of the immigrant population cast for Democrats, the "progressive nonprofit" Mano en Mano envisions, "A stronger more inclusive Down East Maine where the contributions of diverse communities are welcomed, access to essential services, education and housing are ensured, and social justice and equity are embraced."

Plus, think of all that GDP, Republicans! You'll be shocked—*shocked*, I say!—to learn who bankrolls Mano en Mano in addition to the USDA: Goldman Sachs, Charles Schwab, JP Morgan Chase, Elmont-Schwabe Charitable Corporation (donors to the Anti-Defamation League), the Boston Foundation, Maine Women's Fund, the John T. Gorman Foundation, Fidelity Investments, the Emanuel and Pauline Lerner Foundation (of which Eliot Cutler is President of the Board of Directors), C.F. Adams Charitable Trust (whose trustees come from defense contractor Raytheon, law firm Ropes & Gray LLP, and financial advisory firm Lowell, Blake & Associates), TD Bank, the Maine Health Access Foundation, Ian

Yaffe (Executive Director of Mano en Mano and Board Member of Coastal Enterprises, Inc.), Coastal Enterprises, Inc. (CEI), Bowdoin College, the Larsen Foundation (with the Jewish Marc Rosenberg as Administrative Director), Home Depot, the United Way, NAPA Auto Parts, and the People of Color Fund.

Mano en Mano is part of MaineShare, a "progressive social justice network," which partners with Bowdoin College, Cabot, and Coastal Enterprises, Inc., among others, and whose Board consists of members of the University of Maine Law School, IDEXX, Bowdoin College, and Harkins Consulting, LLC, founded in 1992 by the Jewish Marvin Rosenblum. Other organizations in MaineShare include Maine Equal Justice Partners (MEJP), Maine Women's Fund, Maine Center for Economic Policy, the Sierra Club, Maine Access Immigrant Network (MAIN), EqualityMaine, the Maine ACLU, and the Holocaust and Human Rights Center of Maine.

The Maine Access Immigrant Network (MAIN) was originally founded in 2002 as a 501(c)(3) by Mohamud Barre and the resettled Somali community.

The organization was initially named Somali Culture and Development Association and its mission was to embrace the vision of a free-standing community center with staffing to support all Somalis for access to information, resources, and services. It was renamed the Maine Access Immigrant Network in 2014. MAIN has since expanded to serve other African groups, including South Sudanese, Rwandan, Burundian, and Congolese, and continues to expand with services to Middle Eastern and other refugee groups.

It is supported through grants from the Office of Refugee Resettlement Ethnic Community Self Help Grant, Maine Health Access Foundation, and the Maine Community Foundation. MAIN has many partners, including the Greater Portland Refugee and Immigrant Health Collaborative, the University of New England CHANNELS Project, Care Partners, MaineHealth, Mercy Hospital, and others.

The Maine Health Access Foundation is represented by Bernstein Shur and has financial ties to Catholic Charities Maine, EqualityMaine, Maine Immigrants' Rights Coalition (MIRC), Maine Equal Justice Partners (MEJP), Maine Access Immigrant Network (MAIN), the University of Southern Maine Cutler Institute for Health and Social

Policy, Maine Immigrant and Refugee Services, Maine Transgender Network Incorporated, and the list goes on.

Maine Equal Justice Partners (MEJP) is a non-profit legal aid provider dedicated to "finding solutions to poverty and improving the lives of low-income Mainers." MEJP provides direct legal assistance to low-income Maine residents related to public benefits, food, housing, and healthcare.

In addition to direct legal aid, the organization advocates for "fair public policies in the legislature and with governmental agencies," and partners with "diverse low-income communities and agencies through outreach, organizing, and education." MEJP does not accept federal legal services funding and therefore has no limitations based on immigration status for the populations they can assist. MEJP sued former governor Paul LePage when his administration moved to stop welfare payments to illegal aliens.

Hispanics first started to come to the Milbridge area when a sea cucumber processor used a labor contractor to hire migrant labor in 1997; sea cucumbers are similar to starfish and their meat is highly-prized in Asia. The first workers were former blueberry rakers, and network hiring subsequently led to more Hispanic migrants. Wild lowbush blueberries in Maine are "raked" from barrens in the coastal forests of the northeastern ("Down East") part of the state. Cherryfield Foods, Inc. is one of the largest blueberry producers in Maine and provides free housing to its predominantly Mexican workers. Cherryfield is owned by Oxford Foods in Nova Scotia, Canada. Maine produces about $85 million worth of blueberries a year.

Throughout the 1990s and well into the 2000s, most of the seasonal harvesters were Hispanic immigrants or migrant laborers complemented by Micmac Indians from Maritime Canada. According to Maine's Department of Labor, 18% of farm workers in the state are migrants, defined as those who traveled too far from their usual residence to return at the end of the workday. Ed Flanagan, president of Jasper Wyman and Son, a berry harvester, told the *Washington Post* on April 10, 2006 that Hispanic workers are "like migratory birds. I mean, we don't have to do much and they show up every year."

Jasper Wyman and Sons paid $118,000 to the Immigration and Customs Enforcement Agency in November 2010 for failing to properly complete I-9 forms on the 900 seasonal workers hired each year, by the way.

Washington County had almost no Hispanics in 1990, but today they dominate the harvest crews that "rake" berries from their bushes, not to mention the labor force of Aroostook County's major broccoli farms, the coastal seafood processing plants, and other agricultural or seafood-related industries.

The initial batch of migrant workers showed up because, "They say that they left California or Texas to enjoy the higher wages and better benefits associated with fewer newly arrived Mexican workers." The increased use of farm labor contractors is another major factor in the increased use of migrant Hispanic, mostly mestizo, labor in Maine's agricultural industries, but the presence of advocacy groups such as Mano en Mano which are, in their own words, "working hard to alleviate impediments to settlement in the region," is also a contributing factor to be considered.

All of the laborers' (and their families') health care (including dental, eye care, and psychological care), transportation, and translation needs are provided for by another 501(c)(3) called the Maine Mobile Health Program, Inc. (MMHP), which is focused on "equitable healthcare and social justice."

Do you get free housing, healthcare, transportation, and psychological support through your job? MMHP gets a small subsidy from the US Department of Agriculture, and, according to the most recent financial statements I could find, over $1.4 million from the US Department of Health and Human Services. It was recently announced that MMHP—along with twenty other organizations, many of which we have covered such as MEJP, MIRC, and the like— would be receiving a $1.17 million grant from Maine Health Access Foundation.

In a joint project between Mano en Mano and Colby College entitled, "From Sojourner to Settler," published in April 2017, we learn that when Mano en Mano conducted its first HUD-designed (Housing of Urban Development) needs assessment for the area in 2011, "The organization found that 78.5% of the respondents of the HUD survey were born in Mexico; 89% self-identified as Hispanic/Latino. In that year, 93% were employed in farm-work." Further, from the joint study conducted by Mano en Mano and Colby itself:

When asked, 98% of all respondents identified the town in which they live as "home" implying these sojourners have in fact become settled…[of respondents] under the age of 18 years…87% of these were born in the U.S.… Eighty percent of respondents to our survey identify as Latino or Hispanic.

Eighteen percent identify as having two or more racial identities and 1% identify as White. Forty-three percent of respondents report speaking only Spanish in their household, while 45% report speaking both Spanish and English.

Nine percent of households reportedly speak English only at home (note: this is not "diversity," this is an ethnic enclave)…22% of households don't feel comfortable interacting or calling with police (note: we can probably guess why, probably something to do with their immigration status).[195]

What we can see here is that "documented" or not, the migrants are putting down roots and becoming settled, which is an ominous sign for Maine's demographic future. The workers surveyed are already averaging over three children per family, which is well over the US average, but only slightly higher than the local average of 2.7. It doesn't take much imagination to see where this is going, however.

One by-product of the reliance on predominantly Mexican-mestizo labor is that these families have coalesced into communities with a shared culture and language—which has made their ability to organize and demand better working conditions, benefits, and higher wages much easier, especially as, a) their only competition locally is whites who would demand even more and greater protections, and b) there is a paucity of readily-available scab labor to replace these workers.

In the late-1990s and 2000s, we began to see push-back against serious labor abuses as Mexican workers started to understand their rights and interface with local groups about unionization. Let's use

---

195 Donihue, Michael, Betty Sasaki, Ian Yaffe, Julie Olbrantz, Marlen Guerrero, Clare Murray, and Claire Ciraolo, "From Sojourner to Settler," April 2017. Colby College and Mano en Mano.

the saga of Jack DeCoster, farm magnate, as a filter, with a timeline combined from UC Davis's catalogue *Rural Migration News* and Marler Clark's website:

- **1996:** DeCoster was fined $3.6 million for health and safety violations at the family's Turner egg farm, which then-Labor Secretary Robert Reich termed "as dangerous and oppressive as any sweatshop we have seen." Regulators found that workers had been forced to handle manure and dead chickens with their bare hands and to live in filthy trailers.

- **1996:** In Turner, Maine, Mexican immigrants dominate the work force at the DeCoster Egg Farm, the largest brown-egg producer in the US...was fined $ 2 million by the federal Occupational Safety and Health Administration for violations of health and safety laws. This fine and publicity resulted in boycotts of DeCoster eggs, and a law approved in Maine that permits workers on large farms to unionize under state laws. Most farm workers are not covered by the NLRA.

- **1997:** In December, the NLRB announced that it would issue complaints charging that DeCoster unlawfully interfered with workers engaged in union activities, spied on workers and fired union supporters; the United Paperworkers International is attempting to organize DeCoster workers. The charges were filed against the two successor companies, Maine Ag and Quality Eggs of New England. DeCoster paid $2 million to settle a $5.8 million federal fine for health and safety violations, and split into two companies...In the 1980s and 1990s, DeCoster was fined repeatedly for violations of workplace safety laws.

- **1999:** The company paid $5 million to settle wage-and-hour claims involving 3,000 workers.

- **2002:** The Occupational Safety and Health Administration fined the family's Maine Contract Farming operation $345,810 for an array of violations. The same year, DeCoster Egg Farms of Maine paid $3.2 million to settle a lawsuit filed in 1998 by Mexican workers alleging discrimination in housing and working conditions. Afterward, DeCoster subdivided into eight smaller firms on 1,300 acres near Turner.

- **2008:** Maine Contract Farming LLC of Turner, Maine, the successor to DeCoster Egg Farms, was fined $150,000 by OSHA for ordering workers to retrieve eggs from a building with a partially collapsed roof.

Jack DeCoster's Turner and Winthrop Maine egg farms were sued in August 2011 by a plant manager who alleged that DeCoster treated Mexican-born as "virtual slaves." The manager said that DeCoster told him to "get rid of the gringos" because Mexicans accepted his authority.[196,197]

These abuses are just from DeCoster's Maine farms; his farms in Iowa were shockingly worse:

> In 2001, the Iowa Supreme Court ruled that DeCoster was a "repeat violator" of state environmental laws, citing violations involving the family's hog-farming operations. The family was forbidden to expand its hog-farming interests in the state. Also in 2001, DeCoster Farms of Iowa settled, for $1.5 million, a complaint brought by the Equal Employment Opportunity Commission that DeCoster had subjected 11 undocumented female workers from Mexico to a "sexually hostile work environment," including sexual assault and rape by supervisors... n 2003, Jack DeCoster paid the federal government $2.1 million as part of a plea agreement after federal agents found more than 100 undocumented workers at his Iowa egg farms. It was the largest penalty ever against an Iowa employer. Three years later, agents found 30 workers suspected of being illegal immigrants at a DeCoster farm in Iowa. And in 2007, raids in Iowa uncovered 51 more undocumented workers.[198]

What you'll notice is that the suits and fines, with the one exception of the plant manager in 2011, have seemed to dry up over the last decade. Is it that DeCoster suddenly became a responsible and

---

196 "Maine," January, 1998. The University of California-Davis *Rural Migration News*, Vol. 4, No. 1.
197 Marler, Bill, "Wright County Egg owner, DeCoster, seems to be one bad egg," August 21, 2010. Marler Clark.
198 Ibid.

ethical human being, or is it that as the 2000s progressed, Hondurans, Guatemalans, Haitians, Jamaicans, and sub-Saharan Africans started arriving in Maine in appreciable numbers? The uniform ethnic make-up of the migrant workers in Maine throughout the 1990s and into the 2000s allowed the workers to band together and attempt to unionize as well as file class-action law-suits. Clearly this is not beneficial for the agricultural industry, so a more diverse work force had to be imported.

Each success wave breaks the bargaining and organizational power of the group that comes before and keeps wages low. It also harms the domestic population for the aforementioned reasons. I'll say it again: this has nothing whatsoever to do with humanitarianism.

The Mexican enclave in and around Milbridge will not last. Already Mano en Mano is listing Haitian Creole alongside Spanish for the translation services offered, and you will find large numbers of guest workers along the coast from Jamaica and Eastern Europe. This is before considering the huge influx of sub-Saharan Africans or the other mestizo groups from Central America.

The Maine Department of Labor has started to organize job fairs targeting African immigrant communities in Lewiston and Portland, bringing together translators, NGOs, and prospective employers. From the "Immigrant and Refugee Integration and Policy Development Working Group Final Report" for the City of Lewiston, December 2017:

> According to the 2017 Maine Chamber of Commerce report, new immigrants and their children are anticipated to account for 83% of growth in the U.S. workforce between 2000 and 2050…However, as the writers of the report indicate, to incentivize immigrant participation in the Maine economy, "we need to be receptive to the fact that many of the people who will grow our population, workforce, and economy will look different than most of us and have different backgrounds and cultures."… Several area employers, including Staff Management, Aramark, L.L. Bean, Barber Foods, Pionite, Labor Ready, Central Maine Meats, Commonwealth Poultry, Cozy Harbor Seafood, the Harraseeket Inn, Clover Manor,

Conform, St. Mary's Regional Medical Center, HW Staffing, Central Maine Medical Center, TJ Maxx, J.C. Penney, Kohl's, Lowe's, Home Depot, BJ's Wholesale Club, Wal-Mart (both retail and distribution), K-Mart, Hannaford, Shaw's, Belanger Farms, Pineland Farms, and Goodwill, have adopted practices and policies to hire and support a diversified workforce.[199]

What all of this really means is that each successive wave of immigrants breaks the backs of the organizing attempts of the collected group before them, but the power brokers seem finally to have grasped that if you can't even understand or communicate with the person working next to you, you sure as hell cannot propose unionizing to them.

Thus, the more diverse a workforce, the less likely it is to be able to take collective action, and this is before considering long-standing ethnic grievances in addition to linguistic and cultural barriers. They envision a state of unlimited immigration from every nook and cranny of planet earth keeping things perpetually in the black. By extension, the more diverse a country, the less likely it is to be able to take collective action, and will be focused on inter-ethnic quarrels rather than the true power players exploiting everyone.

As discussed with Nestlé, an individual or organization's prior conduct and violations have no negative bearing on their present status unless the ruling class needs a sacrificial lamb. Speaking of Nestlé, under the pretense of spreading "social justice" globally and "empowering women," corporations such as Nestlé endeavor to work with NGOs and governments to produce the kind of semi-literate, cheap workforce they thrive on across the Third World. The stated aim is to, "Strengthen women's economic capacity as entrepreneurs, employees, and producers, and invest in women's leadership development."

Nestlé is also a founding member of the UNHCR Business Council, which "aims to encourage private sector commitment, in programmes on health education…enhancing water delivery systems, promoting sports and education, especially for girls, as well as

---

199 City of Lewiston, "Immigrant and Refugee Integration and Policy Development Working Group," December, 2017.

training skills and access to computers." SwissContact (a joint project between the Swiss government and Nestlé) operates a program of Skill Development, including secretarial or beautician skills, as well as in construction, agriculture, energy, tourism, or media. SwissContact focuses on Asian, African, Latin American, and Central European countries, with the overall objective to "strengthen the private sector, facilitate the generation of sustainable employment for both men and women, and, ultimately, reduce poverty."

This faux-philanthropy is aimed at training a cheap, compliant workforce who will be loyal consumers and not ask questions, and in Central Europe it is to splinter the culture by making women wage-suppressors and "independent"-as-empowered (meaning amenable to the consumerist version of "feminism"), undermining the family and the culture, softening these countries up to the population replacement agenda in full swing in Western Europe and the European-settled countries like Canada and the US. Nestlé also has a number of "global partnerships" and Development Programs:

- **Jamaica:** "On-the-job" training for school leavers and apprenticeship programs in Nestlé operations, e.g. mechanics, industrial and electrical maintenance, welding, etc.

- **Brazil:** An initiative of the government and with GR FoodServices, "First Job" creates 2000 working posts (over 2 years) in the catering field.

- **Philippines:** Cut and Sew Livelihood Project provides jobs to community workers for factory orders for uniforms, hairnets, shoe covers, etc.

- **Kenya:** Ndenderai youth generate income by producing banana-fibre boxes for Nestlé product displays.

- **Thailand:** The "T-Bird" or Thailand Business Group for Rural Development, aims to harness and utilise private sector resources for underprivileged villages in remote areas, via loans to new businesses or contributions for education or infrastructure.

- **South Africa:** More than 1 million SA Rand invested in the Apprenticeship Programme, situated Eastern Cape East London Factory which, in 2004, enrolled 12 people from a nearby disadvantaged community.

- **Dominican Republic:** FORJA Project Training of young farmers, in collaboration with Swiss Association for International Cooperation, to develop business acumen and give technical and practical training in agriproduction techniques, while financing feasible micro-business potential. Includes scholarships to children of farmers and offers on-the-job practical training.[200]

They will be expected to be grateful for being lifted from abject poverty to relative poverty. Meanwhile, in Western countries, the "externalities" of neo-liberalism force young people to flock urban environs to pursue work, where they will be swiftly molded into hedonistic or sexless economic cogs, failing to reproduce and staying on the white-ish collar/barista treadmill to oblivion.

The economic and taxation realities artificially depress white birthrates and "necessitate" the importation of huge numbers of non-whites to fill the labor "needs" of the host country, as one line of propagandistic "reasoning" goes. As Paul Craig Roberts writes:

> The rule of law is dead throughout the West. Democracy is a scam. There is oligarchic rule. Everything is done for organized interest groups. Nothing is done for the people…The number of white children, that is, the group of the next generation of parents, is not only declining relative to the populations of non-whites but also absolutely. During 2010-2018 the number of white children shrank by 2.2 million.
>
> The American middle class, which is largely white, bears the brunt of income taxation which means that white Americans bear the brunt of the cost of the welfare support systems. The white middle class also bears the brunt through property taxes of the public school systems. Many middle class members pay again in private school tuition for the education of their children in safer and more ordered environments. The cost of university education is exorbitant. All of these costs are rising

---

200 Nestlé Public Affairs, "Nestlé, the community and the United Nations Millennium Development Goals," January, 2006. Nestlé SA.

faster than middle class incomes, and this limits white procreation. The decline of people of European descent as a percentage of the US population can only accelerate as the child-bearing ability of the white population evaporates.[201]

All of this is by design. Maximizing profitability means the willful neglect of other considerations such as ethics, which includes commodifying the very misery created by neo-liberalism and marketing and selling it back to the alienated, disaffected population produced by the current system in the first place.

As a second example of the kind of neo-liberal incestuousness that would make Gellius blush, the entire political enterprise of "liberal democracy" is only so much corporatized oligarchic rule.

Let's consider major private equity firm Silver Lake Partners. House Republican Leader Kevin McCarthy's former chief of staff—replaced by Dan Meyer of the Duberstein Group—Barrett Karr is now a managing director and Head of Government Affairs in Washington, DC at Silver Lake Partners, assuming many of the duties of departed CFR member and international security adviser to the United Nations secretary-general Gordon M. Goldstein. Karr's position entails coordinating with lobbyists, trade associations, media contacts, government agencies, and local, state, and federal government officials, working to see to the implementation of policy proposals and ensuring a generally favorable environment for Silver Lake to continue to grow its $43 billion in assets.

Founded by Kenneth Duberstein, White House Chief of Staff to President Reagan and member of the Council on Foreign Relations, the Duberstein Group is a lobbying firm whose services have been retained by the likes of United Airlines, Pfizer, Northrup Grumman, Estee Lauder, Comcast, Hasbro, Bank of New York Mellon, British Petroleum, General Motors, Pepsi, McGraw Hill Financial (now S&P Global), Goldman Sachs, Time Warner, Kellogg's, DeBeers, Lenovo, Sara Lee, Fannie Mae, and Lockheed Martin. During the bailout, the Duberstein Group made in excess of $600,000 lobbying for Fannie Mae and $2.3 million lobbying for Goldman Sachs. The Duberstein

---

201 Roberts, Paul Craig, "The End of White America is Now Assured," September 7, 2019.

Group regularly rubs elbows with firms such as Akin Gump Strauss Hauer & Feld LLP and Verner Liipfert Bernhard McPherson & Hand, as well as the Wexler Group.

One of Silver Lake's founders is Maine native and Lewiston High School graduate David Roux. Bristol Seafood, Inc. in Portland is now positioned for "exponential growth" in the international market, according to former CEO Darrell Pardy, after Roux's decision to invest in the company and provide it with an infusion of capital. With the much-discussed addition of another facility and a consequent spike in its demand for cheap labor, Bristol will likely be using the same Hancock, DeCoster, Wyman, and company playbook. Hancock Foods, along with Coastal Blueberry Service Inc., recently settled a suit over the mistreatment of eighteen Haitian migrant workers who had been recruited by contactor Carol Paul in Florida to come to Maine to pick blueberries in 2008. The suit alleged hundreds of violations of the federal Migrant and Seasonal Agricultural Worker Protection Act involving Paul's promises to the workers. As evidenced elsewhere, these practices are the rule, not the exception, when it comes to these companies.

For his part, Roux will likely see to it that Silver Lake's private equity model be applied to Bristol's seafood harvesting, which will have predictably disastrous consequences affecting wages, demographics, social cohesion and trust, and the Atlantic ecosystem. Silver Lake Partners, like Elliott Management, is representative of the pervasive private equity model, coming to be known as "vulture capitalism," that is destroying this country. This kind of mindset is perhaps no better encapsulated than by notoriously vicious vulture capitalist Paul Singer of Elliott Management. Quoting Tucker Carlson:

> Singer and his firm, Elliott Management, have…made billions by buying large stakes in American companies then firing workers driving up short-term share prices and, in some cases, taking government bailouts, insult to injury…Consider the case of Delphi, the automotive parts supplier. During the last financial crisis, a consortium of hedge funds, including Singer's Elliott Management, purchased Delphi. With Singer and the other funds at the helm, the company took billions of

229

dollars in government bailouts paid for by you. Obama's auto czar compared those tactics to extortion, but they continued anyway. Once they had the bailout money the funds moved most of Delphi's jobs overseas and then either cut retiree pensions entirely or shifted the cost to taxpayers with later financial commitments at home and cheap factories abroad Delphi's stock soared. According to investigative reporter Greg Palast, of the 29 Delphi plants in operation when the hedge fund started buying Delphi's debt, only four were still operating in the United States by 2012. That means tens of thousands of unionized and white-collar workers lost their jobs. Paul Singer's hedge fund cashed out for more than a billion dollars. See how that works? Well, some countries, including the United Kingdom, have banned this kind of behavior. It bears no resemblance whatsoever to the capitalism we were promised in school. It creates nothing. It destroys entire cities. It couldn't be uglier or more destructive. So, why is it still allowed in the United States? The short answer: because people like Paul Singer have tremendous influence over our political process. Singer himself was the second largest donor to the Republican Party in 2016. He's given millions to a SuperPAC that supports Republican senators. You may never have heard of Paul Singer, which tells you a lot in itself, but in Washington he is rockstar famous and that may be why he's almost certainly paying a lower effective tax rate than your average fireman, just in case you're still wondering if our system is rigged.[202]

It's one thing to be lazy, do nothing, expect a handout, and whine that the system is rigged against you. This is quite another thing altogether. Yet someone like Nebraska Senator Ben Sasse has the gall to write a "pull yourself up by the bootstraps" tome called *The Vanishing American Adult* after accepting campaign contributions from someone like the Jewish Singer who's done this to Sasse's Nebraskan constituents:

---

202 Carlson, Tucker. *Tucker Carlson Tonight*, December 3, 2019. Transcript.

Sidney is the long-time home of a sporting goods retailer Cabela's, which sells fishing and hunting gear. In October of 2015 Singer's hedge fund disclosed an 11 percent stake in Cabela's and set about pushing the board to sell the company. Cabela's management apparently fearing a long and costly fight with Singer announced it would look for a buyer. Now at the time Cabela's was a relatively healthy company. It was posting nearly $2 billion a year in gross profits off $4 billion in revenue. There didn't seem to be any immediate need to sell but Cabela's sold anyway after being pushed. So, one year after Singer entered the equation Bass Pro Shops announced the purchase of Cabela's. The company's stock price surged. Within a week literally a week Paul Singer cashed out. He bought the stock for $38 a share. He sold it for $63 a share. His hedge fund made at least $90 million up front and likely more over time. But in Sidney, Nebraska, it was a very different story. The residents of Sidney did not get rich. Oh no. Just the opposite. Their community was devastated, destroyed. The town lost nearly 2,000 jobs; a heartbreakingly familiar cascade began. People left. Property values collapsed and then people couldn't leave. They were trapped there. One of the last thriving small towns in this country went under.[203]

It's a story all-too-familiar to the out-of-work Mainers in dying mill towns across the state. The infamous *New York Times* article about how Maine "needs" African immigrants includes a section where these newcomers are expected to become lumberjacks in the North Maine Woods, which is curious since as a recent *Washington Post* piece notes, northern Maine has been "battered by the closure of its lumber mills."

The conditions that drive away the young and suppress birthrates are of course never discussed; instead, we must import enough "diversity" to drive down wages, increase alienation and consumption, lower trust, and make cross-cultural communication and thus labor organizing impossible.

---

203 Ibid.

Despite the clear disingenuousness of the vested interests declaring a "labor shortage" in the third-most populous country in the world, as David Seminara writes:

> Economists have found no evidence of a labor shortage in the occupational groups that constitute the bulk of H-2B employment. George W. Bush was a vocal advocate for guestworker programs. In 2004, Bush proposed a new guestworker program that, had it been enacted, would have tripled the number of visas issued to seasonal workers. On January 18, 2009, his administration published new regulations that significantly reduced oversight of the H-2B application process and extended the definition of "temporary" in the H-2B context from 10 months to up to three years. The H-2B visa was created in 1986 (the same year of Reagan's illegal alien amnesty), as part of the Immigration Reform and Control Act, which split the H guestworker program into an H-2A visa for agricultural guestworkers, and an H-2B visa for non-agricultural guestworkers. The popularity of the H-2B program for temporary, seasonal, non-agricultural guestworkers has soared from just 15,706 visas issued in 1997 to an all-time high of 129,547 in 2007. American companies filed petitions to request nearly 300,000 H-2B workers in FY 2008. Use of the H-2B program has morphed from its original intent to help employers that need seasonal and/or temporary workers. The majority of the program's current users are neither small nor seasonal employers, but rather mid- to large-sized companies and recruiters that petition for H-2Bs to work for 10 months out of the year, year after year. Many of the businesses filing H-2B petitions for foreign workers are "body shops" that have no actual "seasonal or temporary" need for labor. Body shops can petition for large numbers of workers and then essentially sell them off to companies that either could not get their own H-2B workers or did not know how to do so.[204]

---

204 Seminara, David, "Dirty Work: In-Sourcing American Jobs with H-2B Guestworkers," January 15, 2010. Center for Immigration Studies.

This is very clearly not a partisan issue; the entire Establishment, political and private sector, is in total agreement that more non-white immigration is *always* beneficial. Whether the labor is "specialized" or not is irrelevant.

Unfortunately, as we learn from the Atlantic Council, "In practice, virtually any white-collar occupation qualifies as a specialty occupation for the H-1B program. It is used by employers to fill a variety of occupations, from accountants to reporters to school teachers to salesmen to software developers. There is nothing particularly special about the 'specialty occupations' as defined in the H-1B program."

These, the H-2A, H-2B, and other visas play a significant role in Maine's, and the country's, targeted demographic transformation.

Recently the United States offered to triple the number of H-2A visas issued to Guatemalans "to reduce the pressure on the Southern border"—which will *in no way* incentivize more to come. This comes—like Reagan's IRCA amnesty and the creation of the H-2B visa, the "invade the world, invite the world" ethos of the neo-conservatives, and so on—under a "conservative" regime.

The reader may also be interested to learn that, contrary to the claims that these illegal aliens were doing the farm work that Americans wouldn't, as many as 650,000 "farm workers" amnestied under the Reagan administration had fraudulently listed agricultural work as their profession. As Roberto Suro wrote on November 12th, 1989:

> In one of the most extensive immigration frauds ever perpetrated against the United States Government, thousands of people who falsified amnesty applications will begin to acquire permanent resident status next month under the 1986 immigration law. More than 1.3 million illegal aliens applied to become legal immigrants under a one-time amnesty for farm workers... Now a variety of estimates by Federal officials and immigration experts place the number of fraudulent applications at somewhere between 250,000 and 650,000...The amnesty for farm workers was a last-minute addition to the Immigration Reform and Control Act of 1986, which sought to halt illegal immigration with a two-

part strategy…The agricultural amnesty program was adopted at the insistence of politically powerful fruit and vegetable growers in California and Texas who wanted to protect their labor force. In several respects, the provisions for the program were much less strict than the general amnesty program, which drew 1.7 million applicants. Instead of having to document nearly five years of continuous residence, most agricultural worker applicants had to show only that they had done 90 days of farm work between May 1, 1985, and May 1, 1986… An extensive survey conducted in three rural Mexican communities by the Center for U.S.-Mexican Studies at the University of California in San Diego found that only 72 percent of those who identified themselves as applicants for farm worker amnesty had work histories that qualified them for the program. A similar survey conducted by Mexican researchers in Jalisco in central Mexico found that only 59 percent qualified.[205]

From the US Chamber of Commerce on down, the potential for, and evidence of past, large-scale fraud is blithely ignored. The Maine State Chamber of Commerce has become a leading voice in supporting an increased role for immigrants in the workforce (or on the dole, as the case may be). Republicans are happy to do their part; Jewish Republican State Senator Roger Katz:

Sponsored LD 1492, an Act to Attract, Educate and Retain New Mainers to Strengthen the Workforce…The bill in its original form would have established a state office for "new Mainers" to carry "out responsibilities of the State relating to immigrants in and into the State." The bill also would have funded a second immigrant welcome center for the state, located in Lewiston and modeled on Portland's New Mainers Resource Center, which receives $75,000 a year in state funding. Katz's bill included funding for vocational and workforce training and English-language training, too. All told, the projected

205 Suro, Roberto, "Migrants' False Claims: Fraud on a Huge Scale," November 12, 1989. *The New York Times.*

2018-19 costs were $825,000…"What has changed (about the immigration issue) is that as our workforce challenges have grown—you are hearing an outcry from the business community," says Katz. "Because we need more workers, the voices in the Maine Legislature have changed from the usual social justice advocates. They are now being joined by chambers of commerce and business men and women from around the state. That's starting to really shift the attitude."[206]

Jewish executive director of the Soros-backed immigration advocacy group Welcoming America Rachel Peric concurs, and uses Baltimore, Maryland as one example of an immigration success story. The Partnership for a New American Economy (NAE) and their financial backers and corporate partners—Google, Intel, Microsoft, United Fresh Produce Association, Jewish venture capitalist and Managing Director of the Foundry Group Brad Feld, the National Council of Farmer Cooperatives, the American Farm Bureau Federation, the US Chamber of Commerce, the American Immigration Lawyers Association, Pinterest, the Society for Human Resource Management, the Council for Global Immigration, Western Growers, and eWIC—aver: think of the GDP growth! Also in agreement are Vaishali Mamgain of the University of Southern Maine and Karen Collins, formerly of Catholic Charities Maine Refugee and Immigration Services in Portland: it appears only "white supremacists" object to "policies to facilitate refugee resettlement in Maine."

In November 2016, a proposal to create an Office of Economic Opportunity and Immigrant Integration was forwarded to the City Council with a unanimous recommendation from the city's Economic Development Committee. The budget for the office would be $260,000 and it would be staffed by a director and two program managers. One of the program managers would focus on immigrants and the other on "people of color and young people."

According to David Brenerman, "a Democratic member of Portland's City Council who is Jewish" and Chair of the Economic

---

206 Weed, Peter, "It's cost vs. potential in debate over making it easier for immigrants," May 5, 2019. *Pine Tree Watch*.

Development Committee, and Julie Sullivan, Senior Advisor to the City Manager:

> Immigration is an important part of this city's economic growth strategy and improving immigrant integration is critical to ensuring Portland's work force and vitality... The Committee's research and public input seem to point to creating an Office of Economic Opportunity and Immigrant Integration...to also improve economic opportunity for youth, people of color, and other disadvantaged populations... There would be a Director overseeing the Office, with a Program Manager implementing the Immigrant Integration efforts and a Program Manager implementing the Inclusion and Equity efforts focused on people of color... [plus] proactive, consistent and systematic outreach to employers to identify jobs that are difficult to fill and subsequent partnering with Portland Adult Education, Southern Maine Community College, and the University of Southern Maine to provide those skills... The Director would work on the more macro level issues and would convene partner organizations, build the intern/apprentice/mentor programs, oversee the data tool development, and link with funders.

Who would this matrix of partners and funders include? Among those proposed were: Catholic Charities Refugee and Immigration Services (which "wants to see Portland rebranded as an international city, well-poised to compete for human capital [and] supports an Office of Globalization"), Coastal Enterprises, Inc. (CEI), the University of Maine Law School Cumberland Legal Aid Clinic, Immigrant Legal Advocacy Project (ILAP), Greater Portland United Way, Community Financial Literacy, the University of Southern Maine Muskie School, the John T. Gorman Foundation, Portland Community Chamber of Commerce, IDEXX, SIGCO, Maine Access Immigrant Network (MAIN), Maine Equal Justice Partners (MEJP), Portland Adult Education—New Mainers Resource Center, Portland Development Cooperation, New England Arab-American Organization, the Treehouse Institute's Global Shapers Hub of the

Global Shapers Community founded by the World Economic Forum's (WEF) Klaus Schwab and supported and funded by the WEF,[207] Pine Tree Legal Assistance (PTLA), and the State of Maine Office of Multicultural Affairs. PTLA receives funding from the Sam L. Cohen Foundation, the Harvard University Consumer Project, and the John T. Gorman Foundation, among others. One of the John T. Gorman Foundation's primary financiers is the Jewish Burton Sonenstein, and the Investment Committee Chair is Maggie Keohan, who "advises high net-worth individuals and institutional clients throughout New England from Goldman, Sachs & Co.'s office in Boston."

The John T. Gorman Foundation has donated to Catholic Charities of Maine, Brandeis University, the ACLU of Maine Foundation, Cultivating Community, Immigrant Legal Advocacy Project (ILAP), Maine Access Immigrant Network (MAIN), Maine Equal Justice Partners (MEJP), Pine Tree Legal Assistance (PTLA), and Shalom House, and also has ties to the Annie E. Casey Foundation, which:

> Works closely with the Open Society Institute-Baltimore...In 2005, the Casey Foundation was the largest contributor in a bailout that kept the Open Society Institute-Baltimore from closing. More recently, the two organizations have worked together on programs...to provide legal services for immigrants...In 2017, the Open Society Institute—Baltimore, the Casey

---

207 "The Forum's contribution to the Shapers organization includes significant financial and in-kind contributions for operational support including staff time, technology tools and opportunities to interact and collaborate with its membership network. The Global Shapers Community is governed by a Foundation board that includes leaders from business, government and civil society: Klaus Schwab, Founder and Executive Chairman, World Economic Forum; David M. Rubenstein, Co-Founder and Co-Chief Executive Officer, Carlyle Group; Jack Ma, Executive Chairman, Alibaba Group Holding Limited; Ellyn Shook, Chief Leadership and Human Resources Officer, Accenture; Adrian Monck, Managing Director; Head of Public and Social Engagement, World Economic Forum; Maria Teresa Kumar, President and Chief Executive Office, Voto Latina; Khalid Alkhudair, Executive Vice-President, Riyad Bank; Sharmeen Obaid Chinoy, Chief Executive Officer, SOC Films; Abi Ramanan, Chief Executive Officer, ImpactVision; Juan Jose Pocaterra, Co-Founder and Chief Executive Officer, ViKua; Basima Abdulrahman, Founder and Chief Executive Officer, KESK Green Building Consulting; Akira Sakano, Global Shaper, Osaka Hub."

Foundation, and the city of Baltimore created Safe City Baltimore, a $500,000 legal defense fund that provides legal aid for immigrants and their families, including helping American-born children of immigrants get passports and providing legal assistance for foreigners facing removal from the country...Casey Foundation grants have supported the Baltimore Community Fellows, which has awarded grants to liberal activists since 1998. Currently, the Open Society Institute-Baltimore awards ten activists a year 18-month grants of $60,000...Casey Foundation grants have supported the Baltimore Community Fellows, which has awarded grants to liberal activists since 1998. Currently, the Open Society Institute-Baltimore awards ten activists a year 18-month grants of $60,000...In 2012 Casey continued to give substantial sums to the Center for American Progress Action Fund.[208]

Casey has also donated to the American Enterprise Institute, the Aspen Institute, the Brookings Institution, the Congressional Black Caucus Foundation, the Tides Foundation, and the Tides Center.

Maine Business Immigration Coalition advocates for immigration "from a business and economic perspective," though not without the essential ingredients of ersatz compassion and humanitarianism; its partner organizations include: Barber Foods, Ready Seafood, Coastal Enterprises, Inc. (CEI), MaineHealth, Maine State Chamber of Commerce, SIGCO, several seafood companies, and of course the Partnership for a New American Economy (NAE). Also partnered, in one of the great ironies of this whole affair, is the Portland Buy Local campaign. Ready Seafood:

One of Maine's largest lobster-processing companies, now has a workforce of more than 200 in Portland and Scarborough that's more than half foreign born... Ready Seafood has now developed a pipeline for new workers, making the time-consuming task of recruitment easier... Ben Waxman, co-owner of American Roots, the

---

208 "Annie E. Casey Foundation," Influence Watch entry.

Westbrook clothing manufacturer, echoes Skoczenski's comment about the importance of immigrants to his company's survival… To make it easier for businesses to connect with immigrants and to help coordinate services, the city of Portland created the Portland Office of Economic Opportunity in 2017. Run by Julia Trujillo, its mission is to help integrate immigrants into the economy so that businesses can connect with potential employees…Skoczenski points to the office as the source of Ready Seafood's recruitment success: "Julia is the only reason this program is working for us."[209]

If all of these businesses thrive on cheap labor, well of course it makes sense for them to donate to so-called philanthropic organizations which advocate for "immigrants' rights" and open borders—they do their dirty work without any direct accusations of "dirty money" and lobbying efforts.

---

209 Weed, Peter, "Filling a Severe Gap," May 3, 2019. *Pine Tree Watch.*

Chapter Seven: In Case the Cleaning Lady Has Found My Head

"Just heard there's an ICE checkpoint in Hollywood, just a few blocks from where I live. Everyone better give their housekeepers, nannies, and landscapers a ride home tonight."
—Amber Heard

You may remember that several years ago, Disney became notorious for hiring imported H-1B visa workers to replace their higher-paid American counterparts, and threatening to withhold severance packages if the outgoing American employees refused to train their new replacements. This then-new policy was overseen by the Jewish Partnership for a New American Economy (NAE) member and Disney CEO Bob Iger. Recall the sheer number of powerful executives, major economic players, and prominent politicians among NAE's ranks, as catalogued earlier in this book, and understand that it is no surprise that there has been virtually no resistance to the mass importation of scab labor from either the public or private sectors outside of organized labor and the odd Bernie Sanders (although the "new and improved" Sanders has changed his tune).

NAE's entire *raison d'etre* is to pad corporate profits, and one of the ways they do that is to advocate for increased foreign worker visas. In fact, NAE founder Michael Bloomberg has publicly called for the removal of any cap on H-1B visas issued by the federal government, a sentiment echoed by Bill Gates and others. The burgeoning tech sector in the 21st century has been instrumental in destroying American labor rights and the middle class, and severely undermining national sovereignty. In many ways, it is the catalyst for the accelerating dissolution we are presently witnessing. First, the major players of Silicon Valley worked to violate the Sherman and Clayton Antitrust Acts, and then they lobbied for extensive replacement labor via H-1B visas. As Mark Ames reports:

In early 2005, as demand for Silicon Valley engineers began booming, Apple's Steve Jobs sealed a secret and illegal pact with Google's Eric Schmidt to artificially push their workers' wages lower by agreeing not to recruit each other's employees, sharing wage scale information, and punishing violators... eBay and its former CEO Meg Whitman, now CEO of HP, are being sued by both the federal government and the state of California for arranging a similar, secret wage-theft agreement with Intuit (and possibly Google as well) during the same period...A class action lawsuit [was] filed [by the Department of Justice] on behalf of over 100,000 tech employees whose wages were artificially lowered—an estimated $9 billion effectively stolen... to pad company earnings. Confidential internal Google and Apple memos...clearly show that what began as a secret cartel agreement between Apple's Steve Jobs and Google's Eric Schmidt to illegally fix the labor market for hi-tech workers, expanded within a few years to include companies ranging from Dell, IBM, eBay and Microsoft, to Comcast, Clear Channel, Dreamworks, and London-based public relations behemoth WPP. All told, the combined workforces of the companies involved totals well over a million employees.[210]

In addition to this domestic collusion, Silicon Valley—just like the rest of big tech's co-conspirators in the NAE—is uniform in its support for unlimited foreign worker visas. Regarding H-1B visas specifically, Ron Hira and Bharath Gopalaswamy write:

Technology and financial services firms have taken the lead in the public advocacy, spending millions of dollars on lobbying, creating numerous issue-specific advocacy organizations, and funding favorable studies at think tanks. Unlike traditional policy advocacy—which is typically left to the government affairs departments of

---

210 Ames, Mark, "The Techtopus: How Silicon Valley's most celebrated CEOs conspired to drive down 100,000 tech engineers' wages," January 23, 2014. *Pando*.

corporations—pushing for H-1B expansion has seen CEOs be highly visible. Celebrity CEOs such as Bill Gates, Mark Zuckerberg, Eric Schmidt, Jamie Dimon, and Michael Bloomberg have publicly advocated for expanding the H-1B program—through op-eds, speeches, sponsoring news organizations' events designed to influence lawmakers' views of the program, letters to shareholders, and congressional testimony.[211]

In true Woke Capital fashion, the authors continue, "To broaden the appeal of expanding the program, they have linked their messages to broader advocacy efforts on behalf of Deferred Action for Childhood Arrivals (DACA) recipients and the undocumented." With few exceptions, the entire capitalist structure is in favor of unlimited immigration so long as it serves their needs; organizations such as the NAE, the George Soros- and Ford Foundation-backed National Immigration Forum,[212] the American Action Network, FWD.us, and the US Chamber of Commerce are the rule, not the exception.

Asia, especially India, has been a vast resource for cheap tech sector workers. 70.9% of all H-1B applicants in 2015 were from India, with China in second at 9.7%. Kenneth Rapoza reports:

> The H1-B visa…is the hallmark of every Indian IT company operating in the U.S. Infosys, Wipro. Tata Consultancy, Tech Mahindra and HCL Technologies are the top Indian-owned companies importing foreign workers. In fact, of the top 10 companies that petition for the 85,000 H1-B visas issued annually, five are Indian. Cognizant, Accenture, Amazon, IBM and Deloitte are the biggest U.S. users…Indian IT firms fear Trump will either stop Indian companies from importing workers temporarily, or make it harder to provide evidence that

---

211 Hira, Ron and Bharath Gopalaswamy, "Reforming US' High-Skilled Guestworkers Program," January 15, 2019. Atlantic Council.
212 Executive Director Ali Noorani wrote an open letter to all Republican 2012 presidential primary candidates, citing an NIF report that stated, "The United States could save as much as $2.6 billion per year by implementing common-sense enforcement reforms that focus on real threats to the nation."

Infosys is hiring from Bangalore because it cannot hire from Boston.[213]

The reality of the H-1B visa is that in practice, literally any white-collar occupation is considered a "specialty occupation," so though the tech companies thrive on it, it is used by all kinds of employers to fill a variety of occupations, from salesmen to accountants to reporters to teachers. The H-1B visa worker program is just one of over twenty such worker visas allowing companies to push out American workers in favor of foreign ones, and there are other green card-fast track visas as well, such as the EB-5 "immigrant investor" visa; in 2014, more than 85% of the over 10,000 EB-5 visas issued were for Chinese nationals according to a study by real estate services firm Savills Studley, which also stated that "by 2015, the EB-5 program had become an important source of capital for developers."

In 2013, 450 businesses, chambers of commerce, advocacy groups, immigration attorney groups, and other organizations issued a letter to Congress calling for "Immigration Reform NOW." The letter's signatories demanded a doubling of immigration into the country and full amnesty for all illegal aliens. Disney was of course represented—as were the NAE, FWD.us, the American Action Network, and the National Immigration Forum—and also present were a slew of tech companies from Dell to Google to Microsoft to Facebook to Cisco Systems. Also well-represented were companies that thrive on the cheap labor provided by H-2A and H-2B visas.

The H-2A is designed to import agricultural labor and the H-2B is for general non-agricultural labor (think maids, restaurant employees, etc.). Hence why some seemingly odd names like the Cheesecake Factory, Welch Foods Inc., and the National Christmas Tree Association appeared on the list. As Jon Feere relates:

> The companies apparently looking for more H-2A visas (i.e. cheap agricultural labor from overseas) include the Sun-Maid Growers of California, Welch Foods Inc., the New England Apple Council, Sweet Potato Council of California, National Christmas Tree Association, and various state nursery, landscape, and farm bureau

213 Rapoza, Kenneth, "Here's What's Really On Silicon Valley's Mind Regarding Immigration," February 27, 2017. *Forbes*.

organizations. The companies apparently looking for more H-2B (i.e. cheap non-agricultural labor from overseas) include Hilton Worldwide, Marriott International, and the National Council of Chain Restaurants. Many state Chambers of Commerce also signed on…Santa Clara University also signed on to the letter, the only school on the list. The school bills itself as "The Jesuit University in Silicon Valley," so they likely received pressure from both the Jesuits and the IT industry to support amnesty. And perhaps being the alma matter of Janet Napolitano had something to do with it…Also on the list is FWD.us, a pro-amnesty group created by Facebook's Mark Zuckerberg. The group created an off-shoot called "Americans for a Conservative Direction" aimed at selling amnesty from a conservative perspective (despite the fact that the organization is run by Obama-supporting liberals). It is this group that created the deceptive amnesty ad that starred Sen. Marco Rubio (R-Fla.) earlier this year [2013].[214]

Immigration law firms were also well-represented on the list because, as Ron Hira and Bharath Gopalaswamy explicate:

Immigration attorneys, who have expert knowledge about how the H-1B program operates, have also advocated for H-1B expansion and argued that current safeguards are more than adequate. This should come as no surprise, since H-1B cases are often a large source of revenue for immigration law firms. The more H-1Bs issued, the greater the revenue earned by them.[215]

Outsourcing firms also make billions of dollars in revenue from the current system, and a removal of the cap on foreign worker visas would be a financial windfall. Many businesses enjoy these visas not

214 Feere, Jon, "Yelp Gives Five-Star Review to Amnesty; So Do Virgin America, Overstock.com, E-Bay," October 18, 2013. Center for Immigration Studies.
215 Hira, Ron and Bharath Gopalaswamy, "Reforming US' High-Skilled Guestworkers Program," January 15, 2019. Atlantic Council.

simply because of the lower advertised wages they pay and the fact that the workers typically demand and receive fewer benefits; an unfamiliarity with labor rights and often a language barrier enables employers to exploit these workers by underpayment either through position re-classification or through undocumented overtime, as well as a failure to reimburse workers for expenses normally covered by the employer, such as uniforms.

Bread and Roses Bakery, Inc. in Maine is one such business that checks all of those boxes, and when caught in 2018, the owner flippantly commented that she thought the government had "more important things to do" than to enforce labor law—and in a sense, she's right. The abuses go much further than this one bakery, however. It is vital to understand that the issue is systemic:

> U.S. H-2B employers and the U.S. recruiters they hire often partner with foreign recruiters, and then deny knowledge of the foreign recruiters' tactics when fraud and abuse are alleged. U.S. courts have not shown a willingness to try cases of abuse when the violations occur outside the United States, even if the case involves a job being performed in the United States…Despite credible allegations and even convictions for fraud and abuse of both H-2B workers and the program in general, neither the Department of Labor (DOL) nor the Department of Homeland Security (DHS) has ever barred a U.S. company from filing H-2B petitions. Some repeat offenders continue to have their petitions approved to this day.[216]

Furthermore, write Hira and Gopalaswamy:

> Most of the abuses—whether the low wages for H-1Bs or even the replacement of US workers with H-1Bs—are legal under the current laws and regulations. Increased efforts at enforcement are ineffective when abuse is legal. Even in the high-profile cases of Disney and Southern California Edison, where US workers had to train

---

216 Seminara, David, "Dirty Work: In-Sourcing American Jobs with H-2B Guestworkers," January 15, 2010. Center for Immigration Studies.

their H-1B replacements, government investigations found the practices perfectly legal, leaving US workers with no recourse. Any government investigation of the widespread use of the H-1B for cheap labor would prove similarly fruitless since it too is legal.[217]

And there's the rub: of course illegal immigration into the United States is a massive issue, but even its full curtailment, while necessary, is not sufficient to stop the demographic transformation of the United States and its ultimate destruction.

Nevertheless, the "conservative" Cato Institute, founded by Charles Koch, makes the claim that there are "many upsides and no downsides" to the current immigration policy, which, if you're Jeff Bezos, is probably true. Cato Institute corporate partners and donors include McGraw-Hill Financial/S&P Global, Facebook, Google, the Walton Family Foundation, the Koch Industries Family Foundation, eBay, Microsoft, Walmart, General Motors, ExxonMobil, Time Warner, Verizon, Visa, and Comcast.

The Cato Institute in turn finances organizations such as the Maine Policy Institute, which is part of a network of "conservative" think tanks called the State Policy Network, which has institutions in all fifty states, Washington, DC, Canada, and the United Kingdom. Other than occasionally publishing useful information, their purpose, so far as I can tell, is to exist as punching-bags for the Left and to get obliterated as token opposition.

In short: they're modern conservatives, because apparently scrapping a nation for parts and adopting the basic premises of the Left a decade or two later are conservative values.

Even if there was a moral objection by one company to replacing one's countrymen or outsourcing their jobs for profit, the nature of most industries as things stand would quickly see that company go out of business. The libertarian notion that industries self-regulate in the absence of government is laughable—and destructive.

Just as the media uncritically reprints press releases from the ADL and SPLC as "news," so, too, do lawmakers: in a report published by *USA Today*, over the past eight years, over 10,000 bills introduced

217 Hira, Ron and Bharath Gopalaswamy, "Reforming US' High-Skilled Guestworkers Program," January 15, 2019. Atlantic Council.

before Congress have been almost word-for-word copies of "model legislation" drafted by various corporations and lobbyists.[218]

This doesn't sound like a government by the people for the people, but rather a government by the plutocrats for the plutocrats. For the corporatocracy, the state has become an anachronism, a barrier to maximal profits. Until it can ultimately be dispensed with, the "private companies" and banks will strip-mine everything we have in the exact vein of Bain Capital and leave us with nothing of any true worth.

"Just pull yourself up by your bootstraps!" After all, the "free market" isn't completely rigged, now is it? Trillion-dollar companies paying zero taxes and having their employees receive so little pay they must turn to public services and welfare to make up for it is just the market at work!

It's a *moral* failing more than anything else that explains why wages have stagnated and even declined in several European countries coinciding *exactly* with mass low-skill Third World immigration. It's the buck-toothed hillbillies failing to embrace cosmopolitanism and not learning to code that from Maine to Minnesota hollowed-out former mill towns and industrial centers grapple with opioid addiction, depression, suicide, beleaguered by Third World corruption, crime, and diseases, and made cosmic scapegoats from the media to academia for things they never did. That's *their* fault. It's not that capital gains are taxed at half the rate of labor.

It's not that in addition to the torrent of aliens suppressing wages domestically, scores of American jobs have been shipped overseas. It's not the gas taxes that hit the middle- and working-classes the hardest. It's not the corporations bringing in H-1B visa holders and making you train your cheaper replacements before firing you, it's *you*. As George Monbiot writes:

> So pervasive has neoliberalism become that we seldom even recognise it as an ideology. We appear to accept the proposition that this utopian, millenarian faith describes a neutral force; a kind of biological law, like Darwin's theory of evolution. But the philosophy arose as a conscious attempt to reshape human life and shift

---

218 O'Dell, Rob and Nick Penzenstadler, "You elected them to write new laws. They're letting corporations do it instead." June 19, 2019. *USA Today*.

> the locus of power. Neoliberalism sees competition as the defining characteristic of human relations. It redefines citizens as consumers, whose democratic choices are best exercised by buying and selling, a process that rewards merit and punishes inefficiency. It maintains that "the market" delivers benefits that could never be achieved by planning. The rich persuade themselves that they acquired their wealth through merit...Never mind structural unemployment: if you don't have a job it's because you are unenterprising. Never mind the impossible costs of housing: if your credit card is maxed out, you're feckless and improvident.[219]

This country, as the ruling class sees it, is in effect nothing more than an asset in the portfolios of the major global financial institutions and multi-national corporations. Citizenship is a quaint anachronism at best, an obstacle at worst, to the shareholders. Distinguishing between "legal" and "illegal" immigration, both for their purposes and ours, is irrelevant.

By accepting the premises of Cultural Marxism, many conservatives have unconsciously imbibed this contrived paradigm, with its emphasis on power dynamics and, therefore, "competition," which has served to legitimize neo-liberal economics to the point of religious belief. For liberals, their overt acceptance of Cult-Marx doctrine allows for social agitation that merely greases the wheels of neo-liberalism. Millions of contrived "refugees," who are actually economic migrants and welfare leeches? We owe them a moral debt! Their presence in no way benefits Big Business, it's all about *morality*, you see.

The basic contradictions of neo-liberalism, far from undermining or negating neo-liberalism's pretensions as a moral ideology rather than simply an economic system, paradoxically reinforce the efficacy of the neo-liberal claims to virtue.

This masquerade is of vital importance to the present system, for it cloaks what is at best amoral profit-maximizing, but which is more often than not tinged with, even bathed in malice, and provides

219 Monbiot, George, "Neoliberalism—the ideology at the root of all our problems," April 15, 2016. *The Guardian*.

the totally illegitimate ruling class with a shroud of virtue: the mass importation of wage slaves isn't done to benefit Big Business and the Chamber of Commerce, it is done out of basic human compassion.

The deadly and destructive "wars for democracy" serve the same basic interests. This Orwellian phrase is merely pretext for using the state apparatus to knock down any barriers to the free movement of goods and people, for ultimately "liberalization" doesn't mean more rights—it just means the loosening of mores to buy stuff and go into debt.

What the ruling class really means when they say they are working to "spread democracy" to some foreign land is that their regional particularities and self-determination must be sacrificed in favor of amyl nitrate and sodomy, student loan debt, abortions, sex changes, compound interest, and all the rest of it. This is what constitutes "freedom" in neo-liberalism, so in this sense neo-con warhawks are correct when they say that countries like Iran "hate us for our freedoms." For George Monbiot:

> The freedom that neoliberalism offers, which sounds so beguiling when expressed in general terms, turns out to mean freedom for the pike, not for the minnows. Freedom from trade unions and collective bargaining means the freedom to suppress wages. Freedom from regulation means the freedom to poison rivers, endanger workers, charge iniquitous rates of interest and design exotic financial instruments.[220]

Neo-liberalism is the economic system wearing the mask of liberalism while being anything but liberal.

The weaknesses inherent in liberalism are obvious in much the same way as conservatism; both deal primarily with social norms and culture (the former on faulty premises), and have no real ideological immunity to economic cooption, which is then able to twist the extant ideological framework in the service of not just the protection but the expansion of the economic system and the means of social control and reengineering, not to mention wholesale population change, which is a polite way of saying genocide.

---

220 Ibid.

Liberalism is so open to corruption because it: a) has no defense mechanism, and b) relies on an idealized vision of humanity, to say nothing of the fact that its core ideals were designed by and largely for Europeans. In any case, quoting Michael J. Thompson:

> Neoliberalism is the intensification of the influence and dominance of capital; it is the elevation of capitalism, as a mode of production, into an ethic, a set of political imperatives, and a cultural logic. It is also a project: a project to strengthen, restore, or, in some cases, constitute anew the power of economic elites. Capital is not simply money, property, or one economic variable among others. Rather, capital is the organising principle of modern society. It should be recalled that, in his Grundrisse, Marx explicitly argued that capital is a process that puts into motion all of the other dimensions of modern economic, political, social, and cultural life. It creates the wage system, influences values, goals, and the ethics of individuals, transforms our relation to nature, to ourselves, and to our community, and constantly seeks to mold state imperatives until they are in harmony with its own. Neoliberalism is therefore not a new turn in the history of capitalism. It is more simply, and more perniciously, its intensification.[221]

Liberalism may have "defeated" communism, but the principle actors are largely the same, and this time they've had far longer to manipulate the host population into actively despising itself and facilitating its own demise.

It is a newer and more lethal animal for a new century, having learned the lessons of Weimar (don't accelerate too quickly) and the USSR (don't be too conspicuous, don't under-feed but rather over-feed), and is a terrifying hybrid of the worst excesses of late-stage capitalism and velvet-gloved Eastern Bloc totalitarianism, buttressed by anarcho-tyrannical conditions (Antifa, jihadis, and melanin-enriched criminals terrorize dissidents and even average citizens with

---

221 Thompson, Michael J., "The World According to David Harvey," Winter, 2005. *Democratiya* 3.

impunity on the one hand, while 419 years in prison await you[222] for being in the wrong place at the wrong time with the wrong ideas and skin color on the other) and cult-like self-policing by the ruled.

Additionally, from the mid-twentieth century on, the people of the USSR and its satellites experienced a kind of permafrost, their cultures frozen in time while liberalism and free trade began to corrode the rest of the West into a debased materialism; the removal of impediments to goods also helped facilitate ever-increasing numbers of alien peoples into the West for cheap labor while industry was, in the latter part of the century, dismantled and outsourced. The progenitors of communism, advancing their group interests at others' expense, are they same as those using neo-liberalism as their vehicle; the methodology has evolved but the aims remain.

With the fall of the Soviet Union, the most significant counterbalance to global capital was removed, and the carrion of the USSR was picked over by internationalists and domestic but ethnically alien oligarchs, perhaps most pronounced in Russia. Only with the rise of Vladimir Putin did the "Wild West" period of unbridled capitalism at the price of Russia's soul come to a close. While not perfect, the Putin regime is at present one of the few bastions against neo-liberalism in the world today. To understand the conflict in the Ukraine, it is vital to understand not just the ethnic component, but this fault-line between neo-liberalism and ethnic self-determination.

"Communist" China is not much of an impediment to the spread of neo-liberalism, for though it is insular in many respects and aggressively seeks to advance Han ethnic interests, it remains very much "open for business" while enacting its own neo-colonial agenda. In many crucial ways, the Chinese are actually vital to the neo-liberal system. They're also being given carte blanche to colonize huge swathes of New Zealand, Australia, Canada, and the American West Coast, not to mention the fact that they virtually own countries like Jamaica and Zambia. The West is incessantly treated to a guilt-trip about the ills of colonialism while it's happening again right under our noses. This is before we consider the unprecedented scale of imported colonists facilitated by our ruling class, and the ongoing American military-industrial complex's forever wars.

---

222 "Man gets life plus 419 years in deadly Charlottesville car attack," *CBS News*, July 15, 2019.

Thus Iran, for example, finds itself squarely in John Bolton's crosshairs and why the "classical liberals" screech about women's liberation from mandatory head coverings and modesty laws, totally ignorant of the context of which they speak. To be fair, the genital mutilation practiced in many places across the Islamic and tribal equatorial world is never acceptable, but many of the mores, customs, and laws in place help protect these societies from the corrosive influence of a liberalism gone completely un-hinged. It's why the Eastern European countries have been less susceptible to mass immigration, irreligiosity, decadence, and consumerism. It's also why the European Union threatens member nations like Hungary and Poland with harsh economic sanctions and tries to impose migrant quotas on them and others like Croatia and Bulgaria. All particularist regimes which protect the interests of their people, whether Left or Right, from Cuba to Iran to Venezuela to Russia, must be washed away in the awesome septic tide of neo-liberalism.

China and its abysmal environmental and human rights record is ascendant and we worry about Russia. Speaking of Russia, Mexico and especially Israel actively meddle in our elections and there's no outcry. Some Russian somewhere might've spent a couple thousand dollars on Facebook ads with the help of Macedonian "data farmers" and it's the subject of non-stop media coverage, hysteria, and a federal investigation for two-and-a-half years followed by impeachment. No investigations are launched when China and Israel steal military and trade secrets, though. Israel's foreign policy de-stabilizes the entire Middle East and is directly responsible for the deaths and suffering of millions, but we worry about false flag chemical attacks. We finance the building and maintenance of walls in Tunisia, Jordan, Lebanon, Egypt, and Israel, but we can't get one built here.

The vast majority of the world's environmental degradation and pollution comes from the Third World, India, and China. Over-population, especially a population derived almost exclusively from these regions, makes the self-induced hellscape that is Haiti or the Indian sub-continent or China an inevitability. The infinite growth model of neo-liberalist economics is absolutely ruining the planet, and the Left, once a bastion of concern for Gaia, has abandoned all of its principles—including workers' rights—for iPhones and Mac Books from China and designer clothes made in Bangladeshi and Sri

Lankan sweatshops, where workers in the former make twenty-two cents an hour and in the latter fifty-four cents an hour. You might be interested to know that liberal "icon" Beyoncé's clothing line is made in these Sri Lankan sweatshops. Nothing spells female empowerment like being an eight-year-old girl working her fingers to the bone twelve hours a day for six bucks to supply the consumer capitalist Leviathan!

The *Los Angeles Times* published a multi-part exposé entitled "Product of Mexico" in December 2014 penned by Richard Marosi documenting the horrific conditions on Mexican farms all to supply the American consumer market, courtesy of NAFTA. So we have a situation where American farmers can't compete, Mexican seasonal labor edges out American workers, and back in Mexico, the laborers are literally trapped in a company store cycle of debt and over 100,000 *children* are forced into slave-like working conditions. Marosi reports:

> Children work the fields throughout Mexico's agricultural export regions. They pick tomatillos in Baja California and Michoacan and tomatoes in Zacatecas and San Luis Potosi. They de-stem strawberries in Baja California Sur. They bag coffee beans and cut sugar cane in Veracruz and Chiapas. The chile pepper harvest is especially dependent on underage workers... Pervasive drug violence in Sinaloa, Chihuahua and Michoacan makes site inspections risky...The contractors say children have to work because farm wages are so low that parents can't earn enough to feed their families.[223]

With no border to speak of, what's stopping that pervasive violence—so bad the government can't properly enforce its labor laws—from coming here? The answer is nothing, and criminals and economic migrants alike head for the United States where potential earnings and wages are much higher.

For the ruling class, the criminal element is irrelevant because it doesn't affect them, and foreign scab labor is essential for their swollen profits and maintaining lordship over their would-be serf

223 Marosi, Richard, "Product of Mexico: Child Labor," December 14, 2014. *Los Angeles Times.*

class, whether it's de-stemming strawberries, answering customer query calls in broken English, or "fighting hate" online. We may have more mobility and more technology than ever, but the way workers are treated is downright medieval. That's okay, though, because the fat cats in Silicon Valley need their indentured servants. As Ron Hira and Bharath Gopalaswamy state:

> Employers decide whether to apply for an H-1B visa and select the candidates. Employers also have the power to decide whether the H-1B worker can remain in the country. As a result, employer motivations and behaviors are the primary drivers of the outcomes of the program. Nearly four in five H-1B applications approved by the US Department of Labor were for the lowest two wage levels, far below the average US worker's wage. But, the costs savings run much deeper than just lower wages. Employers have enormous leverage over their H-1B workers, who are, in effect, indentured. A number of economists have recently described how rising monopsony power in the labor market is an important factor in explaining US wage stagnation. One of those economists, Princeton University's Alan Krueger, who served as chairman of the Council of Economic Advisors in the Barack Obama White House, has described how the executives of Silicon Valley technology firms were especially eager to use their monopsony power to keep their engineers' wages low by limiting their opportunities to leave. The executives—including Google's Eric Schmidt, a vocal advocate of H-1B expansion—went so far as to collude with one another by agreeing not to poach each other's engineers. So, especially in the technology industry, employers see limiting worker mobility as an important human-resource strategy to keep wages low. The H-1B rules provide even greater ability for employers to exercise monopsony power over workers. H-1B workers have limited labor-market options, since only a subset of employers is willing to sponsor a work visa. Further, like many others, H-1B

workers are subject to noncompete agreements and, in some cases, are even subject to employment bonds. They are afraid to complain of violations, and can be sued for liquidated damages if they leave, even by employers found to violate H-1B rules.[224]

Silver Lake co-founder and Council on Foreign Relations (CFR) and the Partnership for a New American Economy (NAE) member Glenn H. Hutchins is on the New York Federal Reserve Board of Directors, co-chairs the Brookings Institution and Harvard University's capital campaign, is on the Board of AT&T and Virtu Financial—there is of course no conflict of interest—and like the rest of his plutocratic associates, seems to define this as "progress."

As a case-in-point, speaking of the Brookings Institution, their Hamilton Project is yet another outlet publishing policy papers and memoranda advocating for "a twenty-first century immigration policy." There is near-uniformity in the policy positions of these pro-immigration, GDP-centric organizations like the Hamilton Project or the National Association for Business Economics (NABE), which has featured Hutchins as a speaker at its conferences in the past. Organizations partnering with NABE include Facebook, Google, Netflix, IBM, Amazon, Microsoft, Zillow, Brandeis University, Wells Fargo, Haver Analytics, Ford, Thomson Reuters, the US Census Bureau, Fidelity Investments, Fannie Mae, the McKinsey Institute, FedEx, and the Kingdom of the Netherlands, once again clearly signaling the beneficiaries and supporters of unfettered non-white immigration.

Many of those names are very familiar to us by now. What does their "twenty-first century immigration policy" entail? From the Hamilton Project's May 2012 framing memorandum "The US Immigration System: Potential Benefits of Reform":

> The United States is a nation of immigrants...Even as immigration to the United States continues to rise after a midcentury dip, most agree that America's immigration policy has failed to keep up with changing circumstances.

---

224 Hira, Ron and Bharath Gopalaswamy, "Reforming US' High-Skilled Guestworkers Program," January 15, 2019. Atlantic Council.

The current system does not meet U.S. economic needs, no longer reflects the historic humanitarian goal of reuniting families set out in the landmark 1965 Immigration and Nationality Act, undermines the confidence of Americans in the rule of law, and has produced divisive and fragmented policy responses at the state level... While there are many ways in which both immigrants and U.S.-born citizens benefit from immigration, few are as stark as the fact that when a non-European college-educated immigrant moves from her native country to the United States, her annual productivity and compensation leaps by $57,000.[225]

Right, in the realm of per-capita GDP immigration does have benefits—98% of which accrue to the immigrants themselves. The presumption that natives will experience a net gain is wholly theoretical and is also predicated on wealth re-distribution, that is to say an increased concentration of wealth in the hands of large business owners at the expense of workers and small and even mid-sized businesses.

This particular idea has been thoroughly discredited and yet remains the staid talking point of Koch Brothers types—the re-distribution in question amounts to $531 billion, and the net gain to natives amounts to $54 billion. Furthermore, as Steven A. Camarota, Director of Research at the Center for Immigration Studies reports:

The National Academy of Sciences' comprehensive look at the economic and fiscal impact of immigrants (taxes paid minus services used) found that the net fiscal burden immigrants create (taxes paid minus services used) is actually larger than the immigrant surplus...Whenever the impact of immigration on the labor market is discussed the argument is often made that immigration can fix the problems associated with our aging society, in particular the decline in the share of the population who are workers. However, this is not the case. For example, if

---

225 Greenstone, Michael, Adam Looney, and Harrison Marks, "The Hamilton Project Framing Memo," May 2012. The Hamilton Project.

we remove the 17.3 million immigrants (legal and illegal) who arrived in 2000-2014 and their 3.9 million U.S.-born children from 2014 Census Bureau data, 66 percent of the U.S. population would be of working age (16 to 65); if they are included, 66.2 percent are of working-age—a miniscule difference...Even before the Great Recession, a disproportionate share of employment gains went to immigrants... In the fourth quarter of 2015 only about two-thirds of working-age native-born Americans actually had a job; as recently as 2000 about three-fourths were working. American does not have a shortage of workers, it has a shortage of jobs.[226]

And let's face it: those that we do have suck. The number one employer in this country is Walmart, followed by the US Army, Navy, and Air Force—so you get to go help Genie Energy pump oil out of the illegally-occupied Golan Heights region to make some billionaires even richer and come back possibly maimed or in pieces, if at all, and watch your hometown sink further into blight and despair-induced death. Who knows, maybe your son is now a girl, too.

Other top employers are the Postal Service (if you were keeping track, that means four of the top five employers in America are part of the federal government), Yum! Brands (Taco Bell, KFC, Pizza Hut), UPS, the Kroger Company, Home Depot, McDonald's, Target, and the US Treasury. Nevertheless, Barack Obama decided to attempt to curtail carbon emissions to turn down the global thermostat, as Mark Steyn puts it, based on junk science and cost this country 125,000 jobs and $1.5 trillion dollars; Justin Trudeau's pursuit of similar policies and suffocating regulation is crippling the Canadian economy. Michael Bloomberg wants to do the same thing.

The International Labour Organization (ILO) estimates that globally over 200 million people are unemployed and 1.44 billion people are in vulnerable employment. Both numbers are projected to continue to get worse. Trends in labor force participation also indicate a decline, and wage growth has been suppressed, contributing to a

---

226 Camarota, Steven A., "The Impact of Large-Scale Immigration on American Workers," March 16, 2016. Testimony Prepared for Senate Committee on the Judiciary Subcommittee on Immigration and the National Interest.

long-term decline in the labor share of income. What's more, as Associate General Counsel of the AFL-CIO Lynne Rhinehart explains:

> Under the new rules, employers experiencing a long-term need for a larger workforce could completely avoid the demands of the domestic labor market by serially employing H-2B workers to meet this long-term need. This would drag down wages and working conditions for workers in the industry or region as a whole. The combination of self-attestation, the elimination of the state workforce agencies, and the broadened definition of "temporary" will further depress wages in the industries in which the H-2B program operates, to the detriment of U.S. workers. And, because there is an endless supply of citizens of foreign countries willing to work in the United States ... employers have little or no economic incentive to meet the economic demands of U.S. workers seeking a better wage.[227]

I've dedicated ample space elsewhere to further debunking these dubious claims of economic benefit, to say nothing of the litany of other fallacies—the "nation of immigrants" trope, the acceptance of the 1965 Immigration Act as "humanitarian" in aim, the conception of America as a contract, etc.—so let's look behind the curtain to see who might lend their support to such deeply erroneous claims. Cui bono? Below is the Hamilton Project's Advisory Council with accompanying position(s) at the memo's time of publication:

- George A. Akerlof, Koshland Professor of Economics, University of California at Berkeley
- Roger C. Altman, Founder & Chairman of Evercore Partners
- Alan S. Blinder, Gordon S. Rentschler Memorial Professor of Economics & Public Affairs at Princeton University
- Timothy C. Collins, Senior Managing Director & Chief Executive Officer at Ripplewood Holding, LLC

---

227 Rhinehart, Lynne, "Congressional testimony before the Subcommittee on Commercial and Administrative Law, U.S. House of Representatives, February 4, 2009.

- Jonathan Coslet, Senior Partner & Chief Investment Officer, TPG Capital
- Robert Cumby, Professor of Economics at Georgetown University
- John Deutch, Professor, Massachusetts Institute of Technology
- Karen Dynan, Vice President & Co-Director of Economic Studies, Senior Fellow, The Brookings Institution
- Christopher Edley, Jr., Dean and Professor, Boalt School of Law University of California, Berkeley
- Blair W. Effron, Founding Partner, Centerview Partners LLC
- Judy Feder, Professor & Former Dean, Georgetown Public Policy Institute, Georgetown University
- Roland Fryer, Robert M. Beren Professor of Economics, Harvard University and CEO, EdLabs
- Mark T. Gallogly, Cofounder & Managing Principal, Centerbridge Partners Advisory Council
- Ted Gayer, Senior Fellow & Co-Director of Economic Studies, The Brookings Institution
- Richard Gephardt, President & Chief Executive Officer, Gephardt Group Government Affairs
- Robert Greenstein, Executive Director, Center on Budget and Policy Priorities
- Chuck Hagel, Distinguished Professor, Georgetown University
- Glenn H. Hutchins, Co-Founder, Silver Lake
- Jim Johnson, Vice Chairman, Perseus LLC
- Lawrence F. Katz, Elisabeth Allison Professor of Economics at Harvard University
- Mark McKinnon, Global Vice Chair, Hill + Knowlton Strategies
- Eric Mindich, Chief Executive Officer, Eton Park Capital Management
- Suzanne Nora Johnson, Former Vice Chairman, Goldman Sachs Group, Inc.
- Peter Orszag, Vice Chairman of Global Banking, Citigroup, Inc.
- Richard Perry, Chief Executive Officer, Perry Capital

- Penny Pritzker, Founder, Chairman & Chief Executive Officer of PSP Capital
- Meeghan Prunty, Senior Advisor, The Hamilton Project
- Robert D. Reischauer, President Emeritus of The Urban Institute
- Alice M. Rivlin, Senior Fellow at The Brookings Institution and Professor of Public Policy, Georgetown University
- David M. Rubenstein, Co-Founder & Managing Director of The Carlyle Group
- Robert E. Rubin, Co-Chair, Council on Foreign Relations and Former U.S. Treasury Secretary
- Leslie B. Samuels, Senior Partner, Cleary Gottlieb Steen & Hamilton LLP
- Sheryl Sandberg, Chief Operating Officer, Facebook
- Ralph L. Schlosstein, President & Chief Executive Officer, Evercore Partners
- Eric Schmidt, Executive Chairman, Google Inc.
- Eric Schwartz, 76 West Holdings
- Thomas F. Steyer, Senior Managing Member, Farallon Capital Management
- Lawrence Summers, Charles W. Eliot University Professor, Harvard University
- Laura D'Andrea Tyson, S.K. and Angela Chan Professor of Global Management, Haas School of Business, University of California, Berkeley
- Michael Greenstone, Director of The Hamilton Project

Yes, mass immigration really is great if you're on this list, isn't it? Another fun list is that of the 636 business organizations that signed their approval of a prospective "Immigration Reform" bill in 2014 that enjoyed bipartisan support, and which would have provided for "Dreamer" amnesty and the re-orientation of immigration toward "economic necessity."[228]

This list had it all, from the California Fig Advisory Board to the Brazil-US Business Council to 3 Points Cattle Company to Goldman Sachs, Halliburton, the United States Chamber of Commerce and everything in between! The US Chamber of Commerce has been

---

[228] "Multi-Industry Letter on Immigration Reform," February 25, 2014. US Chamber of Commerce.

relentlessly pushing increased immigration and more worker visas for years.

Two recent examples are illustrative:

1) the Chamber of Commerce's declared support for HR 5038, the "Farm Workforce Modernization Act": "the broader temporary worker program reforms should provide additional sectors of American agriculture, such as meat and poultry processors, with the ability to hire workers under the H-2A program"; and

2) "Today, U.S. Chamber of Commerce Chief Policy Officer, Neil Bradley, released the following statement in regards to the Supreme Court hearing on Deferred Action for Childhood Arrivals (DACA): 'It is extremely disappointing that we've reached a point where Congress has left the future of hundreds of thousands of young people to a decision by the U.S. Supreme Court. Stripping DACA recipients of their ability to legally live and work in the country will harm them, their employers, their families, and their communities,' said Bradley. The Chamber hopes that the U.S. Supreme Court protects these individuals, but the fact remains that only Congress has the power to truly solve this issue."[229,230]

The Chamber's Employment Policy division supports the expansion of worker visas and an amnesty for "Dreamer" illegal aliens. Its "broad coalition" includes, naturally, the National Immigration Forum. NIF's Chairman of the Board is Eddie Aldrete of the International Bank of Commerce, the Vice Chair is Rebecca Tallent of Dropbox, and Members of the Board include Shirley Hoogstra of the Council for Christian Colleges and Universities, Louis Malfaro of the American Federation of Teachers, Akshay Khanna of StubHub, Danielle Burr of Uber, Mustafa Tameez of Outreach Strategists LLC, Rocio Saenz of Service Employees International Union (SEIU), and Arturo Sarukhan, Mexican Ambassador to the United States from 2007-2013.

In another example of how out-of-control the visa situation has gotten in this country, we turn once more to Ron Hira and Bharath Gopalaswamy:

---

229 Howard, Jack, "US Chamber Key Vote Alert! on HR 5038 'Farm Workforce Modernization Act,'" December 11, 2019. US Chamber of Commerce.

230 "US Chamber Statement on the Supreme Court's DACA Hearing," November 12, 2019. US Chamber of Commerce.

The quaint notion that employers will self-regulate has been shattered by dozens of stories of household names replacing US workers with H-1Bs. This common practice has reportedly been used by Disney, Southern California Edison, New York Life, Abbott Labs, Fossil Group, and many other leading firms. Perhaps the most stunning case was when UCSF forced Robert Harrison and his colleagues to train their H-1B replacements. UCSF is part of the University of California (UC) system, one of the largest public university systems in the country. According to Senator Dianne Feinstein (D-CA), the UC system received $8.5 billion in grants and subsidies from the federal government. More astounding, Janet Napolitano, UC's president, previously served as secretary of the Department of Homeland Security, the agency that administers the H-1B program. During an oversight hearing before Congress in 2009, Senator Durbin asked then-Secretary Napolitano what she was doing to ensure that US workers were not being displaced by H-1B workers. She responded, "Our top obligation is to American workers, making sure American workers have jobs…We are going to keep at this to make sure that the intent of that program is fulfilled." Remember, the intent is that H-1B workers are filling positions for which there is a bona fide labor shortage. After the UC H-1B scandal became public in late 2016, about a dozen members of Congress sent letters to Napolitano, urging her to reverse course. In spite of this public admonition, she went forward with replacing her US workers with H-1Bs. The lure of lower-cost, hassle-free workers was too tempting for even for a public university like UC to pass up.[231]

It wasn't just barbarian incursions that un-did Rome; it was an onerous tax code, a bottomed-out birthrate, a civilizational ennui, gross excess and decadence in the moneyed class coupled with its effete softness, and a deeply-misguided foray into multi-culturalism.

---

231 Hira, Ron and Bharath Gopalaswamy, "Reforming US' High-Skilled Guestworkers Program," January 15, 2019. Atlantic Council.

The parallels are striking. In 376 AD, the Romans accepted a massive caravan of Goths "fleeing persecution" into their territory hoping they would become farmers and serve in the legions. Instead, the Eastern Emperor Valens was subsequently killed and the Goths proceeded to loot and ravage Roman lands for years afterward. And no, they never "assimilated."

In Honduras, homicide violence reached a peak in 2012 with an average of *twenty homicides a day*. Out of a population of approximately eight million people, there are a *very* conservatively-estimated 7,000-10,000 street gang members according to official statistics. Since 2010, the US Embassy has recorded 52 murders of US citizens.

In Guatemala, the first country the Last Chance Armada caravan passed through and where it added additional numbers, an average of over one hundred murders per week were recorded in 2016. In the period of 2012-2015, 37% of Guatemala's homicides were attributed to "personal vengeance."

Recall the UNHCR figures from earlier in this book and add to the mix members of ISIS and other international terror groups, as well as any additional number of criminal gangs, and it's pretty clear these are not "refugees" by any stretch of the imagination. They are something else entirely.

Hispanics are the perpetrators in a massive 71% of Hispanic-white interracial violent crimes against women. 50% of the 1.7 million refugees accepted to the United States since 2008 are high school drop-outs and 56% are on food stamps. Roughly one-third have no insurance. So that's how the government is using the "safety net" that is welfare—treating your country and your labor as the world's largest charity *against your will*.

You are financing your own dispossession and probable bankruptcy at gun-point. Previously eradicated diseases and STDs are on the rise, as well, and that's only the tip of the iceberg.

Introduced by Chuy Garcia, and co-sponsored by forty-three other House Democrats including Ayanna Pressley, Ilhan Omar, Rashida Tlaib, Pramila Jayapal, Alexandria Ocasio-Cortez, Ro Khanna, Al Green, and other mostly immigrants and non-white representatives, a bill called the New Way Forward Act would decriminalize illegal border crossings and end the automatic deportation of those caught falsifying passports or those convicted of felonies—in fact, it would remove the possibility of anyone being deported for any reason. Immigration judges would be given blanket authority to nullify any deportation order. ICE would not be able to use an alien's prior criminal record as proof of danger, and special consideration would be given to aliens identifying as gay or transgendered because why not? Lastly, the bill would also allow for a "right of return"—not that of Jewish criminals like Roman Abramovich or Ilan Shor fleeing their respective countries to Israel after committing serious financial crimes to avoid prosecution, but that of deported aliens to return to the US paid for by taxpayers if they would have been allowed to stay under the conditions of the New Way Forward Act.

Whether it be for misguided humanitarian reasons, pro-corporate and financial institution economic reasons, or something infinitely more sinister, there is no question that the post-1965 orientation of America's accelerating immigration policy very clearly does not serve our best interests.

In flagrant disregard for health and well-being, while the rest of the country was on lock-down, the UNHCR, IOM, and US State Department continued to greenlight the re-settling of "refugees" from coronavirus-stricken regions into what's left of your neighborhood despite officially claiming to pause the influx. While corona raged, "refugees" from the Democratic Republic of the Congo, Iraq, Sudan, Somalia, and Afghanistan were dumped into Westbrook, Augusta, and Portland.

Next door in New Hampshire, over the period January 1st, 2020 to April 8th, "refugees" from the Democratic Republic of the Congo were shuttled into Manchester and eleven Congolese and three Somalis were shoved into Colchester, Vermont, just north of Burlington. Eight "refugees" from the Central African Republic were dropped off in Worcester, Massachusetts, and another forty from the Democratic Republic of the Congo were spread out over the state, about half of them in Northampton.

New arrivals also came from South Sudan, Iraq, and elsewhere. Rhode Island was the beneficiary of "refugees" from the Democratic Republic of the Congo, Syria, Rwanda, and Colombia; Bridgeport, Connecticut received twelve Congolese and seven Eritreans. Eight Sudanese arrived in New Haven.

So making New England Africa with a little dash of Latin America and the Middle East is evidently more important than public health. Actions speak louder than words as my mother always said. Way out at the other extremity of the country in Alaska, Anchorage was enriched by some South Sudanese; in Washington state: Eritreans, Afghanis, Congolese, Ethiopians, Iranians, Iraqis, and more. Fargo, meet Somalia, Iraq, and the Democratic Republic of the Congo!

Similarly, Amarillo, Texas apparently was in need of Burmese the same way Memphis, Tennessee and Mission, Kansas have been dying for Afghanis. More Congolese for Wichita? Presto! Over the time period February 1ˢᵗ to April 8ᵗʰ, fifty-four "refugees" from the Democratic Republic of the Congo arrived in Tennessee and another fifty in Idaho.

In the last two weeks of March 2020, while many Americans were sheltering in place, hundreds of "refugees" were dumped off across America in addition to 373 "special immigrant visa" recipients from an Afghanistan we've been at war with for two decades.[232]

From April 1ˢᵗ to April 8ᵗʰ, the US State Department dumped "refugees" from Afghanistan and Burma in Texas, from Pakistan in High Point, North Carolina, and from Vietnam in Salt Lake City, Utah.

In January 2020, 119 Afghani "refugees" arrived in the United States, along with 200 from Burma, seven from Burundi, seven from the Central African Republic, 212 from the Democratic Republic of the Congo, 35 from El Salvador, 92 from Eritrea, 18 from Ethiopia, 14 from Guatemala, 56 from Iraq, 11 from Pakistan, 23 from Somalia, 32 from Sudan, 24 from Syria, 13 from Uganda, and more. This is both criminal and insane. The response, or more appropriately lack thereof, by our leaders shows exactly what they are willing to risk in order for the status quo to be maintained.

April 2020 brought reports of coronavirus in at least one Greek "refugee" camp, and the UNHCR came out and admitted that there were at least ten confirmed coronavirus cases among "refugees" and asylum seekers in Germany, prompting nameless aid officials to worry that "this might undermine future support for taking refugees."

---

232 According to the US State Department, 16,370 Afghanis arrived in the United States on "special immigrant visas" in fiscal year 2017 alone.

I should think so, but our support for this project has never been required.

Donald Trump led off his March 19th, 2020 press conference on the measures being taken to combat the spread of the coronavirus by celebrating the return of "New Hampshire man" Amer Fakhoury from Lebanon to receive medical care for his stage 4 lymphoma. It's not like our medical professionals had other things to worry about, right? Oh, and by the way, Fakhoury collaborated with Israel during their occupation of southern Lebanon.

In the middle of the coronavirus pandemic, the opportunistic Catholic Charities released the following statement on their website:

> Catholic Charities USA (CCUSA) joins the U.S. Conference of Catholic Bishops' Committee on Migration (USCCB/COM), Catholic Health Association of the United States (CHA), and the Catholic Legal Immigration Network, Inc. (CLINIC), in urging DHS and its components to remove barriers to healthcare access so that immigrants may safely comply with government recommendations during this global pandemic health crisis. Specifically, we ask that DHS review all immigration enforcement activities and operations, particularly suspending activities at sensitive locations, and broadly release explicit guidance that the public charge rule does not apply during this COVID-19 outbreak.

Ridiculous and dangerous.

The Great Replacement stops for no virus. The continued funding of the nearly $229,000 from the Department of Homeland Security/USCIS for the Central American Minor Parole Program remained active; this program "was established in 2014 to provide certain minors in El Salvador, Guatemala, and Honduras the opportunity to be considered, while still in their home country, for refugee resettlement in the United States."

The Small Business Administration gave Meredith Immigration Law Offices in Culver City, California a $250,000 loan and a

$226,000 loan in late February to Ibrahim & Rao LLP Immigration and Nationality Law in Atlanta. The continued disbursal of the US State Department's $38.5 million to the IOM for a "refugee and migrant response plan for refugees and migrants from Venezuela" remained active as well.

On February 1ˢᵗ, 2020, the Department of Health and Human Services' Administration for Children and Families announced a $20 million grant to the Lutheran Immigration and Refugee Service (LIRS) for "residential shelters and transitional foster care for unaccompanied alien children" and in January nearly $1 million as part of a matching grant program with LIRS.

Also on February 1ˢᵗ, the Department of Health and Human Services' Administration for Children and Families announced a $2.1 million grant to the Community Action Program for Central Arkansas for a migrant Head Start program "to promote school readiness by enhancing the social and cognitive development of low-income children, including children on federally recognized reservations and children of migratory farm workers." They granted $1.6 million on March 1ˢᵗ to Holyoke-Chicopee-Springfield Head Start in Massachusetts for the same, and $3 million in January to the East Coast Migrant Head Start Project.

On March 15ᵗʰ, the Department of Health and Human Services' Health Resources and Services Administration sent over $57,000 in "supplemental funding" to deal with coronavirus to the Montana Migrant and Seasonal Farm Workers Council. We should also not neglect that in the late March 2020, coronavirus relief package, page 817 of the bill calls for "an additional amount for 'Migration and Refugee Assistance,' $350,000,000, to remain available until expended, to prevent, prepare for, and respond to coronavirus."

As Laura Madokoro, Associate Professor of History at Carleton University wrote in the middle of the pandemic, "Canada has closed its borders to asylum-seekers and non-citizens because of the COVID-19 pandemic. Similar emergency measures over the years should teach us that now is not the time for nationalism." If anything, now, more than ever, is the time for nationalism and an end to globalism, and it is telling that both the "anti-racists" and the mega-capitalists are in lock-step.

There was much weeping, wailing, and the gnashing of teeth north of the border that Canada would have to delay further wage suppression with the start of its Agri-Food Immigration Pilot until mid-May; Canada aims to welcome about 2,750 new permanent residents per year through this pilot. As Nicholas Keung wrote on March 12th, 2020:

> Immigration Minister Marco Mendicino released the much anticipated multi-year immigration plan, which will see the country usher in as many as 1.14 million newcomers between 2020 and 2022. Despite fears of a global recession due to the COVID-19 pandemic, Toronto-based immigration policy analyst Kareem El-Assal said the high immigration intake is justified with more than 9 million Canadians reaching retirement age in the next decade.
>
> "We need to be proactive in immigration policies. New immigrants are not here just to fill immediate job vacancies. With baby boomers retiring in the next 10 years, we need to put ourselves in healthy economic standing by increasing the immigration level," said El-Assal, director of policy and digital strategy at CanadaVisa, an immigration website run by a Montreal-based law firm… In response to the labour market needs of an aging population, especially in remote communities, Ottawa will also raise the annual intake of caregivers, agri-food workers and immigrants willing to settle in smaller communities in Canada's north, from 5,200 in 2020 to 9,500 in 2022.[233]

It is the same story everywhere. According to the Ministry of Business, Innovation, and Employment in New Zealand, 303,453 people were living in the country on temporary work, student, or family visas at the end of February 2020, which is nearly double the amount from a decade prior. There was extreme discomfort in all the places we'd expect that there might be any restrictions whatsoever on cheap labor and demographic replacements. In 2009, there were

---

233 Keung, Nicholas, "Canada to welcome 1 million immigrants over three years despite fears of recession," March 12, 2020. *The Star.*

96,453 work visa holders in New Zealand. At the end of February 2020, there were 220,737.

In the US, as Jessica M. Vaughan reported for the Center for Immigration Studies, "On March 26, the State Department announced that the applications of new and returning farm and non-farm seasonal workers would be immediately expedited by waiving requirements for most visa applicants to be interviewed."[234]

According to the US State Department, "The H-2 program is essential to the economy and food security of the United States and is a national security priority." With millions of Americans suddenly out of work and an international pandemic raging, this was a "national security priority"? Really? This is what happens when your entire existence is predicated on exponential growth: too much is never enough, and in this case one single person is too much.

On March 18th, 2020, an organization called Humanity United sponsored an article in *The Guardian* employing all the familiar tropes: "Groups working with refugees and unaccompanied children in France and Greece implored the authorities in both countries to provide urgent help to refugees and unaccompanied minors, whom they say have been effectively abandoned by the authorities."[235]

Oh the humanity! As one of the cited instances of the kvetching in Europe, NGOs urged the EU and Greece "for a raft of protective measures including an end to deportations and pressing forward with relocation and family reunion programmes for unaccompanied minors across Europe."

The NGOs in question in this instance included the Hebrew Immigrant Aid Society (HIAS), the International Rescue Committee (IRC), and the Danish Refugee Council, which partners with and/or receives funding from the Danish Ministry of Foreign Affairs (Danida), the European Commission's Humanitarian Aid and Civil Protection department (ECHO), the United Nations High Commissioner for Refugees (UNHCR), the US State Department, the UK's Department for International Development (DFID), the Swedish International Development Cooperation Agency (SIDA),

---

234 Vaughan, Jessica M., "Trump Waves in Seasonal Foreign Workers as Pandemic Peaks," April 7, 2020. Center for Immigration Studies.
235 Kelly, Annie, Harriet Grant, and Lorenzo Tondo, "NGOs raise alarm as coronavirus strips support from EU refugees," March 18, 2020. *The Guardian*.

IrishAid, the Norwegian Agency for Development Cooperation (Norad, not to be confused with NORAD), the Swiss Agency for Development and Cooperation (SDC), the Canadian International Development Agency (CIDA), and others including several other UN agencies, national governments, and private sources.

This Humanity United organization was founded and fully funded by the Omidyar Group. Some of its partners include the Clinton Foundation, the Tides Center, the Regents of the University of California at Berkeley, the United Way, the US Holocaust Memorial Museum, Oxfam America, the New Venture Fund, the Pulitzer Center on Crisis Reporting, and more. No agenda there.

The mass importation of these people can only enrich the oligarchs and impoverish and harm the American people. Our common culture and established code of behavior are at present unraveling in the form of social disintegration. The more isolated someone is, the fewer bonds they have, the easier they are to control.

The maintenance of the modern super-state depends on an ever-increasing crack-down on the truth, and a deliberate, coordinated effort to sever all communal, familial, and nationalistic ties via exposure to media-driven propaganda and state-sponsored policies meant to atomize people. The neo-liberal project is an artifice with all of the substance of changing seasonal clothing fashions and no ethos beyond consumerism, blind adherence to authority, and unbridled self-gratification.

The country's demographic transformation bears much of the burden for its atomization, diversity being a primary driver behind distrust, disunity, alienation, and general withdrawal from public life and community involvement. In such an environment, fleeting "pleasures" (or else means of escape) derived from consumption replace more healthy behaviors.

We turn to the superficial in the futile search for some facsimile of a world that vanished decades ago. In this pre-packaged and commodified environment, where people's alienation is only compounded by a deep suspicion of those around them and a fear of random acts of violence and pre-meditated terror—not to mention their purported villainy if they are white—the kind of family-less, community-less, identity-less "individual" that emerges is a grotesquerie of the like classical liberals and their ethos of individualism would not recognize. Even so, that ideological bent has led us here.

Furthermore, the "soaring" contemporary American economy is, like notions of "progress" and strength through diversity, an illusion. Despite the explosion in the FIRE economy, the *real* economies in immigration-heavy countries like the US and the UK are *shrinking*. More people and more GDP, sure, but nothing of any real *value* is being produced.

A few people make a ton from compound interest, fractional reserve banking, financial speculation, and the like and everyone else works in the service economy or is unemployed, subsidized by the government to watch TV all day.

The middle class is now a minority in this country, which is a crossing of the Rubicon for anything resembling stability, and it only continues to shrink.

Pretty much the only thing keeping the fake economy afloat outside of Wall Street is retail, and even then, it's mostly due to population growth in the form of mass Third World immigration as the primary driver of the increase in spending.[236]

---

236 See: Lobaugh, Kasey M., Bobby Stephens, and Jeff Simpson, "The consumer is changing, but perhaps not how you think," May 29, 2019. Deloitte.

Chapter Eight: Transformation Wholesale

"All my friends are brown and red."—Soundgarden, "Spoonman"

What we know is that for both ideological and economic reasons Maine finds itself "suddenly" in the crosshairs of the globalist establishment. From *Time* ("President Trump Betrayed My American Dream by Abdi Nor Iftin, June 20th, 2018) to the *New York Times* ("Maine Needed New, Young Residents. African Migrants Began Arriving by the Dozens." by Kate Taylor, June 23rd, 2019; see also "New Hampshire, 94 Percent White, Asks: How Do You Diversify a Whole State?" by Katharine Q. Seelye, July 27th, 2018 about Maine's neighbor) to *The Christian Science Monitor* ("As US braces for refugees, one Maine town offers a lesson of inclusion" by Jessica Mendoza, February 8th, 2016) to the *Huffington Post* ("Immigration in the Whitest State in America" by Yael Luttwak, October 9th, 2017), we are told in unison that Maine is too old, too white, and in dire need of Haitian nurses, Guatemalan blueberry rakers, Somali who knows what, and all the rest of it. As this sudden media blitz *is totally organic and definitely not coordinated at all*, enter Jeff Bezos's *Washington Post* stage left: In "'This will be catastrophic': Maine families face elder boom, worker shortage in preview of nation's future," written by Jeff Stein, the neo-liberals show their hand to anyone paying attention:

> Across Maine, families like the Flahertys are being hammered by two slow-moving demographic forces — the growth of the retirement population and a simultaneous decline in young workers — that have been exacerbated by a national worker shortage pushing up the cost of labor...The disconnect between Maine's aging population and its need for young workers to

care for that population is expected to be mirrored in states throughout the country over the coming decade, demographic experts say. And that's especially true in states with populations with fewer immigrants, who are disproportionately represented in many occupations serving the elderly…"As the oldest state, Maine is the tip of the spear — but it foreshadows what is to come for the entire country."…Experts say the nation will have to refashion its workforce…The results of not doing so fast enough are already visible in Maine…Care workers in Maine were paid about $11.37 an hour in 2017, according to an AARP report, with a 2019 minimum wage of $11 an hour…"Even Dunkin' Donuts pays you more."… The rising demand for care is occurring simultaneously with a dangerously low supply of workers…"There are simply just not enough people to go around," [Mary Jane Richards, chief operating officer at North Country Associates] said. "We try to elevate our wages, but then the nearest facility brings theirs up."[237]

Oh, the horror of having to pay workers a living wage!

Martha Searchfield of the Bar Harbor Chamber of Commerce echoes the same sentiment: "The [labor] shortage is so acute…other companies have gone so far as to offer higher wages to entice locals." Also of note in this piece is the commentary by Jewish mass non-white immigration advocate and senior fellow in the Urban-Brookings Tax Policy Center at the Urban Institute Howard Gleckman.

Gleckman makes the seemingly apropos-of-nothing argument that, "With climate change, towns get burned down, or people die in fires." We've talked about climate alarmism before—in addition to the monetization of carbon emissions and the creation of a new financial market, "climate change" and open borders are synonymous—because "climate change causes migration," we need to accept any and all (non-white) comers who will be able to increase their consumption while we are expected to confine ourselves to matchbox-sized apartments, sterilize ourselves for the environment, and eat soy and maggot

237 Stein, Jeff, "'This will be catastrophic': Maine families face elder boom, worker shortage in preview of nation's future," August 14, 2019. *The Washington Post*.

sausages, all while remaining great consumers in our own right, just in different ways, from the cradle to the grave. The *HuffPo* article was written by Jewish filmmaker Yael Luttwak, affiliated with the Maine Jewish Film Festival, who says:

> We need to show that diversity works. With one million immigrants making their home in the United States each year, it's urgent that those who believe deeply in America and the notion of diversity as a core American value, find ways to push back against the rising tide of discrimination against "the other." The challenge for all of us now is to look, state-by-state, at how our communities are responding to immigration, and find the good news stories that epitomize the value of immigration and the bridges that have been built between immigrant and non-immigrant communities. A good place to start is Maine—one of the whitest states in America. Since 2015, I along with our documentary filmmaking team, have been following a group of female students—some new immigrants—some not, in South Portland as they navigate life in a public school. I co-directed, along with [Jewish] Abigail Tannebaum Sharon, the new documentary, "Maine Girls" which just premiered at the 2017 Camden International Film Festival and is now on the festival circuit and picked up for distribution by Kanopy—follows immigrant girls from the Congo, Jamaica, Somalia and Vietnam. What's inspiring about these girls is that, even in this anti-immigration environment, teenagers will be teenagers. Through hip hop, culture, and common experiences in a Maine public school, the American and immigrant girls develop trust—with the help of a school curriculum built around tolerance and acceptance who end up enriching life in South Portland.[238]

This is reminiscent of the documentary *One Team* about the 2015 Lewiston high school men's soccer team's "coming together" and

---

238 Luttwak, Yael, "Immigration in the Whitest State in America," October 9, 2017. *Huffington Post.*

"beating the odds" and "championing diversity" on their way to their first-ever Class A state championship. In 2018, Netflix optioned the rights to make a film or series about the same team, based on the book *One Goal.* HBO's *Real Sports* also did a segment on this team entitled "Coming to America—Lewiston Soccer." Laying it on pretty thick.

The Maine Jewish Film Festival (MJFF) works with Colby College, the University of Maine Law School, the University of Southern Maine, the Maine College of Art (MECA), Bates College, the Maine ACLU, Portland NAACP, the Museum of African Culture, EqualityMaine, Interfaith Youth Alliance, and The Holocaust and Human Rights Center.

The Maine College of Art (MECA) sponsored an event entitled "Making Migration Visible: Traces, Tracks & Pathways," with an infusion of funding from several Jewish philanthropic organizations; the tone of the event was very much in line with the seemingly-ubiquitous open borders propaganda we are being conditioned to believe, and there was, as one might expect, a heavy reliance on exhibits connecting the "Jewish experience" to the "struggles" of today's state-, NGO-, and corporate-sanctioned arrivals to Maine. Some of these exhibits included "Dorothea Rabkin: Tragedy to Transformation" about Holocaust refugees; "Maine + Jewish: Two Centuries"; and a documentary series by the Jewish David Grubin "reflecting that 'once, there was no such thing as an illegal immigrant. If you could get here, you could stay,' Prof. [Donna] Gabaccia notes that, from the start of U.S. history, immigrants were recognized as necessary to the country's economic growth."

Colby College in Waterville, Maine held a conference in 2015 entitled, "Maine Migrations, Past and Present," organized in conjunction with Colby's Maine Jewish History Project and co-sponsored by the NAACP, Catholic Charities, Documenting Maine Jewry, and the Jewish Community Alliance (JCA) of Southern Maine, along with several other organizations.

Among the presentations were: "Art, immigrant history, and political engagement" by the Jewish Jo Israelson, Compagna-Sennett Artist-in-Residence at Colby College whose research and art seek to raise awareness of historical Jews in Maine who have helped to "welcome the stranger"; "Children of Holocaust Survivors"; "German Jews of Bangor, 1849-1856"; "Jews in Lewiston-Auburn during the early 20th century" by David Freidenreich, the Pulver Family Associate Professor of Jewish Studies at Colby College and director of its Jewish studies program; and the "Refugees and Asylum-Seekers" symposium moderated by David Greenham, Associate Director of The Holocaust and Human Rights Center of Maine, featuring presentations on the experiences of refugees and asylum-seekers in Maine from Somalia and Burundi, the "experiences of Soviet Jewish Refugees," and a joint presentation by Catherine Yomoah of the Maine State Office of Multicultural Affairs and Tarlan Ahmadov, the State Refugee Coordinator for Catholic Charities of Maine on refugee resettlement and asylum trends.

Greenham organized seminars in the state capital in the summer of 2019 to educate teachers on how to teach the Holocaust and slavery, and how to incorporate advocacy for immigrants' rights into their lesson plans; there were also "anti-bias" training sessions.

Among the Maine Jewish Film Festival's distinguished guests for 2019 were included:

- Lana Alman, HIAS board member, former legal adviser to illegal alien minors, and, as Lead Associate at Booz Allen Hamilton, Lana focuses on projects related to healthcare and immigration, recently overseeing a team of Spanish-language writers and translators for Obamacare to ensure that millions of Spanish-speaking consumers had access to healthcare.

- Alison Beyea, Executive Director at the ACLU of Maine and former employee of the University of Maine Law School.

- Shenna Bellows, state senator and Executive Director of The Holocaust and Human Rights Center; she led the ACLU of Maine as Executive Director for eight years and served as Interim Executive Director for LearningWorks, where Portland Mayor Ethan Strimling served as CEO for 19 years. Most recently, Bellows owned a nonprofit consulting firm providing services to a range of nonprofit organizations ranging from the Maine Women's Lobby to the Maine Immigrants' Rights Coalition. She was a key leader on the successful 2012 marriage equality campaign and co-chaired the successful 2011 statewide ballot campaign to restore same day voter registration.

- Lisa Mayer, former Madison Avenue denizen now residing in Auburn, Maine and contributor to the *Forward* and the *Huffington Post*.

With funding from Hyatt, the Law Offices of Joe Bornstein, the Consulate General of Israel to New England, HeadInvest, Epstein Commercial Real Estate, Alliance Bernstein, the Colby College Center for Small Town Jewish Life, Documenting Maine Jewry, the Sam L. Cohen Foundation, the Robert and Dorothy Goldberg Foundation, the Moser Family Foundation, the Jewish Community Alliance, the Bernard A. Osher Foundation, the Lunder Foundation, the Morris J. and Betty Kaplun Foundation, and the Albert B. Glickman Family Foundation, the MJFF:

> Supports dialogue and engagement across the state by providing a forum for the discussion and exploration of challenging issues...through [its] educational outreach programs and community partnerships, [it] strives to educate and inspire a diverse audience...In recent years, waves of immigration and shifting demographics have reshaped many parts of our state. MJFF regards these changes as an opportunity to create programming and events that celebrate and build community within an increasingly diverse population...Through new outreach initiatives and strategic partnerships [it] will continue to expand [its] reach and remain at the vanguard of Maine's cultural community.

The MJFF's Board of Directors includes representatives of financial institutions, such as Aurora Financial Group Vice President, Chief Compliance Officer, and Investment Advisor Kim Volk. It also includes lawyer Randi Greenwald, short-time Maine resident and volunteer on Obama for Maine and Hillary for Maine Finance Committees, Maine Immigrants' Rights Coalition (MIRC), and "other social justice efforts through Congregation Bet Ha'am." "The Maine Immigrants' Rights Coalition (MIRC) is a unique collaboration of leaders – a majority of whom are people of color – representing diverse ethnic communities across our state." One of its primary financiers is the Sam L. Cohen Foundation. It will also shock you, I'm sure, to learn that Randi Greenwald of the Bet Ha'am Jewish Reform community is on the Board of Directors.

MIRC's extensive network is comprised of: Congregation Bet Ha'am-Tikkun Olam Council, Planned Parenthood, Catholic Charities, the YMCA, the Salvation Army, Diversity Hiring Coalition, Androscoggin Bank, New Ventures Maine, City of Portland-Economic Development Department, Small Business Administration, Coastal Enterprises Inc. (CEI), Southern Maine Workers Center, New Mainers Alliance, Maine People's Alliance, Maine Access Immigrant Network (MAIN), the ACLU of Maine, the NAACP, Maine Business Immigrant Coalition, Mano en Mano, New Mainers PAC, York Diversity Forum, Maine Equal Justice Partners (MEJP), Educate Maine, Portland Friends Meeting, African Women and Development, African Immigrant Association, Angolan Community Association of Maine, Tree Street Youth, Women's Bureau US Department of Labor, Immigrant Resource Center of Maine, My Sister's Keeper, Empower Immigrant Women (EIW), EMERGE Maine, In Her Presence, Women United Around the World, Welcoming Immigrants Our New Neighbors, Maine Community Law, Pine Tree Legal Assistance (PTLA), Cumberland Legal Aid Clinic, Immigrant Legal Advocacy Project (ILAP), Refugee and Human Rights Clinic-Maine Law, Maine Women's Lobby/Maine Women's Policy Center, LearningWorks, Goodwill, Portland Adult Education, IntWork.Co., Upwardly Global, New Mainers Resource Center (NMRC), Center for Immigrant and Community Services, University of Southern Maine-Prior Learning Assessment, Maine Career Center, Maine Association for New Americans (MANA), Welcoming Immigrants Network, Welcoming the Stranger, Maine Immigrant & Refugee Services, Hope Acts, Furniture Friends, the Visible Community, Portland Public Schools Multilingual Multicultural Center, Families First Community Center, Portland Housing Authority, Atlantic Global Aid, Gateway Community Service, Maine Mobile Health Program, Frannie Peabody Center, Healthy Androscoggin, Friends of Mind/Amigos de Mente, Slim Peace, Latinx Family Wellness and Recreation, Portland Diocese-Hispanic Ministry, Light Mission Church, Maine Council of Churches, Roman Catholic Diocese of Portland, First Parish-Faith in Action, Maine Unitarian Universalist State Advocacy

Network, Prosperity Maine, Intercultural Community Center, Maine War Tax Resistance, Southern Maine Community College, Chinese-American Friendship Association of Maine, New Mainers Speak, Portland Public Library, Burundi Community Association of Maine, Djibouti Community and Volunteer Services, New England Djibouti Community, Iraqi Community Association of Maine, Somali Community Center of Maine, the Somali Bantu Youth Association of Maine, South Sudanese Community Association of Maine, Rwandese Community Association of Maine, Congolese Community of Maine, New England Arab-American Org, and Catholic Charities of Maine Refugee and Immigration Services.

This phenomenon of out-of-state Jews (to say nothing of the affiliated banks, firms, corporations, and other organizations) relocating to Maine and promptly working to transform their new environs to become more "cosmopolitan" is a pattern.

The Jewish Judith Sloan is from New York and was drawn to Maine from summering there. She is an immigration advocate and does performances of "Stories of Migration, Refuge and Finding Home...Co-sponsored by the Unitarian Universalist Church of Brunswick and Beth Israel Congregation in Bath...[with] proceeds to benefit EarSay's work with immigrant youth and the The Midcoast New Mainers Support Group...an interfaith collaborative offering resettlement support to asylum seekers and refugees in the Bath-Brunswick area." Also in collaboration is New Mainers Speak, a pro-immigration and -diversity radio show which advocates for the "internationalization" of Maine. Another New Yorker is former Portland Mayor Ethan Strimling. Why does it seem like Maine is not an outlier here and why is it that every reasonable objection to mass transformative immigration somehow leads to Hitler?

As Kevin MacDonald writes, "As usual, Jews see refugee issues in terms of their own history, not what's good for the country, ignoring the fraud and economic motives. 'The Jewish people know what it means to be turned away and to be denied protection.'"

As the Jewish *New York Times* writer Bari Weiss stated in an interview with NPR, "The Jewish connection to the refugee is not a conspiracy. That's something that we're very, very proud of."[239]

---

239 "'New York Times' Opinion Writer On Pittsburgh Synagogue Shooting," *NPR*, October 29, 2018

Never Again Is Now, protestors affiliated with Jewish Activists in Maine (JAM) are adamant that you understand. The Jewish Executive Director of the Capital Area New Mainers Project (CANMP) Chris Myers Asch agrees, saying you should "stand with us for a different America":

> Like many Jews in central Maine, I felt connected to the Jews at the Tree of Life not only through our shared faith but also through our shared commitment to welcoming refugees into our communities. I work with the Capital Area New Mainers Project (CANMP, pronounced "camp"), a local nonprofit that welcomes immigrants and works to build a thriving, integrated community here. Temple Beth El was a founding partner of CANMP, and Jews represent a disproportionate share of our volunteers…
>
> On my computer, I proudly display a HIAS sticker that proclaims, "My people were refugees too." For much of Jewish history, we have indeed been refugees, forced to flee from our homes as one authoritarian leader after another made us scapegoats for economic misery or political scandals.
>
> For me, and for many Jews, being a refugee is not part of the distant past. My grandmother, Berta Asch, escaped from Nazi Germany in the 1930s and made her way to America, a country that promised freedom, opportunity, and, above all, safety…We know what it is like to be driven from our homes, to be a stranger in a new land. That is why we place a high priority on "hachnasat orchim," or "welcoming the stranger."
>
> Embracing refugees and helping them grow comfortable in their new land is part of who we are as Jews. Our history and traditions help explain why Jews are so disproportionately represented in various social movements that seek to build a more just, more equal, more welcoming America. From gay rights to civil rights, Jews are on the front lines fighting for justice and working to help America live up to its ideals…

Like other religious and racial minorities, we need allies
and advocates in the broader community to stand with
us, speak with us, and act with us as we battle against
white supremacists, anti-Semites, and the politicians who
encourage them… Support the values of an egalitarian,
inclusive, welcoming America all year long with your
time, your money, and your votes. The Jews of central
Maine — and all racial and religious minorities — need
you.[240]

Based in Augusta, CANMP "embraces immigrants as New
Mainers who bring much-needed diversity, energy, and vitality to
our area." It was the 2017 Irving J. Fain Award recipient from the
Commission on Social Action of Reform Judaism. It is another of
these 501(c)(3) tax-exempt "charitable organizations."

It is backed by the United Way of Kennebec Valley, one of the most
active organizations in attempting to transform idyllic Maine into a
disaster. Once again we find many of the usual suspects providing
financial support: TD Bank, 3M, Bank of America, Garmin, AT&T,
Allstate, Eli Lilly, Bowdoin College, Bernstein Shur, FedEx, ConAgra
Foods, TJ Maxx, Verrill Dana, Walmart, Sam's Club, Key Bank,
Unum, UPS, the University of Maine, IDEXX, General Electric, and
Target. The United Way of Mid-Maine is partnered with—wouldn't
you know it!—Catholic Charities, the Jewish Alfond family, and the
University of Maine.

The United Way of Androscoggin County? That would be Catholic
Charities, Bates College, and Pine Tree Legal Assistance (PTLA).
Almost its entire board and staff is from the banking and investment
sectors. The United Way of Greater Portland works with Catholic
Charities, ILAP, LearningWorks, MaineHealth, the Opportunity
Alliance, IDEXX, LL Bean, Unum, the John T. Gorman Foundation,
Texas Instruments, Verrill Dana, Sappi, Bank of America, ON
Semiconductor, Bernstein Shur, UPS, Drummond Woodsum, and
the University of Southern Maine.

The following organizations have representatives on their
Board of Directors: Verrill Dana, Portland Public Schools (Xavier

---

240 Asch, Chris Myers, "Community Compass: Stand with us for a different
America," November 1, 2018. *Central Maine.*

Botana), Unum, the John T. Gorman Foundation, Bernstein Shur, MaineHealth, Lincoln Financial, Portland Regional Chamber of Commerce, TD Bank, LL Bean, IDEXX, American Roots Wear, and the University of Southern Maine. The Jewish Community Alliance (JCA) works closely with the University of Southern Maine. The Harvey and Jeanette Weinberg Foundation is another major donor to the United Way, as are a number of other Jewish groups. Again and again you'll find Jewish fingerprints all over the push to import as many people into Maine as possible:

- "Young Rwandan Finds a New Start in South Portland," by Rachel Nusbaum of HIAS, April 13th, 2016 (Note: HIAS sells t-shirts emblazoned with the phrase "My People Were Refugees Too"): "'When I came to this country, I knew there was a way for me to stay legally but I didn't know where to start. I didn't know who to talk to, until I met this lady at church who put me in touch with HIAS.' Wettenhall helped [Yves] apply for asylum—the legal protection Yves was seeking but didn't quite know how to obtain, or even name, back then. It was Wettenhall who prepared Yves for the process, including filing his application and representing him before the Department of Homeland Security Asylum Offices. Yves' application was then referred to the Immigration Court, where he had to wait for two years for a hearing. During that time, Wettenhall continued working to strengthen the case."[241]

- "40 years later, Vietnamese refugees thank Bangor's Jewish community for saving them," by Judy Harrison of the *Bangor Daily News*, June 13th, 2019: "Bangor's Jewish community had welcomed displaced Jews for decades when in the late 1970s its members were asked by the Hebrew Immigrant Aid Society (HIAS) to help a family fleeing Vietnam. The Do family of five arrived in Bangor on a freezing winter day in February or March of 1979 and were met by Bill Miller, then-owner of Miller Drug, and other members of the city's Conservative and Orthodox synagogues. 'HIAS sent us a catalogue,' he said."[242]

---

241 Nusbaum, Rachel, "Young Rwandan Finds a New Start in South Portland," April 13, 2016. HIAS.
242 Harrison, Judy, "40 years later, Vietnamese refugees thank Bangor's Jewish

- "US Jews on Trump's camps: 'Never Again,'" by Hana Sarfan, August 7th, 2019, *The Progressive*: "In the summer of 2015, following my junior year of college, Donald Trump kicked off his candidacy by referring to Mexican immigrants as 'criminals' and 'rapists.' I was filled with dread. Each subsequent bigoted claim…sounded to me like an alarm bell. As the granddaughter of Holocaust survivors, I feel there is something eerily familiar about Trump's scapegoating and dehumanizing rhetoric, which has led to racist policies like the Muslim ban, a dramatic escalation of immigration raids and detention, and the incarceration of children in internment camps…All of this has prompted thousands of Jews across the country, myself included, to join a protest movement called Never Again Action, which is working in partnership with the immigrant-led Movimiento Cosecha. The group is demanding that politicians close the camps, shut down ICE (Immigration Customs and Enforcement), and end raids and deportations. On July 18, more than 1,000 Never Again demonstrators in Washington, D.C., sent ICE headquarters into "lockdown condition," according to a leaked ICE email… Prior to Trump's election, the immigration system was already causing devastating harm to immigrant communities. Since then, human rights abuses by ICE and U.S. Customs and Border Protection have escalated dramatically…Finally, will they wonder what's to stop it from happening again? As a Jewish American, I want my answer to be: us."[243]

- In late 2015, over 1,250 rabbis signed a letter to Congress urging "our elected officials to exercise moral leadership for the protection of the US Refugee Admissions Program," citing the decision to send one ship of Jewish refugees back to Europe in 1939 as reflective of a "climate of fear" and "anti-Semitism" and a mistake we never want to make again. This exercise was repeated in 2019 with over 1,500 rabbi signatures.

America's wide-open borders and the efforts to transform Maine into a cosmopolitan GDP utopia find the same bedfellows entangled

community for saving them," June 13, 2019. WGME.
243 Sarfan, Hana, "US Jews on Trump's camps: 'Never again,'" August 7, 2019. *The Progressive*.

under the covers. In response to Donald Trump's so-called "Muslim Ban" in 2017:

> Jeffery Young, a civil rights attorney, said that as a Jew, he sees Trump's actions as "eerily similar" to actions taken during the Holocaust. At that time, he said, a fear that Nazi spies would infiltrate the U.S. prompted America to heighten security, tighten visa requirements and ramp up screening. As a result, millions of Jews were killed. "When I heard of the president's order, I was reminded of my own ancestors," Young said. "We can't let him do it. We are all immigrants. We are all Muslims. We are all Jews. We are all Americans." Leslie Silverstein, president of the board of directors of the Portland-based Immigrant Legal Advocacy Project, which provides free legal services to immigrants, sought to reassure the immigrant community.[244]

In response to the travel ban, the Maine ACLU issued a statement of open borders pablum co-signed by a number of by now familiar individuals and organizations, including: the Jewish Community Alliance (JCA) of Southern Maine, Congregation Bet Ha'am, Immigrant Legal Advocacy Project (ILAP), former Portland Mayor Ethan Strimling, Immigrant Resource Center of Maine, Planned Parenthood, Welcoming the Stranger, the NAACP, Maine People's Alliance, Maine Women's Lobby, New Mainers Resource Center, Hand in Hand (Mano en Mano), and Maine Equal Justice Partners (MEJP). MEJP's Board of Directors includes representatives of Catholic Charities, Bernstein Shur, TRIO, Verrill Dana LLP, and the Opportunity Alliance. MEJP provides extensive resources to immigrants, refugees, and asylum-seekers, including specific information on how exactly to obtain a panoply of benefits, the kind many struggling Mainers could use, but their well-being is obviously not a priority.

Bernstein Shur, founded by Jewish immigrant Israel Bernstein, provides representation and counsel to a variety of industries,

---

244 Billings, Randy, "Protestors say 'immigrants are welcome here,' as 1,500 rally in Portland to oppose Trump's order," February 1, 2017. *Portland Press Herald.*

including finance, business, real estate, political campaigns, and human resources. Bernstein Shur represented Doctors without Borders nurse Kaci Hickox in her lawsuit when she decided to sue after being held in a state-mandated quarantine when she returned from volunteering to help treat a massive Ebola outbreak in Sierra Leone in 2014. Many Bernstein Shur lawyers also assist with Silverstein's ILAP. The Opportunity Alliance's immigration advocacy is overseen by a Board of Directors staffed almost exclusively by men and women from the worlds of business, finance, law, and real estate. This is neo-liberalism at its finest.

Another Jewish pro-immigration group is the National Council of Jewish Women (NCJW)-Southern Maine Section, which describes itself as "a grassroots organization of volunteers and advocates who turn progressive ideals into action.

Inspired by Jewish values, NCJW strives for social justice by improving the quality of life for women, children, and families and by safeguarding individual rights and freedoms" and "has advocated for immigrants for more than a century," including large numbers of their co-ethno-religionists from Eastern Europe.

They have worked to bring more Sudanese into Maine through the Darfur Project, and have donated ample resources to various immigration advocacy groups as well as to the facilitation of increasing outside immigration into the state. They have also been very active in promoting transgenderism, but that is a topic for another book.

Historically, NCJW has worked on the creation of an interest-free loan fund for other Jews, endorsed legislation for birth control, started the Jewish Refugee Fund, protested the British White Paper restricting Jewish immigration to Palestine and supported the foundation of the State of Israel, advocated for an increase in Jewish "refugees" from Germany around World War II and from the Soviet Union starting in the 1970s, worked with the Maine Civil Liberties Union and the Maine Women's Lobby, took an "active interest in women's issues, civil rights, and Israel," and joined with Temple Beth El for feminist seder. Linda Rogoff, Bobbi Gordan, and Portland-born artist Jo Israelson of the NCJW recently hosted an event that chronicled the organization's work dating back to House Island in the 1920s. Israelson spoke about her multi-media piece "Welcoming the Stranger": "Israelson contrasted the 1923 odyssey of Hungarian immigrant, Bela Gross, with the stories of those newly-arrived in Portland today."

On Thursday, October 12th, 2018, NCJW Southern Maine Section partnered with the University of Southern Maine's Jean Byers Sampson Center for Diversity to host a panel and community discussion about NCJW's history "serving Maine's immigrant populations from the early 1900's through today." The NCJW has a very close connection with the University of Southern Maine.

The majority of the NCJW membership was born and educated outside the state, and they have actively worked to change their new environs to suit their particular goals, particularly in terms of demographics and social policy. On January 8th, 2017, at the Temple Beth El the NCJW held the Equal Justice Forum, featuring presentations on how tikkun olam is vital for "social change" and the importance of "reproductive rights," plus:

> Susan Roche, Executive Director, Immigrant Legal Advocacy Project, outlined ILAP's work with 2,000 clients a year who are new to Maine. Volunteer attorneys help people meet legal residency requirements, and usher their asylum requests through the thicket of the courts. Her biggest concern is expedited deportation if the new administration adopts more aggressive enforcement policies…Zachary Heiden, Legal Director, ACLU of Maine, brought some levity to the event by referencing an optimistic song from the musical "Hamilton." He also took comfort in Martin Luther King Jr.'s observation that: "The arc of the moral universe is long, but it bends towards justice."[245]

Maine Equal Justice Partners were also represented. Temple Beth El sponsors many events and programs advancing the causes of LGBTQ and supporting refugees, asylees, and immigrants to obtain social and economic resources, as well as publicizing the kinds of rose-colored portrayals of migrants to the public we have become so accustomed to

---

245 "Record Turnout for NCJW Equal Justice Forum," National Council of Jewish Women-Southern Maine Section.

Transformation Wholesale

seeing. The president of the Jewish Community Alliance of Southern Maine Bette Novick is a member. The Jewish Community Alliance (JCA) of Southern Maine is the local representative of the Jewish Federations of North America (JFNA); it allocates over $100,000 every year to causes related to "fighting antisemitism and bias and supporting refugees," including donations to the Maine Jewish Film Festival and the Hebrew Immigrant Aid Society (HIAS). The JCA, along with the Michael Klahr Jewish Family Services, was at the forefront of the most recent African migrant influx into Portland with funding, advocacy, press releases, and other donations—as well as the ubiquitous invocation of the Shoah:

> Displacement and migration are central elements of the story of the Jewish people, from antiquity through the modern era.
>
> Whether we draw upon the experience of the Israelites who were "strangers in the land of Egypt" or those who fled the horrors of the Shoah, an ethical and religious commitment to support and welcome immigrants, refugees and asylum seekers is fundamental for many Jews today. With the news last week of record numbers of asylum seekers arriving in Portland, our community sprang into action. We are proud to be a part of a strong network of service providers, including synagogues, that have prioritized this work for many years.[246]

In what possible way do the Holocaust or slavery in Egypt millennia ago have any bearing on bringing Africans into Portland, Maine today? This is preposterous. The JCA might be on to something with Africans, Jews, and eugenics, though, but certainly not the way they're trying to manipulate the public into thinking. As Steve Sailer informs:

> Between 1984 and 1991, Israel achieved a public-relations coup by importing tens of thousands of Ethiopians who claimed to be Jews. Over the last decade, however, Israel has been taking direct action to

---

246 Rowles, Molly Curren, "Refugee and Asylum Seeker Support," 2017. Jewish Community Alliance of Southern Maine.

287

limit its black citizens' fertility...Also unsurprisingly, the Ethiopians have proved increasingly less popular with their Israeli neighbors, who have come to view them and their children as backward and crime-prone. Whether that is due to white Israelis' racism or to the blacks' shortcomings is a matter of dispute... Most interestingly, since 2008 there has been evidence of a widespread resolve within Israeli society to drive down the fertility of its Ethiopian minority through forcefully persuading poorly educated black women into accepting injections of the Depo-Provera contraceptive...In Israel, Ethiopian women have said on camera that Israeli immigration officials told them that they wouldn't be allowed into the country without taking Depo-Provera shots. They claim to have been subsequently browbeaten into staying on the contraceptive. One study found that Ethiopian women account for 57 percent of all Israel's Depo-Provera prescriptions... In contrast to Israelis, who obsess over demographics, Americans are never allowed to think about how proposed policies such as amnesty and guest workers will impact fertility, even though the current interpretation of the 14th Amendment grants instant citizenship to any child born in the US.[247]

Back in Maine, along with the United Way, the JCA was instrumental in propagandizing Ethan Strimling's reckless call for migrants—supplied by Catholic Charities—and seizing the opportunity to use these hapless migrants as both sword and shield. The JCA has also worked with the Maine Association for New Americans (MANA) on "Hope Acts programs including asylum seeker housing, English classes, and individualized support." In 2012, Michael Bloomberg's Partnership for a New American Economy (NAE) paired up with MANA, which:

Has been active not only in combatting anti-Muslim and anti-Islam sentiment but also in working to overcome stereotypes and racial discrimination

---

247 Sailer, Steve, "Israel's Fertility Policy Bears Fruit," January 30, 2013. *Taki's Mag.*

leading to underemployment for (primarily Black) immigrants. Currently, many Black (African) immigrants—despite high-level career experience and English skills—are being placed in cleaning and other manual jobs once they arrive in Maine. MANA has presented employers and other stakeholders with compelling data that contradicts the concept of immigrants as natural-born "service recipients." Rather, we turn this idea on its head by, among other things: pointing out the latent talent and economic power of these (primarily African) immigrants; showing how harnessing and growing this talent can effectively close Maine's workforce gaps, and linking the barriers we see in Maine to cultural nativism, implicit bias (See Implicit.Harvard.edu) and national research on racial bias in hiring. In Spring 2016, MANA leaders took the initiative to lead a statewide "Welcoming Committee," bringing together immigrant leaders with the Maine State Chamber, Maine Development Foundation, CEI, and corporate partners such as Jackson Labs, that is now working with Welcoming America and the Partnership for a New American Economy to build momentum in Maine towards a "Welcoming Maine" initiative... MANA joined the New Mainers' Alliance/New Mainers PAC to ensure that immigrant communities have a voice within civic, non-profit, philanthropic, and government organizations serving immigrants...In Winter/Spring 2019, MANA brought together the elected leaders of Maine' Immigrant Community Associations in a series of meetings to develop a shared Immigrant Leader Vision Board to plan for next steps to advance immigrant success in Maine...We also highlight the success of best practices, such as Welcoming Cleveland and St. Louis Mosaic that have countered this trend and brought economic growth through inclusion.[248]

MANA's Board is comprised of seven Africans, a representative of the Greater Portland Chamber of Commerce, and a Japanese

---

248 "Mission Statement," MANA-Maine, 2019.

"international marketer and diversity coach." It appears to be a "shield" organization. Hope Acts is run by Jewish Executive Director Martha Stein, previously Director of Communications for Maine Equal Justice Partners, Development Director for Tedford Housing, and Development Director for the Maine Council of Churches. Stein also held various management positions at AT&T and Prudential. Vice President of the JCA, Rachael Weinstein Alfond, has made campaign contributions to Representative Jared Golden, and is married to former Democratic State Senator and real estate developer Justin Alfond of the wealthy Jewish Alfond family, who voted against a Penalties for Violent Offenses Against Fetuses bill and sponsored a bill in 2009 which would have allowed non-citizens to vote in local elections state-wide and another to amnesty illegal aliens.

The World Affairs Council of Maine, located on the University of Southern Maine's Portland campus, seeks to educate students to become "global citizens" and have held symposia "problematizing" nationalism, advocating for free trade and the movement of refugees and other migrants into the West, "liberal democracy" for Eastern Europe, climate change, and "women's issues." They are partnered with Verrill Dana, Bernstein Shur, HeadInvest, Maine North Atlantic Development Office, Maine International Trade Center, Unum, Global Ties USA, the World Affairs Councils of America, and the Council on International Educational Exchange (CIEE).

Another representative organization is Maine Initiatives, part of MaineShare, a 501(c)(3) partnered with the Maine People's Alliance, Fair Immigration Reform Movement (FIRM), Center for Community Change (CCC), and National Partnership for New Americans (NPNA), which seeks to "end family separation, build resistance and a unified front, and protect and defend Maine's immigrants and their families" from Trump. Their cohort all have a similar mission and are all part of this vast matrix of organizations dedicated to mass immigration. Maine Initiatives has dispensed over $3.5 million-worth of grants in the last twenty-five years to organizations including:

- Mano en Mano
- Choose Yourself ("a young immigrant-women led organization")
- Indigo Arts Alliance

- The Harriet Tubman Movement Coalition (their mission "is to provide Black Indigenous Women of Color (BIWOC) in Maine sustainable pathways to heal from the soul wounds of racialized trauma and to cultivate their leadership as critically valued stakeholders within their relations and communities"—I didn't know Maine had "black indigenous women of color," certainly they are not indigenous to Maine; I'm reminded here of the liberal contradictions of "everyone's an immigrant" and an insistence on certain groups' indigenousness, such as the Aborigines or the "Native Americans," but not Europeans, who've been on the continent for tens of thousands of years and who *must* learn to become multi-cultural, pace Barbara Lerner Spectre of Paideia, the European Institute for Jewish Studies in Sweden)
- Resources for Organizing and Social Change
- The Third Place (which provides "sustainable community and economic growth within institutions led by and serving Maine's African-American community")
- The Abyssinian Meeting House (which has coordinated with TRIO in the past)
- Maine Community Integration ("MCI helps to support the integration of African immigrants into American society while respecting the integrity of diverse cultural values, identities, traditions and ways")
- CANMP
- League of Women Voters of Maine
- Maine Access Immigrant Network (MAIN)
- New Mainers Public Health Initiative
- Sustainable Livelihoods Relief Organization (which "aims to develop the capacity of New Mainers to become productive members of society and integrate successfully into the labor market as both employees and business owners")
- Kesho Washo
- Black Artists Forum
- Operation Breaking Stereotypes
- Maine Prisoner Advocacy Coalition
- In Her Presence ("organized and led by immigrant women living in Maine")
- Martin Luther King Jr. Fellows

- Tree Street Youth
- Somali Bantu Mutual Assistance Association of Lewiston/Auburn
- Maine Immigrants' Rights Coalition (MIRC)

Board President of Maine Initiatives is the Jewish Suzy Sonenberg and the Jewish "community organizer" Charlie Bernstein recently served as Executive Director. The Jewish Communal Fund, managing an obscene $2 billion in so-called charitable assets, is another financier of organizations active in undermining the way life should be, such as the Jewish Federation of Portland, the NAACP, the National Immigration Forum, Media Matters, HIAS (which has sponsored films at the Maine Jewish Film Festival), CJP-Boston, the American Jewish Committee, and the ADL, as well as Bates College.

Maine's community college system is also corrupted, and works in tandem with a host of groups and organizations to push the immigration agenda in various forms, such as SMCC's new ESOL to EMT course, which is "training new Mainers to become trained EMTs…this *New York Times* article says the course is not only helping the students achieve their personal career goals, it's also helping Maine address its shortage of EMTs."

The *Times* article in question is by Katherine Q. Seelye entitled, "Lacking EMTs, an Aging Maine Turns to Immigrants," on March 27th, 2017. This program and the attendant propaganda is little surprise given the community college system's major sources of their funding: the Jewish Alfond family, Key Bank, the John T. Gorman Foundation, S. Donald Sussman, Bernstein Shur, the Sam L. Cohen Foundation, Unum, TD Bank, Verrill Dana, Nancy Cohen, Elaine Rosen, Pratt & Whitney, LL Bean, IDEXX, Bank of America, Walmart, Shimon Cohen and Rosa Galva de Cohen, the Elmina B. Sewall Foundation, and the Poland Spring Division of Nestlé Waters North America.

At the four-year university level, Colby College is one of the state's premier liberal arts schools. Colby's Maine Jewish History Project, which "promotes sustained Jewish studies programming in small to mid-sized communities" and multi-cultural advocacy derives its funding primarily from Legacy Heritage Fund, Ltd., run by the Jewish Susan Wexner, sister of Les Wexner. Legacy Heritage Fund's CPO, Ari Rudolph, has previously been on the Board of Directors of

HIAS, and has worked for the Jewish Community Relations Council and the Israel Ministry of Foreign Affairs in the Department for Combating Antisemitism.

The Legacy Heritage Fund is a Jewish organization with an endowment of $25 million and has given substantial funding to numerous projects such as the David Project based out of Newtonville, Massachusetts for "educational programming relating to the state of Israel on college campuses." The Legacy Heritage Fund's Board mostly hails from the legal and financial sectors of the economy.

Colby College's Center for Small Town Jewish Life National Advisory Board includes Ellie Miller: board member of the Sam L. Cohen Foundation, former president of Temple Beth El, and, until the fall of 2017, Executive Director of the Jewish Community Alliance of Southern Maine. She also served for 28 years as Assistant Director of Pine Tree Legal Assistance. The Board also includes David Pulver, President of Cornerstone Capital, Inc.

With funding from Berman & Simmons and partnered with the University of Maine Law School, Pine Tree Legal Assistance (PTLA), Maine Equal Justice Partners (MEJP), and the Immigrant Legal Advocacy Project (ILAP— ILAP's Board President Leslie Silverstein spoke at the progressive-minded Day of Hope in 2017 along with Eliot Cutler and Ethan Strimling), the Maine Justice Foundation counts among its bar members Joe Bornstein, Howard H. Dana of Verrill Dana, Kenneth W. Lehman of Bernstein Shur, James I. Cohen, and State Senator Roger Katz. William Harwood of Verrill Dana, LLP is its president, and its mission is identical to those of the aforementioned individuals and institutions. Immigration law is big business and we see many of the big players getting involved in the "activism" side for this very reason.

Potential employers also understand the benefits of the current system. The New Mainers Resource Center (NMRC) in Portland facilitates potential employers' access to migrant labor under, naturally, the guise of humanitarianism and "diversity." The New Mainers Resource Center (NMRC) was created in 2013 by the Maine State Legislature to "develop and execute a strategy to integrate and better utilize the skills of foreign trained immigrants living in Maine." Established as a pilot project at Portland Adult Education (PAE), NMRC's mission is to "support Maine's economic development by meeting employers' demands for a skilled and culturally diverse workforce."

Greater Portland has around 20,000 refugees (double the number of just six years ago) and immigrants from 82 different countries. Portland, mind you, is by far Maine's largest city with just 67,000 people, so this is a huge percentage of migrants we are talking about. NMRC helps expedite asylum applications to get these people into the workforce. Partner organizations include: the City of Portland, Coastal Enterprises, Inc. (CEI), Catholic Charities, Bernstein Shur, New Mainers Fund, Bank of America, the John T. Gorman Foundation, the People of Color Fund, Key Bank, MaineHealth, Barber Foods, Welcoming Immigrants Network, Diversity Hiring Coalition, LearningWorks, H&R Block, Maine Immigrants' Rights Coalition (MIRC), Asylum Seekers Working Group, Francis Hotel, Bowdoin College, Residence Inn Marriott, Taco Bell, Pratt Abbott, Tyco, and ON Semiconductor.

In a nine-month stretch from September 2017 to June 2018, Portland Adult Education had 2,269 migrants, asylum seekers, and the like enrolled in their programs, most of whom were from sub-Saharan Africa or Iraq.

All of that said, a huge percentage of these people do not actually work; in 2009, for example, the national refugee employment rate was between 31.3%-47.1%, depending on the survey. The employment rate for those from the Middle East was 29.1% and from Africa 38.3%, which, along with Haiti and Jamaica, is predominantly where Maine has been sourcing its would-be scab labor from for the past fifteen years. Somali unemployment in Lewiston has consistently hovered around 50% since they started arriving.

Nevertheless, at a recent symposium held at the University of Southern Maine (USM), "Economic Necessity: Workforce Development and Immigrant Integration," the "necessity" of "internationalizing" Portland was echoed by a variety of figures from Ethan Strimling to the Jewish Portland City Council member and Economic Development Committee Chair David Brenerman to David Zahn of Southern Maine Community College (SMCC) who:

> Connected the college with various committees in the Portland metro area (Catholic Charities, One Westbrook,

Maine Immigrant Rights Coalition, etc.). David was instrumental in initiating working relationships with numerous community partners allowing for innovative workforce training initiatives to develop between the college and other entities in the greater Portland, Maine region.

Also present were included: the President of the University of Southern Maine (USM); Xavier Botana, the Superintendent of Portland Public Schools; Quincy Hentzel of the Portland Regional Chamber of Commerce; representatives of SIGCO and IDEXX; and representatives of other NAE-affiliated cities Dayton, Ohio; Louisville, Kentucky; and Aurora, Colorado.

As part of Portland's initial investigation into establishing an Office of Economic Opportunity and Immigrant Integration and/ or an Office of New Mainers, Brenerman's Economic Development Committee concluded that a "broad-based collaborative" must:

> Rebrand Portland as a multicultural, international city… celebrating the mosaic of ethnicities and nationalities here…strengthen Portland's image as multicultural and international…Maine International Trade Center… re-engineer the work force pipeline…[expand] USM (and SMCC?) role with training ESL teachers… support including microfinancing (Opportunity Alliance, Living with Peace, CEI, Community Financial Literacy, Portland Development Corporation, SBA) and proactively connect to employers' needs (Diversity Hiring Coalition)…Ensure optimal coordination of the many service providers.

Tae Chong of CEI and Catholic Charities "wants to see Portland rebranded as an international city, well-poised to compete for human capital [and] supports an Office of Globalization" and recommends "an Office of New Americans to attract and integrate foreign-born populations. One option is to place the office within the Department of Labor so that immigrant integration is aligned with the state's labor and economic development strategies." CEI is:

A [Community Development Finance Institution (CDFI) and] mission-driven lender and investor…and acts as a labor intermediary to help low-income job seekers access employment. The organization also undertakes research and policy development to expand impact… CEI's StartSmartProgram, which began in 1997, provides business assistance and financing to immigrants. More recently in 2014, CEI has coordinated the Portland Jobs Alliance, a City of Portland Community Development Block Grant and John T. Gorman Foundation-funded partnership of service providers who are working to prepare 200 immigrants and other low to moderate-income job seekers for employment in growing Portland businesses over a two-year period.[249]

In a 2016 CEI paper entitled, "Building Maine's Economy: How Maine Can Embrace Immigrants and Strengthen the Workforce," authors Carla Dickstein, John Dorrer, Elizabeth Love, and Tae Chong conclude that, among other factors, racism and discrimination (naturally) present barriers to the exalted "people of color."

Nevertheless, the authors and CEI conclude:

The urgency of Maine's demographics and tightening labor market require immediate action to proactively attract, support, and retain immigrants…Maine's demographic projections and labor force shortages are long-term challenges that require a strategy to develop Maine's human capital over the long run. This includes making sure that immigrant children receive the training and skills to become productive workers… Because immigrants tend to have higher birth rates than native-born residents, they can be a dynamic component of the state's labor force well into the future…Immigrants can also grow Maine's economy through tax-base expansion, increased demand for goods, and business creation.[250]

---

249 Dickstein, Carla, John Dorrer, Elizabeth Love, and Tae Chong, "Building Maine's Economy: How Maine Can Embrace Immigrants and Strengthen the Workforce," 2016. Coastal Enterprises Inc.
250 Ibid.

The paper's lead author Dickstein has made at least eight separate donations to Democratic political candidates as recently as 2018. She also sits on the Research Advisory Board to the Community Affairs Department at the Federal Reserve Bank of Boston. The authors consulted and relied on subjective data from Dr. Paula Gerstenblatt, a "Jewish mother of two black children," from the University of Southern Maine.

Primary funding for their paper was obtained from the Emanuel and Pauline Lerner Foundation, of which Eliot Cutler is president, and the Broad Reach Foundation. Andrea Perry of Broad Reach is a former member of the Maine Philanthropy Center Board of Directors and Erin Cinelli of the Lerner Foundation is its current Chair. Also on the Board are Ian Yaffe of Mano en Mano, Megan Shore of the Elmina B. Sewall Foundation, Ainsley Wallace of the University of Southern Maine Foundation, Joleen Bedard of the United Way of Androscoggin County, Ruta Kadonoff of Maine Health Access Foundation ("Ruta, her husband and their cats re-located from the Washington D.C. suburbs to Belfast, Maine in 2016"), and John Shoos, Executive Director of the Sam L. Cohen Foundation, among others.

The Sam L. Cohen Foundation—committed to "philanthropy, Tzedakah for Tikum Olam, and Jewish culture and traditions"—has an endowment of over $32 million and an annual income of almost $3 million. The Sam L. Cohen Foundation's Board of Directors includes: Co-Director Elinor Miller, Director Treasurer Edward K. Simensky, Director President Jeffery A. Nathanson, Director Chair Jerome F. Goldberg, Chair and Executive Director John Shoos, Co-Director Kenneth Spirer, and Director Secretary Sherry P. Broder.

In addition to the Sam L. Cohen Foundation's deep involvement in the Jewish community, it also "provid[es] support to historically and systematically disadvantaged individuals and communities" and is a primary financier of the Immigrant and Refugee Funders Group.

Other organizations that have been the recipients of the Foundation's largesse include: Catholic Charities of Maine, African Women Development, the Congregation Etz Chaim, the ACLU of Maine (which provides form letters on their website to protest any bills introduced that might interrupt their project in any way, such as Rep. Lockman of Amherst's LD 1833, "An Act to Facilitate Compliance with Federal Immigration Law by State and Local Government Entities"—the reader will recall the *Maine Beacon's* denunciation of Lockman, Isgro, Kawczynski's "white supremacy" for asking that ICE be allowed to do their jobs), Documenting Maine Jewry, Maine Family Planning Abortion Aid, Planned Parenthood, Greater Portland Workforce Initiative, Equality Maine, the Greater Portland Immigrant Welcome Center, Jewish Community Alliance of Southern Maine, Immigrant Legal Advocacy Project, Maine Equal Justice Partners, the Maine Jewish Museum, Maine Jewish Film Festival, Maine Access Immigrant Network (MAIN), New Mainers' Tenants Association, Shalom House, the Maine Center for Economic Policy (their mission: "We need to ensure that the benefits of immigration are available to all parts of the state"), the University of Southern Maine, and the University of Maine School of Law.

The University of Maine School of Law, which received $125,000 from the Sam L. Cohen Foundation in 2018 and $500,000 in 2017, in turn uses its infusion of cash to sponsor events such as the Justice for Women Lecture Series in conjunction with the Maine Jewish Film Festival and Empower the Immigrant Women, as well as the Maine Immigrants' Rights Coalition (MIRC) and several of the state's private colleges.

The lecture series engages in naked political advocacy as well as endeavors to:

> Raise awareness about issues of justice for women and girls in Maine including:
> - the importance of welcoming New Mainers into our communities, our schools, and our homes
> - the impact of federal policies on our lives in Maine
> - the blight that is food insecurity among Maine's children
> - the need for respect for Mainers of all religions and cultures
> - the rights of women and girls within the Muslim religion
> - ONE GLOBAL VOICE.

This one global voice cries out for cheap consumer products and access to white countries. Any barrier to their entry is highly problematic, as Dickstein, et al. explicate in their CEI paper, because it presents a major obstacle to neo-liberalism's utopia/GDP farm:

In this 95% white state, "implicit," and even explicit, bias exists and creates barriers to cultivating and embracing increased diversity. Affirmatively addressing racism and discrimination at the workplace, in schools, and in society as a whole will be an important part of any Maine effort to attract, integrate, and retain immigrants from around the world.

Maine's approach will ultimately define its competitive advantage (or disadvantage) in the U.S. and global economy. The purpose of this study is to understand how Maine can better use the human capital that immigrants— one category of a diverse, multicultural population—bring to the state. Immigrants are one of a number of groups of unemployed or underemployed Mainers who could contribute more to their communities if given an opportunity to work at their full potential.[251]

No evidence of bias of any kind is provided, as we have come to expect. It should also be mentioned that affiliated with this particular paper were the University of Southern Maine, SIGCO (40% of whose labor force is comprised of immigrants), Bates College, IDEXX, Portland Refugee Services, Catholic Charities, and Portland Adult Education and New Mainers Resource Center.

CEI's Dickstein, it should be noted, is also on the Advisory Council of the Frances Perkins Center for social justice, outreach, and advocacy, along with such figures as Jewish registered Democrat and former University of Southern Maine Women and Gender Studies and Economics Professor Susan Feiner, Jewish former Secretary of Labor and UC Berkeley Professor Robert Reich, and Jewish Executive Director of Family Values @ Work Ellen Bravo; Jews Charles M. Wyzanski and Judith Goldstein are on the Board of Directors. CEI's Board includes: Glenn Cummings, the President of the University of Southern Maine; John Dorrer, one of the paper's co-authors (no conflict of interest there); Ian Yaffe, Executive Director of Mano en Mano; Beth Mattingly, of the Federal Reserve Bank of Boston; and other representatives from various private equity firms, construction companies, farms, and universities.

---

251 Ibid.

Beth Stickney, director of the Maine Business Immigration Coalition, was also consulted for the paper, and is of the view that should immigrants or refugees not be welcomed or offered financial assistance in Maine, this shortsighted and counterproductive decision would harm a state facing an aging population and workforce shortage. But you knew that already.

CEI also partners with the Maine Development Foundation (MDF), consisting of elected board members primarily from the worlds of real estate, business, and finance, and which reliably produces "more GDP"-oriented policy suggestions that inevitably recommend more immigration because of Maine's age, whiteness, *ad infinitum*. Their partners are all the usual suspects and more; in addition to CEI, we see: Sam L. Cohen Foundation, the Scarborough Economic Development Corporation, the Maine Restaurant Association, the John T. Gorman Foundation, the Elmina B. Sewell Foundation, the Appalachian Mountain Club, York County Community College, Androscoggin Bank, Bath Iron Works, the Alfond Scholarship Foundation, City of Bangor, the University of Maine system, Maine Treasurer of State, Maine Municipal Bank, Maine State Housing Authority, Maine Department of Transportation, Town of Windham, City of Westbrook, the Wild Blueberry Commission of Maine, Finance Authority of Maine, Maine Department of Health & Human Services, University of Maine Alumni Association, Unity College, University of Southern Maine, WCSH 6/WBLZ 2 (local television), TD Bank, Thomas College, Maine Department of Professional and Financial Regulation, Maine Department of Labor, the US Small Business Association, the United Way, United Insurance, Southern Maine Community College, Systems Engineering, American Red Cross-Maine Region, Anthem Blue Cross and Blue Shield, Bank of America, Bowdoin College, City of Brewer, Town of Bridgton, YMCA, a number of local Chambers of Commerce, Maine Department of Marine Resources, LL Bean, Jackson Labs, Hancock Lumber, Hannaford, Kennebec Savings Bank, Town of Houlton, Housing Initiatives of New England, Husson University, Maine Department of Inland Fisheries and Wildlife, Governor's Office of Policy and Management, Central Maine Power, CEI, Dead River Company, Epstein Properties, Pingree Associates, First National Bank, the Foundation for Maine's Community Colleges, Wright-

Ryan Construction, Maine Department of Agriculture, Conservation, and Forestry, Purdue University Global, Oasis Free Clinics, Portland Public Library, Maine Potato Board, Synergent, Sugarloaf and Sunday River Ski Resorts, St. Germain Collins, Southern Maine Medical Center, Maine Department of Education, Maine Department of Environmental Protection, Maine Department of Community and Economic Development, Mano en Mano, Poland Spring Water, and many more.

Despite the fact that immigration to Western countries today is predicated on economic exploitation and racial animus, it is the host population, seeing their opportunities and way of life evaporate before them, who must adapt, who are "hateful" and must confront the "systemic racism" of a society built by their ancestors for "themselves and their posterity"—not imported peoples from the dark recesses of the equator.

In a recent paper published by Bowdoin College in Brunswick, Maine, entitled "New Mainers' Barriers to Access Healthcare," twenty-five medical professionals were interviewed on "systemic bias and disparities" in healthcare in the state of Maine, despite the fact that, as one informant put it, "Immigrants don't prioritize wellness." Never let facts get in the way of a good narrative.

Now, something about the names of the interviewees stuck out to me: Abshiro Ali, Hassan Mahmoud, Ghassan Saleh, Tho Ngo, Asha Suldan, Nelida Burke, Dancille Nshimimana, Jovin Bayingana, Claude Rwaganje, Tarlan Ahmadov (State Refugee Coordinator for Catholic Charities of Maine), Damas Rugama, Mufalo Chitam (Executive Director of Maine Immigrants' Rights Coalition), Heritier Nosso, Hawa Abdouckader, Sana Osman, and Nadine Twagirayezu.

Of the two authors, one, Darlene Ineza, is from Rwanda, and the other, Kathleen Fairfield, supervises a clinic that works with Catholic Charities to bring refugees into Portland. I cannot imagine what their bias might be. Naturally, according to the authors:

> A perception of scarcity and isolationary beliefs sometimes lead to an environment of xenophobia. Multiple informants shared stories of implicit bias, stereotyping and prejudice by health care providers and community members towards New Mainers. This is

particularly heightened for Muslim immigrants in the current political environment. The instances of violence in Lewiston's Kennedy Park this summer are one example of this (note: in a bit of Orwellian flair here, the authors have seen fit to re-cast the dynamic of violent interactions in Lewiston, as Kennedy Park's violence is almost exclusively perpetrated by Somalis, not whites)... By recognizing the power of societal structures in their own lives, and working on individual bias and stereotypes, then a medical provider can become more attuned and empathetic to a patient from a whole other culture and upbringing.[252]

The conclusions are illustrative as a case-in-point; their acceptance of the premise as axiomatic and providing evidence that relies on this assumption as proof—without first proving the premise—is classic circular reasoning. Most of what passes for academic study and research these days does something similar, hence why it has no validity.

If the population has been trained to think a certain way and/or has not developed critical thinking skills, most of the work is already done, and these "studies" are pushed forth as "proof" when they are not but propaganda. Peter Boghossian calls this "manufacturing their own epistemology," a phenomenon well-documented by Kevin MacDonald in *The Culture of Critique* regarding Boasian anthropology, Freudian psychoanalysis, and other "disciplines."

Similarly illustrative are two other notable names from the paper: "feminist scientist" Heather Shattuck-Heidorn, Lecturer in Studies of Women, Gender, and Sexuality at both Harvard University and the University of Southern Maine, and State Refugee Health Coordinator for the Office of Maine Refugee Resettlement ("I study how our biology is mediated and influenced by our environments - especially our social and gendered environments. I also teach women and gender studies, about feminism and science, and write about how science and society interact.") and Debra Rothenberg: Jewish Democrat, "gun control supporter, marriage equality supporter,

---

252 Ineza, Darlene and Kathleen Fairfield, "Major Barriers to Healthcare Access for New Mainers," 2018. Bowdoin College.

healthcare reform supporter, pro-choice supporter," and recipient of a tidy $90,000-plus salary. The authors of the paper even admit the political purpose of these "New Mainers":

> Right now at the Immigrant Welcome Center, the major focus has been on registering 11,000 eligible immigrants to vote in the upcoming elections. Immigrants themselves consist of a sizeable portion of Portland and Maine's voting population, and thus should be educated and sensitized on policy change so they can have a say in the overall structures shaping their lives.[253]

Interesting that they have a say "in the overall structures shaping their lives" and you don't.

Maine's "whiteness" is oft cited as a problem in these types of studies, but why, exactly, that is problematic is never explicated, beyond vague references to systemic racism, discrimination, and the like—all without concrete evidence. That institutions of higher learning such as the University of Southern Maine and Bowdoin are attached to these papers and symposia lends them a legitimacy they otherwise might not have. The "Culture of Critique" in these places is well-documented and the purposes clear—despite the cooption and even creation out of thin air of different disciplines in the academy the public generally still treats academia with a degree of deference. Using the universities for their propaganda provides an artificial intellectual heft to their arguments while at the same time using the campus as a forward operating base to inject their social engineering and importation of alien peoples into areas far beyond the usual reach of the cosmopolitan urbanite.

This goes for the importation of a "diverse" student body as well—Bowdoin, Bates, and Colby Colleges boast of their commitment to guaranteeing spots for a scant 10% of students from Maine. They also rarely hire from the communities they're actively working to transform for anything other than maintenance or other menial jobs, and even then, immigration helps keep those wages down. Pathetic.

Nevertheless, this is a good thing because old white people and GDP—and the state will pick up the tab for the large numbers of

---

253 Ibid.

imports, padding the bottom lines of the major corporations. That the economic factors that produced the conditions of an aging and/ or absent workforce in the first place are to blame is willfully ignored, and the "necessity" of importing an entirely new population to fill these jobs is a direct consequence of neo-liberal economics.

A necessity it is not, nor is it even desirable for the people of Maine, or any other state or country for that matter. Only a small few stand to gain while the rest are pitted in economic competition against each other and, so distracted with growing resentments, fail to see who has engineered the entire process in the first place.

When you import large numbers of people and inculcate a doctrine of multi-culturalism, which always leaves the host population ceding ground, the new population won't try to change their new environs at all, right? Robbie Feinberg reports in "As Asylum Seekers Relocate Outside Portland, Communities Look to Add Cultural Supports":

> Because of Portland's immigrant population, many of the city's immigrant and community groups have been able to quickly provide services, language supports and cultural brokering to support asylum seekers. But Portland City Councilor Pious Ali says other towns that have never hosted these populations will have to work hard to ensure that new families feel trusted and supported... Claude Rwaganje, executive director of ProsperityME, which provides financial literacy to immigrants, says one concern is ensuring that as families move over the next few months, they stay on top of their address changes to make sure that immigration and court documents don't get lost and jeopardize their asylum cases...Two weeks ago, about 20 asylum seekers moved into two vacant units donated by a developer in Brunswick, rent free for at least three months...A number of organizations have been pushing the town to hire someone to assist the new arrivals and work as a cultural broker. Mufalo Chitam, the executive director of the Maine Immigrant Rights Coalition, says her organization and other advocacy groups will help with that process across Maine in the months ahead. "So we're in there now, basically using

Portland as a blueprint to make sure services are provided for immigrants and asylum seekers," she says.[254]

Isn't it also interesting that a mass infusion of alien people—each more violent and with less education than the last—has led to Portland and Lewiston's public schools being among the most segregated in the nation?

Jewish College of the Atlantic adjunct professor Steve Wessler blames Lewiston's uptick in violence on the working-class whites who are being attacked, bullied, blamed, and forced into economic competition with the mass influx of aliens; while simultaneously being scapegoated, they told that they are "hateful" and need to be more "tolerant." You see how that works, right? They were never asked nor did they ever ask for their hometown to be transformed beyond all recognition, but *they* are the hateful ones.

The media apparatus is uniform in its insistence that Maine, like its neighbor New Hampshire, like the rest of America, like Canada, like the Antipodes, like Europe, is too old and white, and that its vanilla needs some swirl; that contradictory claims of enrichment and punishment for "colonialism," et cetera are never reconciled is of course incidental—good propaganda doesn't need to be logical.

The push to mainline as many non-white immigrants into America as possible is verging on a kind of hysteria, if not psychosis. To quote Bruce Thornton, cultural relativism "makes it impossible to pass judgements on dysfunctional cultures and to stand up for the unique good of one's own when it is under attack."

The host cultures of the West have been rendered at best a blank slate badly in need of enrichment and at worst evil and corrupted. Why you would bring even one person into an evil and corrupted country is beyond me, but again, we are dealing with millions of people who have been brainwashed into facilitating their own destruction.

I am reminded here of Rudyard Kipling's quote about "liberal" ideologues: "If they desire a thing, they declare it is true. If they desire it not, though that were death itself, they cry aloud, 'It has never been!'"

One of George Orwell's great insights in *1984* was that he who controls the language, who has the power to define terms and

254 Feinberg, Robbie, "As Asylum Seekers Relocate Outside Portland, Communities Look to Add Cultural Supports," July 23, 2019. *Maine Public.*

restrict or expand meaning, has the power to shape reality itself, for language is the only means we have to cogently express complex ideas. Control language, control thought, have total control. And from the "intellectuals" in academia to the media-entertainment complex to the Leviathan that is Google, the Establishment has a stranglehold on information and its dissemination, and the tools we use to convey our ideas, including the words themselves.

The media and academia are in the stranglehold of a tight-knit cabal who are hostile toward America—and its Western brethren—and want to see it destroyed for their own profit and out of animus. The demographic war being waged on the state of Maine has received nothing but glowing press and for good reason—certainly not that it has any legitimacy, but that its beneficiaries are not just protected from scrutiny but praised for their efforts to eradicate the indigenous white population from the media establishment to college campuses everywhere.

To quote Vladimir Lenin, "Among one hundred so-called Bolsheviki there is one real Bolshevik, with thirty-nine criminals and sixty fools."

Chapter Nine: Hedging Their Bets

"We all know what happens when men betray their country. But what happens when a country betrays its men?"—Revilo P. Oliver

"There are three kinds of lies: lies, damned lies, and statistics," a quote often attributed to, appropriately enough, Benjamin Disraeli. The salad days of Joe Wilson yelling, "You lie!" at Barack Obama seem so long ago, but here we are with a steady diet of more Joe Biden and Nancy Pelosi. Alas, the more things change, the more they stay the same. Or do they? Was the grass greener or was I? Certainly Emma Lazarus's sonnet wasn't a beacon for the world's wretched refuse when the West was won, and two fratricidal World Wars were still on the horizon. But the rough beast was already slouching toward Bethlehem, and by the time Donald J. Trump was clamoring to see Barack Hussein Obama's birth certificate the beast had been born and grown to adulthood.

In any case, it was a republic and we couldn't keep it; instead, hedge fund managers and plutocrats decide under what guise the neo-liberal machine will continue to operate for it is in fact all window dressing. The reasons may vary—cheap labor, ready votes, "social justice," climate change, anti-white animus, etc.—but the end result is no border and no representation, regardless of the rhetoric.

For billionaires like Michael Bloomberg and Tom Steyer, backing candidates to do their bidding apparently was not enough anymore, or maybe they felt their grip on power becoming more tenuous. Whatever the reason, the Wonderful Wizards moved to center stage for all of America to see in the Democratic Primary for the 2020 Presidential Election.

Having made a killing as a hedge fund manager, Tom Steyer set his sights on the presidency, and spent nearly $48 million of his own money in the process. He didn't need much in the way of campaign donations, but his donors do prove illustrative: Bain Capital (Co-Chair Joshua Bekenstein and CIO Jonathan Lavine are, like Steyer and Bloomberg, Jewish), Hellman & Friedman (a San Francisco-based private equity firm where Steyer was a partner, founded by two Jews—Warren Hellman, former president of Lehman Brothers and Tully Friedman, former managing director of Salomon Brothers[255]), Stanford University (where Steyer received his MBA), MRB Capital (the venture capital firm of Hellman & Friedman senior advisor Matthew R. Barger, who, like Steyer, also received his MBA from Stanford and who, like Hellman, also worked for Lehman Brothers prior to joining Hellman's firm), Pisces, Inc. (described on their LinkedIn page as "an outsourcing/offshoring company" based out of San Francisco), and Twitter.

Of particular note and showing what a ludicrous sham the whole thing is, Steyer's second-largest donor is Farallon Capital, *the very firm he founded*. Steyer also worked as a risk arbitrage trader under Robert Rubin at Goldman Sachs and in Morgan Stanley's corporate mergers and acquisitions department, in addition to Hellman & Friedman, before founding Farallon Capital, named the largest hedge fund in the world in 2005.

Speaking of Goldman Sachs and the mid-2000s, this post-crash snapshot from November 2011 sheds a whole lot of light on the events on the European side of things:

> The new European Central Bank President, Mario Draghi, the newly designated Prime Minister of Italy, Mario Monti, and the freshly appointed Greek Prime Minister Lucas Papademos are totemic figures in this carefully constructed web. Draghi was Goldman Sachs International's vice-chairman for Europe between 2002 and 2005, a position that put him in charge of the "companies and sovereign" department, which shortly before his arrival, helped Greece to disguise the real nature of its books with a swap on its sovereign debt. Monti was an international adviser to Goldman Sachs from 2005 until his nomination to lead the Italian government.

---

255 Michael Bloomberg worked for Salomon Brothers before founding Bloomberg LP.

According to the bank, his mission was to provide advice "on European business and major public policy initiatives worldwide." As such, he was a "door opener" with a brief to defend Goldman's interest in the corridors of power in Europe. The third man, Lucas Papademos, was the governor of the Greek central bank from 1994 to 2002. In this capacity, he played a role that has yet to be elucidated in the operation to mask debt on his country's books, perpetrated with assistance from Goldman Sachs. [Papademos was also Vice President of the European Central Bank from 2002-2010]. And perhaps more importantly, the current chairman of Greece's Public Debt Management Agency, Petros Christodoulos, also worked as a trader for the bank in London. Two other heavyweight members of Goldman's European network have also figured large in the euro crisis: Otmar Issing, a former member of the Bundesbank board of directors and a one-time chief economist of the European Central Bank, and Ireland's Peter Sutherland, an administrator for Goldman Sachs International, who played a behind the scenes role in the Irish bailout.[256]

The Jewish Robert Rubin is on the advisory council of The Hamilton Project, is Chairman Emeritus of the Council on Foreign Relations (CFR), and is a member of the Africa Progress Panel (APP). Rubin is a key Establishment player:

In January 1995, one year after the signing of the North American Free Trade Agreement (NAFTA) and immediately after Rubin was sworn in as Secretary of Treasury, Mexico was suffering through a financial crisis that threatened to result in it defaulting on its foreign obligations. President Bill Clinton, with the advice of Secretary Rubin and Federal Reserve Board Chairman Alan Greenspan, provided $20 billion in US loan guarantees to the Mexican government through the Exchange Stabilization Fund (ESF). In 1997 and 1998,

---

256 Roche, Marc, "Our Friends from Goldman Sachs," November 16, 2011. *Le Monde*.

Treasury Secretary Rubin, Deputy Secretary Lawrence Summers and Federal Reserve Board Chairman Alan Greenspan worked with the International Monetary Fund and others to promote U.S. policy in response to financial crises in Russian, Asian, and Latin American financial markets...

As Clinton's two-term Secretary of the Treasury, Rubin sharply opposed any regulation of collateralized debt obligations, credit default swaps and other so-called "derivative" financial instruments which— despite having already created havoc for companies such as Procter & Gamble and Gibson Greetings, and disastrous consequences in 1994 for Orange County, California with its $1.5 billion default and subsequent bankruptcy—were nevertheless becoming the chief engine of profitability for Rubin's former employer Goldman Sachs and other Wall Street firms.

Rubin sparked controversy in 2001 when he contacted an acquaintance at the U.S. Treasury Department and asked if the department could convince bond-rating agencies not to downgrade the corporate debt of Enron, a debtor of Citigroup... Journalist Robert Scheer claims that the repeal of the Glass-Steagall Act was a key factor in the 2008 financial crisis. Enacted just after the 1930s Great Depression, the Glass–Steagall Act separated commercial and investment banking...Rubin and his deputy Lawrence Summers steered through the 1999 repeal of the Glass-Steagall Act (1933)...It allowed the banks to develop and sell the mortgage-backed instruments that became a principal factor in the financial collapse. In September 2011, the UK Independent Commission on Banking released a report in which it recommended a separation of investment and retail banking to prevent a repeat of the 2008 crisis...

In December 2008, investors filed a lawsuit contending that Citigroup executives, including Rubin, sold shares at inflated prices while concealing the firm's risks.... Writer Nassim Nicholas Taleb noted that Rubin "collected more than $120 million in compensation from Citibank in the decade preceding the banking crash of 2008. When the bank, literally insolvent, was rescued by the taxpayer, he didn't write any check—he invoked uncertainty as an excuse."…

In January 2014, Secretary Rubin joined former Senator Olympia Snowe, former Education Secretary Donna Shalala, former Secretary of State George Shultz, former Housing and Urban Affairs Secretary Henry Cisneros, Gregory Page the Chair of Cargill, and Al Sommer, the Dean Emeritus of the Bloomberg School of Public Health as members of the U.S. Climate Risk Committee.[257]

We know the purposes of this emphasis on "climate change." What we are looking at is the "corporate stranglehold on democracy" that Steyer is supposedly fighting, a rich irony considering. Exemplified here is the neo-liberal establishment at work, operating with impunity, and with obvious and significant in-group preferential treatment and networking.

George Shultz, who was Co-Chair with Tom Steyer on the No to Prop. 23 campaign and was close friends with former Israeli Prime Minister Yitzhak Shamir, was honored at the opening of the Limmud FSU conference for Russian-speaking Jews in November 2017 "for never giving up on Soviet Jews" as Ronald Reagan's Secretary of State with "a leather-bound Book of Psalms from Julius Berman, president of the Claims Conference (which facilitates German government compensation to Holocaust survivors), and another on behalf of Limmund FSU."

In the face of declining support for Israel among Democrat voters, Henry Cisneros joined a number of other Democrat politicians and donors such as Kyrsten Sinema, Bob Menendez, and major party donor, Managing Director with JP Morgan Securities, and former AIPAC staffer Todd Richman in forming the group The Democratic Majority for Israel because if there's one thing America needs, it's more pro-Israel lobbying groups!

Donna Shalala is described by Jackson Richman of the *South Florida Sun Sentinel* thusly:

---

257 Wikipedia entry for Robert Rubin.

Donna Shalala, 77, is no stranger to politics or the relationship between the United States and Israel. She served as Secretary of Health and Human Services under President Bill Clinton, where she traveled to Israel and helped researchers there obtain grants from the National Institutes of Health, in addition to assisting with other initiatives inside the Jewish state. She then went into the private sector: serving as University of Miami president for 14 years and president of the Clinton Foundation for two years. Shalala, endorsed by the Jewish Democratic Council of America, defeated Maria Elvira Salazar in the midterm elections to replace the retiring Republican Rep. Ileana Ros-Lehtinen.[258]

Shalala herself states:

I've been a friend of Israel for a long time. I've been working with the universities within the health-care system for a long time. I first went to Israel to be on Mayor Teddy Kollek's Jerusalem Committee to help plan the city of Jerusalem when I was a young urbanist, a young academic, teaching at Columbia [University]. And I have honorary degrees from the Technion-Israel Institute of Technology, the University of Haifa and from Ben-Gurion University [of the Negev]... I actually worked with Israeli health officials to guarantee the Weizmann Institute [of Science] scientists the opportunity to apply for NIH grants among other things. I worked with women leaders in Israel on health-care issues. I went in and out of Israel four times when I was secretary... Most recently, the University of Miami has helped develop the cancer centers in Israel. Our faculty worked closely with their counterparts in Israel, particularly on cancer interests...[People] should know there's an Arab American with longstanding support of Israel who's just been elected in South Florida.[259]

---

258 Richman, Jackson, "Donna Shalala to bring decades of experience working with Israel to Congress," December 10, 2018. *South Florida Sun-Journal*.
259 Ibid.

It does not, unfortunately, end there. The charade is not always so explicit, however, as Steyer finding the (lime)light, and goes deeper than most people know. It goes right to the very essence of the odious system in place today. As Mark Steyn put it, "No one ever complains about the lack of French restaurants in Mogadishu," but the (former) lack of Mogadishu in Acadian-French regions of Maine is a serious problem the neo-liberal establishment have been more than happy to rectify, even if it means destroying the Acadian-French ethnos.

The ultimate erasure of this unique ethnicity with its own culture, heritage, and the like in the name of "diversity" is tragically just one more of the morbidly-perverse contradictions of "laissez-faire" genocide. As George W. Bush once taunted the Iraqis in his administration's post-9/11 bloodbath by saying, when he may as well have been also talking about his decision to green-light the flood of Somalis into America: "Bring 'em on!"

Would that we had a say in the matter, but in neo-liberal democracy that's simply not possible. That right is reserved for people like Tom Steyer and his friends, associates, and donors such as Lazard, Ltd., the world's leading financial advisory and asset management firm.

Lazard, Ltd. is based out of Bermuda for tax reasons, naturally, and its Chairman and CEO is Kenneth M. Jacobs, another Stanford MBA who is on the Board for the Brookings Institution and is a former member of the Steering Committee for the Bilderberg Group. A number of influential people have worked for Lazard, including: Marcus Agius, Robert Agostinelli, Tim Collins, Disque Deane, Mina Gerowin, Sir Philip Hampton, Hugh Kindersley, Sebastian Kulczyk, Steven Langman, Jean-Marie Messier, Archie Norman, Nelson Obus, Gary Parr, Mark Pincus, Gerald Rosenfeld, Nathaniel Rothschild, Bernard Selz, Johann Rupert, Lars Kroijer, Jaime Bermudez Merizalde, Ron Bloom, Robert Henry Brand, Robert Fred Ellsworth, Vernon E. Jordan Jr., Paul Keating, Robert Kindersley, Anne Lauvergeon, Lord Mandelson, Henrique de Campos Meirelles, Andrew Mitchell, Peter R. Orszag, Vincent S. Perez, Rodrigo de Rato, Jenny Sanford, Simon Sebag Montefiore, Lindsay Tanner, Andres Velasco, Antonio Weiss, Bill White, Frank G. Zarb, Bozidar Delic, Ngozi Okonjo-Iweala, and William D. Cohan. Lazard was founded as Lazard Freres & Co. by three Jewish brothers—Alexandre, Lazare, and Simon:

In the late 1800s and early 1900s, the firm evolved into three "Houses of Lazard" in the United States, France, and England, separately managed but allied. The Lazard partners advised clients on financial matters and built a cross-border network of high-level relationships in business and government.

Noted financial advisor George Blumenthal rose to prominence as the head of the U.S. branch of Lazard Frères and was a partner of Lazard Frères in France. In the economic boom following World War II, the American operations of Lazard expanded significantly under the leadership of the financier Andre Meyer. Meyer and Lazard partner Felix Rohatyn have been credited with virtually inventing the modern mergers and acquisitions (M&A) market...

In 1977, as the health of Meyer began to deteriorate, the firm came to be controlled by Michel David-Weill. Under his leadership, the three houses of Lazard were formally united in 2000 as Lazard LLC. In 2002, David-Weill hired Bruce Wasserstein to be CEO...Following Wasserstein's sudden death in 2009, Lazard's Board of Directors elected Kenneth M. Jacobs Chairman and CEO.[260]

Blumenthal, Meyer, Rohatyn, David-Weill, Wasserstein, and Jacobs are all Jewish. Blumenthal first arrived in the United States on behalf of the dynastic Jewish banking family the Speyers, and along with JP Morgan was one of five bankers whose $65 million gold loans saved Grover Cleveland from giving up specie payments in 1896. At Lazard, André Meyer created SOVAC (Societé pour la Vente à Crédit d'Automobiles), a finance company that in the late-1920s introduced the concept of automobile financing for consumers, ensuring Lazard Frères would become a significant force in consumer credit as well as in product leasing. Meyer and two colleagues would also represent Lazard on the Board of Directors of Citroën. He was also very close with former US President Lyndon B. Johnson, often serving in an unofficial advisory capacity during Johnson's time in office. Rohatyn:

---

260 "Lazard," WikiZero entry.

Joined the New York office of the investment bank Lazard
Frères under André Meyer. He was made partner in
the firm in 1961 and later became managing director.
While at Lazard he brokered numerous, major mergers
and acquisitions, notably on behalf of International
Telephone and Telegraph (ITT), where he became a
director in 1966. He also served on the boards of the
Englehard Mineral and Chemical Corporation, Howmet
Turbine Component Corporation, Owens-Illinois Inc.,
and Pfizer Inc. He served on the Board of the New
York Stock Exchange from 1968 to 1972...In 1996, the
Clinton administration put forward his candidacy for
the post of Vice Chairman of the Federal Reserve...
According to The New York Times, in the 1990s, Rohatyn
described derivatives as "financial hydrogen bombs, built
on personal computers by 26-year-olds with M.B.A.s." In
2006 Rohatyn joined Lehman Brothers as a senior advisor
to chairman, Dick Fuld. On January 27, 2010, Rohatyn
announced his return to Lazard as Special Advisor to
the Chairman and CEO, after a short role at Rothschild.
Rohatyn was United States Ambassador to France from
1997–2000 during the second Clinton Administration...
As ambassador, he also organized the French-American
Business Council (FABC), a 40-member council of
U.S. and French corporate chief executives that met
annually, with meetings held alternately in the United
States and France. FABC meetings included President
Clinton, President Chirac and Prime Minister Jospin, as
well as U.S. cabinet secretaries and French government
ministers and meetings continued during the presidencies
of George W. Bush and Nicolas Sarkozy...[His son]
Nicolas Rohatyn is CEO and Chief Investment Officer
at The Rohatyn Group, an investment firm specializing
in emerging markets, following a 19-year career at J.P.
Morgan.[261]

David-Weill's father, Pierre, was a partner and former Chairman
of Lazard Frères; his grandfather, David, was a partner, and his great-

261 "Felix Rohatyn," WikiZero entry.

grandfather, Alexandre Weill also worked at Lazard Frères, founded by his cousins. David-Weill hired both Bruce Wasserstein and the Jewish "deal-maker" Steven Rattner, a member of the Council on Foreign Relations (CFR) and a previous member of the Brookings Institution's Board. Wasserstein was a First Boston alum who left in 1988 to form Wasserstein Perella & Co.; Wasserstein's private equity firm Wasserstein & Co. specialized in the acquisitions of media. Wasserstein's fourth wife was Angela Chao, sister of Mitch McConnell's wife Elaine Chao. Rahm Emanuel was employed by Wasserstein and his partner Joseph R. Perella at one time (Emanuel was hired in the late 1990s despite not having an MBA or any prior experience working in finance before being appointed to the Freddie Mac Board of Directors in 2000, a brief tenure that was plagued by scandal), as were a number of major Establishment figures such as Robert S. Wiesenthal of Sony, Jeffrey A. Rosen of Lazard, Douglas L. Braunstein of JP Morgan Chase, and more. Jewish psychoanalyst Albert J. Levis married his sister. Rattner:

> Was hired in Washington, D.C., as a news clerk to James Reston, New York Times columnist and former executive editor. After a year, he moved to New York as a reporter to cover business, energy, and urban affairs; there he became friends with colleague Paul Goldberger ("You know, I remember when I was young hearing my grandfather ask, apropos of almost anything—'So, is it good or bad for the Jews?'")...
>
> At the unusually young age of 27, he became the paper's chief Washington economic correspondent. He became close friends with Arthur Ochs Sulzberger Jr....At the end of 1982, Rattner left The New York Times and was recruited by Roger Altman to join the investment bank Lehman Brothers as an associate. After Lehman was sold to American Express in 1984, he followed his boss Eric Gleacher and several colleagues to Morgan Stanley, where he founded the firm's communications group. In 1989, after Morgan Stanley filed for an initial public offering, he joined Lazard as a general partner and completed various deals for large media conglomerates

such as Viacom and Comcast. Alongside Felix Rohatyn, Rattner became Lazard's top rainmaker in the 1990s. Michel David-Weill named him the firm's deputy chairman and deputy chief executive in 1997. In March 2000, Rattner and three Lazard partners, including Joshua Steiner, left the firm and founded the Quadrangle Group. They initially focused on investing a $1 billion media-focused private equity fund. Early investors in Quadrangle included Sulzberger, Mort Zuckerman, and Merrill Lynch. Headquartered in the Seagram Building,[262] Quadrangle grew to manage more than $6 billion across several business lines, including private equity, distressed securities, and hedge funds. The firm also hosted an annual gathering for media executives called Foursquare, where speakers included Rupert Murdoch...

In 2005, Quadrangle made payments to private placement agent Hank Morris[263] to help Quadrangle raise money for its second buyout fund. Morris had come highly recommended to Rattner from U.S. Senator Charles Schumer. Morris was also the chief political advisor to Alan Hevesi, the New York State Comptroller and manager of the New York State Common Retirement Fund (CRF), which invests in many private equity funds. Morris told Rattner he could increase the size of the CRF

---

262 It was designed as the headquarters for what became the Seagram Company with the active interest of Phyllis Lambert, the daughter of scion Samuel Bronfman who acquired Joseph E. Seagram & Sons in 1928. Much of the family's initial fortune was gained from bootlegging. The Bronfmans are Jewish and are immensely powerful and influential from their legacy of having owned and grown the Seagram Company into a multi-billion-dollar enterprise with diverse holdings. The building is owned by the Jewish Aby Rosen's RFR Holdings.

263 "A top New York political consultant who went to prison for masterminding a massive state pension fund scandal has won parole, officials said Tuesday. Hank Morris, the longtime political guru to disgraced state Controller Alan Hevesi, is scheduled to be released no later than June 3 from the Hudson Correctional Facility and be under community supervision until Feb. 18, 2015. 'I'd say that he's very happy,' said Morris lawyer Orlee Goldfeld. 'It's been a long time coming.'" From the *New York Daily News*.

investment in Quadrangle's second buyout fund. Rattner agreed to pay Morris a placement fee of 1.1% of any investments greater than $25 million from the CRF...In 2009, Quadrangle and a dozen other investment firms, including the Carlyle Group, were investigated by the U.S. Securities and Exchange Commission for their hiring of Morris. The SEC viewed the payments as "kickbacks" in order to receive investments from the CRF since Morris was also a consultant to Hevesi. Quadrangle paid $7 million in April 2010 to settle the SEC investigation, and Rattner personally settled in November for $6.2 million without admitting or denying any wrongdoing...In 2008, the firm's asset management division announced it had been selected to invest the personal assets of New York Mayor Michael Bloomberg...Rattner's close friend.[264]

Do you see how all this works? This is how a decadent ruling class, governing for its own benefit, operates. Political affiliation is basically irrelevant in such a context, as we will see with presidential candidate Johnny-come-lately Michael Bloomberg, the former mayor of New York City, who may have run as a Democrat, but is bi-partisan in his support for his co-conspirators and those who will do their bidding. Control is essential, no matter how unethical. As Karl Evers-Hillstrom writes:

Bloomberg, who made his billions as the founder and CEO of financial services firm Bloomberg L.P.,[265] has slammed aggressive regulation of the financial sector...Bloomberg's contributions ebb and flow as the political tides shift...Following the 2010 Supreme Court decision in Citizens United v. FEC, Bloomberg took advantage of his newfound ability to give unlimited sums to super PACs. His Independence USA PAC shelled out millions to back Bloomberg's preferred Republicans and Democrats, and spent roughly 90 percent or more of its money backing winning candidates every cycle since 2014. In 2018, the group spent all of its $38 million

---

264 "Steven Rattner," WikiZero entry.
265 The millions made to establish Bloomberg LP came from his time as a general partner at Salomon Brothers, a Wall Street investment bank.

backing Democrats and opposing Republicans. It helped kick out key Democratic targets such as former Reps. Dana Rohrabacher (R-Calif.) and Pete Sessions (R-Texas) with multi-million dollar ad buys. Bloomberg's other major group, Everytown for Gun Safety, was also successful at kicking Republicans out of Congress. The group spent $4.2 million backing Rep. Lucy McBath (D-Ga.), a gun control activist, and helped gun control groups outspend gun rights organizations on independent expenditures for the first time in 2018. The Bloomberg-funded group was also instrumental in helping Democrats turn Virginia blue…Also during the midterms, Bloomberg poured $20 million into Senate Majority PAC, the super PAC arm for Senate Democrats. He added another $5 million to the League of Conservation Voters.[266]

Notable Democrats who've received funds from Bloomberg in recent years include Cory Booker and Kamala Harris. Interestingly, Bloomberg has never donated to Joe Biden, Elizabeth Warren, or Bernie Sanders. Naturally, though, people like Jerrold Nadler, Chuck Schumer, and Joe Lieberman have also received Bloomberg's largesse. What could possibly unite them?

Rhetorically, Sanders and Warren are very much opposed to the Bloomberg/Steyer *modus operandi*, but their donors are virtually the same as every other major Democratic candidate. Surely there is some in-group tension here regarding Wall Street and venture (vulture) capitalism, but all indications are that it will probably prove either minor or altogether irrelevant.

Sanders may have been a True Believer at one time, but he has clearly been co-opted. Big tech and the major multi-nationals appear to be off-limits completely. Bloomberg has tried to explain his way out of his support for "stop-and-frisk" while mayor of New York to the Woke Golems, but despite the efficacy of such a policy, its "racism" renders it "problematic." As Tucker Carlson says, "'Wokeness' is our Achilles heel."

---

266 Evers-Hillstrom, Karl, "Bloomberg brings the biggest bucks to the Democratic presidential primary," November 8, 2019. Center for Responsive Politics.

On the other side of the aisle, referring to the Center for Responsive Politics, we see that Bloomberg has donated to the Republican National Committee, the Republican Party of Massachusetts, New Jersey Republican State Committee, New York Republican Federal Campaign Committee, and the New York Republican County Committee, as well as current Maine Senator Susan Collins, former Maine Senator Olympia Snowe, Mitt Romney, Orrin Hatch, John McCain, George Bush, George W. Bush, and Rudy Giuliani. He donated $250,000 to Mississippi Conservatives in 2014 and in that same year, donated another $250,000 to West Main Street Values, a single-candidate super-PAC in support of Lindsey Graham.

The following year, while Graham was gearing up for a presidential bid of his own, as Ben Kamisar reported in late July 2015:

> Of the total [$2.9 million raised since March], $200,000 came from a super-PAC that supported Graham's Senate bid, West Main Street Values PAC Inc....Ronald Perelman, the billionaire investor that's a member of Graham's national finance team, also gave a half-million. Access Industries, a holding company that owns Warner Music Group and others, also donated that same sum (note: Access Industries is owned by the Jewish Len Blavatnik)... General Electric CEO Jeffrey Immelt gave $25,000 to the group, as did Boston philanthropist Theodore Cutler. Graham appeared at a fundraiser for the group in March, which was co-chaired by GOP megadonor Sheldon Adelson. Adelson doesn't appear to have given to the super-PAC directly, but another co-chair, former American Enterprise Institute board member Roger Hertog, donated $100,000 a week after the event.[267]

The Jewish Hertog's American Enterprise Institute has been implicated in the horrors wrought on America as a result of the opioid crisis driven primarily by the Jewish Sackler family and their Purdue Pharma. Now entrenched, people like King and Pingree (and Mills and Golden and Collins) are able to shape policy in Maine in such a

---

267 Kamisar, Ben, "Graham super-PAC raises nearly $3M," July 30, 2015. *The Hill.*

way that the state has essentially become a playground for the rich. It is, on a smaller scale, what has happened to countries like Ireland. In addition to tax loopholes and corporate tax breaks, many of these "philanthropic" organizations are tax-exempt, and charitable giving is also tax deductible.

Add to this the fact that the government itself funds many of these organizations, and you have basically created the present situation whereby we pay for our own population replacement and subsidize massive corporate profits—all while buying their commercial products. It's a sick joke.

Steyer, Bloomberg, S. Donald Sussman, the Sacklers...this are the new ruling class of America and they hate you. It's all too easy to retreat to "it's the Democrats" or "it's the Clintons" in the face of this deeply uncomfortable truth, and while in Sussman's case both happen to be part of the picture, it is a woefully incomplete one to leave it at that. Consider that of the top 50 donors to 527's and super-PACs in the 2020 presidential election, eight of the 36 Republicans were Jewish, and of the 14 Democrats, only one was *not* Jewish.

Using the figures for individual donors' campaign contributions to federal candidates, parties, political action committees (PACs), 527 organizations, and Carey committees as reported by the Center for Responsive Politics for the 2018 election, we see that six of the top seven donors were Jews: Sheldon Adelson, Michael Bloomberg, Tom Steyer, S. Donald Sussman, Jim Simons, and George Soros. The Jewish Stephen Schwarzman of the Blackstone Group was also in the top ten. Number ten on that list, Fred Eychaner, is not Jewish, but as *The Times of Israel* reported in late October 2012:

> Eychaner has given $1.5 million to the Priorities USA Action super PAC. He's also given more than $60,000 to the president's re-election committees, and he's listed as a major "bundler" for Obama, having raised at least $500,000 for the president. Eychaner, a gay-rights activist, also has donated millions to other nonprofit groups, including more than $1 million to the progressive EMILY's List organization.[268]

---

268 Zion, Ilan Ben, "Jewish donors prominent in presidential campaign contributions," October 20, 2012. *The Times of Israel.*

More wealthy Jews abound in the top one hundred donors to political campaigns in 2018: Deborah Simon (#14), Bernie Marcus (#18), Dustin Moskovitz (#19), Joshua Bekenstein (#20), Jeff Yass (#21), Paul Singer (#25), Seth Klarman (#26), Amy Goldman-Fowler (#28), and Henry Laufer (#29). Sixteen of the top thirty donors to political campaigns in 2018 were Jewish.

If you continue down the list, you'll continue to see Jews well-represented, including Herbert Sandler, Haim Saban, Irwin Jacobs, Les Wexner, Alexander Soros, Steven A. Cohen, Bernard Schwartz, Sim Daniel Abraham, Richard Rosenthal, Stephen Mandel, Henry Goldberg, Irving Moskowitz, Steven Spielberg, Ronald Lauder, Michael Sacks, David Bonderman, Dan Loeb, and Andrea Soros-Colombel.

We can see how support for rogue state Israel is baked into the cake. Stephanie Schriock, current president of EMILY's List, who the reader will recall has funded several of Maine's prominent politicians and has received extensive funding from S. Donald Sussman, had the following to say on the role of AIPAC in campaign fundraising:

> Before you went to the Jewish community, you had a conversation with the lead AIPAC person in your state and they made it clear that you needed a paper on Israel. And so you called all of your friends who already had a paper on Israel – that was designed by AIPAC – and we made that your paper. This was before there was a campaign manager, or a policy director or a field director because you got to raise money before you do all of that. I have written more Israel papers than you can imagine. I'm from Montana. I barely knew where Israel was until I looked at a map, and the poor campaign manager would come in, or the policy director, and I'd be like, 'Here is your paper on Israel. This is our policy.' We've sent it all over the country because this is how we raise money. … This means that these candidates who were farmers, school teachers, or businesswomen, ended up having an Israel position.[269]

---

269 Weiss, Philip, "'Forward' columnist and Emily's List leader relate 'gigantic,' 'shocking' role of Jewish Democratic donors," April 19, 2016. *Mondoweiss.*

Just as is the case with liberals and conservatives in mainstream political discourse, it is the *apparent* opposition which is most damning. J Street exclusively funded Democrats (and the "Independent" Angus King), to the tune of over $4 million in the 2018 election cycle, whereas AIPAC tends to exert a greater, though not exclusive, influence on the Republicans. Although AIPAC does not technically contribute directly to political candidates, it does require its members to donate to the campaigns of certain candidates in order to receive exclusive membership benefits, and it is able to mobilize donors for their selected candidates. With respect to direct lobbying efforts, their 2018 expenses were in excess of $3.5 million, which is really a rather surprisingly-low figure given its influence. Peter Feld writes:

> In 1988, at the Fairmont Hotel in San Francisco — yes, representing the Dukakis campaign at an AIPAC luncheon is a thing I have done in this life — I heard an AIPAC speaker boast unabashedly about AIPAC's vast influence. In recent cycles, he said, AIPAC had punished enemies of Israel in Congress, like Senator Charles Percy of Illinois, who had lost his 1984 re-election after criticizing Israel's settlements and Lebanon invasion (note: see also Cynthia McKinney)... It cannot be anti-Semitic to say that a lobby that spends large sums of money and boasts (at least to its own supporters) of its influence, is influential through money...Israel also exerts influence in the donations of wealthy individuals like Sheldon Adelson who has given the GOP a reported $100 million and was rewarded by Trump with the Jerusalem embassy move. It's AIPAC, not the evangelicals, who made the Israel Anti-Boycott Act a legislative priority and got 292 House and 69 Senate cosponsors from both parties to place protecting Israel from criticism above their own constituents' constitutional rights to free speech...It was AIPAC who helped force a different anti-BDS bill, S.1, to the Senate floor three times this winter [2018-19] in the midst of a government shutdown.[270]

---

270 Feld, Peter, "No, Ilhan Omar Is Not Anti-Semitic For Calling Out AIPAC," February 11, 2019. *Forward.*

Some of J Street's 2019 lobbying priorities included:

- H.R. 1837 - United States-Israel Cooperation Enhancement and Regional Security Act - Codifying the Obama-Netanyahu memorandum of understanding on US assistance to Israel.
- H.R.6/S.874 - American Dream and Promise Act of 2019 - To authorize the cancellation of removal and adjustment of status of certain individuals who are long-term United States residents and who entered the United States as children and for other purposes.
- H.Res 299 - Condemning White Supremacist Terrorism and the Anti-immigrant Rhetoric that Inspires It Resolution -Expressing the sense of the House of Representatives that immigration makes the United States stronger.
- H.R.2214/S.1123 - the National Origin-Based Antidiscrimination for Nonimmigrants Act or the NO BAN Act - To repeal the three versions of the Administration's Muslim ban, strengthens the Immigration and Nationality Act to prohibit discrimination on the basis of religion, and restores the separation of powers by limiting overly broad executive authority to issue future travel bans.
- Omnibus Appropriations - The final appropriations package provided the full $3.8 billion in annual military aid for Israel promised under the Obama Memorandum of Understanding.
- H.R. 4009/S. 852 - Anti-Semitism Awareness Act of 2019 - Extends protections of Title VI to groups who share a common faith, and includes the definition of anti-Semitism adopted by the International Holocaust Remembrance Alliance, to also include the [c]ontemporary examples of antisemitism identified in the IHRA definition.
- H.R. 336 - Strengthening America's Security in the Middle East Act of 2019 - To penalize activity related to boycotts directed at Israeli settlements in the West Bank.
- H.Res.236/S.Res 120 - A resolution expressing Congressional opposition to the global BDS movement

AIPAC and J Street are far from the only pro-Israel lobbies active in the United States, just the most prominent. We have also discussed

The Democratic Majority for Israel, and the Center for Responsive Politics reports:

> NorPAC, a nonpartisan PAC with the goal of supporting members and candidates who "demonstrate a genuine commitment to the strength, security, and survival of Israel," spent more than $1.1 million in the 2018 cycle, with much of it going to Democrats...A variety of other groups other than AIPAC spend some money on lobbying, such as the Israeli-American Coalition for Action with $550,000...The group which spent the most on Republican candidates was the Republican Jewish Coalition which contributed $501,097 during the midterms. The group's biggest contribution, $42,474, went to the campaign of Sen. Ted Cruz (R-Texas). On the Republican Jewish Coalition board is the largest individual donor from the 2018 cycle, Sheldon Adelson. Also holding a board seat is another big money donor, co-founder of Home Depot, Bernie Marcus (note: one of Turning Point USA's primary financiers).[271]

The other Board members are: Mel Sembler, Fred Zeidman, Bradley D. Wine, Isaac Aplbaum, Wayne Berman, Ronald Weiser, Florence Shapiro, Adam Ross, Alan Sager, Harold Beznos, Ronald H. Blum, Matthew Brooks (Executive Director), Martin Selig, Diane Sembler-Kamins, Norm Coleman (National Chairman), Edward Czuker, Elissa Czuker, Karen Tandy, Jason A. Sugarman, Walter Stern, Abbie Snyder, Richard Sherman, Michael David Epstein, Jeffrey P. Feingold, David M. Flaum, Leonard Sands, Lee C. Samson, J. Phillip Rosen, Robert I. Schostak, Ari Fleischer, Brad D. Rose, Peter Foman, Ronald Plotkin, Larry A. Mizel, Jeff Miller, Earle I. Mack, Alan B. Miller, Richard J. Fox, Shelly Kamins, Linda Lingle, Sam Fox, M. Ronald Krongold, George Klein, Fred E. Karlinsky, Phyllis Greenberg Heideman, Norman Freidkin, Steven L. Friedman, Joel Geiderman, Marc Goldman, Cheryl Halpern, Jason D. Greenblatt, and Sander Gerber. Jeffrey Altman is General Counsel and Eliot Lauer is Treasurer. NorPAC donated $50,000 in the 2020 election

---

271 Arke, Raymond, "AIPAC doesn't contribute directly to candidates. Which pro-Israel groups do?" February 11, 2019. Center for Responsive Politics.

cycle to the [Susan] Collins for Senator PAC alongside many other large donations such as the Republican Jewish Coalition's nearly $24,000.

Mel Sembler personally took Mitt Romney to Israel in 2007 and told the *Jewish Standard* that Romney "gets it":

> Romney said that as president he would "enhance our deterrent against the Iranian regime by ordering the regular presence of aircraft carrier task forces, one in the eastern Mediterranean and one in the Persian Gulf region. I will begin discussions with Israel to increase the level of our military assistance and coordination. And I will again reiterate that Iran obtaining a nuclear weapon is unacceptable." He also said he would centralize U.S. Middle East policy to ensure "that the Arab Spring does not fade into a long winter." The speech came a day after Romney published a list of his foreign policy advisers, including many who have been active in or are close to the pro-Israel community, such as Norm Coleman, the former U.S. senator from Minnesota who is now active with the Republican Jewish Coalition; Dan Senor, the co-author of a book on Israeli technological innovation who often works with the American Israel Public Affairs Committee; and Dov Zakheim, a former top Pentagon official in various Republican administrations who also is active with the American Jewish Committee.[272]

Although the Republican Jewish Coalition does not contribute directly to candidates' campaigns, it does donate money to different SuperPACs supporting politicians who "get it," such as Team Graham (for Lindsey Graham), [David] Perdue for Senate, and the McConnell Senate Committee, which also received over $161,000 over the last half of 2019 from NorPAC.

Other recipients of Republican Jewish Coalition donations include Friends of John McCain, Ted Cruz for Senate, Rick Scott for Florida, Ben Sasse for US Senate, and Tim Scott for Senate. Sasse has received campaign contributions from Paul Singer, Rick Scott signed into

---

272 "Jewish backers enjoy Romney's rise," October 23, 2011. *Jewish Standard*.

law bill SB 86, which prohibits the State Board of Administration from investing in companies that boycott Israel,[273] and Tim Scott is responsible for introducing the Anti-Semitism Awareness Act at the national level in 2019 and getting South Carolina to pass a state-wide Anti-Semitism Awareness Act in 2018.

Pro-Israeli foreign agents registered under the Foreign Agents Registration Act (FARA), which can include lobbyists working on behalf of the Israeli government, companies, political parties, and other organizations, spend tens of millions of dollars annually influencing American policy; the government of Israel has spent over $50 million since 2017, and other agencies such as the World Zionist Organization ($8.6 million in 2018) and the Jewish Agency for Israel ($7.4 million in 2017) have contributed an additional $33 million in that time frame, putting official—and I stress official—Israeli contacts third on the list of foreign entities that've spent the most in the United States over that time frame, almost double the amount spent by Russia.

The mission of both AIPAC and J Street (and their lesser-lights) is clear—protect Jewish interests and the state of Israel at all costs, even at the expense of American national security and civil liberties such as free speech. They are aided in their endeavors by other Jewish organizations like the ADL.

On November 25th, 2019, Governor Andrew Cuomo of the State of New York signed into law a bill sponsored by State Assemblywoman Nily Rozic and State Senator Todd Kaminsky, both Jewish, requiring police across the state to receive mandatory "hate crimes recognition training." The State Division of Human Rights and the Hate Crimes Task Force will now be developing procedures and implementing

---

273 The law "requires the State Board of Administration to identify all companies that are engaged in a boycott of Israel; requires the public fund to create and maintain the Scrutinized Companies that Boycott Israel List; and prohibits a state agency or local governmental entity from contracting for goods and services if the company has been placed on the Scrutinized Companies that Boycott Israel List." According to Governor Scott: "For many generations, Florida and Israel have been close partners and allies. When I was first elected, I led a trade mission to Israel because it is imperative that we further our economic growth between Florida and Israel. I applaud Sen. Joe Negron, Rep. Ritch Workman, Rep. Jared Moskowitz and the many legislative leaders who honored our relationship with the Jewish people by sponsoring SB 86."

them along with its existing training protocol to "identify, report, and respond" to "hate crimes," particularly since, according to Michael Schmidt, Director of the American Jewish Committee (AJC) of New York says, "As we have seen an alarming increase in hate crimes across New York State, particularly in Jewish communities, we are pleased that our police will now be trained to identify and report anti-Semitic and other hate crimes."

Rozic herself, while in the midst of campaigning to have the name of Donald J. Trump State Park changed to Heather D. Heyer State Park, allegedly received "anti-Semitic hate mail containing common white nationalistic phrases." We can only speculate as to the real origin of this "hate mail," but it is eerily reminiscent of the way that right after a proposed bill prohibiting criticism of Israel was struck down some graffiti was miraculously discovered in a Jewish cemetery, "compelling" French lawmakers to hasten through the law and to create a national "anti-hate crime office." In a similar vein, we can probably venture an educated guess on who will advise—or more appropriately, supervise—the Division of Human Rights and the Hate Crimes Task Force on its training and procedures.

Cuomo himself recently made a trip to Israel to "further develop economic development opportunities with Israeli businesses and reinforce solidarity and support for the Jewish community." He declared October 27th a "Day of Action to Combat Anti-Semitism," issuing his proclamation at Central Synagogue in New York at an event organized by the AJC New York Regional Office, the Jewish Community Relations Council, the UJA Federation, and the synagogue itself.

The members of Cuomo's administration were to attend the AJC's #ShowUpForShabbat campaign. In 2016, Cuomo issued an executive order directing the state Office of General Services to create a list of companies determined by the state to "participate in boycott, divestment, or sanctions activity targeting Israel."

In September 2019, the New York State Police, in conjunction with the New York State Division of Criminal Justice Services, the New York State Division of Human Rights, the New York State Hate Crimes Task Force, the Queens County District Attorney's Office, the Anti-Defamation League, and the Jewish Community Relations Council of New York held four separate "hate crime investigation training seminars." Evan Bernstein, regional director of the ADL in New York and New Jersey, has been vociferous in his support for Cuomo's measures, citing, once again, the "increase in anti-Semitic incidents." The ADL trains 15,000 police officers annually and the FBI and the NYPD have already made their training mandatory. Also, according to ADL CEO Jonathan Greenblatt, "We work with the SPLC, for example, and the U.S. Holocaust Museum on some of that training for law enforcement and researching the bad guys…We [also] work with [the] ACLU."

Michael Lieberman, ADL Washington Counsel and Director of the ADL Civil Rights Policy Planning Center, penned a piece for *Dissent Magazine* very much in favor of "hate crime" legislation. Senators Tim Scott (R-SC) and Bob Casey (D-PA) introduced S. 852, the Anti-Semitism Awareness Act in March (South Carolina passed a state-wide Anti-Semitism Awareness Act in 2018), citing ADL statistics in the press release. Indeed, the very concept and origin of "hate crime" legislation emerges from the SPLC and the ADL, the latter especially, as Kamban Naidoo writes:

> As the Civil-Rights Movement gained momentum, civil-society organisations such as the Anti-Defamation League and the Southern Poverty Law Centre began compiling statistical reports to establish the number and frequency of crimes motivated by prejudice, bias and bigotry. In 1981 the Anti-Defamation League, concerned by the rise in crimes motivated by racial and ethnic bias and prejudice in the United States of America, particularly anti-Semitic crimes, and the fact that media exposure, education and law enforcement were ineffective, drafted a model hate-crime statute which recognised racial, religious and ethnic biases…The model statute was intended to influence state legislatures and the Federal government to enact hate-crime laws. The Anti-Defamation League's model hate-crime statute had the desired effect since a number of state legislatures in the United States of America subsequently enacted laws based on the model statute. Shortly after the drafting of the Anti-Defamation League's model

hate-crime statute in 1981, the states of Oregon and Washington passed similar laws…Since the enactment of the Hate Crimes Statistics Act in 1990 a number of federal hate-crime laws have been passed in the United States of America. Contemporary hate-crime laws recognise a wide spectrum of victim characteristics that includes race, ethnicity, religion, disability, gender and sexual orientation. These hate-crime laws include the Hate Crimes Sentencing Enhancement Act of 1994 and the Matthew Shepherd and James Byrd Junior Hate Crimes Prevention Act of 2009. To date, over forty-five American states and the District of Columbia have enacted hate-crime statutes based on the Anti-Defamation League's model statute. *The American trend to enact hate-crime laws has had some international impact, particularly in Western democratic countries. In 1998 the United Kingdom passed the Crime and Disorder Act which is the British equivalent of a hate-crime law and in 2003 France passed its first hate-crime law, which is commonly referred to as la* loi Lellouche.[274]

The ADL's tracking of "anti-Semitic incidents" are uncritically accepted as gospel by the institutions and organizations they influence. Their goal of "combating extremism" is also a ploy for increased revenue; the New York-based "non-profit" has seen revenues climb alongside an increase in reported anti-Semitic incidents. In 2017, the ADL received $72 million in contributions and grants, the most for any year for which information is available, and a 17% increase from 2016. The ADL received a $2.5 million pledge in October 2019 from Facebook COO Sheryl Sandberg to "fight hate." In 2017, the organization acknowledged that it had received a number of contributions from major donors such as JP Morgan Chase, Apple, Uber, and MGM Resorts in addition to a $1 million contribution from the CEO of 21st Century Fox, James Murdoch. Other notable foundation funders have included the Ford Foundation and the Adelson Family Foundation of Sheldon Adelson. The Walter and Elise Haas Fund has also donated to the ADL.

---

274 Naidoo, Kamban, "The origins of hate crime laws," 2016. *Fundamina: Pretoria*, Vol. 22, No. 1.

An interesting note here about the Walter and Elise Haas Fund is that it is one of two major funds run by the Haas family, as well as some smaller ones. The Haas family also founded The Haas Institute for a Fair and Inclusive Society in 2010 at the University of California at Berkeley, which is designed to "produce studies that promote racial equity" and it has partnered up with Race Forward "a nonprofit organization that promotes radical racial policies through research and media," which is bankrolled by the Ford Foundation, Unbound Philanthropy, the W.K. Kellogg Foundation, and the Annie E. Casey Foundation, among others.

They produced the Local and Regional Government Alliance on Race and Equity (GARE). Influence Watch describes GARE thusly: "GARE, as a programming project, is part of a larger network of organizations looking to push radical race-first policies by promising significant financial windfalls should race inequities be removed. In conjunction with PolicyLink and the Program for Environmental and Regional Equity (PERE), GARE is used to convince local lawmakers that the racial mandate 'All-In Cities' should be adopted in their local town or county."[275] GARE's programs also work in conjunction with PolicyLink, which Influence Watch describes as "a radical race-first policy manifesto local municipalities and counties have adopted to view all policies and statutes through the lens of race."

The Walter and Elise Haas Fund and the Evelyn & Walter Haas, Jr. Fund are the two primary funds through which the Haas family disburses donations. The Walter and Elise Haas fund has over $216 million in assets, and in addition to the ADL it has donated to the ACLU, Bend the Arc Jewish Action, the J Street Education Fund, the Tides Center, the SPLC, the New Israel Fund, Horizons Foundation, the Center for Popular Democracy, the National LGBTQ Task Force, National Committee for Responsive Philanthropy, Grantmakers Concerned with Immigrants and Refugees (GCIR), and Mujeres Unidas y Activas (MUA). The Evelyn & Walter Haas, Jr. Fund has almost $464 million in assets and it has donated to La Raza, the Tides Center, the Proteus Fund, the Transgender Law Center, the National LGBTQ Task Force, National Committee for Responsive Philanthropy, MALDEF, the ACLU, and the Asian American and

---

275 "Local and Regional Government Alliance on Race and Equity (GARE)," Influence Watch.

Pacific Islander (AAPI) Civic Engagement Fund. It's unsurprising that so many of these organizations also have ties to George Soros.

Soros's fingerprints are everywhere, and in January 2020 he announced that he was committing $1 *billion* to "transform" higher education, which given its current state as a series of indoctrination mills probably is unnecessary, but Soros feels that it is essential to introduce the same process of inter-connectedness to the academy that has been so lucrative and ideologically successful elsewhere:

> "The Open Society University Network is a new model of global higher education," the Open Society Foundations, a grant-making group founded by Soros, said in a news release. "It will integrate learning and knowledge creation across geographic and demographic boundaries, promote civic engagement to advance open societies and expand access of underserved communities to higher education." Soros said the network will seek to integrate teaching and research across higher education institutions worldwide. It plans to offer simultaneously taught network courses and joint degree programs, both online and in person. The network will focus on neglected populations, including refugees, incarcerated people, Roma and other displaced groups. Bard College and the Central European University, which Soros founded, will be the primary partners of the new network. Other partners include Arizona State University, the American University of Central Asia in Kyrgyzstan and BRAC University in Bangladesh.[276]

Academia is an essential arm of the neo-liberal establishment. Not only do the universities promote the "right" ideas, they serve a variety of networking functions, support for privileged groups, and financial backing at least once-removed from the original source in collaboration with a number of what are euphemistically called pro-immigrant and/or -refugee projects. Once again we can see how enmeshed all of these organizations and institutions are. From the "Immigrant and Refugee Integration and Policy Development

276 Fain, Paul, "Soros to Spend $1 Billion on Higher Ed Network," January 24, 2020. *Inside Higher Ed.*

Working Group Final Report" for the City of Lewiston, December 2017:

A variety of institutions and local colleges including Kaplan University, Maine College of Health Professions, University of Southern Maine's Lewiston Auburn College, Central Maine Community College, and Bates College all serve to connect members of the immigrant and refugee communities to opportunities for higher education in the area...There are a variety of local organizations dedicated to providing support and advocacy services to the immigrant and refugee communities in Lewiston. Organizations such as Trinity Jubilee Center (TJC), Pine Tree Legal Assistance (PTLA), Maine Equal Justice Partners (MEJP), the Immigrant Legal Advocacy Project (ILAP), and Western Maine Transportation Services (WMTS) represent valuable resources for both the native and immigrant and refugee populations, and address basic needs such as food, housing, income support, legal services, and transportation. The City itself provides both services and advocacy through its General Assistance Office.[277]

The Maine Immigrant and Refugee Services (MEIRS), also based out of Lewiston, "promotes a pathway toward citizenship and community engagement, creating opportunities for inclusion and meaningful participation for immigrants and refugees." Its funding is derived from George Soros's Open Society Foundations, which also provides financial support for the Maine People's Alliance, the ACLU, the NAACP, and a slew of other open-borders organizations. The Maine People's Alliance runs the *Maine Beacon*, a propaganda rag committed to libelous accusations of "white supremacy" against anyone who professes pro-white or even immigration restrictionist views, described as "anti-immigration extremists." Consider its anything-but-even-handed treatment of a discussion of a pair of bills brought before the Maine legislature's Judiciary Committee in May 2019:

---

277 City of Lewiston, "Immigrant and Refugee Integration and Policy Development Working Group," December, 2017.

One, by state Rep. Craig Hickman (D-Winthrop), is an attempt to clarify and maintain a distinction between local law enforcement and federal immigration authorities, ensuring local police do not engage in the prosecution or deportation of immigrants. The other, sponsored by state Rep. Larry Lockman (R-Amherst), would do the opposite, threatening large penalties to force Maine law enforcement to focus on investigating immigrants. Lockman's bill…did have its backers, however, including a group of notorious white supremacists who spoke at the hearing. Tom Kawczynski, the former Jackman town manager who was exposed as a white nationalist with plans to create a white "ethno-state" in northern Maine, rallied anti-immigrant activists to the State House on Wednesday to support Lockman's bill and oppose Hickman's. "Our homes are ours, and even worse than the invaders are those who knowingly facilitate this treason," Kawczynski wrote in a social media post to his followers…Kawczynski was also joined at the hearing by Waterville Mayor and Maine GOP vice-chair Nick Isgro, who, adding to a history of racist and alt-right rhetoric, in March attempted to falsely link the spread of disease with immigration.[278]

"A history of racist and alt-right rhetoric," "white nationalist," et cetera, but as usual, not one single counter-factual. Well, Isgro happens to be correct: the fawned-over 2018 "migrant caravan"—our Last Chance Armada—which violently tried to force its way across the border in Tijuana was not only riddled with lice, Hepatitis, tuberculosis, respiratory infections, and HIV/AIDS, but many had no vaccinations of any kind, and by the way, it was 80% male—and hundreds of them have criminal records. Further, they trashed Tijuana, leaving bottles of urine and mountains of trash for the locals to have to clean up.

Illegals crossing the border between Mexico and Arizona discard in excess of four million pounds of trash in the desert annually, per

---

278 Neumann, Dan, "White supremacists rally for Rep. Lockman's anti-immigrant bill," May 22, 2019. *Maine Beacon.*

the Center for Immigration Studies. This might even be a low figure, for Arizona's Bureau of Land management estimated the volume of discarded trash from the period 2003-2005 at twenty-five million pounds. The aforementioned caravan's LGBTQ-etc. members had to leave it for the sheer amount of abuse and harassment they were receiving, yet the "liberals" who paint a rainbow flag over everything insist we accept the totality of not just this caravan, but any other that happens to show up. The words and deeds indeed do not match, but again, this is unsurprising. Misguided liberal crusades typically cause far more harm than good; Iain Murray catalogues just a few such instances:

> Environmentalists have covered up the polluting effects of contraceptive and chemical abortion drugs—did you know that estrogen from birth control and "morning after" pills is causing male fish across America to develop female sex organs? Funny how "pro-choice" and "environmentalist" liberals never talk about that. Or how about this: the Live Earth concert to "save the planet" released more CO_2 into the atmosphere than a fleet of 2,000 Humvees emit in a year?[279]

A lot of hot air? Returning to the *Maine Beacon*'s naked propaganda:

> "This is making sure that the people who have chosen to be here for whatever reason are not targeted or discriminated against, are free to have an education, are free to not have to look over their shoulders," Hickman told the Judiciary Committee…He continued, "I don't believe any of us want our esteemed law enforcement agencies to have to participate with a corrupt federal immigration agency any more than is required by federal law. We can't change federal law in this room. But what we can do — like we said in 1855 when we said we would not enforce The Fugitive Slave Act — is not use our resources to participate in modern-day slave catching."…

---

279 Murray, Iain Hamish. *Really Inconvenient Truths: Seven Environmental Catastrophies Liberals Don't Want You to Know About—Because They Helped Cause Them*. Regnery Publishing. 2008.

The bill would also require reporting to Maine's attorney general all arrests made for the purposes of immigration enforcement…"Over the last couple of years we have seen increased fear and anxiety in Maine's immigrant population," explained Julia Brown, advocacy and outreach attorney for the Immigrant Legal Advocacy Center of Maine…"These fears stem from a marked rise in indiscriminate immigration enforcement activity nationwide and here in Maine."…"No one is illegal," testified state Rep. Rachel Talbot Ross (D-Portland) in favor of Hickman's bill.[280]

"Nativist" attitudes like Hickman's are highly problematic, and Maine's racism and xenophobia are the only reason individuals from places like Somalia, culturally about as different from Maine as one can get, aren't *immediately* achieving parity (that and the fact that Maine's average IQ is 103.4 according to Michael McDaniel and as reported by *The Washington Post*, and Somalia's is 68). The ACLU believes Lewiston needs more diversity (and spending on special programs) to cope with its diversity, and Lewiston's superintendent of schools agrees:

In February of 2017, the American Civil Liberties Union (ACLU) of Maine, in partnership with Disability Rights Maine and Kids Legal at Pine Tree Legal Assistance, released a well-publicized study that investigated racial disparities and identified five primary areas of concern: lack of teachers who share the cultural background of students; discipline disparities; differences in special education identification; programming for ELL students; and insufficient interpretation services… Lewiston Superintendent Bill Webster has confirmed the district's need for more black and minority teachers, and conversations are taking place in relation to the recruitment and hiring of a more diverse workforce within Lewiston Public Schools. The district is seeking to work in partnership with the University of Southern

280 Neumann, Dan, "White supremacists rally for Rep. Lockman's anti-immigrant bill," May 22, 2019. *Maine Beacon.*

Maine and other partners to design a recruitment program to attract more minority instructors. The district also seeks to promote careers in education to Lewiston High School graduates of color.[281]

Their importation of diversity must beget more diversity to cope with the diversity. See how that works? Curious, though, that the lack of diversity in the first place is such a problem when:

> Anaam Jabbir…a refugee from Iraq…and her family first settled in Georgia. They moved to Maine in 2009 because she heard that the schools are better in Maine… Secondary migrants move to Maine for various reasons, including a belief that it's safer here than in urban areas like Atlanta or Philadelphia.[282]

Because Maine so safe and has such good schools, and is therefore such a desirable destination for immigrants and refugees, it stands to reason that it must be a rotten place with systemic racism and all kinds of obstacles for the saintly people of color we're reminded at every turn are so morally superior to us whites. Ipso facto, the ACLU of Maine is strongly in favor of more immigration into the state because…racism? In a September 2017 paper entitled, "We Belong Here," author Emma Findlen LeBlanc concludes:

> That our state (note: not "our," as LeBlanc is not from Maine) remains overwhelmingly white does not mean that we do not have an urgent problem with racial discrimination that demands collective action. In fact, the centrality of whiteness to Maine's cultural identity often exacerbates the obstacles that immigrants and other people of color face. There are special challenges associated with being non-white in one of the whitest states in the nation, from greater ignorance about multiculturalism to fewer specialized services. Being a less diverse, whiter state doesn't exempt our schools from

---

281 City of Lewiston, "Immigrant and Refugee Integration and Policy Development Working Group," December, 2017.
282 Weed, Peter, "Filling a Severe Gap," May 3, 2019. *Pine Tree Watch*.

the responsibility of grappling with race and racism; in fact, it demands a greater commitment.[283]

Because of course it does. LeBlanc's offering is nothing more than a fifty-two page onslaught against whites for every Cultural Marxist, critical race theory invention you've been smashed over the head with for what feels like forever—insufficient diversity anywhere and everywhere, racial disparities in discipline and performance, the injustice of Maine formerly requiring a perfect score to test out of ELL classes, et cetera, et cetera.

Don't believe me? LeBlanc concludes:

> The structural and personal discrimination that this report documents is alarming, and we hope it will disrupt any complacency about the state of our schools. No person, and certainly no child, should feel as vulnerable, excluded, and victimized as many immigrant students in Maine described themselves as feeling.[284]

And of course it's not just immigrants and refugees who experience pernicious racism while living *voluntarily* amongst whites; "Black Girl in Maine" blogger and Executive Director of Community Change, Inc., Shay Stewart-Bouley ("a Chicago-born, Chicago-raised chick") moves about the state with the nation's lowest crime rate in abject terror seeing all those white faces.

Offering the typical takes you'd expect to find at race-baiting publications such as *The Root*, Stewart-Bouley aims to solve "the white problem" while her blackness serves as a substitute for intellect or even coherent thought in "our" (post-) modern "discourse."

Stewart-Bouley also works closely with The Mindfully Queer Collective, which aims to push LGBTQ sexuality programming on minors in schools and libraries, as well as in "shared spaces."

They use the CM Bailey Public Library in Winthrop for "drop-ins." This group is bankrolled by Resources for Organizing and Social Change (ROSC), a 501(c)(3) founded in 1977 with the mission to,

---

283 LeBlanc, Emma Findlen, "We Belong Here," September, 2017. ACLU report.
284 Ibid.

"build and support a movement for nonviolent social change that will educate, activate, and empower all Maine people through grassroots community organizing." ROSC also helps fund the Portland Racial Justice Congress, African Youth Alliance, Maine Prisoner Advocacy Coalition, Sunlight Media Collective, Konbit Sante (Haiti Health Development), and the NAACP of Maine, among others.

That Stewart-Bouley's organization Community Change, Inc. was founded by the Jewish Horace Seldon (who refers to himself as a "fellow white" in their mission statement), utilizes the space and resources of the Yvonne (Blumenthal) Pappenheim Library ("a free lending library of materials about racism and white privilege in the United States") also established by the organization's founder, and is affiliated with the Boston Foundation is utterly unsurprising.

The Boston Foundation (TBF), Greater Boston's community foundation, is one of the largest community foundations in the nation, with net assets of over $.13 billion. President and CEO Paul S. Grogan is on the Board of Trustees at Brandeis University. Grogan used to be a part of the Local Initiatives Support Foundation, financed by the Ford Foundation. TBF finances such projects as the Immigrant Family Services Institute and receives major funding from a host of local universities, Fidelity Investments, Combined Jewish Philanthropies, and the United Way of Massachusetts Bay, which is itself funded by Bain Capital, Raytheon, the Federal Reserve Bank of Boston, Bank of America, Ropes & Gray LLP, Gillette, Wells Fargo, Berkshire Partners LLP, Liberty Mutual, the Federal Home Loan Bank, Fidelity Investments, and JP Morgan Chase, among others.

The Chairman of the Board for the United Way of Massachusetts Bay is Steven D. Krichmar, Founder and Managing Principle of Krichmar & Associates and Independent Trustee of the Goldman Sachs Trust II Funds—as well as a member of the Board of Directors of Combined Jewish Philanthropies of Boston.

ooooo

"So you see, my dear Coningsby," Jewish 19th century British Prime Minister Benjamin Disraeli wrote in his novel *Coningsby* (1844), "that the world is governed by very different personages from what is imagined by those who are not behind the scenes."

Indeed.

339

Chapter Ten: A Tale of Two Senators

"We can dance, we can dance, everything is under control."
—Men Without Hats, "Safety Dance"

Perhaps no two figures better epitomize the rock-and-a-hard-place Mainers—Westerners in general, really—find themselves than the personages of former Maine Senators George J. Mitchell and William S. Cohen, Democrat and Republican, equal and complementary slices of kosher bread in the neo-liberal order. They are, as we shall see, really quite perfect avatars.

George Mitchell

Following his stint in the US Senate from 1980 through the end of his term on January 3rd, 1995, Mitchell was asked by the Jewish Michael Eisner to join Disney's Board of Directors; he also joined Verner Liipfert Bernhard McPherson & Hand (where the Jewish Elliott Abrams—yes, *that* Elliott Abrams—worked before joining the Reagan administration), a law firm and lobbyist organization that in September 2002 merged with Piper Rudnick LLP, which would itself soon be part of the merger that would form DLA Piper.

Mitchell is currently a consultant and Chairman Emeritus of DLA Piper's Board, and has been on or is presently on the Boards of Staples, Unum, Unilever, Starwood Hotels (owned by Marriott), Xerox, FedEx, and others; Mitchell was also on the Board of the American Security Project, which is not as innocuous as the name sounds.

The American Security Project takes a very antagonistic stance toward Russia and works to advance interventionism in order to combat "climate change."

They also use climate change as a bogeyman for causing "ethnic conflict" in and mass migration from sub-Saharan Africa. The implications are obvious, and with people like John Kerry on the Board and former "luminaries" including Susan Rice, this is unsurprising. As one example, the same UNICEF that declares the West must open itself up to an indefinite number of "migrants" receives well north of $100 million annually from the United States government and also has a multi-million-dollar partnership with DLA Piper.

Curiously, however, despite the carbon-driven mass migrations from the equatorial world, Mitchell's Bipartisan Policy Center, of which he is co-founder and co-chair, receives a substantial amount of funding from companies like BP, Chevron, ConocoPhillips, and Shell, not to mention General Dynamics, Northrop Grumman, the American Bankers Association, Citigroup, and the Nuclear Energy Institute. It also receives funding from FedEx, which is *surely* a coincidence.

In 2004, Mitchell defended the Board's ouster of Roy Disney and, as one might expect, was rewarded as Chairman of Disney from March 2004 to December 31ˢᵗ, 2006. Roy Disney and Stanley Gold were vocal in their criticisms of Mitchell as former CEO Michael Eisner's puppet. "Giving the company's chairmanship to former US Senator George Mitchell, Eisner's lap dog, is a fig leaf covering Eisner's continuing control of the company," wrote one observer. Additionally, as Gold wrote in his letter of resignation from the Board:

> Senator Mitchell was appointed Presiding Director, despite having been recently employed as a Company consultant and notwithstanding that the law firm of which he was chairman received in excess of $1 million for legal services on behalf of the Company in fiscal 2001.

No conflict of interest there. It gets better, as Wesley B. Truitt reports in his book *The Corporation*:

> After retirement, [George Mitchell] became a partner in a prominent Washington, DC law firm and accepted Michael Eisner's invitation to join Disney's board of directors and those of eight other companies. As a nonemployee director at Disney, he was paid $45,000 annually, plus $1,000 per meeting he attended. Disney

also hired him as a $50,000-per-year consultant, and he became a consultant to six of the other companies on whose boards he served. Two of those firms, Federal Express (FedEx) and Staples, for which he was both director and consultant, also employed his law firm, as did Disney. This is all pre-2002. In that year, with corporate governance reforms occurring, Disney dropped Mitchell's law firm, having paid it $2.6 million in fees over the previous seven years, and required Mitchell to give up all other board seats except three. He kept FedEx, Staples, and Starwood Hotels.

He continued to take consulting fees, amounting to $175,000 annually from FedEx and Staples. His consulting fees from Disney had brought him $300,000 over seven years.

In March 2005, Disney's board of directors, following a search in which only one outsider was interviewed (in Eisner's presence), announced their choice of Robert Iger, then president of Disney and Eisner's handpicked insider choice, to succeed him as CEO later that year.[285]

In 1998, Verner Liipfert et al. received $1 million in compensation from Starwood Hotels for their lobbying efforts; that number was $430,000 in 1999, $380,000 in 2000, $380,000 in 2001, and $300,000 in 2002, when they merged with Piper Rudnick. Starwood retained Piper Rudnick, and then what became DLA Piper after the merger, into 2016, at which point Starwood was acquired by Marriott.

As the ultimate "team player," Mitchell earned high praise from former ADL National Director Abe Foxman while serving as Special Envoy for Middle East Peace under Barack Obama. As if he could be any more of a living cliché, Mitchell is also in the Bilderberg Group.

In documents unsealed on August 9th, 2019 by federal prosecutors in New York at the US Attorney's Office for the Southern District of New York, Mitchell was among those named by Virginia Roberts Giuffre in a lawsuit against Jeffrey Epstein and Ghislaine Maxwell as one of the men she was forced to have sex with while she was

285 Truitt, Wesley B. *The Corporation*. Greenwood Guides to Business and Economics. 2006. p. 209.

allegedly being trafficked for sexual acts as an underage girl by the Jewish duo. Mitchell denies the accusation, however a sworn affidavit by a former Epstein employee, Juan Alessi, affirms Giuffre's claim. Mitchell was absolutely an associate of Epstein's—Mitchell called Epstein a "friend and supporter" in a 2003 *New York Magazine* profile and Epstein referred to Mitchell as "the world's greatest negotiator." Giuffre named Mitchell in a 2015 defamation suit against Ghislaine Maxwell and again in a sworn deposition in 2016, saying she was instructed to give him a "sexual massage" while he was visiting Epstein in Palm Beach.

From these documents, we learn:

> American liberal icon, President Obama's Middle East peace envoy Senator George Mitchell, frequently visited Epstein's New York residence. Mr. Mitchell...was very close to Jeffrey, Virginia recalled. "He is very clean-cut. You wouldn't think of him being part of Jeffrey's crew."

Though Mitchell cited work commitments as the reason and not the atrocious optics of an accused sex abuser's affiliation with a fund for those abused by the clergy, he resigned in May 2019 from the oversight committee of the Philadelphia archdiocese's Independent Reconciliation and Reparations Program (IRRP), a fund handled by administrators Kenneth Feinberg and Camille Biros. Feinberg made at least $3.3 million representing British Petroleum after their massive spill, and, per Judicial Watch:

> Uncovered U.S. Treasury Department documents...reveal President Obama's "Special Master for TARP Executive Compensation" Kenneth Feinberg received a $120,830 annual salary to establish executive compensation levels at companies bailed out by the federal government. These documents contradict multiple press reports that Feinberg would not be compensated for this work for the Treasury Department.

Feinberg makes his living deciding on what, if any, financial compensation victims of tragedies like 9/11 are entitled to. There's really not much else to say about that—it says it all, really.

William Cohen

William Cohen and George Mitchell were concurrent Maine Senators for all of Mitchell's time in office. The Jewish Cohen was a Senator from 1979 through the end of his term on January 3rd, 1997.

Cohen and his wife Janet Langhart have made a tidy profit from advertising their interracial marriage, first with the 2006 memoir *Love in Black and White*, and next with Langhart's one-act play *Anne and Emmett*, which—I kid you not—debuted at the US Holocaust Museum and is about "an imagined conversation between Anne Frank and Emmett Till."

After serving as the Secretary of Defense during Bill Clinton's second term, Cohen founded the Cohen Group, a lobbyist organization and "business advisory firm providing corporate leadership with strategic advice and assistance in business development, regulatory affairs, deal sourcing, and capital raising activities," of which Cohen remains Chairman and CEO.

The Cohen Group has lobbied on behalf of special interests such as VR military training technology company Raydon, commercial satellite operator SES Americom, and technology-defense contractor Alion Science & Technology. William Cohen himself and members of the Cohen Group have donated extensively to Senator Susan Collins, and former Senator Olympia Snowe has also received a number of donations from the Cohen Group. Tellingly, Cohen rebuked Donald Trump during Trump's 2016 campaign and endorsed Hillary Clinton for president.

In the 2016 election cycle, the Cohen Group's largest donation recipient was Hillary Clinton, although Republicans Susan Collins, John McCain, and Jeb Bush were also among the top donation recipients from the Group.

This speaks volumes about the truly bipartisan nature of not just the Cohen Group, but of the DC Beltway—and the entire Establishment for that matter: they're all pretty much on the same page. Also consider that Cohen was John McCain's Best Man in his second marriage, and the picture increasingly comes into focus. For further illustrative purposes, however, let's look at some of the top donation recipients from the Cohen Group in other election cycles:

- **2014:** Susan Collins, Cory Booker, Mitch McConnell, John McCain, Joe Kennedy III (a supporter of the New Way Forward Act)
- **2012:** Susan Collins, Barack Obama, Mitt Romney, Joe Kennedy III, Tim Ryan
- **2008:** Hillary Clinton, Barack Obama, Susan Collins, Mitch McConnell, Ted Stevens
- **2004:** John Kerry, Joe Lieberman, Howard Dean, Arlen Specter, John Edwards

You get the idea. What many do not know, however, is that Cohen's former chief of staff and top political strategist Bob Tyrer (who by the way is now co-President of the Cohen Group) was tasked with running Susan Collins's campaign for Senate in 1996 as Cohen's hand-picked replacement—a position she enjoys to this day. The substantial and consistent donations to Collins especially make much more sense in this light. As you'll recall, DLA Piper is also a major campaign donor to Collins, as are companies like FedEx. You can see how the pieces fit.

Cohen is also on the Advisory Board of the Partnership for a Secure America, which, like Mitchell's American Security Project, considers "climate change" to be a "threat multiplier." Other organizations of which Cohen is currently or has been involved with include ViacomCBS, the Council on Foreign Relations, AIG, MIC Industries, the Brookings Institution, the Atlantic Partnership, Thayer Capital, and the Trilateral Commission.

The Kosher Sandwich

The most obvious connection between Cohen and Mitchell, aside from the fact that they were concurrent Senators from Maine for a decade-and-a-half and clearly worked closely together is their co-authored book on the Iran-Contra affair published in 1988.

Not-so-obvious would be the other aspects of their working relationship. Presently, DLA Piper has established, "a strategic alliance with The Cohen Group, a business consulting firm, to help clients identify and achieve global business and strategic opportunities." The first identifiable financial ties are from 2003, when the Cohen

Group's lobbying services were retained by Piper Rudnick for $250,000; in 2004 that number rose slightly to $280,000, but in 2005, when a three-way merger created DLA Piper, the Cohen Group's compensation fell to $80,000.

The working relationship persisted, however, with the Cohen Group's compensation for their lobbying efforts on behalf of DLA Piper totaling $110,000 in 2006 and $140,000 in 2007. Though DLA Piper is listing as having retained the Cohen Group in 2008, I could not find the amount, at which point the financial record of the Cohen Group's explicit lobbying endeavors on behalf of DLA Piper appears to vanish. As indicated above, however, this did not end the Cohen-DLA Piper working relationship, but rather precipitated what would grow into a major partnership.

Cohen was a featured speaker at DLA Piper's annual Global Real Estate Summit in Chicago in 2019 and Ambassador Nick Burns serves as Senior Advisor to DLA Piper through the firm's exclusive relationship with the Cohen Group, where he is a Senior Counselor. DLA Piper and the Cohen Group have collaborated on "independent reports" designed to influence policy—for which they were financially compensated—and a litany of other projects both domestically and globally.

One such project may potentially have involved a coup attempt in Turkey. A large percentage of the Cohen Group's leading figures are ex-diplomats and military figures; there is a curious paucity of "traditional" business or legal acumen at the top. Oh, and by the way:

> We know, from sworn testimony given by FBI whistleblower Sibel Edmonds, that former Undersecretary of State Marc Grossman committed treason when he divulged classified information to Turkish operatives in the summer months of 2001, included in that information was the fact that Brewster Jennings & Associates and Valerie Plame were CIA...Marc Grossman's former boss at the State Department, Richard Armitage...The ATC helps facilitate billions in defense contracts between the Turkish government and FBI Director James Comey's friends at Lockheed Martin, where Comey used to be VP and Senior Counsel. Lockheed Martin's Board of

Directors also includes Joseph Ralston and James Loy who work with Grossman at the Cohen Group.[286]

Lockheed Martin is a major donor to both Maine Senators Susan Collins and Angus King, and House Representative Chellie Pingree—Republican, Independent, and Democrat.

There are deep ties not just between the Cohen Group and DLA Piper, but between the Council of Foreign Relations (CFR) and both the Cohen Group and DLA Piper, as Laurence Shoup relates:

> The Cohen Group was founded by former Defense Secretary and CFR director William S. Cohen when he left the Clinton administration in early 2001. The objectives of the firm are: "helping multinational clients explore opportunities overseas as well as solve problems that may develop. The Cohen Group has the unique ability to provide our clients with truly comprehensive tools for understanding and shaping their business, political, legal, regulatory, and media environments." The Cohen Group has a strategic alliance with the international law firm DLA Piper, one of the largest law firms in the world. Both the Cohen Group and DLA Piper have multiple connections to the CFR. Besides Cohen himself, Marc Grossman, a vice chair at the Cohen Group, is a Council member, and former ambassador and undersecretary of state Nicholas Burns is both a CFR member and a senior counselor at Cohen. Former Senator George J. Mitchell, DLA Piper's former chairman, was a Council director, and former U.S. senator and CFR member Tom Daschle is a policy adviser at this law firm.[287]

But why does it matter that Mitchell, Cohen, and their associates have these connections to the CFR? There are dozens of these think tanks that recycle the same old "bureaucratic tape-worms," to borrow

---

286 Souchak, Ernie, "Valerie Plame Wilson's friend, Marc Grossman, guilty of Treason!" August 3, 2013. Illinois Pay to Play.
287 Shoup, Laurence. *Wall Street's Think Tank: The Council on Foreign Relations and the Empire of Neoliberal Geopolitics, 1976-2014.* Monthly Review Press. 2015. p. 124.

Tucker Carlson's phrase, in between governmental appointments. As Shoup explains in his excellent book *Wall Street's Think Tank: The Council on Foreign Relations and the Empire of Neoliberal Geopolitics, 1976-2014*:

> The CFR's own leaders, in their own publication, [state] that U.S. foreign policy in the twentieth century was made by a "professional class" (their term for a ruling capitalist class) of only "several hundred" people, augmented by a number of "experts" beginning in the 1960s. Almost all of these people were members of the CFR, which actively promoted a foreign policy suitable to the U.S. capitalist class...The Council is the most important U.S. and global center of "deep politics" and the "deep state" that rules behind the scenes, a way that the 1 percent conducts their unrelenting class war against the 99 percent. Despite pretensions to "democracy" and endless attempts at instructing the world, U.S. "democracy" is, in reality, largely a fraud, a hollowed-out shell, devoid of any substantive content. The fact is that the U.S. government—led behind the scenes by the CFR—is largely run in an anti-democratic fashion by and for the interests of a financialized capitalist class, their corporations, and the wealthy families that control and benefit from these corporations. No matter who is elected, people from the Council propose, debate, develop consensus, and implement the nation's key strategic policies. The deep state, in the form of the CFR, operates behind the scenes, making and enforcing important decisions outside of those publicly sanctioned by law and society. A focus on the Council on Foreign Relations is a key way to understand concretely the central sector of the ensemble of power relations in the United States and its informal global empire.[288]

The Cohen Group—which was among the organizations represented at the World Bank Group's 2019 annual meeting that also included the CFR—and DLA Piper each feature both current

288 Ibid. p. 7.

and former members within or affiliated with the CFR, as well as other major geo-political players; these connections are anything but incidental.

Major DLA Piper alumni include: A.B. Krongard, former Executive Director of the CIA; Mel Martinez, former Senator, member of the Bipartisan Policy Center, and JP Morgan Chase's Chairman of the Southeast US and Latin America; and Harry Cummings McPherson, Jr., who served as counsel and special counsel to Lyndon B. Johnson from 1965 to 1969 and was Johnson's chief speechwriter from 1966 to 1969.

DLA Piper has a "global pro bono initiative" called New Perimeter, where the President of the NGO the Public Welfare Foundation (PWF)—endowed by the Tides Center, the ACLU, and Van Jones's Color of Change, among others—Mary McClymont serves on the Advisory Board; McClymont was previously Chairwoman of the Board for the Migration Policy Center, National Director for Legalization at the Migration and Refugee Services of the US Catholic Conference of Catholic Bishops, President and CEO of InterAction (an alliance of US-based "international development" and "humanitarian" NGOs that subscribe to the UN's Sustainable Development agenda), a trial attorney for the US Department of Justice's Civil Rights Division, and she performed various functions for the Ford Foundation and Amnesty International. She is the also the co-founder of Grantmakers Concerned with Immigrants and Refugees.[289]

---

289 From the Louis Freedberg with assistance from Ted Wang report to the Ford Foundation, "The Role of Philanthropy in the US Immigrant Rights Movement": "The creation of these [post-Regan amnesty IRCA] organizations was a central element in the evolution of what McClymont called an 'infrastructure of organizations' that operated on the international, national, state and local level to advance immigrant rights...Muzzafar Chisti, who now directs the Migration Policy Institute's office at the NYU Law School [said,] 'It suddenly galvanized the field, in terms of advocacy, in terms of new people entering the field, in terms of philanthropy's role. It changed the field completely.' The major shift was to move the locus of activity, Chisti said, 'not away from Washington, but in addition to Washington.'... The [Ford] Foundation's Board of Trustees quickly agreed to spend $2.1 million on IRCA implementation... For the Rosenberg Foundation, IRCA provided a vehicle to achieve gains that had eluded it for years, including improving working conditions for the largely undocumented workforce in the California fields. 'We saw IRCA as a great

Also on New Perimeter's Advisory Board are included: Mark S. Ellis, Executive Director of the International Bar Association; Marc Grossman of the Cohen Group; Maha Jweied, a member of the American-Arab Anti-Discrimination Committee's Board and a law clerk to Judge Mohamed Shahabuddeen of the Appeals Chamber of the International Criminal Tribunal for the former Yugoslavia; Sheldon Krantz, Retired Partner in Residence at DLA Piper; David Weiss, member of the Board of Directors of InterAction, the largest alliance of US-based NGOs; and Philip Zeidman, partner in DLA Piper's Franchise and Distribution practice. New Perimeters has an extensive global presence, including offices in Mali (Promoting Financial Inclusion for African Women), Nepal (Enhancing the Skills of Women Lawyers in Nepal), Kosovo (Supporting Women Lawyers in Kosovo; Strengthening Kosovo's Legal Profession; Supporting Law Reform in Kosovo), Guyana (Modernizing Guyana's Justice Sector), Georgia (Assisting Georgia with Climate Change Negotiations), South Africa (Teaching About Special Economic Zones in South Africa), Timor-Leste (Supporting Economic Development in Timor-Leste), Tanzania (Training Tanzanian Government Lawyers), and Mexico (Advocating for Unaccompanied Children at the Border).

Additionally, DLA Piper represents over 150 Israeli companies and investors. From the firm's website:

> The firm has also assisted over 75+ of its foreign clients who require legal assistance in Israel...Our Israel Country Group delivers all the benefits of a global elite law firm through a team of lawyers dedicated to the Israel market. Our broad knowledge and access to local advice has led

---

opportunity,' recalled Kirke Wilson, Rosenberg's long time president who retired in 2005. In the year following IRCA's enactment, Rosenberg set aside $750,000 for implementation, a huge grant for a foundation of its modest size. Rosenberg made 130 grants, mostly on the West Coast, to church groups, unions, civil rights organizations, and others. 'We funded everyone,' Wilson said... On May 15, 1987, barely a week after IRCA went into effect, the Ford Foundation hosted a "Funders' Briefing Session" on IRCA at its New York headquarters to mobilize support for the Fund for New Citizens. Ford contributed $150,000. The New York Community Trust contributed a similar amount. Other donors included the New York Foundation, the BoothFerris Foundation, Trinity Church and Morgan Guaranty Bank... Ford committed an additional $1 million for IRCA activities in 1988.

to us becoming a key address for advising Israeli clients as they do business across the globe. Recent involvement has included advising on M&A transactions in Japan, Norway, Spain and South Africa; HR matters in Brazil, Singapore and Italy; real estate deals in the US, Germany and the UK; IP and tax in Turkey, Dubai, Australia and Czech Republic; fund formation in Poland and the US; commercial and mining advice in Africa; and litigation advice in the UK, Africa and the US.

Don't forget that George Mitchell of DLA Piper was an associate of Jeffrey Epstein, a Mossad asset. Recall also the "changing role" of the NSA following 9/11 and the fact that the NSA has been providing Israel raw, unfiltered data on US citizens for years. This all dovetails rather nicely, as, returning to Shoup:

> William J. Clinton was himself a CFR member before he became president...Of Clinton's three secretaries of the treasury, the first, Lloyd M. Bentsen, was not a CFR member, but Robert E. Rubin and Lawrence H. Summers were, with Rubin later becoming a director and co-chair of the Council. All three of Clinton's choices for Secretary of Defense, Les Aspin, William J. Perry, and William S. Cohen, were CFR members, and Aspin and Cohen were directors. Cohen was a director when Clinton called on him to serve in the government...
>
> George W. Bush was never a member of the CFR, but... his vice president, Richard B. Cheney, was a longtime member and was a two-time director between 1987 and 1995. Both of Bush's secretaries of state, Colin L. Powell and Condoleezza Rice, had long been members of the Council when they were appointed, and Powell became a CFR director in 2006...
>
> George W. Bush had two secretaries of defense, Donald H. Rumsfeld and Robert M. Gates. Rumsfeld was a CFR member during the 1970s but later dropped out of the organization. Gates has been a continuous Council member since 1985. Bush's appointees to head the

CIA, Porter J. Goss and Michael V. Hayden, were CFR members prior to entering office, as were both of his appointees to head up the World Bank, Paul Wolfowitz and Robert Zoellick, who had also been a Council director.

Three of the four men Bush appointed to be UN ambassador, John D. Negroponte, John R. Bolton, and Zalmay Khalilzad, were CFR members prior to their appointments...

Susan E. Rice, who also served as Obama's first UN representative, has been active in the organization for years... Obama's second secretary of state, John Forbes Kerry, became a CFR member in the early 1990s. He married his second wife, the near billionaire Teresa Heinz (who inherited the Heinz food fortune), in 1995, the same year she was elected to Council membership.[290]

Among William J. Clinton's many "accomplishments" includes the pardoning of the Jewish Marc Rich of federal charges of tax evasion and making oil deals with Iran during the Iran hostage crisis at the behest of Rich's many powerful Jewish connections.[291]

There's also that thorny little matter of the Bill Clinton-Jeffrey Epstein connection. Among Epstein's many connections, including that with George Mitchell, includes Bowdoin College trustee James Staley, who spent over 30 years at JP Morgan Chase and is now CEO of Barclays. Bowdoin's Chairman of the Board of Trustees is Robert F. White, who:

Spent the 1980s as one of the architects of Bain Capital,

---

290 Ibid. p. 97-98.

291 Including Michael Steinhardt, the son of Sol Frank Steinhardt, a compulsive high-stakes gambler, New York's leading jewel fence per then-DA Frank Hogan, convicted felon, and close friend of Jewish underworld crime boss Meyer Lansky, who, along with another Jewish gangster Moe Dalitz, was a major funder and benefactor of the Anti-Defamation League. Theodore Silbert worked simultaneously for the ADL and the Sterling National Bank (a Mafia operation controlled by the Lansky syndicate) and Lansky's granddaughter Mira Lansky Boland was the ADL's liaison to law enforcement. Michael Steinhardt wrote a letter to Clinton advocating the pardon of Rich, and was an early promoter of the possible presidential candidacy of the Jewish Michael Bloomberg in 2008. He and Charles Bronfman co-founded Taglit-Birthright Israel.

a private equity firm notorious for its pioneering use of corporate dividends to accumulate massive profits for itself while processing the cash-starved companies under its control through the more Byzantine corners of the bankruptcy code. This practice sent hundreds or thousands of workers at a time into unemployment and hollowed out businesses once ingrained in their communities, while pocketing millions for White and others, so they could move on to the next acquisition. This is where the money comes from.[292]

Speaking of Bain Capital and Maine's higher education system, in yet another perfect microcosm, the University of Maine system advertises heavily out-of-state to recruit its students, and then wonders aloud why young people won't (read: can't) stay in their home state to live and work. Hence why old and white Maine needs Somalis and "urban youths" from Massachusetts and Connecticut, apparently. But their business model is not influenced by educating the next generation of real Mainers, it is, beyond the obvious need to indoctrinate the youth, about exponential growth.

This is utterly unsurprising for a whole host of reasons discussed previously in this book, but the nail in the coffin is the Bain of our existence: in 2018, the University of Maine system hired Bain Capital to manage about $18 million in bank loan portfolios for the system's $317 million managed investment pool of six endowment funds and $30 million pension fund. Oh, and Bain Capital's Jonathan Lavine, like fellow Jewish vulture capitalist Seth Klarman, is a major donor to Boston's Combined Jewish Philanthropies. In fact, Bain Capital itself helps fund The Boston Foundation and the Combined Jewish Philanthropies of Greater Boston, so central to Catholic Charities' shuttling of migrants into Maine. Lavine is also a member of the Boston Celtics professional basketball franchise ownership group.

Where else does Bain Capital get its money? Well, lately by investing in methadone clinics, adding more "assets" to the "nationwide methadone clinic empire being assembled by private equity giant Bain Capital." Mental health facilities and other kinds of facilities

---

292 Hamilton, Andrew, "Bowdoin's moral entanglements are bigger than the Epstein case," September 20, 2019. *The Bowdoin Orient.*

and clinics are also joining private equity portfolios along with these rehab clinics:

> Places like Gosnold are being gobbled up by private equity companies and publicly-traded chains looking to do what is known in Wall Street jargon as a roll-up play. They take a fragmented industry, buy up the bits and pieces and consolidate them into big, branded companies where they hope to make a profit by streamlining and cutting costs.
>
> One company that advises investors listed 27 transactions in which private equity firms or public companies bought or invested in addiction treatment centers and other so-called behavioral health companies in 2014 and 2015 alone. Acadia Healthcare is one national chain that has been on a shopping spree. In 2010 it had only six facilities, but today it has 587 across the country and in the United Kingdom.
>
> What's driving the growth? The opioid addiction crisis is boosting demand for treatment and two relatively recent laws are making it easier to get insurers to pay for it. The Mental Health Parity Act of 2008 requires insurers to cover mental health care as they would cover physical health care. "Mental health parity was the beginning. We saw a big benefit. And then the Affordable Care Act was very positive for our industry," says Joey Jacobs, Acadia's CEO... Suddenly there's a huge stream of cash for Acadia and other companies to tap into. Addiction treatment isn't all that Acadia does. It has residential schools for teenagers, inpatient psychiatric facilities, and centers for people eating disorders...But addiction is certainly a big part of the business. It has more than 100 inpatient detox and rehab centers and runs 110 opioid treatment programs, better known as methadone clinics, which it bought from private equity firm Bain Capital in 2014 for $1.18 billion. Bain, which was founded by Mitt Romney, had purchased CRC Health, a chain of treatment centers, in 2005 for $720 million.

It then bought at least 20 more rehab centers and then added a Massachusetts-based chain of methadone clinics in 2014 for $58 million, just before selling the entire package to Acadia…The company referred to the rising use of heroin as a "favorable industry tailwind" and predicted its revenue would continue to grow.[293]

"Addiction services" represent a $35 billion a year and growing market:

> "The appetite among private equity firms for these assets tends to be greater because there is less payer reimbursement risk and the growth opportunities are so great," said James Clark, a managing director at investment bank Harris Williams & Co.
>
> The latest wave of investors includes Goldman Sachs Group Inc's private equity arm, which gave tens of millions of dollars to two healthcare industry veterans Mitch Eisenberg and Lewis Gold at a company called Advanced Recovery Systems late last year [2013] to acquire and develop rehabilitation clinics.[294]

The Establishment profits off the very crises they create. The Jewish Sackler family claimed their prescription opioids were non-addicting, knowing full well they were, and they've also now seen fit to open their very own opioid rehabilitation clinic—profiting off people's misery at every stage. There's something else about so many of these names, like Eisenberg and Gold, I can't quite put my finger on… Consider the following, from Jane Mayer's March 2017 piece "The Reclusive Hedge-Fund Tycoon behind the Trump Presidency" in *The New Yorker* about libertarian Robert Mercer, formerly a main stakeholder in Breitbart and CEO of Renaissance Technologies:

> David Magerman, a senior employee at Renaissance, spoke out about what he regards as Mercer's worrisome

---

293 Kodjak, Alison, "Investors See Big Opportunities In Opioid Addiction Treatment," June 13, 2016. *NPR Digital Media.*
294 "Obamacare helps private equity get its rehab clinic fix," December 8, 2014. Brentwood Capital Advisors.

influence. Magerman, a Democrat who is a strong supporter of Jewish causes, took particular issue with Mercer's empowerment of the alt-right, which has included anti-Semitic and white-supremacist voices. Magerman shared his concerns with Mercer, and the conversation escalated into an argument. Magerman told colleagues about it, and, according to an account in the *Wall Street Journal*, Mercer called Magerman and said, "I hear you're going around saying I'm a white supremacist. That's ridiculous." Magerman insisted to Mercer that he hadn't used those words, but added, "If what you're doing is harming the country, then you have to stop."[295]

David, I could not agree more.

---

[295] Mayer, Jane, "The Reclusive Hedge-Fund Tycoon behind the Trump Presidency," March 17, 2017. *The New Yorker.*

Conclusion

"Globalization...knows the price of everything and the value of nothing. Without borders the world will become—is visibly becoming—a howling desert of traffic fumes, plastic, and concrete, where nowhere is home and the only language is money."—Peter Hitchens

The many service providers and NGOs described in this book are absolutely essential to the vast matrix of "philanthropic capitalism," and it should be abundantly clear by now that all of these organizations from the "charitable" to the state- and corporate-sponsored are inter-connected and their machinery is geared toward first splintering and then eradicating the native populations of the Western world, indeed all unique races, ethnicities, and cultures under the heel of the neo-liberal oligarchy. Understanding these mechanisms is absolutely essential in counter-acting the Establishment's destructive agenda.

Neo-liberalism's masquerading as a vehicle of "social justice" is a complete sham, and even the most basic claims of equality and empowerment fall apart with just a little scrutiny. There is also the matter of not just outsourced and internalized Jewishness, but the very essence of Judaism forming the back-bone of neo-liberal capital, as evidenced by Erika Karp's own admission.

What we are witnessing is the next stage in Judeo-neo-liberalism's evolution; from "internationalism" and communism in the first half of the twentieth century—financed primarily by Jewish capitalists such as Olof Aschberg and Jacob Schiff in its early Soviet days and supported into the 1950s as an extension of Judaism—to Cultural Bolshevism and the dawn of neo-liberalism in its second half, this third act is far more dangerous for its pervasiveness and intrusiveness, and the fact that an induced paralysis of government and consumer at best, an active facilitation of their own destruction at worst, gives the primary drivers carte blanche to act with impunity and steamroll what little resistance they presently encounter. The tab we are stuck with continues to balloon, and they expect us to never stop paying until we are all, in every sense, totally bankrupt.

In the face of severe over-population and environmental degradation we are instead treated to an array of platitudes about how migration "is a human right" and that, despite the consternation of the Justin Trudeau's of the world over the carbon footprint of Western nations, there are economic benefits to be had from untold millions more people from parts unknown pouring in and adding to the pollution, crime, alienation, and atomization of those of us who live here.

We were never asked, and even if we were, the ruling class wouldn't have listened. We don't even live in a society anymore. We live in a market. Though carbon-trading, for example, is framed as "green business," the only green here is greed, and perhaps nausea at the ruling class's depravity.

The "elites" do not view themselves as accountable to the people they would deign to govern—for the out-facing functionaries and beneficiaries are bought and sold, for one, and most of the true power brokers are not of the same stock, for another. The ruling class is beyond redemption, and nothing short of a replacement of the kind they envision for us will suffice to save any semblance of an America worth saving.

The ruling class hates you; they want you dead, and they are profiting off your misery and destruction. What kind of government does that to its people? A government not by and for the people, but a hostile occupation government.

Anaconda-like, Mammon encircles the globe and slowly squeezes to death all free and independent people, all unique and diverse cultures, all dissent, all opposition—the "melting pot" a tepid soup. There is nothing "compassionate" or "tolerant" about the ideology of liberalism. It is only the vehicle through which the ruling class has chosen to manipulate well-meaning people into accepting servitude. To paraphrase Rich Barlow, neo-liberalism may now be the sun of our solar system, but it is a bloated, unstable, dying one. A red giant.

To my mind, the end goal must be to allow for the self-determination of all peoples, respecting the environment and human bio-diversity so that *all* may have a healthy and happy homeland to call their own. I am reminded here of Maine's seal and attendant state motto, *Dirigo*— translation, "I direct," "I guide," or "I lead"—which I take to be a call to action:

> Supporters: on dexter side, a husbandman, resting on a scythe; on sinister side, a seaman, resting on an anchor. In the foreground, representing sea and land, and under the shield, shall be the name of the State in large Roman capitals, to wit:

MAINE.

> The whole shall be surrounded by a crest, the North Star. The motto, in small Roman capitals, shall be in a label interposed between the shield and crest, viz.:--DIRIGO

The motto, *Dirigo*, extends the character of the North Star—the Polar Star:

> As the Polar Star has been considered the mariner's guide and director in conducting the ship over the pathless ocean to the desired haven, and as the center of magnetic attraction; as it has been figuratively used to denote the point, to which all affections turn, and as it is here intended to represent the State, it may be considered the citizens' guide, and the object to which the patriot's best exertions should be directed.

Acknowledgements

Special thanks to William Triumph for serving as a sounding board and for providing invaluable insights into this project. Special thanks as well to the New Albion group in general and Tom Kawczynski in particular for their feedback and information. A deep and sincere thanks to everyone who has helped me get to this point and for your efforts on behalf of our people, including but by no means limited to: Skeptical Hippo, Spectre, Pikachu, Apache, Coach Finstock, the Mannerbund men, Dark Enlightenment, Ash Sharp and Patriot, Laura Towler, Musonius Rufus, Mr. X, the After Party fellas, Richard Houck, all of the great Cocktail Hour guests and Anatomically Correct Banana contributors and readers, and for the donors who helped make those projects a reality. Special thanks to Luca, the "Croatian Idiot" who put me in touch with Dr. Kevin MacDonald, and an extra special thanks to Dr. MacDonald for publishing my pieces at *The Occidental Observer* and in *The Occidental Quarterly*, as well as for his kind words and central role in not just this project, but in all of his efforts for the Occidental peoples of the world. The same goes for all of the aforementioned men and women, and Arthur Kemp for both publishing this book and for his tireless efforts, and a final thanks to all of you for reading!

Index